International Tourism Development and the Gulf Cooperation Council States

This book examines the challenges facing the development of tourism in the six member states of the Gulf Cooperation Council (GCC): Bahrain, Kuwait, Oman, Qatar, Saudi Arabia and the United Arab Emirates (UAE). This region, which largely comprises the Arabian Peninsula, possesses some of the fastest growing economies in the world and is remarkably unique. It shares similar associations and affinities: tribal histories, royal kinship, political associations, Bedu cultural roots, Islamic heritage, rapid urbanization, oil wealth, rentier dynamics, state capitalist structures, migrant labour, economic diversification policies and institutional restructuring. Therefore, this volume takes the study of tourism away from its normative unit of analysis, where tourism in the region is being examined within the context of the Middle East and the wider Islamic and Arab world, towards an enquiry focusing on a specific geo-political territory and socially defined region.

Although international tourism development in the region embodies a range of challenges, complexities and conflicts, which are deeply contextualized in this volume, the approach overall does not endorse the normative 'Gulf bashing' position that has predominated within the critical enquiries in the region. It presents a forward-looking and realistic assessment of international tourism development, examining development potentialities and constructive ways forward for GCC states and the region as a whole. This edited volume provides a real attempt to examine critically ways in which tourism and its development intersect with the socio-cultural, economic, political, environmental and industrial change that is taking place in the region. By doing so, the book provides a theoretically engaged analysis of the social transformations and discourses that shape our contemporary understanding of tourism development within the GCC region. Moreover, it deciphers tourism development's role within the context of the GCC states undergoing rapid transformation, urbanization, ultra-modernization, internationalization and globalization. In addition to state-specific illustrations and destination case studies, the work provides insights into relatable themes associated with international tourism development in the region, such as tourism's relationship with religion, heritage and identity, the environment and sustainability, mobility and cross-border movements, the transport industry, image production and destination branding, mega-development and political stability and instability. The book combines theory with diverse case study illustrations, drawing on disciplinary knowledge from such fields as sociology, political economy and social geography.

This timely and original contribution is essential reading for students, researchers and academics in the field of tourism studies and related subject areas, along with those who have regional interests in Middle East studies, including Gulf and Arabian Peninsula studies.

Marcus L. Stephenson is a Professor of Tourism and Hospitality and Head of the School of Tourism and Hospitality Management at the University of the South Pacific. Previously, he was Associate Professor of International Tourism Management and the Chair of Research at Middlesex University Dubai (UAE). Marcus holds a PhD in Social Tourism from Manchester Metropolitan University (UK) and he has published extensively on the sociology of tourism, especially concerning nationality, race, ethnicity, culture and religion. His current research interests focus on Islamic hospitality and tourism, and tourism development in the GCC and South Pacific region. He is co-author of *Tourism and Citizenship: Rights, Freedoms and Responsibilities in the Global Order*, a Routledge publication (2014).

Ala Al-Hamarneh is an Assistant Professor of Human Geography and Senior Researcher at the Centre for Research on the Arab World (CERAW), Johannes Gutenberg University of Mainz, Germany. He is also a visiting professor at the University of Sharjah (UAE). He holds a Masters in Human Geography and a PhD in Economic and Social Geography from Kiev State University, Ukraine. Ala co-edited *Islam and Muslims in Germany* (2008), which was the December 2008 Choice Magazine Outstanding Academic Title Award Winner (USA). Currently he is involved in research on intra-regional mobilities in the GCC region and neo-liberal urban developments in the Arab world.

Contemporary Geographies of Leisure, Tourism and Mobility

Series Editor: C. Michael Hall, Professor at the Department of Management,
College of Business and Economics, University of Canterbury, Christchurch, New Zealand

The aim of this series is to explore and communicate the intersections and relationships between leisure, tourism and human mobility within the social sciences.

It will incorporate both traditional and new perspectives on leisure and tourism from contemporary geography, e.g. notions of identity, representation and culture, while also providing for perspectives from cognate areas such as anthropology, cultural studies, gastronomy and food studies, marketing, policy studies and political economy, regional and urban planning, and sociology, within the development of an integrated field of leisure and tourism studies.

Also, increasingly, tourism and leisure are regarded as steps in a continuum of human mobility. Inclusion of mobility in the series offers the prospect to examine the relationship between tourism and migration, the sojourner, educational travel, and second home and retirement travel phenomena.

For a full list of titles in this series, please visit www.routledge.com/series/SE0522

The series comprises two strands:

Contemporary Geographies of Leisure, Tourism and Mobility aims to address the needs of students and academics, and the titles will be published in hardback and paperback. Titles include:

9   **An Introduction to Visual Research Methods in Tourism**
Edited by Tijana Rakic and Donna Chambers

10 **Tourism and Climate Change**
Impacts, Adaptation and Mitigation
C. Michael Hall, Stefan Gössling and Daniel Scott

11 **Tourism and Citizenship**
Rights, Freedoms and Responsibilities in the Global Order
Raoul V. Bianchi and Marcus L. Stephenson

Routledge Studies in Contemporary Geographies of Leisure, Tourism and Mobility is a forum for innovative new research intended for research students and academics, and the titles will be available in hardback only. Titles include:

66 **Tourism and Gentrification in Contemporary Metropolises**
International Perspectives
Edited by Maria Gravari-Barbas and Sandra Guinand

67 **Co-Creation in Tourist Experiences**
Edited by Nina K. Prebensen, Joseph S. Chen and Muzaffer Uysal

68 **International Tourism Development and the Gulf Cooperation Council States**
Challenges and Opportunities
Edited by Marcus L. Stephenson and Ala Al-Hamarneh

International Tourism Development and the Gulf Cooperation Council States

Challenges and Opportunities

Edited by Marcus L. Stephenson and Ala Al-Hamarneh

Routledge
Taylor & Francis Group

LONDON AND NEW YORK

First published 2017 by Routledge

2 Park Square, Milton Park, Abingdon, Oxon OX14 4RN

605 Third Avenue, New York, NY 10017

Routledge is an imprint of the Taylor & Francis Group, an informa business

First issued in paperback 2022

British Library Cataloguing-in-Publication Data
A catalogue record for this book is available from the British Library

Library of Congress Cataloging-in-Publication Data
Names: Stephenson, Marcus L., editor. | Al-Hamarneh, Ala, editor.
Title: International tourism development and the Gulf Cooperation Council States: challenges and opportunities/edited by Marcus L. Stephenson and Ala al-Hamarneh.
Other titles: Contemporary geographies of leisure, tourism, and mobility.
Description: Milton Park, Abingdon, Oxon: Routledge, 2017. |
Series: Contemporary geographies of leisure, tourism and mobility |
Includes bibliographical references and index.
Identifiers: LCCN 2016059047 (print) | LCCN 2017007998 (ebook) |
ISBN 9781138023277 (hardback) | ISBN 9781315776576 (ebk) |
ISBN 9781315776576 (master eBook) | ISBN 9781317690887 (pdf) |
ISBN 9781317690870 (epub3) | ISBN 9781317690863 (Mobipocket)
Subjects: LCSH: Tourism–Persian Gulf Region. | Tourism–Government policy–Persian Gulf Region.
Classification: LCC G155.P47 I58 2017 (print) | LCC G155.P47 (ebook) |
DDC 915.30068–dc23
LC record available at https://lccn.loc.gov/2016059047

ISBN: 978-1-138-02327-7 (hbk)
ISBN: 978-1-03-233960-3 (pbk)
DOI: 10.4324/9781315776576

Typeset in Times New Roman
by Deanta Global Publishing Services, Chennai, India

Contents

Illustrations

Figures

Tables

Contributors

Ala Al-Hamarneh is an Assistant Professor of Human Geography and Senior Researcher at the Centre for Research on the Arab World (CERAW), Johannes Gutenberg University of Mainz (Germany). He is also a visiting professor at the University of Sharjah (UAE). He holds a Masters in Human Geography and a PhD in Economic and Social Geography from Kiev State University (Ukraine). Ala co-edited *Islam and Muslims in Germany* (Brill, 2008), which was the December 2008 Choice Magazine Outstanding Academic Title Award Winner (USA). Currently he is involved in research on intra-regional mobilities in the GCC region and neoliberal urban developments in the Arab world.

Hafidh AlRiyami is a Lecturer at the Rustaq College of Applied Sciences, Oman. He holds a Bachelor of Tourism (Dist.) from Sultan Qaboos University (Oman) and a Master of Business (International Travel and Tourism Management) from the University of Queensland (Australia), and has worked for an international tour company in Oman for several years. He is currently undertaking his doctorate at University of Queensland. His research interests include sustainable tourism development and cross-cultural consumer behaviour.

Nicholas J. Ashill is a full Professor in the Department of Marketing and Information Systems, American University of Sharjah (UAE). He also holds the position of Chalhoub Group Professor of Luxury Brand Management. His research interests include topics related to services marketing, customer satisfaction, brand management, job performance and human resource management practices. He is highly research active and has published articles in many of the world's leading journals in marketing and management. Nicholas is currently Associate Editor for two leading marketing journals – the *European Journal of Marketing* and the *Journal of Services Marketing*.

Samer Bagaeen is Associate Director with the Rockefeller Foundation's 100 Resilient Cities initiative and is Professor of Architecture and Urban Planning at the University of Jordan. He led on town planning education at the University of Brighton and served as Visiting Professor of Real Estate at the Institute of Urban Economy in Lima (Peru). He recently co-edited *Sustainable Regeneration of Former Military Sites* (Routledge, 2016) and *Beyond Gated Communities* (Routledge, 2015). Samer is a Fellow of the Royal Society of Arts and a Trustee of two leading urban planning organizations in London, the Town and Country Planning Association and the Royal Town Planning Institute.

Arnd N. Bätzner is a researcher and consultant specializing in the integration of demand-responsive transport with high-capacity transit. Based in Switzerland, his PhD research at the University of St Gallen concerns the last-mile linkage role of elevated connectors in dense urban environments. Arnd is a non-executive director of the nationwide Swiss car-sharing operator, Mobility, and is a member of several standing committees of the Transportation Research Board of the US National Academies of Science, Engineering and Medecine. He has previously been involved in economic research at Credit Suisse and in corporate strategy at Swiss International Air Lines. He holds an MSc in Particle Physics with a minor in Railway Engineering and Public Transport Management.

Lyn Bibbings is an independent academic and consultant. She has worked in the public sector as a Planner and Tourism Research and Development Manager. At Oxford Brookes University (UK), she developed and managed a bespoke programme for British Airways, taught strategic thinking to managers as part of the TUI Academy and was National Liaison Officer for Tourism for the Higher Education Academy (HEA) Subject Network. Subsequently, Lyn became National Subject Lead for Tourism, Hospitality, Leisure and Events. She chaired the UK Association of Tourism in Higher Education and in 2012 was one of the first in the country to be awarded Principal Fellowship of the HEA. In 2013, her outstanding work was recognized by the Higher Education Funding Council for England by the award of National Teaching Fellow.

Peter Burns is Professor of Tourism and International Development and Director of the Institute for Tourism Studies (INTOUR) at the University of Bedfordshire (UK). As a consultant, he specializes in tourism master planning for developing countries and emerging markets. He has undertaken research and consultancy assignments in over 30 countries, including in the Middle East and North Africa region. Peter's research interests concern strategic policymaking for sustainable human development. He is co-editor of *Tourism Planning and Development*, a panel member of the United Nations World Tourism Organization (UNWTO) Global Tourism Barometer, and a judge of the World Travel and Tourism Council's 'Tourism for Tomorrow' award. He was made an Academician of the Academy of Social Sciences in 2006.

Prakash Chathoth is a full Professor in the Department of Marketing and Information Systems, American University of Sharjah (UAE). He has published in such top-tier journals as *Annals of Tourism Research, Tourism Management, Journal of Sustainable Tourism, Journal of Travel and Tourism Marketing, Journal of Hospitality and Tourism Research, International Journal of Hospitality Management* and *International Journal of Contemporary Hospitality Management*. He serves on the editorial board of nine international research journals and is currently the Regional Editor – Middle East and Africa for the *International Journal of Contemporary Hospitality Management*.

Erdogan Ekiz is an Associate Professor in the Tourism Institute at King Abdulaziz University, Kingdom of Saudi Arabia (KSA). He received his PhD in Tourism and Hospitality Management from Hong Kong Polytechnic University. He also has an MBA in Services Marketing from Eastern Mediterranean University in North Cyprus. He is a Certified Hospitality Educator from the American Hotel and Lodging Educational Institute and has over 15 years of teaching experience in Hong Kong, Taiwan, Cyprus, Turkey, Malaysia and KSA. Erdogan has over 170 published journal articles, book chapters and conference papers. His areas of expertise include service failure, consumer complaining behaviour and tourist behaviour and culture.

William G. Feighery is an independent scholar whose research interests embrace visual studies, ethnicity, signification/representation and critical discourse studies. Currently based in Switzerland, he has previously lived and worked in the United Kingdom, the Middle East and China. He has published his research in a range of international peer-reviewed journals, including *Annals of Tourism Research*, *Tourism Analysis*, *Policy Research in Tourism, Leisure and Events*, *Historic Environments (ICOMOS)*, *Current Issues in Tourism* and *Critical Discourse Studies*. William currently serves as Editor-in-Chief for the journal *Visual Methodologies*.

Matthew Gray is Associate Professor in the School of International Liberal Studies, Waseda University, Tokyo (Japan). From 2005 to 2016 he was at the Australian National University (ANU) in Canberra, and from 1997 to 2005 he held various positions in trade promotion, defence and immigration with the Australian government. His research and teaching focuses on the politics, political economy and international relations of the Arab world. He is the author of *Global Security Watch − Saudi Arabia* (Praeger, 2014), *Qatar: Politics and the Challenges of Development* (Lynne Rienner, 2013) and *Conspiracy Theories in the Middle East: Sources and Politics* (Routledge, 2010). Matthew has a PhD from the ANU and an MA from Macquarie University in Sydney.

Waleed Hazbun is Associate Professor in the Department of Political Studies and Public Administration at the American University of Beirut (AUB), Lebanon, where he teaches international relations and political economy. He has a PhD in Political Science from the Massachusetts Institute of Technology. Before joining AUB in 2010, Waleed taught international political economy at the Johns Hopkins University in Baltimore, Maryland. He is author of *Beaches, Ruins, Resorts: The Politics of Tourism in the Arab World* (University of Minnesota Press, 2008), and has published work on US foreign policy and international relations of the Middle East. He is currently developing a book project on the global politics of air travel in the Middle East.

Joan C. Henderson is Associate Professor at Nanyang Technological University's Nanyang Business School in Singapore, where she has worked since 1997. Previously, she lectured in the travel and tourism field in the UK, after periods of employment in the public and private tourism sectors. Her University of Edinburgh PhD thesis concerned social tourism, and she holds an MSc in Tourism. Joan has published on a variety of tourism-related topics, encompassing studies of pilgrimage travel and destination development within a Middle Eastern context. She currently sits on the editorial board of six international journals.

Jafar Jafari is Professor Emeritus of the University of Wisconsin-Stout School of Hospitality Leadership. He is the Founding Editor of *Annals of Tourism Research: A Social Sciences Journal*; Chief Editor, *Tourism Social Science* (book) series; Co-Chief Editor, *Bridging Tourism Theory and Practice* book series; Chief Editor, *Encyclopedia of Tourism*; Co-Founding Editor, *Information Technology & Tourism*; Co-Founder, TRINET: Tourism Research Information Network; and Founding President, International Academy for the Study of Tourism. He is a cultural anthropologist and has a PhD from the University of Minnesota (USA). Jafar is a Hotel Administration graduate, with a BS and MS from Cornell University (USA). He was the recipient of the 2005 UNWTO Ulysses Award.

Marjorie Kelly was an Associate Professor at the American University of Kuwait where she taught anthropology for 8 years as one of the founding faculty of the institution. Her research specialties are the Arab world, museums and the anthropology of the arts. Marjorie has consulted on contemporary culture exhibits for the National Museum of Qatar. She has published numerous articles and reviews on the presentation of culture for museum and tourist audiences, as well as an edited volume on Islamic civilization. Her most recent project, *Kuwait at 50*, is a visual ethnography of Kuwait in its fiftieth year of independence.

Zafer Öter is Associate Professor of Tourism at İzmir Katip Çelebi University, Ismir (Turkey). His research interests include tourism marketing, heritage interpretation and cultural tourism, and the Middle East and North Africa and Francophone regions. He is the author of *Valorisation du Patrimoine Culturel: Commercialisation Touristique de l'Artisanat d'art en Turquie*, published by *Éditions Universitaires Européennes* in 2011. He has published and communicated his academic work through the media of Turkish, English and French, and published widely in such journals as *Annals of Tourism Research*, *Milli Folklor*, *Journal of Heritage Tourism*, *European Journal of Tourism Research*, *Anatolia*, *SOID* and *Procedia*.

Cody Morris Paris is the Deputy Director of Middlesex University Dubai (UAE) and an Associate Professor in the School of Law. He is also a Senior Research Fellow in the School of Hospitality and Tourism at University of Johannesburg in South Africa. He holds a PhD in Community Resource Development at

Arizona State University. His primary research interests include geopolitics and tourism, technology and tourism, sustainable development, tourism mobilities and experiential learning. Cody is on the executive board of the Association for Tourism and Leisure Research and Education (ATLAS) and the Travel and Tourism Research Association Asia Pacific Chapter.

Ahmad M. Ragab is a Lecturer at the Faculty of Tourism and Hotels, Minia University (Egypt). He obtained his PhD in Tourism Studies with emphasis on tourism statistics. He is acting as an advisory committee member at the Tourism Satellite Accounts Unit, Egyptian Ministry of Tourism, as well as the manager of Tourism Demand Surveys project in KSA. Ahmad's research interests include tourism statistics, tourism satellite accounts and tourism market analysis.

Nadine Scharfenort is an Assistant Professor at the Institute of Geography, University of Mainz (Germany). She holds a PhD in Urban Geography from the University of Vienna (Austria), where her dissertation focused on oil urbanization and post-oil city development in Abu Dhabi, Dubai and Sharjah (UAE). She has authored a number of articles on urban and socioeconomic development in the UAE and Qatar, conducting research since 2001. Nadine is involved in research on inbound tourism from GCC countries to Germany and Austria, and neoliberal transformation processes in GCC cities.

Noel Scott is a Professor at Griffith Institute for Tourism, Griffith University, Gold Coast (Australia). His research interests include tourism experiences, destination management and stakeholder organization. His recent work has examined the design of tourism experiences in visitor attractions and how to create stronger memories through emotion, co-creation and use of symbols, myths and legends. Noel has completed tourism consultancy projects in a number of countries including Chile, China, Fiji, Saudi Arabia and Peru, and represented such organizations as the Association of Southeast Asian Nations and the Organization for Economic Cooperation and Development. Noel has published over 200 academic articles and 13 books and supervised 18 doctoral students.

Marcus L. Stephenson is a Professor of Tourism and Hospitality and Head of the School of Tourism and Hospitality Management at the University of the South Pacific. Previously, he was Associate Professor of International Tourism Management and the Chair of Research at Middlesex University Dubai (UAE). Marcus holds a PhD in social tourism from Manchester Metropolitan University (UK), and he has published extensively on the sociology of tourism, especially concerning nationality, race, ethnicity, culture and religion. His current research interests focus on Islamic hospitality and tourism, and tourism development in the GCC and South Pacific region. He is co-author of *Tourism and Citizenship: Rights, Freedoms and Responsibilities in the Global Order*, a Routledge publication (2014).

Dallen J. Timothy is Professor of Community Resources and Development, Director of the Tourism Development and Management Program at Arizona

State University (ASU) (USA), and Senior Sustainability Scientist at the Julie Ann Wrigley Global Institute of Sustainability at ASU. He also holds four different visiting professorships at universities in Asia and Europe. Dallen serves on the editorial boards of 16 international journals and is the current and Founding Editor of the *Journal of Heritage Tourism*. He is currently involved in research in Asia, North America, the Middle East, the Caribbean and Europe, focusing on issues relating to cultural adaptation, souvenir meanings, heritage politics, migration and diasporas, identity and food, international borders, geopolitics and religious tourism.

Anuradha Vyas holds two master's degrees – the first was in Mathematics from Kurukshetra University (India), and the second was in Business Administration from Middlesex University, London (UK). Anuradha has been an educator in higher education for the past 16 years. She is a Lecturer in Foundation Studies at Middlesex Univeristy Dubai (UAE), and previously worked for 10 years at Skyline University College, Sharjah (UAE). Her research interests include tourism marketing, strategic management and sustainable tourism.

Sarina Wakefield is an Adjunct Lecturer in the College of Arts and Creative Enterprises at Zayed University, Dubai (UAE). She holds a PhD from the Open University, UK, where her research focused upon the heritage industry in Abu Dhabi (UAE), and the inter-relationship between franchised and autochthonous heritage. Sarina guest lectured at UCL Qatar and has worked on museum and heritage projects in the United Kingdom and Bahrain. In addition to her work on hybrid heritage and cosmopolitanism in the Emirate of Abu Dhabi, she has published work on falconry as heritage in the UAE. She is the Co-Founder and Director of the international conference *Museums in Arabia*.

Paul Williams is a full Professor in the Department of Marketing and Information Systems, American University of Sharjah (UAE). He holds a PhD in Marketing from the University of Western Australia and has been teaching marketing courses for over 20 years at universities in the Middle East, United States, United Kingdom, Australia and Hong Kong. His teaching and research interests focus on the services marketing field, where he has published extensively and gained an international reputation for his work on customer attitudes such as satisfaction, value and service quality in the services sector.

Acknowledgements

The idea for this edited volume evolved out of an international workshop co-chaired by the volume's editors, entitled 'International Tourism Development in the GCC Countries: Opportunities and Challenges'. As this workshop formed part of the Third Annual Gulf Research Meeting (2012), held at the University of Cambridge (UK), the editors would like to thank the event's organisers: the Gulf Research Centre (Geneva, Cambridge). Although only five of the 15 chapters presented in this volume originated from this conference, we are grateful to all contributors in participating in the project and are appreciative of their energy, enthusiasm and patience. Given that all submissions and contributions went through a double-blind peer review process, we express our gratitude to the many referees who provided constructive comments and useful advice. Thanks also to Raoul Bianchi, Shaun Goldfinch, Mathew Gray and Nazia Ali for their intellectual support, and to the librarian staff at both Middlesex University Dubai and the University of the South Pacific. Given that this book, from start to finish, has indeed been a long journey, we would like to acknowledge help and assistance from our Routledge colleagues, Emma Travis and Carlotta Fanton. The first editor of this volume is indebted to his colleagues at the School of Tourism and Hospitality Management, University of the South Pacific (Fiji). Importantly, he would like express warm appreciation to his partner Golnoosh Najafi-Sohi, for her constant patience and unwavering support.

Introduction

Deciphering International Tourism Development in the GCC Region

Marcus L. Stephenson

Academic scholarship has started to pay serious attention to the study of the Arabian Peninsula over the past two decades, supported by the advancement of quality-based publications and the proliferation of institutions sponsoring academic exchange (Peterson 2014). The study of tourism development has largely focused on the wider context of the Middle East and the Arab and Islamic world (see especially Almuhrzi *et al.* 2017; Daher 2007; Hazbun 2008; Timothy 2017), rather than within the Gulf Cooperation Council (GCC) regional context. However, several preliminary enquiries focusing on tourism industry dimensions do exist (Karolak 2015; Mansfeld and Winckler 2007; 2015), along with emerging enquiries dealing with the urban and built environment (Wippel *et al.* 2014), and the museum and cultural heritage industry (Exell 2016; Exell and Rico 2016; Exell and Wakefield 2016). The current volume evaluates international tourism development and its relationship to the GCC region, dealing with the challenges faced and identifying the future potentialities for tourism destinations in the region. The endeavour is to provide an analysis exposing the socio-cultural, economic, political, environmental and industrial transformations that have an impact on tourism development within the GCC region. The work as a whole recognizes ways in which the impacts and outcomes of rapid change, urbanization, ultra-modernization, internationalization and globalization significantly shape and determine tourism development in the region. This introduction thus contextualizes the GCC and the region, leading to an explanation of the reasons for GCC states embracing diversification practices and embarking on tourism development, as well as identifying the influencing factors, specific challenges and ongoing realities of destination development in the region.

Gulf Cooperation Council: the regional context and commonalities

The Gulf states of Bahrain, Kuwait, Oman, Qatar, Saudi Arabia and the United Arab Emirates (UAE) signed the 'Charter of the Cooperation Council' in May 1981, forming the GCC. Although this intergovernmental and regional union is formally termed the 'Cooperation Council for the Arab States of the Gulf' (CCASG), the GCC as a label is popularly applied and is the term and acronym that will be used in this volume. All GCC member states are monarchies with variations in their patterns of governance. The UAE, composed of seven emirates governed by separate royal families, is a federal monarchy. Saudi Arabia and Bahrain are kingdoms, Kuwait and Qatar are ruled by emirs and Oman is a sultanate. These states are located on the Arabian Peninsula (see Figure 0.1), situated northeast of Africa and located between the Red Sea to the west and the Persian Gulf to the northeast. It is the largest peninsula in the world, with a land mass of around 3,237,500 square kilometres. It also includes Yemen in the south as well as the southern parts of both Jordan and Iraq in the north. The region is largely desert terrain and is the original homeland of the Arabs. It is the historic centre of Islam, introduced to the region in the seventh century through the teachings of Prophet Muhammed, who was born in Makkah in 570 and had initiated the Islamic religion after his migration to Medina in 622 (see Wynbrandt 2010). The popularized significance of Arabia concerns the folk tales and stories of the 'Arabian Nights' (or 'One Thousand and One Nights'), as well as the production of legendary figures, from the Queen of Sheba in antiquity through to Lawrence of Arabia in the twentieth century (see Hodson 1995). Nonetheless, the GCC region has experienced rapid socio-economic and urban transformations, which have determined, structured and impacted tourism development.

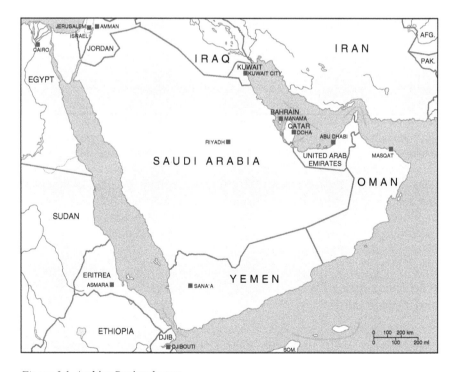

Figure 0.1 Arabian Peninsula map.

Source: Produced by Hermes Peter Furian (www.shutterstock.com/pic-196664717.html).

One reason for the establishment of the GCC concerned 'common strategic and ideological worries' over the political intentions of Iran and Iraq in the region (Pinfari 2009: 3). Another influencing factor was the region's post-colonial circumstance. The British withdrew from the region in 1971, with full independence granted to Bahrain, Qatar and the UAE. Kuwait became independent a decade earlier, in 1961, and Oman two decades earlier in 1951, while Saudi Arabia had always maintained de facto independence since its formation as a modern nation state in 1932. Self-rule followed a period of political discontent, where anticolonial sentiment was manifest in national strikes taking place from the 1950s in such states as Bahrain, Kuwait and Qatar. The sympathy of the regional states towards the Palestinian issue, and a realization that these states needed more control and ownership over oil production, expedited the challenge towards colonial authority (Hanieh 2011).

The Charter of the GCC comprises the Supreme Council, the Ministerial Council and the Secretariat General. The latter body is composed of six Directorates: (1) political affairs, (2) economic affairs, (3) military affairs, (4) environmental and human resources, (5) legal affairs and (6) financial and administrative affairs. The 1982 'Unified Economic Agreement' established the main measures for economic cooperation, including the coordination of banking, financial and monetary policies, and the free movement of GCC citizens. Although some anticipated initiatives have been achieved, other proposals crucial for cooperation and unification have not yet reached fruition (Sturm and Siegfried 2005). Accordingly, differences of opinion continue to afflict the GCC; for instance, Oman and the UAE are reluctant to work with the other states towards closer economic integration, unconvinced with the ongoing plan for a single currency (Marzovilla 2014). Nonetheless, the GCC agreed, in principle, to introduce value added tax by 2018, expected to be around 5 per cent on certain goods and services (Maceda 2016). Saudi Arabia and Bahrain favour closer integration, including the need to strengthen regional security. However, the GCC has a defence capability known as the 'Peninsular Shield Force' (see Patrick 2012), formed in 1984 and deployed during the Arab Spring uprising in Bahrain in 2011 (Fahim and Kirkpatrick 2012). The twentieth century witnessed territorial conflicts over state borders, such as those existing between Bahrain and Qatar over the ownership of several islands and the enclave of Zubarah (Al-Arayed 2003). The speculation of oil companies in the early to mid-twentieth century meant that land accumulated economic value and, thus, was subsequently contested, territorialized and safeguarded as part of a political system (Zahlan 1989).

One important regional directive indicating mutual forms of cooperation concerns the free movement of GCC nationals, who can freely travel between member states without visas, and reside and work in other GCC states. Given the high disposable incomes of nationals, GCC tourists are a lucrative source market for GCC tourism destinations and one that can help strengthen tourism numbers during difficult periods, as Bahrain witnessed as a consequence of the Arab Spring uprisings (see Chapter 5). Therefore, there is substantial mobility between states. Dubai, for instance, received 3.3 million tourists from other GCC states in 2015: around

1.54 million of these came from Saudi Arabia, representing the highest source market in the region, followed by 1 million tourists from Oman (*Saudi Gazette* 2016a). Qatar has also experienced an increasingly significant GCC tourism market, where arrivals doubled from 2010 to 2015 (*TTN* 2016). GCC tourists are also an important source market for other international destinations. The International Passenger Survey (IPS) indicated that a record number of 723,773 GCC travelers visited the United Kingdom in 2015, contributing a total spending of US$2.3 billion (*TTG Media* 2016). Although the current volume focuses on tourism within the context of tourist-receiving societies rather than tourist-generating societies, buoyant tourism mobility rates signify the capacity of significant sections of the national (and regional) citizenry to be able to access the 'good life' through claiming touristic privileges. This is reflective of the socio-economic rights associated with being a citizen of the modern state, whose disposable incomes are relatively high (Bianchi and Stephenson 2014).

Provision for the freedom of movement, however, excludes those who have resident status, that is, expatriates. The adoption of a liberalized visa regime through the introduction of a unified tourist visa could be advantageous to both tourists and residents alike, emulating the practices found in Europe through the Schengen Agreement and in Southeast Asia through the Association of Southeast Asian Nations. The president and chief executive officer of the World Travel and Tourism Council claims, 'If you create a common visa zone for people who live in the GCC countries it has a huge, huge positive impact on job creation and economic development' (*Saudi Gazette* 2016b). This remains a pressing concern, especially as available data indicate that 49 per cent foreign nationals live in the GCC region compared to 51 per cent nationals. Non-nationals represent 89.9 per cent in Qatar, 88.5 per cent in the UAE, 69.4 per cent in Kuwait, 52 per cent in Bahrain, 45.4 per cent in Oman and 32.7 per cent in Saudi Arabia (GLMM Programme 2016). Therefore, although the GCC does acknowledge the importance of developing a visa similar to Europe's Schengen visa (Khan 2015), the practical concerns have yet to be resolved, as mobility restrictions set limits for non-nationals working in the private sector, especially in areas involving cross-border transport and trade in services (Sturm and Siegfried 2005). The free movement of residents/expatriates could, thus, adversely affect job nationalization in the region, marginalizing nationals in private sector employment (*Arab News* 2014). Nevertheless, geo-political issues do contribute to influencing cross-border mobility (see Chapter 2). Currently, however, GCC states are adopting their own mechanisms to either control tourism mobility (as in the case of Saudi Arabia, for instance) or ease mobility (as in the case of the UAE, for instance). The UAE thus has a more liberal approach to mobility regulation, where there is now provision for visas on arrival for Chinese visitors (*Gulf News* 2016), and multiple-entry visas for cruise ship tourists (Algethami 2014). In fact, the UAE is leading the way in terms of globally advancing its tourism development portfolio.

Socio-economic levels of cooperation between GCC states are not as penetrative as those forms of cooperation that emerged from such politico-economic federations as the European Union (EU). This is not surprising, since the EU has a longer history of proactive cooperation, with its roots entrenched within the pan-European movement from the 1920s (see Weigall and Stirk 1992). Nonetheless, the GCC region presents itself as a useful unit of examination to comprehend how tourism development can be determined and contextualized across (and within) state boundaries, influenced by common and distinct socio-economic and political attributes.

Oil wealth and economic diversification

The discovery of oil and subsequent production revitalized and advanced Gulf economies, which partly suffered since the decline of the pearling industry from the early 1930s (see Al-Sayegh 1998). Today, GCC states collectively produce around 20 per cent of the world's oil, with 60–90 per cent of state revenues derived from petroleum exports (Lahn 2016). Data from the World Bank and the International Monetary Fund indicate that these states rank among the world's 22 richest countries in relation to GDP based on purchasing power parity per capita. The rankings are as follows: Qatar – 1 (with a GDP per capita of US$146,011); Kuwait – 2 (US$71,600); UAE – 7 (US$67,201); Saudi Arabia – 11 (US$56,253); Bahrain – 12 (US$52,830); and Oman – 22 (US$44,903) (Tasch 2016).

Unsurprisingly, the GCC region has developed a global image as a 'land of opportunity'. Such populist envisioning came to the fore recently, when a 16-year-old Chinese boy evaded security and hid in the cargo hold of Emirates flight EK303, which was travelling from Shanghai to Dubai. Apparently, he heard via social media that 'even beggars in the city (*Dubai*) can earn several hundred thousand yuan a month' (*Gulf Business* 2016). Ironically, government-led anti-begging initiatives have been the norm in most major GCC cites (Agarib 2012; *Peninsular* 2016; Toumi 2016). These initiatives, together with an emphasis on 'city beautification', 'greening projects' and 'public hygiene' (Khalaf 2006: 258), contribute to the production and representation of aestheticized, sanitized and clinical spaces and places. These destination attributes are some of the main tourism 'pull factors' of GCC destinations, manufactured on the basis that the 'tourist gaze' partly depends on a common desire for aesthetically pleasing experiences (Urry 1990).

The Human Development Index (HDI) indicates noticeably lower rankings for GCC states than their global wealth rankings, despite ultra-modern appearances and economies of wealth. From a ranking of 188 countries and based on three human development indicators – life expectancy at birth, literacy levels and standard of living (Chonghaile 2015) – the GCC states are positioned as follows: Qatar – 32; Saudi Arabia – 39; UAE – 41; Bahrain – 45; Kuwait – 48; and Oman – 52. In enhancing the human conditions of the population at large, especially given the challenges faced by lower socio-economic groupings and migrant workers (see Chalcraft 2012; Dresch 2006; Khalaf *et al.* 2015), one progressive approach would be to work towards an allocative approach to the welfare of others, irrespective of nationality and economic status.

The GCC region has one of the highest rates of population growth in the world, seven times faster than China, particularly given the large inflow of expatriates

(Accad 2015). A recent World Bank report indicates that nine out of ten people in GCC countries will live in cities by 2050 (*BQ Magazine* 2016a). In comparison to other Middle East and North Africa countries, GCC countries have economically advanced more quickly and integrated more rapidly into the global economy. The GCC's real GDP expanded by an average of 5.2 per cent over a 12-year period from 1998 (*Economist* 2009). During the second oil boom (2002–8), GCC states accumulated an estimated US$2.4 trillion in oil revenues, with an estimated US$1.5 trillion invested in regional sovereign wealth funds (Held and Coates Ulrichsen 2012: 17). However, at the time of writing, oil prices remain low, with global demand being uncertain and existing stock levels high (ICAEW 2016). This presents challenges for the region, as public cuts have been an inevitable result of low oil prices. In 2016, the Saudi Arabian government announced a year-on-year decline in planned spending for the first time in 14 years, and Oman announced a 16 per cent cut in spending (Nagraj 2016).

The *BP Statistical Review of World Energy* noted that, if production continued at the 2007 rates, then within a 100-year period most GCC oil reserves would be depleted, with the exception of Kuwait (cited in Reiche 2010: 2398). Accordingly, economic diversification involves the need to broaden the private sector and reduce dependency on the hydrocarbon sector (see Fasano and Iqbal 2003). As the oil sector is not labour intensive, the need for states to diversify and create more labour-intensive industries is imperative. In the 1990s, when oil prices were low and states experienced rapid population growth, those countries with the highest GDP growth rates were less dependent on oil. Such states were Bahrain (with a 4 per cent growth rate) and the UAE (with a 3.9 per cent growth rate), in contrast to the oil dependency countries of Saudi Arabia (with a negative growth rate of -0.8 per cent) and Kuwait (with a negative growth rate of -0.6 per cent) (Mansfeld and Winckler 2007: 339). Bahrain has moved forward as a financial hub, notably through Islamic banking, aluminum production and tourism (Mansfeld and Winckler 2008). UAE followed a similar pattern, though it is arguably developing a stronger international tourism profile. Oman diversified into manufacturing with some tourism infrastructure, and Saudi Arabia expanded into manufacturing and construction, although it has a strong and well-established pilgrimage tourism sector. Qatar has diversified into tourism, especially the conference and event market (Sturm et al. 2008). Kuwait, however, is more dependent on commodities and finance, and much less so on tourism (see Chapter 6).

Traditionally, GCC states have been economically and politically determined by the rentier system, characterized by high rent influx from oil exports and natural gas (see Beblawi and Luciani 1987), where some of this wealth has been redistributed through public spending (including tax-free incomes) in exchange for political compliance (DeVriese 2016). Oil wealth legitimized and strengthened the 'socio-political status quo' (Abdulla 2012: 109) of GCC states. Nonetheless, economic returns from oil and gas enable these states to diversify their economic assets through investing in service sector industries. According to Gray (2011: 24), the entrepreneurial intentions of GCC states and their open approach to development have influenced the movement towards diversification, supported by the fact that these states are 'more responsive, globalized, and strategic'. Diversification involves GCC states moving away from an 'energy-centric' economy, involving a complete rentier system based on the over-reliance on revenue gained from oil and gas exports, towards an 'energy-driven or energy-underwritten' economy that is characteristic of the 'late rentier' era (Gray 2011: 31) (see also Chapter 1).

International tourism development in the GCC region: key influences

Mansfeld and Winckler (2007: 341–343) identify six factors influencing GCC states to focus on tourism as a diversification directive: (1) 'Tourism provides a new source of employment opportunities for nationals', (2) 'Tourism promotes the construction industry', (3) 'Tourism promotes private sector activities' and attracts local investment, (4) 'Tourism promotes local industries and services', (5) 'Tourism can be used as a means to gain political advantage' and alleviate negative images of the region, especially those associated with terrorist activities and (6) 'The basic contradiction between oil prices and the tourism industry'. Regarding the latter point, the authors explain that tourism development emerged from the early 1990s when oil prices were low, thus benefitting tourism development as energy costs were also low. Prior to this period, however, tourism development was not an overwhelming priority for GCC states. Smith (2015: 154) notes that in the 1970s the region had 'little to offer', and Ritter (1986: 240) observes that in the 1980s GCC cities were disorganized, where hotels were built in isolation from other amenities and utilized mainly by 'business travellers' and 'weekenders' rather than by tourists per se.

In realizing the influencing factors of tourism diversification, the role of the airline industry should not be underestimated. Most GCC states are investing heavily in airport infrastructure, especially as the region connects to major tourism markets. Accordingly, there are significant ongoing developments and investments across the region. In the UAE, for instance, the following major projects are taking place: the construction of Al Maktoum International Airport (Dubai), involving a US$8 billion investment; the expansion of Dubai International Airport, costing US$7.8 billion; and the building a new international airport in the Emirate of Ajman, involving a US$600 million investment. Airport developments costing US$6.1 billion are planned at two international airports and four regional airports in Oman, with further initiatives in place at the King Abdulaziz International Airport in Jeddah (Saudi Arabia) and Bahrain International Airport (Menon 2016). Consequently, GCC states are expectant that tourism development has a significant future in the region.

Held and Coates Ulrichsen (2012: 10) emphasize the GCC's role in 'the fundamental reshaping of the map of global aviation power', epitomized by the ambitions of three major players in the region: Emirates Airlines, Etihad Airways and Qatar Airways. Qatar's ambition is to be a global leader in the airline industry. Its ever-expanding fleet size is perhaps a testimony to such determination, with

36 aircraft being delivered in 2016 (*ETN* 2016a). The *Economist* emphasizes the value of national carriers and their global approach to aviation, claiming that 'The ubiquity of UAE and Qatar air carriers in Western geographies has led the globalization of their national brands' (2014: 19). Low-cost airlines have also grown in popularity over the past decade. Emirates-owned Flydubai, for instance, produced annual profits of US$27.4 million and a revenue totalling US$1.33 billion in 2015 (*ETN* 2016b).

Nonetheless, there are prevailing concerns facing GCC airlines. There were three major airline incidents in the UAE in 2016: (1) a Flydubai aircraft crashed as it was landing in Rostov-on-Don in Southern Russia, killing 61 people; (2) Emirates Airline's Boeing 777 made an emergency landing in Mumbai on its way to the Maldives; and (3) another Boeing 777 belonging to Emirates Airlines crash-landed at the Dubai International Airport (*Guardian* 2016). These incidents could have a medium-term impact on public confidence and customer perceptions of airline safety. Also, increased congestion of airspace is an emerging regional concern. However, as will be indicated in Chapter 4, plans to advance a GCC rail route represent constructive ways to embrace cooperation in the region, integrate mobility structures and encourage greater transnational, socio-cultural affinities.

Nevertheless, the region's geographic location as a stopover point between the Far East and Europe is a considerable comparative advantage of GCC-based tourism (Mansfeld and Winckler 2007). Bahrain, to some extent, and then Dubai, very aggressively, were the first destinations in the region to focus on the stopover market and develop retail tourism. The Dubai International Airport, for instance, contained the world's largest stock list by 1993 (Laws 1995: 179). In fact, hotel developers strategically select locations zoned for retail space (Salama 2008), particularly as large shopping malls become a key motivational component of the 'tourist gaze', as seen in Dubai and elsewhere in the GCC region (see Chapter 8). The shopping experience signifies the integration of Gulf cities into the globalized economy. Thomas (2013: 22) describes the common recreational experience in the region:

> On visiting shopping malls across the Gulf States you are likely to encounter the same fast food outlets, boutiques and coffee shops you would find in most industrialized western nations. It's not uncommon even to find the same sequence of shops; Costa Coffee, for example, always within eyeshot of Starbucks; global brands going head-to head for market hegemony on the world stage. During your walk through the mall you will also encounter the costumes of acculturation: baseball caps, jeans and t-shirts abound. The full flamboyant spectrum of globalized teen culture is on parade.

The socially liberalized atmosphere of GCC states represents another destination 'pull factor' for international tourists, particularly for the non-Muslim segment. With the exception of Saudi Arabia and Kuwait, non-Muslims living in and travelling to the UAE, Qatar, Oman and Bahrain can legally purchase alcohol and pork products. In the latter state, members of Parliament (MPs) had voted to ban pork (Shane 2013). Najjar (2005) is sceptical of Arab communities being able to maintain their cultural identity and independence when they are gradually embracing modernization. He highlights that the 'hegemony of globalization' (2005: 105) is challenging the cultural, religious and traditional values of the Arab-Muslim world. Future enquiries ought to consider more the direct impacts of tourism upon social and cultural life. There has been little attempt to deal with these concerns in the region, with the exception of a few enquiries focusing on tourism impacts in specific GCC states (see El Amrousi and Biln 2010; Mershen 2007; Stephenson 2014; Stephenson and Ali-Knight 2010). Although the chapter contributions of this volume do not directly centralize their enquiries on such impacts, social enquiry should consider the 'local voices', including the perspectives of both expatriates/residents and nationals/citizens. This would help to provide critical insights into levels of local tolerance relative to rising visitor numbers. Despite the pervading force of globalization and the substantial oil wealth-fuelling Western forms of public consumption, there is still hope for some GCC destinations to pursue Islamic forms of hospitality and tourism; notably Sharjah (see, especially, Chapter 10) and Saudi Arabia (see Chapter 7).

Mansfeld and Winckler (2007: 344–345) identify other notable comparative advantages of GCC tourism products: the region's religious, cultural, historic and 'winter sun, sand, sea' appeal; its potential to expand the domestic tourism market; its capacity to combine the business and leisure components; and its perception as a safe destination. Ironically, the region benefitted from tourist flows by international and Arab tourists during the Arab Spring uprisings. Operators in tourist-generating countries were actually redirecting their customers to the more stable destinations in the region (Stephenson 2014; see also Mansfeld and Winckler 2015). As a relatable destination attribute in the region, the leisure component, noted here, would appeal to the cruise ship market. Although cruise ship tourism is still in its infancy in the GCC region, it has started to develop in the past few years and, thus, has market potential (Karolak 2015). However, as its positive economic contribution to tourism destinations has been contested (see Chin 2008), the degree to which this form of tourism is being fully integrated into the leisure (and retail) market in GCC states would require detailed evaluation.

International tourism development: challenges and ways forward

Nonetheless, the region is still vulnerable to security threats and safety risks, which will inevitably test its ultimate tourism potential. Further conflicts penetrating deeper within the GCC region could be detrimental to the buoyancy of the tourism industry. As Coates Ulrichsen (2016: 188) claims, 'The Gulf remains an extremely volatile sub-region of the Middle East, with multiple interlinking threats to internal and external security alike'. GCC states dropped substantively in the 2016 Global Peace Index (GPI) rankings, with the Middle East and North Africa classified as the least peaceful region in the world. This classification covers three dimensions: (1) ongoing domestic and international conflict, (2) safety and security in society and (3) militarization (Institute for Economics and Peace 2016: 2). Bahrain fell from a ranking of 107 in 2015 to 132 in 2016, which is low considering that Syria occupies the bottom-ranking position of 162 in 2016. UAE fell from 49 in 2015 to 61 in 2016, Kuwait dropped from 34 to 51 and Saudi Arabia plunged from a ranking of 95 to 129 over the same period. Oman, however, remained unchanged in 2016, ranked 74. Qatar ranked 34 in 2016 and was the highest-ranked state in the Middle East and North Africa region (King 2016). Although Saudi Arabia's involvement in the war in Yemen could impact the perception of the country as a peaceful destination, this situation would be aggravated by the July 2016 attacks on security forces by suicide bombers outside the Prophet's Mosque in Medina (Saudi Arabia) (Shaheen 2016). Nonetheless, Saudi Arabia's image as a safe and secure destination is of paramount importance to the state, especially given that the government launched 'Vision 2030' in 2016, involving a plan to extend its tourism offering beyond pilgrimage tourism (see Chapter 7).

Despite a general recognition within the GCC that tourism development is an inevitable outcome of economic diversification, there is substantial opportunity for the region to become more globally competitive. Accordingly, the World Economic Forum's (2015) 'Travel and Tourism Competitiveness Report 2015' indicates that of the 141 economies noted, GCC's rankings were low overall: Saudi Arabia – 69; UAE – 75; Oman – 93; Qatar – 114; Bahrain – 131; and Kuwait – 137. The current volume concerns ways in which the development of international tourism faces significant problems and challenges, despite degrees of optimism. Destination branding is certainly one strategic mechanism by which GCC states can move forward in the global tourism market. Various chapters in this volume advertently or inadvertently concern ways in which destination branding can be, or is being, internationally and strategically mobilized (see especially Chapters 1, 5, 7, 8, 10 and 14).

In 2015, 'Strategy &' found that business tourists in the GCC states represent around one in three of all visitors in the region, which is considered to be relatively high, given that only 2 per cent of global exhibitions take place in the Middle East (*BQ Magazine* 2016b). The UAE aims to strengthen its presence and competitive spirit as an event destination. Dubai's Meetings, Incentives, Conferences and Events (MICE) market represents nearly 27 per cent of the share of the GCC MICE market, worth US$1.3 billion in 2015 (*Trade Arabia* 2016). The region is preparing for a 'golden decade' (Pivac 2015) of events, represented by two prominent mega-events: the Expo 2020 in Dubai and the 2022 FIFA World Cup in Qatar.

Alpen Capital (2016) forecasts the hospitality markets of Qatar and the UAE to have the fastest annualized growth rate of over 10 per cent from 2015 to 2020, while Oman, Saudi Arabia and Kuwait are likely to experience a less than average regional growth of 5–6 per cent. However, Bahrain is likely to produce a growth rate consistent with the regional average. Most GCC governments aim to increase the visitor numbers through setting very ambitious targets. The Oman Ministry of Tourism, for instance, intends to double tourist arrivals to 5 million by 2040 (*Times of Oman* 2016).

Within the context of a newly developed region, the development of the hospitality industry mirrors the realities of most developing tourism regions in that major international companies have a strong foothold in GCC states, where the likes of Accor, Hilton, Hyatt, InterContinental, Marriot and Starwood have dominated. Nonetheless, there is an increasing involvement of homegrown brands which are overwhelmingly, though not exclusively, from the UAE, for instance Al-Ansar Hotel Company, Al Habtoor Group, Emaar Hospitality Group, Hospitality Management Holdings, JA Resorts and Hotels, Jumeirah Group, Majid Al Futtaim Properties, Mubarak Group, Rotana Hotels and TI'ME Hotels Management. Dubai's Jumeirah Group, which has significant interests across the GCC region and beyond, launched an expansion project in 2014 expected to cost 8 billion dirham (US$2.18 billion) (*Khaleej Times* 2014). However, given the level of hotel expansion in the region, matching the supply of rooms with lower than anticipated demand could be a challenge, placing pressure on hotel occupancy and average daily rates; as well as, perhaps, a potential skills shortage due to increased property openings. Low oil prices can also affect the business climate, and the possible depreciation of currencies can make travel more expensive (*Times of Oman* 2016). What strengthens the GCC's globalized strategy to tourism development is the way in which GCC states and interested bodies invest substantially in the international hotel industry, especially through sovereign wealth funds. Qatar Holdings, for instance, owns high-class hotels in London, while Qatar investors have lucrative interests in France, the Netherlands (Barnard 2016), Singapore, Myanmar and Laos (Buller 2012).

Although diversification into tourism is to be encouraged as it represents a source of employment for nationals, as noted by Mansfeld and Winckler (2007), the realities on the ground are quite different. GCC nationals have overwhelmingly taken up positions within the public sector and far less so in the private sector, particularly the tourism and hospitality industry (see Chapter 11). Despite arguments concerning the importance of GCC nationals working in the industry, such as the role of GCC nationals as cultural ambassadors and role models, this industry is not fully perceived as an attractive source of employment in the GCC region (see Sadi and Henderson 2005; Stephenson *et al.* 2010). In Oman, however, there have been some positive outcomes concerning the Omanization of the tourism and hospitality industries (Winckler 2007).

The hospitality industry has been far more visibly dominant than the cultural heritage industry in the region. There were just 12 United Nations Educational, Scientific and Cultural Organization (UNESCO) Heritage Sites across all GCC states registered in February 2017, which is quite low when compared to Iran, for instance, possessing 21 recognized sites. Oman and Saudi Arabia have four sites each, Bahrain has two sites, Qatar and UAE have one site each and Kuwait has no registered sites. As all of these sites are cultural sites; no registered UNESCO natural site exits in the region (UNESCO World Heritage List 2017). Nevertheless, there is growing recognition of heritage preservation as an important cultural and national resource for most GCC states. As Exell and Rico (2013: 675) assert, 'The nation-states of the Arabian Peninsula are now becoming openly and aggressively involved in the preservation, representation and invention of their own individual and distinct tangible national culture and heritage'. Tourism representations arguably serve to represent the national and dominant cultural identity of the state, rather than signify ethnic and cosmopolitan diversities (see Chapter 3). That is not to say that heritage projects do not have the capacity to reflect global and transnational elements. The development of two major museum projects in the UAE, Guggenheim Abu Dhabi and Louvre Abu Dhabi, indicate the growing awareness of hybrid heritage (see Chapter 14). Nonetheless, as Chapter 14 also implies, as the state has structured and controlled hybrid heritage production, the manufacture of heritage can characterize a de-colonial agenda. Stephenson's (2014) observations of tourism development in Dubai indicate how de-colonialism operates. He notes of the exploitative relations embodied within the pearl trade during British colonial rule and emphasizes Dubai's contemporary quest to be 'bigger and brasher' (2014: 727) than the 'West and the rest' (2014: 730). Accordingly, such spectacular architecture and tourism-based infrastructure in some way negates the realities of a difficult past and indicates 'self-determination' and 'economic freedom' (2014: 729).

The ultra-modernized image of the GCC region is overriding the perception of these states as having meaningful heritage resources. However, in their observations of the heritage industry in Qatar, Exell and Rico (2013) challenge the assumption from the West that the state has 'no heritage' and emphasize that the country is taking a serious approach to heritage development (see also Chapter 8). Arguably, the region is slowly witnessing a heritage awakening (see Exell and Rico 2016). Sharjah (UAE), for instance, has developed a proactive policy to revitalize itself as an Islamic city as well as a centre for culture and education (Fox *et al.* 2006: 285). Nonetheless, not all GCC destinations are following the same pathway, particularly as ultra-modernization and development represent a threat to heritage – as seen in Saudi Arabia (see Chapter 13) and Failaka Island (Kuwait) (see Chapter 15). However, Stephenson's (2014: 8) observations of Dubai point to a rather progressive conceptualization of 'heritage', indicating how heritage is becoming re-constituted. He notes:

> The endeavour is to break new ground by investing in a new cultural fabric based on the manufacture of novel experiences and the strategic advancement of global patterns of consumption, as well as being innovative in the development of monumental and architectural grandeur. In an inimitable way, its [*Dubai's*] new cultural landscape indicates that heritage is indeed in 'the making': invented and created rather than preserved and conserved in a familiar western sense.

The heritage industry does not fully communicate and explain all significant historical events and circumstances that have helped to define the socio-cultural, political and economic fabric of the GCC region. The greatest challenge for GCC countries is to deal directly with sensitive pasts and social complexities, such as the cosmopolitan heritage of recent migrant groupings, including their unique contributions to economic and cultural life; tribal rivalries and distinctiveness; ancient Arabian Christianity; the historical Jewish presence in Arabia, including the legendary travels on Benjamin of Tudela in the Arabian Peninsula (see Daniel 1998; Shatzmiller 1998); and the Arab slave trade (see Gordon 1989). However, there are some emerging signs that particular GCC states are rethinking ways to embrace and engage with the past. The recent opening of the Bin Jelmood House Museum in Doha (Qatar), for instance, the former home of a well-known slave trader, presents new historical narratives of slavery in the region (Khan 2016). In the current context of the state undergoing scrutiny for the living and working conditions of migrant construction workers (Meier 2015), such heritage and tourism initiatives could work to symbolically pacify perceived social imbalances within the state itself.

One major tourism development challenge concerns 'environmental sustainability', where the GCC region occupies a low-ranking position for this component in the World Economic Forum's (2015) Travel and Tourism Competitiveness Report 2015. This component covers such aspects as 'environmental regulations', 'sustainability of travel and tourism industry development', 'baseline water stress', 'threatened species' and 'wastewater treatment'. The rankings were as follows: UAE (41), Qatar (50), Oman (74), Bahrain (104), Saudi Arabia (121) and Kuwait (136). The environmental concerns for the region (see Raouf and Luomi 2016) could have a notable effect on the tourism industry in the future. One specific concern, for instance, is the quality of the shoreline environment. Although the GCC has a significant coastline, only the UAE has Blue Flag certification (Kader 2014). Nonetheless, there are still opportunities for the region and for tourism industry stakeholders to seriously consider eco-alternatives (see Chapter 9), sustainable directives and a responsibility-based agenda (see Chapter 12).

Structure of the book and chapter summaries

Most of the chapters in this volume concern enquiries that are conceptually based. However, given that the study of tourism development within the context of the GCC region is still evolving, with significant scope for academic advancement, all chapters, crucially, identify implications for future research. Part One, 'Tourism development and the Gulf Cooperation Council region', looks collectively at the GCC region and the situation of tourism development within a wider international context, particularly in relation to the following components: the political economy; geo-politics of tourism, mobility and border issues; cultural, national and tourism representations (and images) of GCC states; and transport structures and networks within and across GCC states. Part Two, 'The challenges of international tourism development at a national level', critically scrutinizes the concerns and problems faced by GCC states. Chapter contributions in this section consider why such challenges exist and continue to persist, despite the fact that tourism development is deemed to be economically viable. The challenges identified are multifarious, focusing on such issues as socio-cultural environment, political climate, ultra-modernization, cultural sensitivities, environmental issues, policy implementation, physical infrastructure and infrastructural capacities, and the tourism and hospitality industry itself. Part Three, 'Destinations and opportunities', concerns the needs of particular destinations in terms of identifying real prospects and potentialities. The work focuses on ways forward, operationally and strategically, concentrating on such elements as marketing and branding, destination awareness and product development, national employment, education and training, environmental sustainability and responsibilities, transnational heritage formations, and heritage management and conservation. The book concludes with an Afterword from Waleed Hazbun, commenting significantly on the implications and ramifications of the chapter contributions. In addition to reflecting on emerging issues, conceptual advancements and research prospects, the Afterword acknowledges where the main topic of enquiry can and should travel to in the future.

Part One: Tourism development and the Gulf Cooperation Council region

In Chapter 1, Gray examines how key theoretical approaches to the political economy of the GCC states apply and link to the dynamics of tourism. The chapter investigates three main areas of political economy theory. The first is rentier state theory, focusing on how oil wealth, or any large external 'rent', corrupts or reshapes state-society relations. Originally designed to explain the durability of Gulf regimes in the absence of democratic processes, this theory covers other dynamics relevant to tourism, such as the business-government relationship and the politics of economic reform. Rentier dynamics relate to the second body of theory comprehending a Gulf 'type' of state capitalism. This 'new' state capitalism still privileges the state but encourages efficient and profitable state-owned enterprises through openness to the global economy. The third area of theory considers the links between tourism and the political economy of national 'branding' and differentiation. Gray draws attention to how national branding, through the strategic enablement of the tourism industry, serves to legitimize the international image and profile of the state, including cultural representation and image.

In Chapter 2, Timothy addresses some of the most pressing elements of the geo-politics of tourism in the GCC region. The chapter initially highlights the barriers of tourism and human mobility, including challenges to the potential of using GCC state borders as tourist attractions. The discussion acknowledges that border regions create differential tourism growth between member states, with some states focusing on different forms of tourism than others. Furthermore, unique border histories also create fragmented states or exclaves, which have implications for particular types of tourism. Although visa restrictions and borders do limit people from visiting certain countries in the region, Timothy considers ways in which geo-politics impacts tourism through encouraging cross-border cooperation and supranational alliances. In addition to the introduction of common visas for nationals, potential elements of commonality are identified: common passports; regional transportation networks; and a single currency. The work further indicates how the implications of cross-border collaborative efforts can influence tourism in a variety of contexts.

In Chapter 3, Feighery utilizes critical discourse analysis to determine representations of 'national' and/or 'regional' identity of three GCC states (Oman, Qatar and Saudi Arabia) through state-sponsored tourism promotional films. His assessment acknowledges that within and among the states of the Arabian Gulf, there is a diversity of inter- and intra-ethnic, linguistic, sectarian and tribal cleavages which have long influenced the social, economic and political development of the region. More recently, state responses to the perceived cultural threat from non-nationals and an emerging regional or '*Khaleeji*' ('*of the Gulf*') identity have focused on 'national identity' as a state-building tool, which has also been encouraged through the recent emphasis on the state funding of heritage. Accordingly, representations in and through state-sponsored tourism promotion support such undertakings. Feighery's analysis thus suggests that tourism promotional films transmit performative power and, potentially, play a constitutive role in personifications of the state. One implicit concern is the way in which formal and official state narratives are not addressing the cultural, ethnic and religious diversities of the region. The discussion thus insinuates that Western perceptions continue to influence representations and images.

In Chapter 4, Bätzner and Stephenson examine ways in which transport structures can serve the purpose of both fostering tourism and strengthening cooperation within the GCC region. The work welcomes GCC plans to develop a trans-GCC rail network, especially in light of past challenges to connect the region as a whole. The authors believe that this planned development could encourage regional mobility and new holiday experiences for many, as well as assisting the socio-economic process of unification within the region. The chapter determines the major challenges to the expansion of ground transportation, such as increased car dependency, sustainability concerns and transport comfort. Although the discussion does highlight the regional and global influence of GCC carriers, some state carriers have not been economically successful, indicating that the airline industry is not particularly unified in the region. One other concern raised is increased airspace congestion, especially as passenger movement intensifies. The latter part of the chapter highlights how integrated transportation networks can foster political, social and cultural ties between states, as well as add value to the region's image.

Part Two: The challenges of international tourism development at a national level

In Chapter 5, Bagaeen addresses key challenges facing tourism development in Bahrain, particularly in the context of the 2011 Arab Spring uprisings and the aftermath. Therefore, the discussion recognizes that socio-political transformation is affecting destination strategy. One implicit challenge identified concerns Bahrain's reliance on one dominant market, Saudi Arabia, rather than a multitude of markets. However, the author's observations indicate a paradox, as this market encouraged Bahrain to recuperate gradually from the loss of tourism numbers due to political unrest. The discussion highlights how culture and sport can be (and, to some extent, are being) leveraged for international tourism development, though it raises further concern over the need to represent Bahrain's cultural and religious diversity. This is, arguably, a germane issue because of the existing religious divisions and the need to pacify conflict though tourism development. Bagaeen concludes by claiming that the emotive values of the destination brand of Bahrain should concern 'cultural plurality' and 'cosmopolitan diversity'.

In Chapter 6, Kelly examines the reasons why tourism development has not moved significantly forward in Kuwait. She utilizes the World Economic Forum's 'Travel and Tourism Competitiveness Report: Growth through Shocks in 2015' to explain the reasons for Kuwait's low rankings in such areas as prioritization for travel and tourism, government policy and support, marketing tourism, tourism employee training and natural and cultural resources. The subsequent discussions concern such challenges as lack of tourism investment in Kuwait, environmental degradation, cultural sensitivities and the lack of national value placed on tourism employment. Kelly emphasizes that within the context of a conservative society, the 'tourist gaze' could be too intrusive. The final section discusses the Master Plan and its potential for implementation, evoking a concern that Kuwaitis may wish to pursue more localized versions of tourism development.

In Chapter 7, Ekiz, Oter and Stephenson address the challenges that the Kingdom of Saudi Arabia faces in developing an international tourism industry, beyond pilgrimage tourism. This is despite the fact that the government is becoming increasingly aware of the need to diversify its economy, as reflected in the recent plan, *Saudi Vision 2030*. This chapter provides an initial synopsis of tourism trends and demand factors, including the significance of domestic tourism and outbound travel by nationals. The evaluation identifies factors that can facilitate travel, predominantly the religious tourism infrastructure, economic investment, accumulated oil wealth, political stability and an established knowledge economy. The key inhibitors and challenges are addressed: the state's austere visa system; the need for an advanced public transport system; low representation of nationals working in the tourism industry; personal safety concerns at pilgrimage sites; re-emerging political tensions; low oil prices; and modernization's impact on the environment and the culture. To reconcile the challenges, the authors recommend particular ways forward: market differentiation and niche market development; utilization of natural and archaeological resources; and the strengthening of public transport options. The discussion recommends that Saudi Arabia should logically embrace Islamic tourism development, targeted at Muslim and non-Muslim tourists, and ensure that the destination brand signifies societal values. Capacity building and localized training and employment are considered imperative if the industry is to become more culturally representative and contribute to the national development framework.

In Chapter 8, Scharfenort probes into the difficulties faced by Qatar in terms of its plans to become a globally renowned tourism destination. The chapter initially contextualizes the state's strategic intentions to advance the tourism industry, particularly in light of hosting the 2022 FIFA World Cup. The discussion implicates disparities in the availability of non-luxury hotels and the need for infrastructure to support the expansion of retail, entertainment and leisure facilities. The author identifies the rationale behind the state's emphasis on the development of cultural resources and events, recognizing the potential drawback of the 'boosteristic' approach to infrastructural developments, including the capital-intense nature of rapid modernization. Finally, the work identifies future challenges in developing market segments, monopolizing on the passenger transit market and competing with more established destinations.

In Chapter 9, AlRiyami, Scott, Ragab and Jafari consider how Oman practices sustainable tourism and ecotourism, in particular. The chapter evaluates the performance of ecotourism practices in the state, based on the six common principles of ecotourism: (1) nature-based activities, (2) preservation and conservation, (3) environmental and cultural education, (4) distribution of benefits, (5) ethics and responsibility and (6) sustainability. In examining the challenges faced by each of these components, the following improvements are recommended: consistency in the provision of ecotourism attractions having basic facilities; all protected areas to be well resourced and managed; more on-site and localized forms of interpretation of heritage, history and nature; more localized tourism services and locally involved staff; guidelines and standards in place for dolphin and whale watching trips; and more opportunity to retain and represent Omani authenticity and Arabian culture. The authors indicate that some principles of ecotourism are still poorly implemented, requiring significant resources and determined action.

Part Three: Destinations and opportunities

In Chapter 10, Ashill, Williams and Chathoth examine the destination of Sharjah (UAE), assessing the marketing challenges facing tourism development and then identifying the marketing opportunities. The chapter contemplates how well the Emirate is positioned in terms of future growth as an Islamic tourism destination, especially if it continues to be strategic in orientation and outlook. This position recognizes Sharjah's wealth of Islamic cultural attractions and services sensitive to the needs of Muslim travelers. The discussions, however, raise concern over road traffic congestion and the decline in specific national tourist segments. Given negative perceptions of the Middle East, the work infers that the Emirate should focus on developing a stronger brand image and greater destination awareness. Marketing attention directed to Sharjah's cultural offerings is one way forward to ensure brand consistency. The discussion recognizes the potential of the destination to target the family market and attract those tourists who are appreciative of the destination's conservative values. Despite Dubai's mature profile as a tourism destination, the authors believe that Sharjah can benefit from its geographic proximity to Dubai.

In Chapter 11, Burns and Bibbings investigate Kuwait and are optimistic that tourism development can move away from the conception of Kuwait as an anomaly in the annals of tourism history. The authors assess the rationale for tourism development, aligned in part to wider policy matters, and provide a conceptual model for identifying potential conflicts arising from the co-presence of tourists and communities. They indicate that there is a need to generate private sector employment to mitigate the consequences of youth unemployment and a bloated public sector. This chapter speculates on the socio-cultural implications and the opportunities of tourism development, especially tourism's potential to strengthen social unity and national identity as well as the need to develop a localized educational framework in tourism and hospitality education.

In Chapter 12, Stephenson and Vyas study the enviromental impact of tourism development in Dubai (UAE) and explicate the challenges that tourism development presents to Dubai's increasingly fragile environment, especially rapid hotel and resort developments, intensified tourism infrastructural developments, expanded transport networks, land reclamation schemes, artificial island developments, and increased recreational developments. Accordingly, the work further discusses problems concerning excessive water consumption, desalination and high-energy consumption, and land, sea and air pollution. The authors question the ambiguous intentions of an aesthetic management approach to the environment and environmental modification practices. They argue that because urbanism, consumerism and capitalistic-driven development activities not only commoditize the environment but fuel tourism development, capitalist enterprise represents an ultimate threat to the physical environment. Despite some environmentally friendly initiatives being pursued at public and private sector levels, it is asserted that these initatives need to be embraced more at the community level. Moreover, the argument emphasises that a sustainable tourism development platform should adopt an 'environmental citizenship' framework, involving elements of corporate and civic responsibility.

In Chapter 13, Henderson examines pilgrimage (Hajj and Umrah) as a form of tourism development and discusses the performative elements of pilgrimage tourism, issues concerning the management and operational dynamics of Hajj and future prospects of pilgrimage tourism. The chapter initially implicates the Kingdom of Saudi Arabia as a leading centre for religious tourism but observes how a large number of people on the move create practical problems for the authorities. The formidable challenges in managing the Hajj are identified: overcrowding and fatal accidents; traffic congestion and logistical difficulties; physical upgrading of facilities; and capacity enlargement concerns at primary pilgrimage sites. The work, importantly, indicates the unresolved conflicts between development and heritage conservation. Given that these challenges could intensify in light of the expanding Muslim population worldwide, the chapter identifies future ways forward, particularly to minimize safety concerns and develop stronger educational awareness concerning natural and cultural heritage conservation.

In Chapter 14, Wakefield presents a case study of Abu Dhabi (UAE) and examines the role of transnational heritage. The emirate is prioritizing cultural tourism as one of the ways to diversify its economy by 2030 and is developing two high-profile global heritage institutions through the process of cultural heritage franchising, namely the Louvre Abu Dhabi and the Guggenheim Abu Dhabi. This chapter analyzes the interrelationship between globalization and hybrid heritage, understanding how this connects to the transnational economy. It then provides a theoretical discussion on how cultural heritage franchising relates to globalization, cosmopolitanism and soft power. Wakefield argues that despite an emerging cosmopolitan discourse concerning global heritage formations and cultural heritage franchises, it is not entirely inclusive of the heritages of other groupings and, thus, does not stretch beyond official state versions of heritage. Another contention raised in the latter part of the chapter indicates that because the state is branding this kind of heritage, it has control over something interpreted and produced by the West. The work thus suggests that Abu Dhabi's transnational outlook and desire to preserve the past is leading to the creation of a transnational heritage industry based on hybrid heritage processes.

In Chapter 15, Paris evaluates the potentiality of tourism and destination development in the context of the ongoing plan to develop Failaka Island (Kuwait). As the author describes, the island looked towards significant tourism development in the early 1980s, but the subsequent Iraqi invasion halted this ambition. The chapter initially uncovers the historical and cultural importance of the island and the current work done to discover and preserve its broad-based heritage, which has historical connections to such diverse places as the Indus Valley, Mesopotamia, Dilmun, Oman, Greece and Portugal. However, the discussion notes that plans to redevelop the island since 2003 manifest disagreements between the private sector and the state concerning which stakeholders should be ultimately responsible for the cost of the infrastructure. The author implicates the range of challenges that the island faces, such as how this large-scale project could threaten archaeological sites and those yet to be uncovered, the need for water management projects and the importance of a sustainable coastal development approach to island planning. However, Paris observes that a vocal and visible group supporting the preservation and conservation of the island's historical sites has started to emerge, where the identification of sustainable ways forward is now possible.

Afterword

Hazbun outlines the emerging themes arising from this volume, interlinking his own evaluation of tourism development issues in the GCC region. He calls for tourism enquiries to make a unique contribution to 'Khaleeji Tourism Studies', which in turn could strengthen tourism studies globally. He acknowledges that scholars in the region face a number of challenges, such as visa restrictions, transportation, language barriers and a harsh climate, as well as limitations in the free flow of information. He asserts that petrodollars have been fundamental to international tourism development in the region, more so than other determining factors. The discussion implies that tourism scholars should continue to be aware of how globalization affects tourism in the GCC region, undertaking research enquiries concerning tourism immobilities and tourism's relationship to migrant and expatriate communities. The Afterword provides valuable advice concerning the application of ethnographic studies in the field and the importance of studying the political economy of tourism, as well as transnational and transregional processes and networks. Hazbun emphasizes that future studies should deal more with how tourism development intersects with everyday cosmopolitanism and cosmopolitan values, not simply in terms of petrodollars purchasing (or commodifying) cosmopolitanism but in terms of customary experiences and encounters.

References

Abdulla, A. (2012) 'The Arab Gulf moment', in D. Held and K. Coates Ulrichsen (eds) *The Transformation of the Gulf*, London: Routledge, pp. 106–124.

Accad, C. (2015) 'Opinion: GCC population growth is a blessing and a curse', *Albawaba Business*, 2 July. Available online at www.albawaba.com/business/opinion-gcc-population-growth-blessing-and-curse-714266 (accessed 28 May 2016).

Agarib, A. (2012) 'Dubai policy launch anti-begging drive', *Khaleej Times*, 16 July. Available online at www.khaleejtimes.com/nation/crime/dubai-police-launch-anti-begging-drive (accessed 15 June 2016).

Al-Arayed, J. S. (2003) *A Line in the Sea: The Qatar v. Bahrain Border Dispute in the World Court*, Berkeley, CA: North Atlantic Books.

Algethami, S. (2014) 'UAE multiple entry cruise visa to boost passenger growth', *Gulf News*, 5 December. Available online at http://gulfnews.com/business/sectors/tourism/uae-multiple-entry-cruise-visa-to-boost-passenger-growth-1.1422548 (accessed 23 July 2016).

Almuhrzi, H., N. Scott and H. AlRiyami (eds) (2017) *Tourism in the Arab World*, Clevedon: Channel View Publications.

Alpen Capital (2016) 'Strong fundamentals drive long-term growth of the GCC hospitality industry, says Alpen Capital in its latest report', *Alpen Capital*. Available online at www.alpencapital.com/news/2016/2016-August-23.html (accessed 15 September 2016).

Al-Sayegh, F. (1998) 'Merchants' role in a changing society: the case of Dubai, 1900–90', *Middle Eastern Studies*, 34(1): 87–102.

Arab News (2014) 'Citizens, expatriates to be allowed free movement across GCC', *Arab News*, 7 August. Available online at www.arabnews.com/news/saudi-arabia/612861 (accessed 5 July 2016).

Barnard, L. (2016) 'Arabia Gulf funds find Europe's finest hotels still attractive as ever', *The National*, 31 January. Available online at www.thenational.ae/business/travel-tourism/arabian-gulf-funds-find-europes-finest-hotels-still-attractive-as-ever (accessed 20 February 2016).

Beblawi, H. and G. Luciani (1987) *The Rentier State*, London: Routledge.

Bianchi, R. V. and M. L. Stephenson (2014) *Tourism and Citizenship: Rights, Freedoms and Responsibilities in the Global Order*, London: Routledge.

BQ Magazine (2016a) 'City bus segment a preferred area for investment by GCC transport authorities', *BQ Magazine*, 27 April. Available online at www.bq-magazine.com/industries/transportation-industries/2016/04/city-bus-segment-a-preferred-area-for-for investment-by-gcc-transport-authorities (accessed 15 June 2016).

BQ Magazine (2016b) 'Business visitors account for over 30% of tourists to the GCC region', *BQ Magazine*, 28 February. Available online at www.bq-magazine.com/industries/hospitality /2016/02/business-visitors-account-for-over-30-of-tourists-to-gcc-region-mere-2-of-exhibitions-held-in-middle-east (accessed 18 March 2016).

Buller, A. (2012) 'GCC to invest billions in ASEAN region', *Gulf Business*, 5 November. Available online at http://gulfbusiness.com/eastern-promises/#.V2njqct96Ul (accessed 16 June 2016).

Chalcraft, J. (2012) 'Migration politics in the Arabian Peninsula', in D. Held and K. Coates Ulrichsen (eds) *The Transformation of the Gulf: Politics, Economics and the Global Order*, London: Routledge, pp. 66–85.

Chin, C. B. (2008) *Cruising in the Global Economy: Profits, Pleasure and Work at Sea*, London: Ashgate Publishing.

Chonghaile, C. N. (2015) 'Make it work: jobs hold key to achieving development goals, says UN report', *Guardian*, 14 December. Available online at www.theguardian.com/global-development/2015/dec/14/un-human-development-index-report-2015-employment-selim-jahan (accessed 7 March 2016).

Coates Ulrichsen, K. (2016) *The Gulf States in International Political Economy*, New York: Palgrave Macmillan.

Daher, R. F. (2007) *Tourism in the Middle East: Continuity, Change and Transformation*, Clevedon: Channel View Publications.

Daniel, F. (1998) 'A Jewish tombstone from Ra's Al-Khaimah', *Journal of Jewish Studies*, 49(1): 103–107.

DeVriese, L. (2016) 'Genie out of the bottle: social media and the expansion of the public sphere in the Arab Gulf', *NIDABA: An Interdisciplinary Journal of Middle East Studies*, 1(1): 72–82.

Dresch, P. (2006) 'Foreign matter: the place of strangers in Gulf society', in J. W. Fox, N. Mourtada-Sabbah and M. al-Mutawa (eds), *Globalization and the Gulf*, London: Routledge, pp. 200–222.

Economist (2009) *The GCC in 2020: Outlook for the Gulf and the Global Economy*, Economist Intelligence Unit. Available online at http://graphics.eiu.com/marketing/pdf/Gulf2020.pdf (accessed 3 April 2014).

Economist (2014) *GCC Trade and Investment Flows*, Economist Intelligence Unit. Available online at www.economistinsights.com/sites/default/files/GCC%20Trade%20and%20investment %20flows.pdf (accessed 5 March 2016).

El Amrousi, M. and J. Biln (2010) 'Muscat emerging: tourism and cultural space', *Journal of Tourism and Cultural Change*, 8(4): 254–266.

ETN (Global Travel Industry News) (2016a) 'Qatar Airways ranked among world's most powerful brands', *ETurbo News*, 10 February. Available online at www.eturbonews.com/68403/qatar-airways-ranked-among-worlds-most-powerful-brands (accessed 22 July 2016).

ETN (Global Travel Industry News) (2016b) 'Flydubai, Fourth full-year of profitability and 25 per cent increase in passenger numbers', *ETurbo News*, 10 February. Available online at www.eturbonews.com/68404/flydubai-fourth-full-year-profitability-and-25-percent-increase- (accessed 22 July 2016).

Exell, K. (2016) *Modernity and the Museum in the Arabian Peninsula*, London: Routledge.

Exell, K. and T. Rico (2013) '"There is no heritage in Qatar": Orientalism, colonialism and other problematic histories', *World Archaeology*, 45(4): 670–685.

Exell, K. and T. Rico (eds) (2016) *Cultural Heritage in the Arabian Peninsula: Debates, Discourses and Practices*, London: Routledge.

Exell, K. and S. Wakefield (eds) (2016) *Museums in Arabia: Transnational Practices and Regional Processes*, London: Routledge.

Fahim, K. and D. G. Kirkpatrick (2012) 'Saudi Arabia seeks union of monarchies in region', *New York Times*, 14 May. Available online at www.nytimes.com/2012/05/15/world/

middleeast/saudi-arabia-seeks-union-of-monarchies-in-region.html?_r=2 (accessed 25 September 2015).

Fasano, U. and Z. Iqbal (2003) *GCC Countries: From Oil Dependence to Diversification*, Washington, DC: International Monetary Fund.

Fox, J. W., N. Mourtada-Sabbah and M. al-Mutawa (2006) 'Heritage revivalism in Sharjah', in J. W. Fox, N. Mourtada-Sabbah and M. al-Mutawa (eds) *Globalization and the Gulf*, London: Routledge, pp. 266–287.

GLMM (Gulf Labour Markets and Migration) Programme (2016) 'Percentage of nationals and foreign nationals in the GCC countries' populations' (2010–2016). Available online at http://gulfmigration.eu/media/graphs/graphGCC%201%20April%202016.pdf (accessed 15 August 2016).

Gordon, M. (1989) *Slavery in the Arab World*, New York: New Amsterdam Books.

Gray, M. (2011) *A Theory of 'Late Rentierism' in the Arab States of the Gulf*, Qatar: Centre for International and Regional Studies, Georgetown University School of Foreign Service in Qatar.

Guardian (2016) 'Emirates plane in "accident on landing" in Dubai', *Guardian*, 3 August. Available online at http://guardian.ng/news/emirates-plane-in-accident-on-landing-in-dubai/ (accessed 15 August 2016).

Gulf Business (2016) 'Chinese stowaway found on emirates flight', *Gulf Business*, 1 June. Available online at http://gulfbusiness.com/chinese-stowaway-found-on-emirates-flight/ (accessed 27 June 2016).

Gulf News (2016) 'Visas on arrival in UAE for Chinese tourists', *Gulf News*, 4 September. Available online at http://gulfnews.com/news/uae/government/visas-on-arrival-in-uae-for-chinese-visitors1.1890575 (accessed 9 October 2016).

Hanieh, A. (2011) *Capitalism and Class in the Gulf Arab States*, New York: Palgrave Macmillan.

Hazbun, W. (2008) *Beaches, Ruins, Resorts: The Politics of Tourism in the Arab World*, Minneapolis, MN: Minnesota Press.

Held, D. and K. Coates Ulrichsen (2012) 'Editors' introduction: the transformation of the Gulf', in D. Held and K. Coates Ulrichsen (eds), *The Transformation of the Gulf: Politics, Economics and the Global Order*, London: Routledge, pp. 1–25.

Hodson, J. C. (1995) *Lawrence of Arabia and American Culture: The Making of a Transatlantic Legend*, London: Greenwood Press.

ICAEW (2016) *Economic Insight: Middle East*, ICAEW (The Institute of Chartered Accountants in England and Wales) produced with Oxford Economics. Available online at www.icaew.com/-/media/corporate/files/technical/economy/economic-insight/middle-east/me-q2-2016-web.ashx (accessed 4 June 2016).

Institute for Economics and Peace (2016) *Global Peace Index 2016*. Available online at http://static.visionofhumanity.org/sites/default/files/GPI%202016%20Report_2.pdf (accessed 15 June 2016).

Kader, B. A. (2014) '7 more UAE beaches receive Blue Flag certification', *Gulf News*, 10 December. Available online at http://gulfnews.com/news/uae/environment/7-more-uae-beaches-receive-blue-flag-certification-1.1425051 (accessed 15 December 2014).

Karolak, M. (2015) 'Analysis of the cruise industry in the Arabian Gulf: the emergence of a new destination', *Journal of Tourism Challenges and Trends*, 8(1): 61–78.

Khalaf, S. (2006) 'The evolution of the Gulf City type, oil, and globalization', in J. W. Fox, N. Mourtada-Sabbah and M. al-Mutawa (eds) (2006) *Globalization and the Gulf*, London: Routledge, pp. 244–265.

Khalaf, A., O. AlShehabi and A. Hanieh (eds) (2015) *Transit States: Labour, Migration and Citizenship in the Gulf*, London: Pluto Press.

Khaleej Times (2014) 'Jumeirah Group rolls out Dh8 billion global expansion', *Khaleej Times*, 11 May. Available online at www.khaleejtimes.com/business/local/jumeirah-group-rolls-out-dh8-billion-global-expansion (accessed 10 December 2015).

Khan, G. A. (2015) '"Schengen-style" GCC visa likely by mid-2016', *Arab News*, 11 October. Available online at www.arabnews.com/news/818686 (accessed 17 February 2016).

Khan, T. (2016) 'Doha slavery museum confronts past to help Qataris shape future', *The National*, 23 May. Available online at www.thenational.ae/world/middle-east/doha-slavery-museum-confronts-past-to-help-qataris-shape-future (accessed 17 September 2016).

King, N. (2016) 'Gulf states drop down global peace index', *Gulf Business*, 9 June. Available online at http://gulfbusiness.com/gulf-states-drop-global-peace-index/ (accessed 17 September 2016).

Lahn, G. (2016) 'Fuel, food and utilities price reforms in the GCC: a wake-up call for business', Research Paper, Chatham House, London: The Royal Institute of International Affairs.

Laws, E. (1995) *Tourist Destination Management: Issues, Analysis and Policies*, London: Routledge.

Maceda, C. (2016) 'UAE, other GCC firms urged: get ready for VAT now', *Gulf News*, 19 August. Available online at http://gulfnews.com/business/economy/uae-other-gcc-firms-urged-get-ready-for-vat-now-1.1848598 (accessed 8 August 2016).

Mansfeld, Y. and O. Winckler (2007) 'The tourism industry as an alternative for the GCC oil-based rentier economy', *Tourism Economics*, 13(3): 333–360.

Mansfeld, Y. and O. Winckler (2008) 'The role of the tourism industry in transforming a *rentier* to a long-term viable economy: the case of Bahrain', *Current Issues in Tourism*, 11(3): 237–267.

Mansfeld, Y. and O. Winckler (2015) 'Can this be spring? Assessing the impact of the "Arab Spring" on the Arab tourism industry', *Tourism Review*, 63(2): 205–223.

Marzovilla, O. (2014) 'Economic diversification in GCC countries and the optimality of a monetary union', *European Scientific Journal*, June: 1857–7881.

Meier, B. (2015) 'Labor scrutiny for FIFA as a world cup rises in the Qatar desert', *New York Times*, 15 July. Available online at www.nytimes.com /2015/07/16/business/international/senate-fifa-inquiry-to-include-plight-of-construction-workers-in-qatar.html?_r=0 (accessed 16 September 2016).

Menon, A. (2016) 'Top airport projects in the GCC: massive airport developments in Middle East to push global aviation growth', *Infrastructure Middle East*, 21 January. Available online at http://infrastructureme.com/2016/01/top-airport-projects-in-the-gcc/ (accessed 15 February 2016).

Mershen, B. (2007) 'Development of community-based tourism in Oman: challenges and opportunities', in R. F. Daher (ed.) *Tourism in the Middle East: Continuity, Change and Transformation*, Toronto: Channel View Publication, pp. 188–214.

Nagraj, A. (2016) 'Low oil prices impact: GCC growth "challenging", but no recession expected', *Gulf Business*, 6 March. Available online at www.gulfbusiness.com/articles/industry/finance/low-oil-prices-impact-gcc-growth-challenging-but-no-recessionexpected/ (accessed 15 August 2016).

Najjar, F. (2005) 'The Arabs, Islam and globalization', *Middle East Policy*, 12(3): 91–106.

Patrick, N. (2012) *Nationalism in the Gulf States*, London: Routledge.

Peterson, J. E. (2014) 'The Arabian Peninsula in modern times: a historiographical survey of recent publications', *Journal of Arabian Studies*, 4(2): 244–274.

Pinfari, M. (2009) Nothing but failure? The Arab League and the Gulf Cooperation Council as mediators in Middle Eastern conflicts, Working Paper No. 45, *Crisis States Working Papers Series No. 2*, London: Crisis States Research Centre, Development Studies Institute, LSE.

Pivac, D. Z. (2015) 'Lucrative budget hotel market attracts investors to the GCC', *BQ Magazine*, 2 January. Available online at www.bq-magazine.com/industries/hospitality/2015/01/lucrative-budget-hotel-market-attracts-investors-gcc (accessed 18 March 2016).

Raouf, M. A. and M. Luomi (eds) (2016) *The Green Economy in the Gulf*, Abingdon: Routledge.

Reiche, D. (2010) 'Energy policies of Gulf Cooperation Council (GCC) countries – possibilities and limitations of ecological modernization in rentier states', *Energy Policy*, 38(5): 2395–2403.

Ritter, W. (1986) 'Tourism in the Arabian Gulf region – present situation, chances and restraints', *GeoJournal*, 13(3): 237–244.

Sadi, M. A. and J. C. Henderson (2005) 'Local versus foreign workers in the hospitality and tourism industry', *Cornell Hotel and Restaurant Administration Quarterly*, 46(2): 247–257.

Salama, V. (2008) 'New hotels look to locate near emerging retail space', *The National*, 5 May, p. 6.

Saudi Gazette (2016a) 'Visitors from KSA still biggest in volume of Dubai tourists in 2015', *Saudi Gazette*, 31 January. Available online at http://saudigazette.com.sa/business/visitors-from-ksa-still-biggest-in-volume-of-dubai-tourists-in-2015/ (accessed 7 March 2016).

Saudi Gazette (2016b) 'GCC single visa to boost tourism', *Saudi Gazette*, 2 May. Available online at http://saudigazette.com.sa/business/gcc-single-visa-boost-tourism/ (accessed 17 June 2016).

Shaheen, K. (2016) 'Suicide bombers attack sites in Saudi Arabia including mosque in Medina', *Guardian*, 5 July. Available online at www.theguardian.com/world/2016/jul/04/saudi-arabia-bombings-jeddah-medina-prophets-mosque-qatif (accessed 27 August 2016).

Shane, D. (2013) 'Bahrain MPs vote to ban pork in Kingdom', *Arabian Business*, 22 May. Available online at www.arabianbusiness.com/bahrain-mps-vote-ban-pork-in-kingdom-502595.html#.V_tEDY997IU (accessed 7 September 2016).

Shatzmiller, J. (1998) Jews, Pilgrimage, and the Christian Cult of Saints: Benjamin of Tudela and His Contemporaries. *After Rome's Fall: Narrators and Sources of Early Medieval History*, Toronto: University of Toronto Press.

Smith, B. (2015) *Market Orientalism: Cultural Economy and the Arab Gulf States*, Syracuse, NY: Syracuse University Press.

Stephenson, M. L. (2014) 'Tourism, development and destination Dubai: cultural dilemmas and future challenges', *Current Issues in Tourism*, 17(8): 723–738.

Stephenson, M. and J. Ali-Knight (2010) 'Dubai's tourism industry and its societal impact: social implications and sustainable challenges', 'Middle East and North Africa Special Issue', *Journal of Tourism and Cultural Change*, 8(4): 278–292.

Stephenson, M. L., K. A. Russell and D. Edgar (2010) 'Islamic hospitality in the UAE: indigenization of products and human capital', *Journal of Islamic Marketing*, 1(1): 9–24.

Sturm, M. and N. Siegfried (2005) 'Regional monetary integration in the member states of the Gulf Cooperation Council', *Occasional Papers Series*, No. 31, June 2005, Frankfurt am Main, Germany: European Central Bank.

Sturm, M., J. Strasky, P. Adolf and D. Peschel (2008) 'The Gulf Cooperation Council countries - economic structures, recent developments and role in the global economy', *Occasional Paper Series*, No. 92. July, Frankfurt am Main, Germany: European Central Bank.

Tasch, B. (2016) 'The 25 richest countries, ranked', *Business Insider*, 31 March. Available online at http://uk.businessinsider.com/the-richest-countries-in-the-world-2016-3 (accessed 25 April 2016).

The Peninsula (2016) '35 patrols to nab beggars during Ramadan', *The Peninsula*, 30 May. Available online at www.thepeninsulaqatar.com/news/qatar/383576/35-patrols-to-nab-beggars-during-ramadan (accessed 15 July 2016).

Thomas, J. (2013) *Psychological Well-being in the Gulf States: The New Arabia Felix*, Basingstoke: Palgrave Macmillan.

Times of Oman (2016) 'Oman's hospitality market to reach $1b in 2020: report', *Times of Oman*, 23 August. Available online at http://timesofoman.com/article/90866/Business/Oman's-hospitality-market-to-reach-$1b-in-2020:-Report (accessed 15 September 2016).

Timothy, D. J. (ed.) (2017) (in press) *Routledge Handbook on Middle East Tourism*, London: Routledge.

Toumi, H. (2016) 'In anti-begging drive, 112 arrested in Riyadh in one day', *Gulf News*, 22 July.

Trade Arabia (2016) 'GCC to pump $100bn into airport construction projects', *Trade Arabia*, 23 June. Available online at www.tradearabia.com/news/TTN_309196.html? (accessed 15 July 2016).

TTG Media (2016) 'Britain welcoming record number of GCC tourists', *TTG Media Online*, 30 May. Available online at www.ttgmena.com/britain-welcoming-record-number-gcc-tourists/ (accessed 25 June 2016).

TTN (Travel and Tourism News Middle East) (2016) 'GCC guests double in Qatar', *TTN*, June. Available online at www.ttnworldwide.com/Article/16659/GCC_guests_double_in_Qatar (accessed 15 July 2016).

UNESCO World Heritage List (2017) United Nations Educational, Scientific and Cultural Organization. Available online at http://whc.unesco.org/en/list (accessed 2 March 2017).

Urry, J. (1990) *The Tourist Gaze: Leisure and Travel in Contemporary Societies*, London: Sage.

Weigall, D. and P. Stirk (eds) (1992) *The Origins and Development of the European Community*, London and Leicester: Leicester University Press.

Winckler, O. (2007) 'The birth of Oman's tourism industry', *Tourism: An Interdisciplinary Journal*, 55(2): 221–234.

Wippel, S., K. Bromber, C. Steiner and B. Krawietz (eds) (2014) *Under Construction: Logics of Urbanism in the Gulf Region*, London: Routledge.

World Economic Forum (2015) *The Travel and Tourism Competitiveness Report 2015*, Geneva: World Economic Forum. Available online at www3.weforum.org/docs/TT15/WEF_Global_Travel&Tourism_Report_2015.pdf (accessed 15 August 2016).

Wynbrandt, J. (2010) *Saudi Arabia: A Brief History of Saudi Arabia*, New York: Infobase Publishing.

Zahlan, R. S. (1989) *The Making of the Modern Gulf States: Kuwait, Bahrain, Qatar, the United Arab Emirates and Oman*, London: Routledge.

Part One

Tourism development and the Gulf Cooperation Council region

1 Theoretical approaches to the political economy of tourism in the GCC states

Matthew Gray

This chapter examines some key theoretical approaches from the sub-field of political economy which can be utilized to explain the tourism dynamics of the Gulf Cooperation Council (GCC) states – Bahrain, Kuwait, Oman, Qatar, Saudi Arabia and the United Arab Emirates (UAE) – and the context in which tourism occurs. It argues that three main approaches, each developed for wider explanatory usage, are valuable in this regard: rentier state theory; ('new') state capitalism; and arguments about the nexus between national branding and political economy. These are outlined and explored as approaches that frame and explain the political economy of tourism in the GCC states. What follows, after some brief contextual discussion, is an explanation of the contribution that each of these approaches potentially makes towards explaining Gulf tourism. This paper does not propose one of these approaches over all others, although it biases rentier arguments in explaining the highest-level dynamics of Gulf state-society relations, including by briefly diverging into a discussion about the rentier characteristics inherent in tourism itself. Ultimately, a conglomeration of all three approaches forms the ideal framework through which to understand the political economy of tourism in the GCC states. As the conclusion notes, however, research into Gulf tourism is in its infancy. Therefore, more work is needed concerning the more nuanced and opaque aspects of both tourism and the political economy dynamics in these states, particularly to refine political economy approaches to tourism.

Theorizing the political economy of Gulf tourism: approaches, assumptions and caveats

Before examining the best theoretical approaches to the political economy of Gulf tourism, three points should be noted. These confirm the distinctiveness of the GCC states' tourism sectors and economic profiles, and imply an extremely limited potential for cross-regional comparative studies involving the GCC states. They begin laying the foundation for the more overarching argument that, while the expansion of tourism in these states appears to be driven by neoliberalism, it is, in fact, very different, almost the opposite; a product of the rentier, state capitalist structures of the small but wealthy GCC states.

The first issue is that of the nature of tourism in these states. All six have tourism sectors of some importance, albeit varying in their economic significance, but lost in any statistical comparison is the marked variation in the nature and profiles of the tourists they variously receive. In Saudi Arabia, for example, arrivals are overwhelmingly pilgrims on the Hajj and Umrah (see Chapter 13), who are on specific-purpose visas yet may also engage in tourism-like activities. Saudi Arabia also has a substantial domestic tourism sector (see Chapter 7), catering to nationals and expatriates. In contrast, Bahrain receives large numbers of tourists from other GCC states, especially short-term visitors from Saudi Arabia who cross the causeway to Bahrain (see Chapter 5); thus, the absolute tourist number for Bahrain is a more impressive figure than, say, the total tourist nights one. Kuwait also receives some Saudis, and prior to the 1990 invasion it used to host large numbers of Iraqis, but in many respects Kuwait has been slow to encourage tourism and has struggled to attract high-value arrivals in large numbers (see Chapter 6). The country receives many business and some stopover visitors, but its high costs, less dynamic national airline and proximity to Iraq probably deter many leisure tourists. All these cases are a reminder that a range of variables differentiate GCC tourism sectors from each other and from leisure tourism sectors elsewhere, even where their tourism industries are large, valuable or otherwise important.

A second point to note about GCC tourism is that its relation to the international tourism industry, and to globalization broadly, is very different to the rest of the world. It is widely accepted that tourists are commonly motivated by a search for cultural 'authenticity' (Silver 1993), and yet, at least in an economic sense, tourism experiences are deliberately constructed and artificial, not authentic. Accordingly, the experiences of tourists 'in' the Middle East are a construct driven by economic incentives and reinforced by fabricated, managed experiences and interactions (Daher 2007: 3–11). This is amplified by the increasing commodification of tourism (Shaw and Williams 1994: 97–105) globally, and no less in GCC states than elsewhere. Yet, the GCC region mostly lacks the mass tourism found in more established destinations, despite the fact that its economies are closely interconnected with globalization or, at least, selected components of it; especially its economic features.

Therefore, in seeking to expand tourism, the GCC states have permitted greater and further commodification and homogenization of it, even though they have sought an exclusive or up-market niche within the international tourism industry. The hyper-luxuriousness, cosmopolitanism and use of historical symbols in emerging centres such as Dubai (Hazbun 2008: 205–225) are examples of tourism commodification and the artificial construction of visitors' experience. Many observers, even scholars specializing in the region, assume that the imagery and commodification of tourism, leisure and even public space are the product of neoliberalism (for example, Kanna 2011: 135–143, 166–170, 200–202). The GCC economies are linked to and shaped by the global economic system, certainly, and have introduced specific reforms in response to it, as other authors note (such as Hanieh 2011). Compared to much of the world, however, GCC political economies have, quite unusually, commodified tourism not for reasons of neoliberal-driven mass tourism marketization, but for the very different goal of controlling tourism and organizing it within the region's (albeit entrepreneurial and profit-minded) state capitalist, regime-managed political economies.

The third point to make is on the approaches to the political economy of tourism in the GCC states and the issues they raise. First, no matter how central the disciplinary or sub-disciplinary approach used, the interdisciplinarity of tourism impacts the nature of scholarship on it. In the past, fields such as geography and anthropology have produced more tourism scholarship than political science, but from different, often more microcosmic, angles than political science usually adopts. Furthermore, tourism studies has long suffered from a contest common in the social sciences, wherein some scholars want it to become more quantitative and 'scientific', while others want it to be more qualitative and critical (Cooper 2003: 2–4). This is related to the complaint by some scholars that tourism studies is hamstrung by a positivist tradition. Valid or not, such comments are worth noting, given how many studies examine tourism in relative isolation or are reductionist in their analyses (Cooper 2003: 1–4). Approaches to political economy, too, are as contested as those of tourism studies. To some, political economy suggests a critical counter-approach to economic issues; to others, it should offer progressive arguments about the politics of economics, as several arguments imply (e.g. Payne 2006: 1–10). Still others treat it as a more neutral term, seeking to capture and explain the actors, forces and dynamics that create a linkage between the economic and the political, in the process touching on a diverse range of topics such as economic policymaking, development debates, the socio-political structures in which economic activity takes place and how economic and political outcomes each, in turn, impact the other. This latter approach is the more common in Middle Eastern studies, even though much area studies scholarship concerns a radical or progressivist approach. Key recent texts have, arguably, been closer to this more neutral approach (such as, among many, Held and Coates Ulrichsen 2012; Hertog *et al.* 2013; Kamrava 2012), and this is also the intent in this chapter.

A final point concerns the uniqueness of the Gulf states and the scopes and limitations that this presents in drawing on work elsewhere, or engaging in cross-regional comparative studies, especially to inform discussions about both political economy and tourism. The GCC states stand out in the Middle East by virtue of their comparative wealth, mostly from oil and gas exports, and the distinct impacts that this has had on, among other variables, their political structures, their economic importance within and beyond the Middle East and their selective, state-led globalization (Lawson 2012: 13–38). This is, arguably, why the Gulf is a bastion of powerful, sometimes autocratic monarchies, but also why these monarchies remain not only durable but for the most part stable, even popular. This is why the region appears to be engaging in ambitious economic liberalization, even though it is actually pursuing far more modest reforms that will support and enrich its novel, relatively efficient, entrepreneurial form of state capitalism (see Gray 2011: 18–36). It is also why the GCC states' politics is dominated by middle-class concerns, why there is a strange concomitance of the global and the local in its public spaces and political economy profiles and, yet, also why social, religious and historical variations in these states have created notable differences in their approaches to both political and economic change (Abdulla 2012: 109–119). They are all energy-driven economies, all changing in important economic and social respects, all linking increasingly to the forces of globalization and all trying to expand tourism, but they are not all the same as each other, either in the finer details of their political economies or in the profiles and potential of their tourism industries.

Tourism and rentierism in the GCC states

One of the most common theoretical frameworks with which the GCC states are analyzed is 'rentier state theory' (RST) and its variants. RST, at its core, argues that 'rents', which are externally derived and usually concern unproductively earned income from natural resources or other assets innate or inherent to an economy, have an impact on the state-society relationship. Specifically, rents make states 'allocative' rather than 'extractive', the former distributing externally earned income to society and the latter imposing taxes on economic activity and then redistributing those funds. As a result, an extractive (taxing) state must make a bargain with society, perhaps a democratic one, or at least a deal on how taxes will be redistributed. The allocative or rentier state needs to do no such thing. Once it has co-opted (or, put crudely, 'bought off') society, the state becomes autonomous from society while also having the means at hand for an expansive state repressive capacity. It needs no bargains with society, the argument goes, usually not even an economic or development policy (Luciani 1990: 71–72, 76). The early literature on RST by Mahdavy (1970), Beblawi (1987) and Luciani (1990), among others, all argued along these lines.

Such arguments had, and retain to this day, considerable validity, but they were also simplistic. They explained the absence of democracy in basic, some would say reductionist, terms, and usually claimed or assumed that the autonomy of the state was virtually absolute. The theory is also broadly applicable, yet insufficiently analytical, for the case of the GCC states over the past 20–25 years. A more sophisticated approach to rentierism treats it as a *dynamic* rather than a *structural explanation* for a political economy. The idea of the GCC states as 'late' or 'late-stage' rentier states is based on this less ambitious approach to rentierism (Gray 2011). It acknowledges that the state is never fully autonomous from society: rentier regimes normally maintain ties with the elites most crucial to their survival, be they merchants, clerics, tribal leaders or others. Moreover, the post-2010 Arab uprisings have reinforced to Gulf leaders the need for an even wider responsiveness to society at large (Peel and Blas 2011). Certainly, this does not mean a democratic bargain is required. Rents always allow a state more repressive and co-optive means than it otherwise would possess. At best, however, these states have partial autonomy from society, but still need a basic level of legitimacy or toleration by society. They must respond effectively to the changes brought by globalization, in which case responsiveness also means addressing unemployment and other socio-economic pressures. They must have solid development strategies and plans.

Further, and at the same time, older established political mechanisms remain important. In the rentier case, perhaps the most obvious and important is the relationship between the ruling family elite and other elites, the latter coming from various political and civic institutions, as well as representing an array of social forces. Most commonly, political leaderships face the greatest potential threat from the key merchants, clerics and tribal leaders; those who have either their own sources of legitimacy with society, or who have the capacity to generate their own income and gain financial independence from the state. Thus, leaders typically use neopatrimonial webs to build and maintain elite networks, and with which to ensure that most elites either remain reliant on the regime and the state, or at least are encouraged to link into it and not oppose it. As Bill and Springborg (1990: 152–161) note in some detail, in a neopatrimonial structure leaders build an inner network of core elites to whom they send favours, access and funds which, in turn, are distributed to those elites' institutions or networks further out from the centre of this neopatrimonial web. In exchange, these elites join and support the political order, and feed information up to leaders. Smart leaders also play these elites off against each other, or at least ensure that no one actor gains enough power or support base to become a political threat. A leader will often also make clear that access and favour are very easily withdrawn. Beyond large-scale welfare such as subsidies, health spending or education investment, these networks are a primary pathway through which rents are disbursed, but otherwise patrimonialism (the modern version is "neo" because modern institutions and processes are also incorporated) is a political tactic for managing politics that predates the oil era by centuries.

This explains some paradoxes inherent in contemporary GCC states. It makes a strong case as to why the GCC monarchies are as flooded with rents as ever, yet have tried to diversify their economies – including through the development of tourism and related sectors – and, at certain levels, have appeared to embrace economic and social change. It also explains why state decision-making remains so personalized and opaque. Compared to the decades prior to the 1990s, the late-stage rentier states have become very open to tourism, as well as promoting major events, investing in infrastructure and building global, transcontinental state-owned airlines (Gray 2011: 23–36). This has signified a new openness to certain types of tourism, albeit on certain conditions. Tourism is both encouraged and supported by the nature and features of late rentierism, and in return reinforces many of its features.

There is a very strong tourism/late rentierism relationship therefore, especially as tourism outcomes can demonstrate state responsiveness to society. Apart from the newly reinforced limits of state autonomy, pressures from population growth (Burns 2007: 231–232; Malik and Niblock 2005: 103) and social and technological change (Foley 2010) are all driving GCC leaderships to develop their tourism sectors. Tourism development strategies are a sign of responsiveness to these pressures and a state attempt to alleviate them. Tourism links strongly to the international economy and globalization, yet it can offset some of the very problems created by globalization and the change it brings. It is labour intensive, important in creating employment both directly in the tourism sector and more widely through the investment that tourism requires and the circulation of tourists' spending. It supports economic diversification because of the breadth of economic activity it generates: hotels, tour companies, transport networks, touristic facilities, shops, sports stadia and heritage sites. Such infrastructure is increasingly demanded as tourism expands.

Tourism is also a politically attractive sector, often underdeveloped and with few pre-existing elite interests embedded in it. It is, thus, relatively straightforward for the leaderships to open and expand it under their sponsorship and to their political ends, with less contestation than would occur in long-established sectors and areas such as foreign trade or certain manufacturing industries. As a result, in the GCC the state, above all the regime at its summit, has promoted tourism expansion for not just economic but also social and political purposes. It has used rents to pay for massive state investment into national airlines, convention and business facilities and new socio-economic infrastructure, while rents have also created many of the dynamics and issues that a tourism development policy is seeking to address.

Bahrain provides an example of tourism supporting economic diversification and employment-generation strategies. Since the 1970s, Bahrain has sought to compensate for the long-term decline in oil revenues with economic diversification and a stronger private sector (Mansfeld and Winckler 2008: 246–247, 252; Smith 2015: 232–238). Oil wealth has been recirculated into new economic sectors, including tourism, creating a range of local and regional Arab firms in tourism and tourism-related businesses (Hazbun 2008: 203–205). Bahrain relies heavily on transit visitors flying Gulf Air and on short-term tourists driving in from Saudi Arabia, but a key reason why it has such dominance of the regional Saudi leisure tourism market, in particular, is that it moved first, quickly and deliberately to build this base. The state was integral in driving this initiative and in funding it. Many Bahraini tourism firms are world class in their management and strategy, but they would never have originally emerged without oil wealth and rentier dynamics as drivers. A very similar argument exists for Dubai, where tourism and other service sectors have been salient features of the so-called Dubai model of development since the mid-1980s (Foley 2010: 145), and where tourism has been state-led and funded for similar aims such as economic diversification.

Tourism as rentierism: is the tourism sector itself a rentier economic activity?

A further point worth making, albeit briefly, is that not only are there strong correlations between rentierism and state tourism policies and strategies, but an argument can be made that tourism itself is rentier or contains rentier-like elements. This may seem strange at first glance, given the array of productive economic activities supported by tourism: preparing and serving meals in a restaurant; building a hotel or tourist facility; tour guiding services; transportation activities; and involvement in a range of retail services and other activities – which are all productive and not inherently rentier. Yet, at the most fundamental level, tourism is about earning income by drawing visitors to a state's natural assets or cultural heritage. Without these attractions, tourism income would be substantially lower or much more difficult to generate. Such assets are, for the most part, inherited. They are natural features within a state's territory (as with beaches, mountains and waterfalls) or are bequests from past generations (as with archaeological sites, historic buildings and old townscapes). Most such sites and features cannot be created. At best, wealthier states may be able to construct contemporary alternatives, such as Dubai's indoor ski slope and other fabricated spectacles (Simpson 2012), or Qatar's rebuilt and somewhat reimagined public spaces (Gray 2013: 175–177).

A second rentier type of feature to tourism is the surplus income often generated by (or, more often, *tapped from*) it. In the retail sector of some states, tourists often pay a price that is separate from and higher than that paid by locals; in effect, the difference in the two prices is a form of rent. The re-sale of imported products, likewise, includes an element of rent in the mark-up that could not be charged in a completely free market or if tourists had full market information available to them. The fees and charges at historical sites, museums and other sites – which often go directly to the state, a feature of rentierism – may also be higher than the underlying cost of profitably providing them, and thus include a rent component.

The politics of tourism overlaps with the political dynamics of broader rentierism, prominently but not exclusively in the GCC states. Their tourism industries have been deliberately developed, and are evolving, such that lower-level jobs are held by foreign workers, but the senior and professional roles are mostly held by nationals. It is nationals, too, who are the main investors in tourism and allied sectors such as leisure and retail, and who stand to gain the most from tourists arriving and spending their money. These opportunities, whether in employment or investment related to tourism, provide rentier-like outcomes. In the case of employment, relatively prestigious positions become available which the state does not have to offer elsewhere in the bureaucracy or help generate elsewhere in the private sector. Investors, intermediaries and agents operating in the tourism sector often have an even more obvious rentier approach, seeking to extract income from economic activity that is happening only because of the expansion of the tourism industry. For the rentier state, this is an alternative to sharing more of the rents earned from other sources, and may also allow the state to avoid making adjustments to how rentier wealth is allocated. Tourism also helps the state to avoid or reduce trade deficits and improves, among other things, national income and tax revenue, as Richter and Steiner (2008: 953) noted in the case of Egypt; to varying degrees, these are motivations for the GCC states in developing tourism. This all indicates that GCC leaderships support tourism not only to diversify away from traditional rents such as those from energy exports, but also because tourism, as it expands, is quasi-rentier, or at least provides the state with a set of political benefits that are rentier-like and do not upset the extant political economy order.

Thus, while tourism arguably is *generically* quasi-rentier, it has particular appeal for states that are already rentier.

Terms like *quasi-rentier* or *rentier-like* are probably the most appropriate answer to the question of how rentier in nature GCC tourism might be. Tourism is not as substantially rentier as oil and gas exports, of course, and in the Gulf (and everywhere except for a few Caribbean islands) tourism does not account for national wealth at a level that is anywhere close to that delivered from energy exports. Tourism income, moreover, does not exclusively flow through the state or political elite out to society; some does, but some accrues directly to other non-state economic actors. However, the manifestations of tourism also contain some features very similar to those of rentierism, including earnings that are the result of natural assets, earnings beyond what would otherwise be accepted for a product or service and political goals in the mind of the state that are similar, whether for energy rents or tourism activity.

New state capitalism arguments and Gulf tourism

Another political economy approach linked to Gulf tourism is the region's specific state capitalist structure. If rentierism is more a process than a structure, then state capitalism, conversely, is more a structure than a process: it dictates many of the transactions that occur in the political economy but also helps define the nature of the state itself. 'State capitalist', here, means that the state allows market-price mechanisms to operate and the private sector to play a (controlled) role in the economy, but with the state being the key actor in the economy and a disproportionate owner of the means of production. This is the case at a basic level with all state capitalist systems. However, in the GCC states in recent decades, there has existed a specific type of state capitalism that is 'entrepreneurial' (Gray 2013: 11–16, 63–70), 'new' (Bremmer 2009; Bremmer 2010) or conceptually similar to these ideas (MacDonald and Lemco 2015). In such a system, the state is an activist and ambitious actor, willing and even keen to engage economically with the outside world. It has also sought to operate, in an efficient and profitable manner, the economy and such institutions as state-owned firms. The GCC state is very different to older state capitalisms, such as those in the post-independence Arab republics, where the state sought dominance over old social classes and pursued heavy industry development and import substitution.

The GCC's dynamic and entrepreneurial state capitalism shares some similarities with Schlumberger's (2008) concept of 'patrimonial capitalism'. Neopatrimonial dynamics are, for example, powerful pathways for political negotiation, and they enhance elite solidarity and informal consultation as well. Champion's description of Saudi Arabian '*asabiyya* capitalism' (Champion 2003: 10–12, 182–191), which stresses the importance of social bonds and informal networks in dictating economic patterns and outcomes, is also of some insight. However, the 'entrepreneurial state capitalism' described here, while acknowledging the importance of elite and class dynamics, has a far stronger emphasis on the role of the state as an owner of assets in the economy, as a driver of a clear and articulated development strategy and as the initiator of an opening (albeit a conditional and selective one) to globalization and, above all, international trade and investment. Still, as with 'patrimonial capitalism' and '*asabiyya* capitalism', the summit of 'the state' is occupied by a regime that rules more opaquely and informally, and through more complex elite networks, than do most legal-rational states. The GCC's state capitalism makes the state a force for 'late-late-development' (Hvidt 2009) or similar explanations (MacDonald and Lemco 2015: 101–110). Here, the state bypasses industrialization rather than focusing on it, sets strategic goals rather than prices in the economy, publishes visions rather than central plans and nurtures old social elites rather than ideologically trying to undermine them. It is not a neoliberal system, even if some policies occasionally make it appear so, since the state's power is not in any significant decline, and the economy is not fully marketized.

The Gulf's state capitalism relates to tourism in several ways. First, it means that the private sector is encouraged in some areas (e.g. hotels, tours and smaller-scale retailing), but the state retains a centrality in other areas (e.g. airlines and major event infrastructure). It also explains why the state appears reformist yet retains a strong regulatory role and dominates tourism marketing, standardization and planning (Mansfeld and Winckler 2008: 253–255). It further accounts for the power of state-owned firms, but at the same time for their efficiency and profitability. Accordingly, Hertog (2010: 261–301) and others (such as Marcel 2006) have noted that GCC state-owned firms may still have some political goals behind them, but they also are usually better run and more profitable than those of state capitalist systems. This is, arguably, why airlines such as Emirates and Etihad are profitable, as are most other established GCC tourism and leisure firms owned by the state. These firms operate similarly to private sector ones, competing at a global level, informed by market forces and responses and motivated by profit and market share. In such a setting there is, moreover, no reason why tourism firms, whether state-owned or private sector, would not want to see tourism commodified, as indeed it has been, above all in Dubai (Hazbun 2008: 195–196). There, this has included the creation of enclaves structured for the tourism profit, and with increasingly sophisticated company networks emerging to package and otherwise manage tourists' activities and experiences (Hazbun 2008: 197–198). To a lesser extent, this is an increasingly prominent feature of tourism in other Gulf destinations. Commodification, however, is still under the control of the state, and tourism is not as homogenized as it would be in a neoliberal political economy, but instead it is being strategically and purposefully commodified towards the types of tourists and the tourism outcomes being sought.

The economic diversification and employment creation strategies discussed earlier are also linked closely to state capitalism and tourism, because they are designed to ensure the political and commercial viability of the system both in the current period of rents and, arguably, into the post-rent future too. For the moment, diversification helps support new state capitalism by flattening out economic cycles and fluctuations in income, and especially by minimizing the painful impacts of periods of sustained low rents. Longer-term rents flow into new sectors and thereby diversify the economy, essential for the post-rent future. At the same time, the new state capitalism is like the old, in that it sustains patterns of ownership and reinforces the structure of economic power and existing patterns of privilege. The state-owned firms that Bremmer calls 'national champions' (Bremmer 2010: 67–69) are, in the GCC states, nearly all wholly or partly state-owned (Luciani 2005: 144–181), as in other state capitalist systems. This does not preclude genuine private sector activity in both the indigenous and international sectors (including tourism), but the private sector is not permitted to challenge the political order in any significant way. Moreover, the private sector is usually constrained if it will impact sensitive geographical, cultural or social areas, as of course tourism regularly does. The GCC's state capitalism thus serves to maintain the political order, making it similar, perhaps, to rentierism in its impacts, but very different in its mechanisms and dynamics.

The features of this state capitalism set it apart from neoliberalism, even where elements of the latter are occasionally a component of Gulf economic policy. There is a business-friendly policy orientation of the Gulf's state capitalism, but with business ultimately subservient to the state and the highest levels of the private sector elite. This approach stems from the shock of low oil prices from 1986 and into the 1990s (Maloney 2008: 133), where there was a general impression that too much of the oil wealth generated in the 1970s and 1980s was actually wasted (Maloney 2008: 133). Moreover, there was a general recognition that an active and entrepreneurial state better maintains the political order than other forms of state capitalism or other economic systems (Bremmer 2010: 51–81). This is why GCC tourism has developed emphatically but also somewhat cautiously, broadly concomitant with the globalization era of the post-1980s. Tourism is pursued for particular economic and ultimately political reasons rather than simply for blunt commercial ones. Accordingly, GCC states have expanded and commodified tourism but have not encouraged uncontrolled tourism development. Mass-market leisure tourism has very deliberately been eschewed by most of the Gulf and is unlikely to be developed in the foreseeable future: even Dubai, which has tourism arrival numbers that would make many mass-market destinations jealous, has an expensive, relatively up-market tourism sector and, thus, is not the same sort of 'mass-market' destination as, for example, some Caribbean islands, coastal Spain or even certain US cities such as Las Vegas or Orlando. There is no evidence that any Gulf state will transform into such a tourism destination in the foreseeable future, even if they continue to attract increasing numbers of leisure visitors.

The state, national 'branding' and the political economy of Gulf tourism

Integral to how the GCC states pursue tourism for political and economic purposes is the dynamic of 'branding' (Gray 2013: 159–184; Peterson 2006). Branding is partly a security strategy, raising both the profile and the international legitimacy of the state (Peterson 2006: 746–748). Given the activism of the GCC states and their entrepreneurial state capitalism, branding is also intended to serve economic security needs and deliver commercial opportunities. Put crudely, if a royal family and its closest allies own and control a large proportion of the economy, then branding, image and security are all interlinked into, in effect, a nation-state business development strategy. In such contexts, tourism has become crucially important. Qatar's focus on major events (Smith 2015: 239–254; also see Chapter 8), for example, or Dubai's efforts at branding itself as a safe yet up-market destination, bring new opportunities for the (state-owned) airlines of these emirates and for a tourism sector which the state is deliberately, and in very specific ways, trying to promote. This brings income to the state as charges and as profits from state-owned firms, while also offering the chance to promote the country or even gain some new commercial opportunities, especially if tourists return as investors or trading partners.

The example of Qatar Airways, the Qatari government's tourism strategy and the links between the two are illustrative here. Previously, tourism was mostly centred on business travellers and, later, on visitors to major sporting and cultural events. These remain important, and Qatar is unlikely to give up its emphasis on higher-end tourism. A US$20 billion tourism and culture strategy was unveiled in mid-2010, which aimed to further develop and expand the tourism sector (Smith 2010). The strategy encouraged cultural-oriented inward visits and high-end travellers, and included a target of 5 per cent of airline transit passengers staying for 2 days more than the usual layover. Qatar Airways now explicitly pursues this stopover target in its marketing material. In such ways, the airline marketing goals are linked, explicitly and intentionally, to the state's tourism strategy; a reminder of both the new state capitalism and the tourism-related branding of which Qatar is a consummate example. This varies somewhat from the also up-market but more leisure focused strategies of Dubai and Bahrain. Yet, although the strategies are different, strong links are always evident between branding, tourism and development in all of the GCC states.

The cultural element of the branding-tourism nexus link is also important. Major events and cultural infrastructure not only earn income, but create both a domestic and an international image. Domestically, they enhance the sense of shared purpose or identity in and with society, and internationally, they are a form of advertising for the country, its economy and the existing order. Tourism has always been about cultural representation and image to some extent, but this is especially the case when potential visitors or investors lack understanding of a state or confuse them culturally with each other, as arguably is the case with those of the GCC states. In Qatar, efforts to host major sporting events such as the successful bid for the 2022 World Cup and continuing attempts to host a Summer Olympic Games have such goals, among others, in mind (Smith 2015: 239–254). Doha's hosting of the Asian Games in 2006 was the first time it deliberately used a major event to showcase the country and raise international awareness of Qatar (Anon. 2005). The aim was to send a message to both Qataris and foreigners that Qatar is not meekly accepting globalization and economic change, but is positively and creatively embracing it (Amara 2005: 501–505). Likewise, Qatar's grand arts and cultural initiatives since the late 1990s have been designed, at least in part, for the same reasons.

In Bahrain, there are several examples where image, tourism and politics inter-link. These include at Dar al-Naft, the Oil Museum; Bayt al-Qur'an, a museum of Islamic calligraphy; and attractions such as the Lost Paradise of Dilmun Water Park. Dar al-Naft is a deliberate attempt to remind the population and visitors alike about the wealth and opportunity generated by oil rents, with a historical narrative that praises the country's oil income and the ruling family that has distributed it since 1932. Bayt al-Qur'an, however, is an indirect assertion and reminder of the Islamic credentials of the regime and its support for Islamic scholarship (Nawwab and Al-Ramadan 2000: 24–31). The Lost Paradise of Dilmun Water Park is not only a major recreational venue and a place for family social interaction, but a place of symbolic gesture and cultural significance as it alludes to Bahrain's claim to be the original site of the biblical Garden of Eden (Lewis 1984). It thus con-structs a unique historical narrative and at the same time legitimizes the small island's existence as a modern nation state.

At the same time as tourism brings about cultural change and potential threats, states continue to endorse its development. Oman has an emphasis, as Valeri has noted, on 'selective quality tourism', by which it means, in effect, as Valeri some-what dryly puts it, 'tourism reserved to wealthy and easily controllable elites of the West' (2009: 216). This may be a slight exaggeration, but there is no doubt that the Omani government wants tourism that will serve its economic and brand-ing goals but have a minimal impact on Oman's culture or environment.

Saudi Arabia has, like Oman, developed tourism for economic reasons, while also – in fact, even more so – seeking to protect cultural and religious values (Burns 2007: 225). It is often presumed to be very different from the five other GCC states because of its custodianship of Mecca and Medina and given the puritanical Wahhabi Islam of central Arabia. While these are valid, Saudi Arabia nonetheless has begun to more actively promote tourism for the same economic and socio-economic reasons as other Gulf states. This has been done cautiously, with mass international leisure tourism deliberately avoided, and with only cer-tain types of tourism actively promoted, such as domestic tourism, supplementary travel by visiting pilgrims and tightly controlled guided tours (Okruhlik 2004: 203–205). Yet tourism is a feature, nonetheless, of Saudi Arabia's economic, branding and political strategies.

Conclusion and research implications

Notwithstanding all the numerous ways to approach the study of tourism, it is always a highly economic and political affair. Using political economy as either a point of theoretical departure for the study of tourism, or a point of reference for examining its ramifications, is not only effective but essential, even if the debate still needs to occur over the exact approaches within political economy that might best be utilized. The case for political economy is as true for the GCC states as anywhere, since GCC tourism has been comparatively state-led and only recently encouraged and nurtured. Above all, as argued here, is that across all the GCC states, tourism has been driven by the late-stage rentier dynamics of political economies, the particular state capitalist structure of these political economies and the importance of economic security, branding and political stability and the nexus between all these. Tourism has featured prominently in, and helped to serve, strategies of economic diversification, selective globalization, greater indigenous employment and deeper trade and investment with the outside world (Herb 2014: 161–165). For these reasons, a single approach to the political economy of the GCC states cannot adequately explain the emergence of tourism and the dynamics that shape and modify it.

The approaches discussed in this chapter have their unique role: rentier arguments are salient in explaining the GCC's state-society dynamics; state capitalism is central to understanding the development approaches of the sub-region's leaderships and in distinguishing their economic policies from neoliberalism; and branding and its links to political economy provide insights into the many connections between politics, economics and tourism. Ultimately, a conglomeration of all three approaches is the best, if not only, comprehensive framework through which to explain the political economy of the GCC states' tourism strategies and outcomes.

The arguments here have identified some fundamental political-economic dynamics of GCC tourism, which also act as a starting point for future scholarship. Indeed, much about the political economy of tourism, both generally and in the GCC states, remains to be investigated and explained. The arguments herein elucidate some unusual properties of tourism: in the GCC states, for example, tourism may have lower profit margins than many sectors, but appeal politically because of its ability to generate a large number of jobs. Investment in the sector, as in the case of Dubai, may be encouraged by the state for its own commercial gain, or because of the rentier-like characteristics of private investment in emerging economic sectors. These ideas, however, deserve further focus from researchers.

These are relatively preliminary arguments. Important as they are to make, the finer characteristics of the GCC states' tourism all remain unexplained. A research priority in this regard should be to scrutinize business-government relations in the tourism sector, important because the sources and extent of private sector influence are likely, in the coming years, to dictate the nature and pace of wider changes to economic policy or to overall tourism strategy. A strong, independent set of wealthy merchants is more able to mount support or opposition to state policy than is, say, a relatively weak or controlled private sector that is operating subordinate to a state or royal family in an overwhelmingly state capitalist structure. The impacts of tourism expansion on actors in other economic spheres are also awaiting scholarly investigation. While tourism may be designated by regimes as a promising sector to promote as it has few pre-existing elites or interests engaged in it, this is likely to change as the size of the sector grows more prominent in some states. Research into how this might challenge state power in the sector, or into how new business elites in the tourism industry might challenge key established merchants in other sectors, would be difficult to develop because of political sensitivities. The rewards, however, would include new insights into a unique sub-region's tourism sector and, more broadly, new depth and nuance on the political economy of the GCC states.

References

Abdulla, A. (2012) 'The Arab Gulf moment', in D. Held and K. Coates Ulrichsen (eds) *The Transformation of the Gulf: Politics, Economics and the Global Order*, London: Routledge, pp. 106–124.

Amara, M. (2005) '2006 Qatar Asian games: a "modernization" project from above?' *Sport in Society*, 8(3): 493–514.

Anon. (2005) 'Bright horizons', *Middle East Economic Digest*, 14 October.

Beblawi, H. (1987) 'The rentier state in the Arab world', in H. Beblawi and G. Luciani (eds) *The Rentier State: Nation, State and the Integration of the Arab World*, London: Croom Helm, pp. 63–82.

Bill, J. and R. Springborg (1990) *Politics in the Middle East*, 3rd edn, Glenview, IL: Scott, Foresman/Little, Brown.

Bremmer, I. (2009) 'State capitalism comes of age', *Foreign Affairs*, 88(3): 40–55.

Bremmer, I. (2010) *The End of the Free Market: Who Wins the War Between States and Corporations?* New York: Portfolio.

Burns, P. (2007) 'From Hajj to hedonism? Paradoxes of developing tourism in Saudi Arabia', in R. F. Daher (ed.) *Tourism in the Middle East: Continuity, Change and Transformation*, Clevedon: Channel View Publications, pp. 215–236.

Champion, D. (2003) *The Paradoxical Kingdom: Saudi Arabia and the Momentum of Reform*, New York: Columbia University Press.

Cooper, C. (2003) 'Progress in tourism research', in C. Cooper (ed.) *Classic Reviews in Tourism*, Clevedon: Channel View Publications, pp. 1–8.

Daher, R. F. (2007) 'Reconceptualizing tourism in the Middle East: place, heritage, mobility and competitiveness', in R. F. Daher (ed.) *Tourism in the Middle East: Continuity, Change and Transformation*, Clevedon: Channel View Publications, pp. 1–69.

Foley, S. (2010) *The Arab Gulf States: Beyond Oil and Islam*, Boulder, CO: Lynne Rienner.

Gray, M. (2011) 'A theory of "late rentierism" in the Arab States of the Gulf', *Center for International and Regional Studies Occasional Paper No. 7*, Doha: Georgetown University School of Foreign Service in Qatar.

Gray, M. (2013) *Qatar: Politics and the Challenges of Development*, Boulder, CO: Lynne Rienner.

Hanieh, A. (2011) *Capitalism and Class in the Gulf Arab States*, Basingstoke: Palgrave Macmillan.

Hazbun, W. (2008) *Beaches, Ruins, Resorts: The Politics of Tourism in the Arab World*, Minneapolis, MN: University of Minnesota Press.

Held, D. and K. Coates Ulrichsen (eds) (2012) *The Transformation of the Gulf: Politics, Economics and the Global Order*, London: Routledge.

Herb, M. (2014) *The Wages of Oil: Parliaments and Economic Development in Kuwait and the UAE*, Ithaca, NY: Cornell University Press.

Hertog, S. (2010) 'Defying the resource curse: explaining successful state-owned enterprises in rentier states', *World Politics* 62(2): 261–301.

Hertog, S., G. Luciani and M. Valeri (eds) (2013) *Business Politics in the Middle East*, London: Hurst & Company.

Hvidt, M. (2009) 'The Dubai model: an outline of key development-process elements in Dubai', *International Journal of Middle East Studies* 41(3): 397–418.

Kamrava, M. (ed.) (2012) *The Political Economy of the Persian Gulf*, London: Hurst & Company.

Kanna, A. (2011) *Dubai: The City as Corporation*, Minneapolis, MN: University of Minnesota Press.

Lawson, F. (2012) 'The Persian Gulf in the contemporary international economy', in M. Kamrava, *The Political Economy of the Persian Gulf*, London: Hurst, pp. 13–38.

Lewis, P. (1984) 'Eden on the isle of Bahrain', *New York Times*, 18 November. Available online at www.nytimes.com/1984/11/18/travel/eden-on-the-isle-of-bahrain.html (accessed 26 May 2014).

Luciani, G. (1990) 'Allocation vs. production states: a theoretical framework', in G. Luciani (ed.) *The Arab State*, London: Routledge, pp. 65–84.

Luciani, G. (2005) 'From private sector to national bourgeoisie: Saudi Arabian business', in P. Aarts and G. Nonneman (eds) *Saudi Arabia in the Balance:* Political Economy, Society, *Foreign Affairs*, London: Hurst, pp. 144–181.

MacDonald, S. B. and J. Lemco (2015) *State Capitalism's Uncertain Future*, Santa Barbara, CA: Praeger.

Mahdavy, H. (1970) 'The patterns and problems of economic development in rentier states: the case of Iran', in M. A. Cook (ed.) *Studies in Economic History of the Middle East*, London: Oxford University Press, pp. 37–61.

Malik, M. and T. Niblock (2005) 'Saudi Arabia's economy: the challenge of reform', in P. Aarts and G. Nonneman (eds) *Saudi Arabia in the Balance:* Political Economy, Society, *Foreign Affairs*, London: Hurst, pp. 85–110.

Maloney, S. (2008) 'The Gulf's renewed oil wealth: getting it right this time?', *Survival*, 50(6): 129–150.

Mansfeld, Y. and O. Winckler (2008) 'The role of the tourism industry in transforming a *rentier* to a long-term viable economy: the case of Bahrain', *Current Issues in Tourism*, 11(3): 237–267.

Marcel, V. with J. V. Mitchell (2006) *Oil Titans: National Oil Companies in the Middle East*, London: Royal Institute of International Affairs.

Nawwab, N. I. and H. A. Al-Ramadan (2000) 'Beit Al Qur'an: Religion, art, scholarship', *Saudi Aramco World*, 51(3): 24–31.

Okruhlik, G. (2004) 'Struggles over history and identity: "opening the gates" of the Kingdom to tourism', in M. Al-Rasheed and R. Vitalis (eds) *Counter-Narratives: History, Contemporary Society, and Politics in* Saudi Arabia *and Yemen*, Basingstoke: Palgrave Macmillan, pp. 201–228.

Payne, A. (2006) 'The geneaology of new political economy', in A. Payne (ed.) *Key Debates in New Political Economy*, London: Routledge, pp. 1–10.

Peel, M. and J. Blas (2011) 'Saudi spending could require high oil price', *FT.com*, 31 March. Available online at www.ft.com/cms/s/0/87d60044-5bbb-11e0-b8e7-00144feab49a. html#axzz1K6WbamI0 (accessed 21 April 2011).

Peterson, J. E. (2006) 'Qatar and the world: branding for a micro-state', *The Middle East Journal*, 60(4): 732–748.

Richter, T and C. Steiner (2008) 'Politics, economics and tourism development in Egypt: insights into the sectoral transformations of a neo-patrimonial rentier state', *Third World Quarterly*, 29(5): 939–959.

Schlumberger, O. (2008) 'Structural reform, economic order, and development: patrimonial capitalism', *Review of International Political Economy*, 15(4): 622–649.

Shaw, G. and A. M. Williams (1994) *Critical Issues in Tourism: A Geographical Perspective*, Oxford: Blackwell.

Silver, I. (1993) 'Marketing authenticity in third world countries', *Annals of Tourism Research*, 20(2): 302–318.

Simpson, T. A. (2012) 'Tourist utopias: Las Vegas, Dubai, Macau', *Asia Research Institute Working Paper No. 177*, Singapore: Asia Research Institute, National University of Singapore.

Smith, B. (2015) *Market Orientalism: Cultural Economy and the Arab Gulf States*, Syracuse, NY: Syracuse University Press.

Smith, P. A. (2010) 'Qatar pledges $20 billion for tourism and culture', *The Middle East* (London), 413: 36–37.

Valeri, M. (2009) *Oman: Politics and Society in the Qaboos State*, London: Hurst.

2 Tourism and geopolitics in the GCC region

Dallen J. Timothy

Political geographers have long been interested in how human geography affects international relations (Agnew and Muscarà 2012; Kasperson and Minghi 2011). Geopolitics as a field of study seeks an understanding of political behaviour based upon geographical variables. Scholars who study geopolitics have widespread interests in many social, economic, cultural and ecological spheres of influence (e.g. the formation of states, colonialism, migration, gender, power, conflict and territory). Three of the most pervasive elements of geopolitics that touch on each of these are political boundaries, territorial conflict and supranationalism and their effects on social space and human activity (Glassner and Fahrer 2004).

From this perspective, borders, conflict and cross-boundary collaboration sway human behaviour and govern economic development. They determine where and when certain events occur, and they dictate the limits of power and sovereign jurisdiction of nation states. These and other characteristics of borders have substantial consequences for tourism as an economic, political and social phenomenon throughout the world (Timothy 2001). In particular, political borders create competitive conditions and legal advantages, such as relaxed laws, differing taxes or price differentials, where certain types of tourism thrive. These include shopping, gambling and medical tourism and, in some situations, unique heritage-based tourism when geopolitics determines the most prominent heritage of the destination, as is the case in many borderlands throughout the world (see Arreola and Curtis 1993; Silverman 2011; Sofield 2006). At the same time, borders erect barriers to tourism, as both physical obstacles and psychological impediments to travel. As physical barriers, borders can prevent certain people from entering a country or make entry difficult. They can also change how tourism develops physically and result in differing tourism landscapes on opposite sides of a frontier, especially when it inhibits collaborative planning and the development of a cross-boundary tourism region with similar resources. The perceived barrier can typically affect travellers, who may be dissuaded by restrictive travel policies or arduous entry requirements (Timothy 1995).

Although geopolitics in general, and borders in particular, influence tourism in various ways, this chapter will focus on only a few of the most pertinent geopolitical concerns in the Gulf Cooperation Council (GCC) region. The chapter first describes the primary ways in which borders and conflict affect human mobilities and tourism development in the GCC states from the perspectives of creating tourist attractions, as well as functioning as barriers to tourism growth and development. The second part of the chapter examines the emerging trend of supranationalism and other forms of cross-border cooperation as they pertain to tourism in GCC.

Geopolitics, borders and the potential for tourism in the GCC region

In practice, sovereignty refers to absolute control of state territory unfettered by outside interference and is the legal mechanism by which a country can exercise legitimate control of all socio-cultural, economic, physical and political activities that occur within its boundaries. One of the most influential elements of sovereignty concerns the state border, which is the limit up to which a country can exercise its sovereign authority. Importantly, state borders have major implications for tourism development. Scholars have recently begun exploring the relationships between borders and tourism, with most attention being devoted to boundaries as tourist attractions (Gelbman 2010; Sofield 2006; Timothy 1995) or barriers to travel (Canally and Timothy 2007; Wachowiak 2006).

Borders have the potential to create socio-economic and political situations that are conducive to tourism development. On one hand, differential tax laws, permissive shopping or gaming regulations on opposite sides of a border, as well as the development of interesting boundary-related landscapes, can all contribute to the growth of, and demand for, tourism in border areas. On the other hand, however, restrictive visa regimes and other administrative mobility controls, such as passport requirements, quarantine prohibitions and import limits on goods, can prevent the growth of tourism and create cognitive barriers in the minds of potential travellers, or actual obstacles to travel for people of certain nationalities (Brabandt and Mau 2013).

The GCC region is replete with interesting historic sites, modern cities, wildlife parks, marine activities, oases and desert safaris, so there is much that appeals to foreign visitors. Unlike political boundaries in Europe, North America and much of Asia, however, the GCC's international borders have yet to create significant tourist attractions. In fact, the borders of the GCC states have been more effective in erecting barriers to tourist mobility and the development of tourism than they have in stimulating tourism. These obstructionist implications will be discussed later in the chapter. Nevertheless, GCC states have potential to develop certain types of tourism that relate to current border and sovereignty situations in the Middle East: differential tourism development, international enclaves and cross-border peace parks.

Perhaps the most visible impact of borders from an attraction perspective is the differential development of tourism between GCC member states (Fasano and Iqbal 2003; Mansfeld and Winckler 2007; Ritter 1986). While business travel related to oil production is widespread in most of the states, and religious pilgrimages have long been a tourism mainstay in Saudi Arabia, pleasure travel is skewed overwhelmingly towards the United Arab Emirates (UAE), Oman, Bahrain and

Qatar. In this regard, borders are meaningful because they determine the types of tourism that will be developed and the extent to which they are allowed to grow. Owing to plentiful oil reserves and potential conflict between the conservative religious traditions of nationals and the hedonistic behaviour of tourists, Kuwait and Saudi Arabia have shown the least interest in developing large-scale leisure tourism (see Chapter 6 and Chapter 7). Even within the UAE, there is a significant difference between the tourism policies and plans between the seven emirates, where each emirate has different development priorities. Dubai clearly has had the most aggressive tourism development agenda and is now known as a truly global tourism destination for its resorts, shopping facilities, festivals and events, busy international airport and superlative architecture and attractions, such as the tallest building in the world and the only downhill ski slope on the Arabian Peninsula (Lew *et al.* 2011). Other emirates have remained more conservative in their tourism growth endeavours, although Sharjah, Abu Dhabi and Ras al Khaimah are all encouraging foreign and domestic investments in tourism development (see Chapter 10 and Chapter 14).

The second unique border phenomenon is exclaves, or enclaves. More than 200 exclaves have appeared through history in various parts of the world as a result of land tenure histories, cross-border battles, changes in sovereignty, physical topography, misunderstandings in bilateral treaties, and various other historical reasons (Robinson 1959). These unique phenomena are small pieces of one nation's territory completely surrounded by the territory of a neighbouring state. Several European enclaves have become significant tourist destinations in their own right (Gelbman and Timothy 2011; Timothy 1995; Vinokurov 2007). For example, shopping is a primary draw for visitors to Baarle-Hertog (Belgium), which is entirely surrounded by the Netherlands. Llivia (Spain), situated within France, has become an important bedroom community for skiing in the Pyrenees. Campione d'Italia (Italy) is an enclave located inside Switzerland, best known for casino gambling and boating races on Lake Lugano. The primary advantage of these small spaces is that they are part of another country's sovereign territory and are, therefore, able to offer unique shopping, entertainment or other recreational opportunities. Exclaves are able to offer product diversity, and tax and legal advantages, and they typically lack border controls so that people from the surrounding (enclaving) state are able to enter and participate in the enclave's unique offerings without having to possess passports or visas (Timothy 1995, 2001).

GCC is also home to two similar exclaves: Madha (Oman), which is completely surrounded by the UAE; and Nahwa (UAE), which is inside Oman's Madha exclave, making Nahwa a 'counter-enclave', or an exclave within an exclave. This geopolitical situation alone makes the two exclaves a curiosity for map and historical geography aficionados (Henzell 2012; Vinokurov 2007). Visitors crossing into Madha receive a mobile phone text to inform them they are under the service of Omantel and no longer in the UAE. According to Henzell (2012: n.p.):

> If not for the text, the unobservant might not even notice the crossing of an international boundary. Indeed, unlike the UAE's other borders with Oman and Saudi

Arabia, there is no secure barrier restricting access ... Madha, with its different architecture and narrower roads, has the feel of another country, that goes beyond the familiar ensign of the Emirates being replaced by the Omani flag.

Thus, while Madha and Nahwa have potential to become at least a secondary tourist destination for shopping and because of their geopolitical heritage, no efforts have been made to capitalize on their unique frontier situation or the lack of need for passports and visas to enter, or the missing barbed-wire fences that might otherwise hinder tourism development (Figure 2.1).

Although the Musandam Peninsula is not a true exclave, it is a part of Oman separated from its motherland by the UAE. This is, itself, an interesting geopolitical curiosity, and Musandam appears to be more popular as a destination among residents of the UAE and foreign visitors in the UAE than it does for visitors and residents of Oman. Musandam has substantial potential as a tourist destination for diving, boating, four-wheel driving and hiking. Efforts so far have begun capitalizing on the region's unique environment as a significant tourism resource (Dietl 2013; Funsch 2015), but more can be initiated by Oman to promote its separated territory (i.e. Musandam) as a destination for tourists who visit Muscat and other parts of Oman. For some tourists, outlying territories and peripheral regions with smaller populations and somewhat 'undiscovered' landscapes exude a unique appeal that might attract an international clientele (Brown and Hall 2000).

Another situation that bears some similarity to that of enclaves is free trade zones (or special economic zones), which are emerging throughout the world, primarily for manufacturing and transshipment industries. In most cases, free trade zones are established as customs-free areas where products can be landed from abroad, controlled, produced or assembled, and re-exported without interference or regulation by customs authorities (Levien 2013). Hundreds of these 'free zones' have emerged in recent decades, including in the GCC region, and some

Figure 2.1   Omani-UAE border marker and welcome sign to the Madha exclave.

Source: D. Timothy, May 2009.

of them have important implications for tourism, such as tax-free development, the growth of shopping and commerce-based tourism, less government interference, freer travel and, in some cases, resort-based tourism. Several (e.g. in Belize and China), in fact, have emerged as free trade zones for traditional trade, as well as tourism as an industry. Although Iran is not a member of the GCC, it is very close geographically and well connected to several GCC states. Kish (Iran), a small island and free trade zone in the Persian Gulf, is a center for tourism activity in Iran and, statistically, one of the most visited destinations in the Gulf region (Mohajerani and Miremadi 2012). There are no visa requirements to visit Kish, even for people who normally need visas to enter Iran (Kish Free Zone Organization 2014; Riasi and Pourmiri, 2016). Both of these facts make the island rather appealing for Western tourists who might not otherwise have an opportunity to visit Iran. The island resort is especially popular among Iranian domestic travellers, but it is growing in popularity among Western tourists as well, with frequent connections from Abu Dhabi and Dubai. There are several free trade zones in the GCC, but these focus on the more traditional treatment of manufactured products and have yet to promote tourism and serve as visa-free vacation destinations, the way Kish has done in Iran. There is considerable potential for this sort of tourism-related, visa-free development to take place in designated parts of the GCC states, especially in countries that normally have strict visa requirements for foreigners.

Another prospective element of tourism development is transboundary nature preserves and peace parks. This has become a normative approach to taking advantage of demilitarized zones (DMZs) or borderlands that have gone without direct human interference for many years. Calls have been made in recent years to establish linear peace parks and nature preserves along the former East-West Germany divide and within the DMZ between the two Koreas (Cramer 2008; Healy 2007; Westing 2001). Similar calls have been made to establish a cross-border peace park in the DMZ at the Kuwait-Iraq border. This DMZ is 240 km long and 15 km wide, and because it is off limits to most human intrusion, it has a diverse and healthy ecosystem. According to Alsdirawi and Faraj (2004: 53), the creation of a nature-oriented peace park would serve a variety of purposes: to conserve biodiversity; promote more peaceful relations and political stability between Kuwait and Iraq; and serve as a mechanism for bilateral cooperation and economic development. Although the peace park is a promising concept, such efforts may be hard to establish and maintain between feuding states. Similar efforts, however, could be considered at certain spots along inner-GCC boundaries, such as between Saudi Arabia and its GCC neighbours and between the UAE and Oman, although in both cases border fortifications have recently been erected as barriers to human movement.

Borders, geopolitics and tourism barriers

The borders and geopolitics of the GCC have functioned more as constraints to tourism than as instruments for its development (Hazbun 2006; Henderson 2006).

The international borders within the GCC region have long been barriers to human mobility and tourism development in a variety of ways. Perhaps the most notable of these has been the territorial and border disputes that have prevailed since the decolonization of the Gulf states (Okruhlik and Conge 1999).

The current borders of GCC states have evolved considerably during the past century. The gradual collapse of the influence of the Ottoman Empire in the Arabian Peninsula and wider Persian Gulf region ended in the early twentieth century, when the British exerted control over several parts of the region (i.e. today's Bahrain, Kuwait, Qatar and parts of the UAE) until their independence from British rule, or their consolidation into modern states from various tribal factions and individual kingdoms (i.e. Saudi Arabia and Oman) (Stewart 2013). One of the remaining effects of colonialism in the region from both the Ottomans and the British is the state boundaries. Although they have long been defined, many had not been demarcated until recently. Like other colonial regions, border definitions imposed upon the GCC lands occupied by various tribes, factions and ethnicities were somewhat arbitrary, favouring the colonialists (including the Ottomans) rather than citizens and largely ignoring local conditions and history (see Carapico 2004; Okruhlik and Conge 1999; Schofield 1994).

This seemingly wanton disregard for local identities and traditional tribal boundaries has, together with disputes over oil and water resources, resulted in a significant number of boundary and territorial conflicts. The legal contest between Bahrain and Qatar over the Hawar Islands, resolved in 2001, retarded travel and cooperation in development initiatives between the two countries for many years. Relations were also soured between Saudi Arabia and its GCC neighbours, Qatar and the UAE, over border zone oilfields, oases and maritime waters, even leading to armed conflict between Saudi Arabia and Qatar in the 1990s (Okruhlik and Conge 1999; Wiegand 2012). This territorial disagreement was resolved in 2001, and the Saudi-Qatari border was subsequently delineated and demarcated. With this bilateral agreement, all territorial disputes between GCC member countries were resolved. Until that time, however, cross-border cooperation had been difficult to achieve in all areas of economic development, including petroleum production, security and tourism. Earnest collaboration between the two states in the tourism realm only truly began after 2001.

Despite most of the GCC countries sharing cultural and religious similarities, there are some socio-economic incongruities between them. As a result, and because of broader security concerns, thousands of kilometres of barbed-wire fences have been erected that keep less-affluent people from filtering through the borders illegally in search of work or other economic advantages, and ostensibly for security purposes to thwart terrorist activity (Jellissen and Gottheil 2013). Nonetheless, borders and barriers create not only physical obstacles to cross-border tourism development but also psychological obstacles to cross-border travel by individual tourists (Figure 2.2).

One recent example illustrates this point. Al Ain (UAE) and Al-Buraimi (Oman), neighbouring oasis cities on opposite sides of the border, are important tourist destinations in both countries. Until 2006, the border between them was

Figure 2.2   Barbed-wire fence and boundary marker in Dibba, on the UAE side adjacent
          to Oman (the Musandam Peninsula).

Source: D. Timothy, May 2009.

open, and tourists were permitted to cross the border without visas. In the early
2000s, however, the border was demarcated and a barbed-wire fence erected
between the two cities. As part of the region's broader security measures and to
thwart the flow of illegal immigration from Oman to the UAE, the border was
closed to free movement in September 2006, for both locals and tourists; passport controls were initiated, and visas are now required from non-GCC nationals
(Kalimat Group 2014).

Austere visa regimes have played a role in hindering some elements of tourism.
Cruise tourism is one of the best examples of this. Cruises have increased in the
region in recent years, with several countries having expressed interest in developing this activity to support their burgeoning tourism economies (Baporikar 2012).
Persian/Arabian Gulf cruises are becoming more popular, with most departing
from Dubai or Abu Dhabi and stopping at ports in Oman, Bahrain, Qatar and the
UAE. While the climate, outdoor activities and shopping are important elements
of an Arabian Gulf cruise, much of their appeal lies in calling at rather exotic
ports that most people would not otherwise visit on their own (Bryant 2014). The
blossoming of cruise tourism in the GCC region has been hindered somewhat by
visa restrictions, as well as religious conservatism and concerns about inappropriate tourist behaviour. While cruise passengers in other parts of the world (e.g. the
Caribbean and Latin America) typically do not require visas (or passports, for
that matter) for each port on the itinerary, this is not the case in the Gulf (Timothy
2006a). Acquiring visas ahead of time for the UAE, Oman, Qatar and Bahrain can
be a painstaking and expensive process that prevents many people from purchasing Gulf cruises (Peisley 2000). Saudi Arabia's visa restrictions have presented
this state from being fully included in the cruise ship circuits. However, given the
national objectives of some GCC states to meet visitor number targets, the introduction of a multiple-entry visa system for cruise tourists in the UAE should help

to attract increased numbers. This system, introduced in 2014, aims to bring more tourists from such places as Brazil, China, India, Russia, South Africa and the Commonwealth of Independent States, who may have been discouraged by the previous single-entry permit system, as it was more costly and administratively cumbersome (Algethami 2014).

Another geopolitical issue has been Saudi Arabia's reluctance to issue general tourist visas. Although certain types of tourists have been issued visas for many years (e.g. business travellers, family visitors and religious pilgrims), leisure travel has been virtually shunned by the Saudi government, despite the state's recent interest in increasing foreign visitation to its cultural sites and natural landscapes. The contradictory policies of encouraging and promoting tourism through such official 'destination marketing organizations' as the Saudi Commission for Tourism and Antiquities (SCTA) (which changed to the Saudi Commission for Tourism and National Heritage in 2014), while at the same time not issuing tourist visas, is rather puzzling (Burns 2007). However, SCTA's efforts have been geared towards domestic tourism, visitors from other GCC countries, expatriates and other non-Saudis spending time in the country on other types of visas. The Kingdom began issuing a limited number of group visas in 2006, but this is an inconsistent policy as no individual tourist visas are allowed (Zamani-Farahani and Henderson 2010). However, the situation is changing, as there is an Umrah Plus Programme being introduced, encouraging pilgrims to stay for a month in the country to participate in tourism activities (see Chapter 7).

Other travel restrictions have limited the number and types of tourists that have been allowed to enter the Kingdom, including women, who are not permitted to travel alone without permission from a male head of household or without being accompanied by a close male relative. Strict visa requirements for non-GCC states have also affected travel to GCC by nationals of other countries in the Middle East, such as Egypt, Turkey and Iran.

Another issue related to regional conflict and travel restrictions, which has at its core colonialism, borders and sovereign territory, is the lack of recognition of Israel among GCC states and the varying degrees of acceptance of travel to and from Israel. Many predominantly Muslim countries do not allow entry to Israelis, although several permit or encourage Israeli tourists to visit (e.g. Egypt, Indonesia, Morocco, Tunisia, Turkey and Jordan). The majority of GCC countries do not allow Israeli citizens to enter, with the exception of Bahrain. Several countries do allow entry for people with Israeli stamps in their passports, with the exception of Kuwait, Saudi Arabia and UAE, which restrict passports bearing evidence of travel to Israel. While these restrictions derive primarily from a non-acceptance of Israel and its occupation of Palestinian lands, as well as a sign of solidary for Palestine (Shlaim 2001), from a purely economic standpoint the majority of GCC states could benefit from a potentially lucrative regional travel market.

Regional conflict and geopolitics create obstacles to successful tourism, as adverse travel advice by market source countries may diminish the attractiveness of the GCC destinations. Travel alerts can have profound impacts on tourism in destination countries, as citizens take heed of their home country's warnings or alerts regarding personal safety (Kim *et al.* 2007; Timothy 2006b). Based on political expediency, international relations or threat level, countries are listed or delisted periodically, while many remain on warning lists for many years.

At the time of writing (May 2016), only Saudi Arabia of the GCC countries was on the US State Department's list of travel warnings, owing to the potential for terror activities against US interests and citizens in the country (US Department of State 2016). Australia's Department of Foreign Affairs and Trade cautioned Australians regarding travel to the GCC region. In Kuwait, Australians are advised to 'exercise a high degree of caution', while their citizens are strongly encouraged to 'reconsider [their] need to travel' to Bahrain and Saudi Arabia because of potential terrorist concerns. There were no Australian warnings for Oman, the UAE or Qatar (Department of Foreign Affairs and Trade 2016). Similarly, British citizens were warned to exercise caution and vigilance in all GCC countries, for general threats of terrorism, public protests and crime, with less emphasis placed upon Oman and Qatar (Foreign and Commonwealth Office 2016). There is little doubt that these sorts of travel warnings influence some latent travellers' perceptions of GCC destinations and affect their travel decisions, as they do for many destination countries (see Löwenheim 2007). While this does not imply an endemic problem in the GCC region, it is certainly something that potential visitors might consider in their travel decision-making.

Cross-border cooperation and supranationalism

Shortly after the Second World War, countries in Europe began to realize that acting alone in economic development would not produce the desired development outcomes. As a result, they began to work together across their common boundaries to counteract the devastating effects of the war and develop their economies. Since that time, the world has undergone a process of supranationalization and other collaborative measures. International collaboration can occur at many different scales, including global (e.g. World Trade Organization), regional/multilateral (e.g. European Union (EU)) and bilateral (e.g. two countries agreeing on rainforest conservation measures) (Timothy and Teye 2004).

Most countries today understand that only through bilateral or multilateral cooperation can they achieve their modern development goals. Supranationalism is the process of countries forming regional alliances, usually for economic development purposes. The most common and effective manifestations of these are customs unions, trade blocs and economic alliances. There are a number of regional and supranational alliances to which various GCC members belong (e.g. Arab League, Muslim World League, the Organization for Islamic Cooperation and the Greater Arab Free Trade Area). However, the GCC is the best integrated of these in terms of plans for integrating infrastructure development, transportation and a single currency.

Multilateral supranational alliances have many implications for the development of tourism (Timothy 2003, 2004); three of these are highlighted here. First is the flow of people between member states. Many blocs have as their ultimate goals common passports, common visas and a shared customs regime (e.g. the EU and the Schengen Accord). As part of efforts to improve human mobility within the bloc, GCC citizens are free to travel across inner-GCC frontiers without visas, although passports or national IDs are still required. In 2003, a common GCC e-passport was, in theory, approved for travel outside the union, but it has yet to come to fruition as of mid-2016. Taking this a step further, the council has begun to consider a common GCC tourist visa, which aims to attract visitors from countries outside the GCC and permit them to move more freely between member countries (Rejimon 2013). Advocates of the pan-GCC visa argue that it will boost tourism in the region and spread its benefits to a wider range of destinations. However, prior to such a visa taking affect, some issues will have to be resolved. One major issue might include foreign policy changes to be more consistent between countries. The common visa has practical implications, such as the need for shared electronic linkages throughout the GCC to be installed to keep track of visitors from abroad and to share blacklists with the names and biometric information of people who are banned from entering any GCC member country. As well, the diverging policies regarding admitting Israeli citizens or people with Israeli stamps in their passports will have to be worked out, while maintaining the sovereign authority of each member state.

The second major tourism-related consideration within supranational alliances is transportation (Timothy 2004). Shared budgets and the development of common-use transportation resources (e.g. highways, airports, railways and air traffic policies), and the growth of transport hubs are typical examples of multinational alliance transportation concerns. Plans have been initiated for developing a GCC railway, especially for the purpose of connecting the six member states, enhancing economic development in the region and transporting goods and passengers across the Arabian Peninsula (see Chapter 4). The cost of the rail line will be partly carried by all members, depending on the portion of the line within their individual boundaries. There has also been a great deal of cooperation in developing common standards for road construction, connecting highways of member states and setting forth safety regulations, as well as treating drivers from any member nation as nationals of the country where they are driving (GCC Secretariat General 2014).

The third major tourism-related consideration within supranational alliance is a single currency. Few supranational alliances have been able to achieve a common currency, although this is a conventional desire among trade alliances (Timothy and Teye 2009). Since its inception, the GCC has aimed to establish a common currency, the *Khaleeji* (GCC Secretariat General 2014), but several economic and political discrepancies have weakened these efforts. As of 2009, the UAE and Oman withdrew from the unified currency agreement, although there are plans for Saudi Arabia, Qatar, Kuwait and Bahrain to continue moving forward with the motion. If the common currency eventually comes to fruition an economic boost for tourism and trade could result, as regional tour operators will function more economically under one currency, and it will be more convenient for tourists not to have to exchange currencies each time they cross a border (GCC Secretariat General 2014).

The council has begun to look at many other areas of cooperation that also touch on tourism either directly or indirectly, but most of these are at varying levels of implementation. These include efforts to standardize environmental education and youth and sport exchanges, improve telecommunications facilities and standardize costs (e.g. transportation and taxation) between member states and organize joint training and seminars related to museums, culture and folklore (GCC Secretariat General 2014). Besides these pan-GCC initiatives, other efforts are underway at a smaller scale within the GCC region to cooperate across political boundaries, with salient implications for tourism. The building of the King Fahd Causeway between 1981 and 1986, connecting Saudi Arabia and Bahrain by wheeled traffic, was a huge boost for tourism between the two countries (Aljarad 1995; Dar and Presley 2001).

With the success of the King Fahd Causeway and the 2001 resolution of the Hawar Islands dispute, efforts were made to plan and build an even longer causeway between Bahrain and Qatar. Work was set to begin on the construction of the 40 km bridge in 2009 to support a highway and a railway, but the project was since put on hold for various reasons, including financial concerns and souring relations between the two states. When the Qatar Bahrain Causeway was originally envisaged, there were no direct flights or ferry services between the two countries; the only way to travel between Qatar and Bahrain was via a third country, usually Saudi Arabia. Thus, the bridge was seen as a vital means of cross-border travel that would allow non-GCC citizens to access Bahrain without having to go through Saudi Arabia, where strict transit visa regulations were necessary (Wiegand 2012). Today, however, there are multiple nonstop flights each day on Gulf Air, Qatar Airways and British Airways, so the bridge has become a lesser priority for both countries involved.

Conclusion and research implications

This chapter examined the role of borders and geopolitics in tourism in the GCC region. It described the role of borders in creating tourist attractions, as well as understanding geopolitical issues as barriers to tourism development. State borders within the GCC have untapped potential to create a variety of attractions and destinations that can expand the resource base for tourism in several countries of the region. Regional borders create competitive advantages, differential development and unique exclaves, all of which can result in shopping and heritage destinations. In common with other regions of the world, the GCC's free trade zones can also become visa-free tourist zones, where special rules and policies (e.g. visa-free entry and resort development) are applied. Likewise, establishing transborder nature preserves/peace parks will stimulate increased levels of nature-based tourism and help protect delicate desert ecosystems in transfrontier areas. All of these have found considerable success in other parts of the world and are efforts the GCC states might consider in their tourism planning objectives.

Territorial conflict, difficult geopolitical relations and travel restrictions have also created salient obstacles to tourism development equally throughout the region. However, these are only symptoms of larger political issues. Standing in the way of the potential border-induced appeal of the GCC region is an array of geopolitical concerns. Nonetheless, these concerns are not necessarily endemic to the GCC, especially as they can be found in all areas of the world and within all supranationalist organizations (Chapman 2011; Timothy 2003). The most salient of these is a lack of political will. Most countries would rebuff the idea of devolving a degree of sovereignty in the name of progress for the greater good, which creates a common impediment to collaborative efforts across political boundaries (Timothy 2001). This stifles many efforts to develop tourism related to exclaves, free trade zones and peace parks, and it is just as formidable a barrier to the goals of supranationalism (e.g. single currencies, common passports and common visas).

There may well be mistrust by GCC states towards particular neighbours, resulting in complete bans on travel to and from said countries or restricting entry of people who have visited such states. Age-old cultural conservatism also erects barriers to people entering some countries as leisure tourists, even while neighbouring states are pushing a more liberal tourism agenda. In their efforts to develop tourism, a few GCC countries will need to assess the degree to which their desire for tourism earnings will overpower the desire to remain on the tourism periphery as a means of protecting long-held cultural, religious and political positions. Strict travel requirements, even among citizens of countries in the general region, are thought to be symbolic of a common mistrust of others (cf. Salter 2006).

Resource rights (e.g. oil) are jealously guarded and sometimes claimed by more than one state party, resulting in conflicts that are difficult to resolve and which may lead to armed conflict (Okruhlik and Conge 1999). This, almost inevitably, leads to downturns in arrivals and the tourism industry's ability to recover. Wealth disparities between GCC states and their populations have also led to the erection of new physical barriers during the past decade in an effort to quell illegal immigration. In the process, however, these new fences have also erected new visa and passport regimes for people who have traditionally been free to cross some common borders, such as the Oman-UAE border, including residents and tourists. Supranationalism is not a panacea for the deep cultural norms and power relations that create intraregional socio-economic differences and conflict. However, supranationalism and other configurations of cross-frontier collaboration have started to show promise in levelling the tourism playing field between GCC states, alleviating some of the barriers that have existed since most of them gained independence from Britain in the late twentieth century. Cross-border cooperation is essential for transportation and infrastructure development, environmental conservation, common currencies and human mobility. With the exception of the recent erection of fences along many inner-GCC borders, nascent efforts at cross-boundary cooperation are slowly eroding the traditional barriers that have heretofore hindered the growth of tourism.

There are many geopolitical conditions in the region that merit additional research attention. While GCC treaties encourage a great deal of cooperation on many fronts that affect tourism, we still know relatively little about how these are playing out on the ground. Studies are needed to help understand the operationalization successes and failures of GCC regulations and to assist in formulating regional policies towards tourism development. Gauging cross-border collaboration in terms of human movement, tourism development and planning, transportation and infrastructure growth, equitable resource use and cultural and natural resource protection are all crucial concerns throughout the world that we know relatively little about in the GCC context.

Similarly, cross-boundary tourism marketing of physically contiguous regions has found considerable success in other strategic alliances (e.g. the EU and the Association of Southeast Asian Nations), and it would behoove scholars and industry leaders to study how these successes could be replicated in the Gulf region. This would have salient repercussions for the tourism industry, for the countries involved and for further academic knowledge. Much of the geopolitical landscape of the GCC, including international conflicts, trade globalization, mobility barriers and potential attractions (spurred by international boundaries), is unique to this region. The distinctive characteristics of GCC's geopolitics are in desperate need of additional empirical and theoretical research, to understand not only how tourism is influenced by these specific variables but also how tourism affects regional geopolitics, and why.

Saudi Arabia, Kuwait, Qatar, Bahrain, the UAE and Oman as a common trading bloc and customs union have come a long way in their tourism development goals. The establishment and function of the GCC has facilitated much of this growth. Nonetheless, there are still many conflict-related and border-induced concerns (and other geopolitical impediments) that need to be managed prior to the full introduction of an integrated tourism system on the lines of other supranational alliances. Additional research can make significant strides in helping this region overcome some of the obstacles to tourism development and realize greater success, and help illuminate the reasons for both.

References

Agnew, J. and L. Muscarà (2012) *Making Political Geography*, Landham, MD: Rowman & Littlefield.

Algethami, S. (2014) 'UAE multiple entry cruise visa to boost passenger growth', *Gulf News*, 5 December. Available online at http://gulfnews.com/business/sectors/tourism/uae-multiple-entry-cruise-visa-to-boost-passenger-growth-1.1422548 (accessed 26 May 2016).

Aljarad, S. N. (1995) 'Modeling Saudi Arabia-Bahrain corridor mode choice', *Journal of Transport Geography*, 3(4): 257–268.

Alsdirawi, F. and M. Faraj (2004) 'Establishing a transboundary peace park in the demilitarized Zone (DMZ) on the Kuwait/Iraq borders', *Parks*, 14(1): 48–55.

Arreola, D. D. and J. Curtis (1993) *The Mexican Border Cities: Landscape Anatomy and Place Personality*, Tucson, AZ: University of Arizona Press.

Baporikar, N. (2012) 'Emerging trends in tourism industry in Oman', in P. Ordóñez de Pablos, R. Tennyson and J. Zhao (eds) *Global Hospitality and Tourism Management Technologies*, Hershey, PA: Business Science Reference, pp. 116–135.

Brabandt, H. and S. Mau (2013) 'Liberal cosmopolitanism and cross-border mobility: the case of visa policies', *Global Society*, 27(1): 53–72.

Brown, F. and D. Hall (2000) *Tourism in Peripheral Areas: Case Studies*, Clevedon: Channel View.

Bryant, S. (2014) 'Cruise critic: eight reasons to cruise the Arabian Gulf'. Available online at www.cruisecritic.com/articles.cfm?ID=1232 (accessed 4 March 2014).

Burns, P. (2007) 'From Hajj to hedonism? Paradoxes of developing tourism in Saudi Arabia', in R. F. Daher (ed.) *Tourism in the Middle East: Continuity, Change and Transformation*, Bristol: Channel View, pp. 215–236.

Canally, C. and D. J. Timothy (2007) 'Perceived constraints to travel across the US–Mexico border among American university students', *International Journal of Tourism Research*, 9(6): 423–437.

Carapico, S. (2004) 'Arabica incognita: an invitation to Arabian Peninsula studies', in M. Al-Rasheed and R. Vitalis (eds) *Counter-Narratives and History: Contemporary Society and Politics in Saudi Arabia and Yemen*, Basingstoke: Palgrave, pp. 11–34.

Chapman, B. (2011) *Geopolitics: A Guide to the Issues*, Santa Barbara, CA: Praeger.

Cramer, M. (2008) *German-German Border Trail*, Rodingersdorf: Esterbauer.

Dar, H. A. and J. R. Presley (2001) 'The Gulf Co-operation Council: a slow path to integration'? *The World Economy*, 24(9): 1161–1178.

Department of Foreign Affairs and Trade (2016) 'Advice for travellers'. Available online at http://smartraveller.gov.au/ (accessed 25 May 2016).

Dietl, G. (2013) 'Musandam: creating a new region across the water', in S. Wippel (ed.) *Regionalizing Oman: Political, Economic and Social Dynamics*, Dordrecht: Springer, pp. 279–288.

Fasano, U. and Z. Iqbal (2003) *GCC Countries: From Oil Dependence to Diversification*, Washington, DC: International Monetary Fund.

Foreign and Commonwealth Office (2016) 'Travel advice'. Available online at www.gov.uk/foreign-travel-advice (accessed 26 May 2016).

Funsch, L. P. (2015) *Oman Reborn: Balancing Tradition and Modernization*. New York: Palgrave Macmillan.

GCC Secretariat General (2014) 'The charter'. Available online at www.gcc-sg.org/eng/ (accessed 3 March 2014).

Gelbman, A. (2010) 'Border tourism attractions as a space for presenting and symbolizing peace', in O. Moufakkir and I. Kelly (eds) *Tourism, Progress and Peace*, Wallingford: CAB International, pp. 83–98.

Gelbman, A. and D. J. Timothy (2011) 'Border complexity, tourism and international exclaves: a case study', *Annals of Tourism Research*, 38(1): 110–131.

Glassner, M. I. and C. Fahrer (2004) *Political Geography*, New York: Wiley.

Hazbun, W. (2006) 'Explaining the Arab Middle East tourism paradox', *The Arab World Geographer*, 9(3): 201–214.

Healy, H. (2007) 'Korean Demilitarized Zone: peace and nature park', *International Journal on World Peace*, 24(4): 61–83.

Henderson, J. C. (2006) 'Tourism in Dubai: overcoming barriers to destination development', *International Journal of Tourism Research*, 8(2): 87–99.

Henzell, J. (2012) 'Madha village's pledge of allegiance changed the map forever', *The National*, 27 January. Available online at www.thenational.ae/lifestyle/

madha-villages-pledge-of-allegiance-changed-the-map-forever (accessed4 March 2014).

Jellissen, S. M. and F. M. Gottheil (2013) 'On the utility of security fences along international borders', *Defense and Security Analysis*, 29(4): 266–279.

Kalimat Group (2014) 'The 4,000-year-old cradle of UAE's heritage', *Travel Arabia*. Available online at www.ontravelarabia.com/living-arabia/arabian-experience/al-ain (accessed5 March 2014).

Kasperson, R. E. and J. V. Minghi (eds) (2011) *The Structure of Political Geography*, New Brunswick, NJ: Transaction.

Kim, S. S., D. J. Timothy and H. C. Han (2007) 'Tourism and political ideologies: a case of tourism in North Korea', *Tourism Management*, 28(4): 1031–1043.

Kish Free Zone Organization (2014) 'Kish, the family paradise'. Available online at www.kish.ir/ Homepage.aspx?lang=en-US&site=DouranPortal&tabid=1 (accessed 24 May 2014).

Levien, M. (2013) 'Regimes of dispossession: from steel towns to special economic zones', *Development and Change*, 44(2): 381–407.

Lew, A. A., C. M. Halland and D. J. Timothy (2011) *World Regional Geography: Human Mobilities, Tourism Destinations, Sustainable Environments*, Dubuque, IA: Kendall Hunt.

Löwenheim, O. (2007) 'The responsibility to responsibilize: foreign offices and the issuing of travel warnings', *International Political Sociology*, 1(3): 203–221.

Mansfeld, Y. and O. Winckler (2007) 'The tourism industry as an alternative for the GCC oil-based rentier economies', *Tourism Economics*, 13(3): 333–360.

Mohajerani, P. and A. Miremadi (2012) 'Customer satisfaction modeling in the hotel industry: a case study of Kish Island in Iran', *International Journal of Marketing Studies*, 4(3): 134–152.

Okruhlik, G. and P. J. Conge (1999) 'The politics of border disputes on the Arabian Peninsula', *International Journal*, 54(2): 230–248.

Peisley, T. (2000) 'The cruise industry in the Arabian Gulf and Indian Ocean', *Travel and Tourism Analyst*, 1: 3–17.

Rejimon, K. (2013) 'Common GCC tourism visa will boost economy, income', *Times of Oman*. Available online at www.timesofoman.com/News/Article-24429.aspx (accessed 3 March 2014).

Riasi, A. and S. Pourmiri (2016) 'Examples of unsustainable tourism in the Middle East', *Environmental Management and Sustainable Development*, 5(1), 69–85.

Ritter, W. (1986) 'Tourism in the Arabian Gulf region – present situation, changes and restraints', *GeoJournal*, 13(3): 237–244.

Robinson, G. W. S. (1959) 'Exclaves', *Annals of the Association of American Geographers*, 49(3): 283–295.

Salter, M. B. (2006) 'The global visa regime and the political technologies of the international self: borders, bodies biopolitics', *Alternatives: Global, Local, Political*, 31(2): 167–189.

Schofield, R. N. (ed.) (1994) *Territorial Foundations of the Gulf States*, London: University College of London Press.

Shlaim, A. (2001) *The Iron Wall: Israel and the Arab World*, New York: Norton.

Silverman, H. (2011) 'Border wars: the ongoing temple dispute between Thailand and Cambodia and UNESCO's World Heritage List', *International Journal of Heritage Studies*, 17(1): 1–21.

Sofield, T. H. B. (2006) 'Border tourism and border communities: an overview', *Tourism Geographies*, 8(2): 102–121.

Stewart, D. J. (2013) *The Middle East Today: Political, Geographical and Cultural Perspectives*, London: Routledge.

Timothy, D. J. (1995) 'Political boundaries and tourism: borders as tourist attractions', *Tourism Management*, 16(7): 525–532.

Timothy, D. J. (2001) *Tourism and Political Boundaries*, London: Routledge.

Timothy, D. J. (2003) 'Supranationalist alliances and tourism: insights from ASEAN and SAARC', *Current Issues in Tourism*, 6(3): 250–266.

Timothy, D. J. (2004) 'Tourism and supranationalism in the Caribbean', in D. T. Duval (ed.) *Tourism in the Caribbean: Trends, Development, Prospects*, London: Routledge, pp. 119–135.

Timothy, D. J. (2006a) 'Cruises, supranationalism and border complexities', in R. K. Dowling (ed.) *Cruise Ship Tourism*, Wallingford: CAB International, pp. 407–413.

Timothy, D. J. (2006b) 'Safety and security issues in tourism', in D. Buhalis and C. Costa (eds) *Tourism Management Dynamics: Trends, Management and Tools*, Oxford: Butterworth Heinemann, pp. 19–27.

Timothy, D. J. and V. B. Teye (2004) 'Political boundaries and regional cooperation in tourism', in A. A. Lew, C. M. Hall and A. M. Williams (eds) *A Companion to Tourism*, London: Blackwell, pp. 584–595.

Timothy, D. J. and V. B. Teye (2009) 'Regional alliances and cross-border tourism in Africa: border implications and the Economic Community of West African States', *Tourism Review International*, 12(3/4): 203–214.

US Department of State (2016) 'Travel alerts and warnings'. Available online at http://travel.state.gov/content/passports/english/alertswarnings.html (accessed 25 May 2016).

Vinokurov, E. (2007) *A Theory of Enclaves*, Lanham, MD: Lexington Books.

Wachowiak, H. (2006) *Tourism and Borders: Contemporary Issues, Policies and International Research*, Aldershot: Ashgate.

Westing, A. H. (2001) 'A Korean DMZ park for peace and nature: towards a code of conduct', in C. H. Kim (ed.) *The Korean DMZ: Reverting Beyond Division*, Seoul: Sowha, pp. 157–191.

Wiegand, K. E. (2012) 'Bahrain, Qatar, and the Hawar Islands: resolution of a Gulf territorial dispute', *Middle East Journal*, 66(1): 79–96.

Zamani-Farahani, H. and J. C. Henderson (2010) 'Islamic tourism and managing tourism development in Islamic societies: the cases of Iran and Saudi Arabia', *International Journal of Tourism Research*, 12(1): 79–89.

3 Discourses of tourism and identity in the Arabian Peninsula

William G. Feighery

The states of the Arabian Peninsula emerged out of the struggle for authority which took place during the pre-independence phase and continue to be led by the dominant families of ruling tribes who were in the ascendancy prior to these new formations. Since gaining independence, the ruling elites of these states have been confronted with pressures of socio-economic and political development while attempting to retain 'traditional values' and build 'national' identity ('*haweeya al-watani*'). The outcome of these aspirations has often been an oscillation between radical change in the drive towards 'modernity' and a resurgence of essentialist impulses.

The 'post-oil' era has witnessed the development of modern institutions, which are often involved in the production, reproduction or representation of national and regional myths of origin. As Exell and Rico (2013: 675) note, 'The nation-states of the Arabian Peninsula are now becoming openly and aggressively involved in the preservation, representation and invention of their own individual and distinct tangible national culture and heritage'.

Newly constituted ministries or institutes, many of which are concerned with tourism either directly or indirectly, have been charged with collecting and curating symbolic and material artifacts which can be deployed, not merely to buttress preferred interpretations of 'an authentic national culture' or even to maintain 'a cultural link between the modern changing society and the old cultural lifeways' (Khalaf 1999: 102), but to construct a homogenized, unified and romantic past around which a collective national identity can be assembled. One of the difficulties with such imaginaries in the context of the states of Arabian Peninsula is that 'political borders are not the borders of identity' (Partrick 2009: 11).

Nations as cultural artifacts are maintained through a wide variety of discursive institutions (First 2002), including those of tourism. Officially sanctioned promotional videos are an important part of the content and modalities through which dominant and powerful groups within nations promote themselves and their perceived interests. Yet, despite several decades of critical reflection, narratives of tourism (including visual narratives) continue to essentialize and eroticize. National tourism organizations (NTOs) expend a great deal of resources constructing images of the nation (i.e. the 'tourist destination image' (TDI)) which are deemed to appeal to their target tourism markets while, at a minimum, maintaining social acceptance among the dominant population(s) within the state. NTOs and related agencies potentially act to inscribe and communicate national stories, which allow people to confirm and/or affirm (or contest) their belonging to the nation. Such a sense of belonging is potentially achieved in and through promotional discourses, within which fantasy and reality are fused into a form of 'hyperreality' (Eco 1987).

In promoting their territories for tourism, state authorities increasingly use visual images in multiple forms to disseminate national myths of origin and fraternity. In an era where visual culture is dominated by expanding technologies of representation, tourism promotion can be regarded as a significant node for the deployment of these visual rhetorics. The advantage of such visual arguments over print or spoken communication lies in their evocative power (Hill and Helmers 2012: 51). Yet, despite the importance of such representational and significatory practices in and through tourism, the analysis of visual images (Burns 2004; Crouch 1999; Rakić and Chambers 2011), and of moving images in particular (Feighery 2012; Yan and Santos 2009), has only recently begun to receive sustained scholarly attention and, to some extent, remains something of a marginal activity. Yet, as Yan and Santos (2009: 299) note, visual practices in tourism 'form ideological spaces where socio-cultural powers are affirmed, challenged or contested'.

In seeking to contribute to this impoverished arena, the current chapter explores the contemporary practices of image creators in the Arabian Peninsula and considers whether, as Daher (2006: 9) suggests, state agents continue to read from an Occidental script, perpetuating oppositional perspectives of us and them, the familiar and the strange and the dynamic and the atrophied. The discussion here focuses on representation and signification in the promotional images of three Gulf Cooperation Council (GCC) member states: the Sultanate of Oman, Qatar and the Kingdom of Saudi Arabia. Specifically, the analysis and discussion employ a discourse studies approach, which focuses on state-sponsored tourism promotional videos for the three countries.

Critical discourse analysis

The recent upsurge of critical interest in language in contemporary society, as exemplified by the 'critical turn', is, in part at least, a response to those conscious interventions which control and shape language practices in the service of dominant economic, political and institutional objectives (including those in/of tourism). Part of that response has grown out of the roots of the Frankfurt project of 'critical theory' and the emergence of Critical Linguistics (CL) and the subsequent development of Critical Discourse Analysis (CDA). CDA approaches have been adopted by a number of scholars in relation to aspects of tourism, including national tourism promotion (Feighery 2006, 2012; Yan and Santos 2009), representation of protected areas (Stamou and Paraskevopoulos 2006) and in-flight magazines (Small *et al.* 2008). While a full discussion of CDA is beyond the scope of this chapter (the author has provided a detailed account elsewhere (Feighery 2006)), the following discussion provides a brief outline of the approach.

CDA is concerned with the relationship between discourse and power. Is seeks to explain the processes by which power is legitimated, reproduced and enacted in the talk and texts of dominant groups and institutions. Scholars working within critical discourse frameworks view discourse as a form of social action. They are concerned with the analysis of power and dominance associated with specific social domains, professional elites and institutions, and the rules and routines that form the background of the everyday discursive reproduction of power in such domains and institutions (Feighery 2012).

The discursive practices associated with tourism promotion have ideological effects through the ways in which they represent, signify or silence particular views or position particular individuals or groups. Thus, for scholars probing the cultural political economy of tourism, CDA approaches can be deployed to interrogate a raft of cultural, economic, environmental or political discourses which are mutually constituted in, and constitutive of, contemporary society. CDA is particularly useful for analyzing phenomena such as the communication patterns of public institutions, media discourse and the constitution of individual and group identity. Language is only one variety of the available semiotic modes in creating meaning. Visual elements, including moving images, are a major part of the rhetorical environment. Rose (2011) argues that there are three sites at which the meanings of an image are made: (1) the sites of production, (2) the site of the image itself and (3) the site of its audiencing (Rose 2011: 20). In the discussion here, analysis is focused on the site of 'audiencing'.

CDA can, potentially, inform an understanding of the role of language (in its broadest sense) in/of tourism promotion in the making and marking of identity. In the context of the current study, discourse analysis represents a subjective and interpretative approach to research, not necessarily a method or set of techniques (Feighery 2012). Here, the scholarly analysis of a 'text' does not seek to identify the intended message of the text's author. Further, the adoption of a rhetorical perspective on promotional film/video, which comprises the visual artifacts analyzed in this chapter, does not regard the creator's intentions (even if these are only implied) as determining the 'correct' interpretation of the work, but instead can be viewed as 'independent of its creator's intentions' (Hill and Helmers 2012: 308).

The corps

Excerpts from three official promotional 'texts' (videos) of the aforementioned GCC states provided the corps of data for the forthcoming discussion. The corps includes both linguistic and visual text. The following 'texts' are analyzed:

- *Qatar: Where Dreams Come to Life* (Qatar) (see www.youtube.com/watch?v=g4Atnii-8hM).

- *Saudi Tourism: An Enriching Experience* (Kingdom of Saudi Arabia) (see www.youtube.com/watch?v=YKVKunwcGBM).
- *Welcome to My Country* (Sultanate of Oman) (CD, Ministry of Tourism, Sultanate of Oman).

These 'texts' were either produced directly by the state tourism organization of the concerned state, or commissioned by state authorities. The CDA approach to analysis taken here is 'close reading' within a multimodal framework (van Leeuwen 2005). First, a short description of the three videos is provided, followed by a critical discussion of the 'texts' in the context of broader socio-political and socio-cultural impulses within the three GCC states. The conclusion seeks to draw together insights that such an analysis offers, as well as to hint at potentially productive avenues of future research concerning this aspect of contemporary tourism discourse in the Arabian Peninsula.

'Qatar: where dreams come to life'

Qatar, with its relatively short history as an independent state, has adopted a high-profile independent stance within the Gulf region. Such state-sponsored stimuli as the projects of the recently established Qatar Museums Authority have been shaped by Western heritage discourse and foreign expertise, significantly raising Qatar's international profile in recent years. Such investments in the cultural sphere bring 'increased awareness of and legitimacy accruing to Qatar – in domestic and external terms', which 'enhances the prospects of the state's survival' (Peterson 2009: 748). The state's branding strategy is certainly evident in the video 'Qatar: where dreams come to life'. The opening scenes of the video depict the architectural modernity of Qatar through scenes of the Doha skyline, while the foreground portrays traditional dhows. Although there is no oral narrative in this production, the visual narrative device of the video features an adult male in a short-sleeve shirt and trousers. This device introduces a level of ambiguity as to whether the 'figure' is a local Qatari, a tourist or both. Driving an open-top BMW motorcar in the midst of skyscrapers, this figure acts as a signifier of leisure, luxury and modernity. The scene moves quickly to the same male astride a speedboat, with the modern skyline still in the background, and then cuts to shots of camel racing before returning to the male figure entering a shopping mall (i.e. City Centre Doha). Two unveiled women walking in an outdoor precinct are then depicted, prior to the narrative returning to the male character in a museum displaying traditional swords and other artifacts. The narrative then moves to sporting activities, with depictions of horseracing, golf, dune 'bashing' and falconry. The production also features short cuts of castles, beaches and nightscapes of the skyline.

Branding Qatar as a sophisticated destination for business and leisure travellers not only underpins the state's economic development strategy, but, more fundamentally, it lends support to the legitimacy of the micro-state and, in particular, serves to mediate the historical myths which serve to maintain the ruling Al Thani family's grip on power. Such representational practice conceals the intricate and multi-layered nature of heritages and identities in the state. Fromherz (2012: 2) argues that the ruling Al Thani family sought to construct Qatar as having a homogeneous, timeless and 'legendary' past, serving to conceal potentially contradictory and politically awkward tribal histories. In 'Qatar: where dreams come to life', the melding of representations of cultural heritage with those of modernity can be regarded as a 'regime of globalisation' (Fibiger 2011: 189) and, perhaps, an indication of a shift from the deployment of heritage as a counterbalance to the impacts of globalization, to one which co-opts globalized heritage in its quest for legitimacy. The pearling town of Zubara, located on Qatar's north coast, is a useful example of such transition. The site serves not only to represent Qatar's local heritage, but also to validate the lineage of the current ruling family, and as a desired United Nations Educational, Scientific and Cultural Organization (UNESCO) World Heritage Site, it has become a symbolic authorization of Qatar's presence on the world heritage stage (Exell and Rico 2013: 678).

'Saudi tourism: an enriching experience'

The visual narrative device of this video is a young girl wearing a black headscarf and dress. This visual narrative embeds sweetness, nostalgia, history and mysteriousness (Yan and Santos 2009: 303). The opening scenes of the video depict a rising sun reflected in still water. The next immediate image is of a male figure wearing traditional headdress and sunglasses, holding a falcon amidst sand dunes. The pace of the production is slow at first, but with the depiction of the sun now high in the sky the mood quickens, and the shots are cut short (1 or 2 seconds each). The next sequence depicts a young boy and girl sitting under a stone arch, then the scene moves to two smiling females wearing black *abaya* and *hijab*. The images then comprise short cuts depicting Islamic-style buildings, camels, souks with traders offering woven baskets, ancient buildings and groups of men wearing *dishdashas* around campfires.

The narrative moves to modernity, with scenes of women shopping for luxury items, then returns to the central figure, the young girl, now having her hands and arms adorned by henna designs. The scene proceeds to an elderly man cycling in front of a modern building, then to young men in *dishdashas* running through a series of buildings. Subsequently, we see representations of historic buildings in the desert. With depictions of sunset, the mood slows to the young girl now alone aboard a boat in the harbour, the sun setting over sand dunes, shepherds, the face of a smiling young woman and a mosque. A series of cuts that are extremely short are then presented, leading to the final scene depicting the young girl swinging on a large rope inside the shell of a traditional dhow. The video concludes with a male voice narrating: 'Saudi tourism, an enriching experience'. Accordingly, Saudi Arabia is discursively constructed in a Western imaginary through the myth of the 'unchanged' (Echtner and Prasad 2003), or what Said (1985: 93) refers to as a 'kind of pragmatic fossilization', with little reference to the modern urban reality of the majority of Saudis.

'Welcome to my country'

One of the cornerstones of Oman's tourism promotional effort and its first tourism promotional film was *Welcome to My Country*, produced for the Ministry of Tourism in 2003. The film, which runs for some 14 minutes, introduces Oman to a global tourism audience as well as supporting the development of an Omani 'tourism brand'. It has five distinct sectioned parts or narratives: 'introduction', 'heritage', 'hospitality', 'culture' and 'adventure'. The film includes footage taken from various regions of the Sultanate, including representations of land and seascapes, people and artifacts. There is only brief narration by a female voice on five separate occasions, facilitating the transition between the various sections and at the conclusion of the film. In the English version of the film, 'on-screen' texts appear throughout the film. The production seems to follow a chronological progression, representing aspects of the country closely connected to the particular theme.

The introductory sequences depict misty mountains, deserts, underwater scenes of marine life, including beaches, and coastal sunset scenes with seabirds in the foreground, as well as green wooded hills and wildflowers. As the introductory scenes 'run', a female voice narrates the words '*my land is beautiful*', while the on-screen representation (image) depicts an ancient map of Oman inscribed with the words '*Arabia Felix*'. The textual and visual narrative appeals to a timeless land, devoid of human habitation, with the exception of representations of 'primitive man' confined to archaeological sites. The viewer is presented with a 'lost land' fixed in a timeless present, waiting to fulfil the fantasies of the tourist/ explorer (see Exemplar 1). Here, an orientalist fantasy of 'empty lands' and 'discovery' (see Exemplar 2) await the mythical hero: the Western tourist.

Exemplar 1

1   *Since the dawn of man*
2   *Tales were told of lost cities and a land of legendary beauty*
3   *Such a land was known as Arabia Felix*
4   *Today ... the legends live on*

Exemplar 2

1   *Tradition flows through the blood, reaching the heart of a nation*
2   *The essence of Oman is as diverse as its people*
3   *Get close to the real Arabia*

Reading the 'introduction' through a politico-national lens, it can be argued that the film constitutes a narrative of unfolding national truth-making through appeal to ancient origin and a shared history and culture. This is particularly apparent through the textual association with longevity, unity, history, national pride and heritage while visually representing the seat of the Imamate in Nizwa, the historical (and, some would argue, the contemporary) source of opposition to the Said regime and an area bombed by the British air force during the last major opposition to the Said dynasty in 1955. Under the current Qaboos regime, there has been a national quest for heritage preservation, from textile and craft traditions to its maritime history, and this has been utilized to anchor the new nation in its history through the celebration of an idealized past (Valeri 2009: 140).

Welcome to My Country is unique among the corps in providing a depiction of women in hospitality service roles. The paucity of representations of women at work in the films signals deeper socio-cultural and socio-political cleavages in the region relating to women's labour and entrepreneurial ambition (OECD 2013).

Pedagogies of identity in the Arabian Peninsula

The visual rhetoric of the 'texts' explored here potentially plays a constitutive role in identity formation and affirmation through their pedagogic role. These state-sponsored promotional videos can be regarded as part of the 'performance strategy' (Wodak 2011) of the concerned state and are part of a political process which encodes and reinforces dominant ideologies structuring touristic relations (Mellinger 1994). Such promotion is a form of autoethnography in the sense that the videos attempt to construct authoritative representation of *our*selves, *our* landscape, *our* traditions and *our* lifeways. As has been noted in other jurisdictions in the region, ministries of tourism in the Middle East tend to define the region 'mainly through its classical traditions marginalizing local regional realities in the recent past in particular' (Daher 2006: 9). Representations in the three 'texts' explored here, to some extent, support a discourse of 'universalising historicism' (Said 1978), in which a diversity of experience is compressed both temporally and spatially and represented through the beautification of settings and the simplification of characters as timeless, lost and forever waiting. Such representations enable the construction of points of cultural identification and, in this sense, are critical exercises of socio-cultural power and normalization (Hall 1996; Yan and Santos 2009).

In the production of these visual texts, we can observe the utilization of a number of significatory tropes, for instance, a young girl, an apparently affluent and leisured young man, old men in traditional dress and desert scenes. These tropes work as visual metaphors, in which tradition and modernity are signified within an authorized narrative of the nation state. In all three videos, we find tropes associated with the construction of rural Arab identity. Representations of camels, desert camps and falcons are a common feature of these often simplistic, inaccurate and falsely nostalgic discourses (see Hull 2000), sanctioned and perpetuated by contemporary state institutions. They are part of what Appadurai (1996) refers to as the 'imagined worlds' constituted by and through the historically situated imaginaries of dominant individuals and groups within the territories in question. Such tropes perform a rhetorical function in re-shaping both self-identity and external perceptions of these territories and their peoples (Hawker 2002). Perhaps, representations such as the 'desert warrior' are indeed evidence of adherence to an Occidental script. This makes analysis of the relationship between tourism representations and 'national' identity problematic in the context of the historical and cultural evolution of states on the Arabian Peninsula.

Visual narratives, such as those explored here, become both a source and repository of cultural knowledge. While Frew and White (2011: 1) argue that 'the tourist may develop a deeper appreciation of a destination by understanding it through the lens of national identity' and 'marketers and planners may be better equipped to promote and manage it', many questions arise as to whose history, heritage and cultural artifacts constitute the 'national story'. Accordingly, three notable questions prevail: (1) Who (and under what authority) has been sanctioned to be the arbiter of these choices? (2) Whose interests are being promoted? (3) Who or what is excluded or silenced? As Hazbun (2004: 331) notes, states have used a wide variety of symbolic representations to 'promote political interests such as state legitimacy, for example, by projecting images of domestic tranquility for foreign investors or promoting national mythologies'.

The homogenous representations of state territories and peoples apparent in the texts tend to obscure the diversity of cultural identity/identities therein. For example, much of the state-sponsored discourse on tourism in Saudi Arabia elides the cultural, religious and ethnic diversity of the territory, while also referencing Wahhabism as the state religion and a cornerstone of national identity (Delong-Bas, 2004). However, given that the modern state of Saudi Arabia emerged from the conversion of tribal lands into the monarch's property, including all resources under the land of the whole country (Khoury and Kostiner 1990; Sharara 1981), the construction and/or representation of such homogeneity may prove elusive and, more importantly in the contemporary context, more divisive. As Al-Hassan (2006) points out, 'Saudi society is heterogeneous, varied and divided on religious, regional and tribal basis; it is a society of religious and regional minorities, which used to belong to independent emirates, or even independent states' (2006: 8–9).

He goes on to suggest that in Saudi Arabia:

> religion, in its Wahhabist version, has become an element of deep internal divisions, undermining the very bases of the building of national identity, and has perhaps become an element of political disintegration. In Saudi, sub-identities are still far stronger than the national one, and loyalty to region is stronger than loyalty to the state, or to Wahhabism (2006: 10).

In constructing the notion of a homogenous Saudi homeland, the House of Saud continues to uphold the legacy of their political compact with the '*ulama*' – the leading scholars of Islamic traditions and Islamic law. While this historic pact may secure control over the land and its resources in the contemporary period, alongside state sanctioned and orthodox visions of Saudi Arabia, there is a cacophony of cultural strands impeding those visions officially sanctioned by the state. These diverse strands of dissent potentially provide the seeds of disintegration of a state sustained by the use of force and dependent on foreign powers (Blanchard 2010: 17). Awareness of such potentialities seems to be a key driver of initiatives such as the Saudi 'national dialogue', which acknowledged that 'contradictory internal pressures were threatening national cohesion, especially in the wake of heightened internal and regional sectarian tensions' (Partrick 2009: 2). Representations in and through tourism, as evidenced in video *Saudi Tourism: An Enriching Experience*, may appeal to the notion of 'Arabia' but do little to acknowledge the diversity of inheritances circulating in the lifeworld of the peoples of the territory. The Saudi text, in common with many tourism promotional media, excludes most identity groups who are likely to find the representations of little meaning or relevance and, thus, can be regarded as a form of collective disavowal (see Khalaf (2000) for a pertinent discussion on the reconstruction of national cultural identity in the UAE).

As already noted, across the 'texts' we find topoi such as camels, falcons, tents and campfires. To varying degrees, these visual topoi of Bedouin *signs* have become a culturally powerful, if somewhat complex, appellation in the Arabian Peninsula. As Peutz (2011: 338) suggests, the 'Bedouin have been substantially abstracted from their variant occupational and political foundations and are reemerging as a rather generic – and, yet, eminently marketable form of cultural identity and national heritage'. The Bedouin are represented as tradition bearers confined to the expression of the past and located outside of modernity, but within the contact zone of tourism. This stereotype of Bedouin lifeways is 'wielded by an indigenous minority that holds the reins of power and that projects the stereotype as a representation of the collective self rather than of the collective other' (Hawker 2002: 1). While coastal fishing and farming were the traditional occupations of the majority of the population, it is the armed desert warrior who provides the romantic allusions to the Arabian Desert. Compounding these nostalgic imaginations is the practice of representing the 'Bedouin' as a single group from the past, which ignores complex tribal and ethnic differences. In a sense, the Bedouin have acquired what Barbara Kirshenblatt-Gimblett (1998: 50) calls a 'second life' as heritage: a 'Bedouinness' positively transvalued through its emphasis on 'pastness, exhibition, difference, and, where possible, indigeneity' (quoted in Peutz 2011: 338).

In the CD *Welcome to My Country*, Omani modernity is mainly confined to the sections focusing on hospitality and/or adventure activities. Importantly, urban Oman is virtually 'written out' of the narrative and contrasts sharply to the video concerning Qatar, which foregrounds contemporary architecture and social interaction in an urban setting. Representations of people in *Welcome to My Country* are predominantly of Omani men and Western women. The representation of children in the film is primarily confined to the 'culture' section, which depicts Omani children reading the Qur'an, sitting with family groups, playing in the desert or on the beach and engaging in camel racing. The children are represented in Bedouin dress and in the more common *dishdasha* worn throughout Oman. In the Qatari video, the images are predominantly of men, with only one scene depicting children – two boys with a male adult. The one scene where women are depicted shows two women walking outside, neither of whom are wearing head-dress. Interestingly, the women are passing a large advertising poster showing a group of young women and men, all of whom are smiling and do not wear any form of headdress. This poster, a representation of a representation, is the only depiction of women and men together in the video.

As linguistic and visual narratives, there is a striking similarity between the content of the representation across the three texts representing the same 'selective aspects of reality' (van Leeuwen 2005: 95). The promotional discourses of the three states can be read as part of their political imaginaries as unified, stable and welcoming, while simultaneously commodifying aspects of their heritage, culture and natural environments in support of government sponsored, neo-liberal tourism development agendas. The scale and pace at which these states have embraced transnational corporations in the hospitality sector, especially to construct and operate such facilities as conference, hotel and resort developments, is certainly evidence of that. For example, while Oman can still be characterized as a 'rentier state', the emphasis on tourism development clearly indicates Oman's movement towards a Arabian-style liberal economic model, signalled by foreign ownership of property in designated tourism resorts, deregulation, privatization and place marketing.

If nationalist discourse is built around the nodal point of the 'nation', envisaged as a limited and sovereign community existing through time and linked to a certain space (de Cleen 2013), then we can say that in the process of socio-economic development and nation building, the ruling elites of the Arabian Peninsula states have interpolated a diversity of tribal peoples and cultures into a 'national' identity; especially to maintain legitimacy over entire territories and peoples. Heritage representation has been instrumental in providing a linear narrative that links current rulers to a long history of progress and technological evolution (Exell and Rico 2013: 677). In Oman, for example, this is achieved through an autochthonous perspective in producing a past as well as a place where that past can be located, thus providing a lens through which people understand the present historically. This primordial perspective (see Geertz 1977; Smith 1991, 1994) foregrounds ethnic ties and the uniqueness of the heritage. However, for some, the production also entails learning to forget and the construction of religious, tribal and trade allegiances, which defined their social landscape.

The representations projected to attract tourists to a given national territory also act to validate a national identity sanctioned by, and foregrounding the values of, hegemonic cultural producers (Pretes 2003), as well as contributing to the imagining which feeds the myth of fraternity (Anderson 2006). Therefore, tourism promotional films such as the corps explored in this chapter can be interpreted as pedagogic texts, narrating a vision of the concerned states as anchored in prehistory and extending into modernity/postmodernity. The productions explored here elide any hint to the social memory of alternative, competing conceptions of the political, religious or social organization of the concerned state, all of which have been 'silenced' in these productions.

Conclusion and research implications

Scholarly work on the Arabian Peninsula has been dominated by the role of elites and leaders, tribal influences, the struggle between the *badu* (tribal) and the *hadar* (city dwellers), the role of women in society and the diversity of religious and ethnic minorities. All of these important areas of concern intersect with tourism (production and consumption) at many levels. This chapter has focused on the seemingly unproblematic signification at work in and through tourism promotional videos. Officially sanctioned representations of culture and heritage, such as the visual texts discussed here, can be located at a social, cultural and political nexus. These texts are fragments of the institutionally grounded imaginaries, or symbolic matrixes, within which people imagine and act as world-making collective agents (Gaonkar 2002) of the concerned state. Representation of stereotypical topoi such as falcons, camels and desert campfires is part of a ritually constructed theatre in which the political elite celebrate their own political ideology framed within, for example, Bedouin poetics and cultural aesthetics. Such significatory practices appeal to the idea of '*asala*' (cultural authenticity) within the context of rapid integration into the global politico-cultural economy (Khalaf 2000). Qatar's recent cultural policy or Oman's liberalization of property law in tourism resorts are clear examples of this.

While the historical and cultural inheritances of the three territories discussed here are very different, their representation in these tourism promotional texts is strikingly similar and contributes to the construction and internalization of stereotypes about what states on the Arabian Peninsula 'are like'. For example, the instrumentalization of memory through the rehabilitation of heritage in accordance with contemporary political discourse is prevalent throughout the three states discussed here. All manner of historic remains have come under the gaze of state officials seeking material evidence, deployed to bolster imaginaries of continuity and belonging. Here, the link between national mythology and historic preservation is evident, as buildings and artifacts serve as concrete manifestations of mythical abstractions (see Maass *et al.* 1976). However, while such rehabilitation may represent a significant drawcard for the increasingly important international tourism sector, it often silences their historical testimony if, as so often is the case, they are mediated devoid of the complex, contested histories which they have witnessed but to which, under state authority, they do not bear witness (see Layne 1989; Limbert 2010; Valeri 2009).

When the same ways of thinking and talking appear across a range of texts or at a number of different institutional sites such as NTOs, they can be regarded as belonging to the same 'discursive formation'. Analysis of promotional 'texts' tends to support the notion that states construct national identity through a narrative of the nation, with emphases on 'traditions', 'myths of origin', 'continuity' and 'timelessness'. These characteristics are clearly apparent in the lexical and visual elements of the productions explored here (as illustrated in the previous Exemplar 1 and 2). Yet, these texts do not significantly acknowledge the tribal, ethnic, religious or linguistic diversity of the represented territories. The representation of women in these texts is limited when compared to that of men and in the context of the wider debate in the region of the role of women in society (OECD 2013). Further critical inspection would be useful to decipher the gendered implications of such representation in relation to specific states of the Arabian Peninsula.

Another noteworthy silence across all three 'texts' is the paucity of representations of the significant non-national populations of these states. Such silences are a common feature of discursive formations, which not only 'rule in' what can be talked about or represented but 'rule out' or restrict what can be said. The representation, misrepresentation or silencing of the non-nationals in states on the Arabian Peninsula also presents an important agenda for tourism researchers in the region. While the political discourse relating to non-nationals within the Gulf states is concerned with 'demographic imbalances' rather than on how these communities might be imagined in(to) the national narrative, it is nonetheless the members of these diverse communities that visitors are most likely to encounter as part of their visitor experience. This highlights the need for the development of research agendas to explore not only the representation of identity groups within and across the region but also the role and position of the significant non-national, non-Arab populations who are likely to remain an indispensable component of the region's future economic, political and social development.

This study has focused on the site of 'audiencing', but there is a need to explore the other 'sites of meaning' noted by Rose (2011), namely, the sites of production and the sight of the image itself. The role and deployment of image in and through tourism, and in support of political regimes, is insufficiently theorized. Here, the work of Baudrillard (1994) provides a useful point of intersection in relation to simulation, spectacle and seduction, which today characterizes much state (and elite) sanctioned promotional discourse. The development of 'country image' (CI), which also embraces TDI, is becoming a key concern for national governments across the globe. While the literature on TDI is well developed, there is a paucity of studies focusing on the visual rhetoric of NTOs and other state agencies concerned with tourism development and promotion. In the field of tourism studies, the analysis of promotional video is particularly impoverished, despite the fact that most countries now produce national promotional films. Herein lies an opportunity for the development of research agendas seeking to critically examine the 'politics and poetics' (Lidchi 1997) of CI as well as TDI. The work presented here only concerns issues of representation in and through the visual rhetoric of state tourism organizations. There is a need to develop this strand of analysis to other contexts and to the diversity of visual data currently available. There is also a need to explore the editorial gaze(s) as well as the strands of power that discipline such productions and communications. In addition, there are significant opportunities for scholars to critically explore how such 'imaginaries' are perceived and/or internalized by the populations of the territories in question, as well as by external populations.

An important concern, which presents both challenges and opportunities for the development of such work in the field of tourism studies/tourism management, is the paucity of critical work by scholars from the region. While significant numbers of local scholars in the Arabian Peninsula have received research training at doctoral level (many at prestigious foreign universities), this does not seem to have resulted in sustained critical output thereafter, with many pursuing non-scholarly occupations, or getting 'caught in a social environment that deadens the scholarly impulse' (Peterson 2009: 3). Of course, we must respect that scholars in the Arabian Peninsula often operate within a domestic political culture which could be characterized by the 'forbidden' ('*mamnû*'), which clearly brings into view the disciplinary effects of discourse so eloquently inspected in Foucault's writings on power-knowledge and subjectivity (Foucault 1980; Rabinow 1991).

References

Al-Hassan, H. (2006) 'The role of religion in building national identity (case study: Saudi Arabia)'. Unpublished PhD Thesis, London: University of Westminster.

Anderson, B. (2006) *Imagined Communities: Reflections on the Origin and Spread of Nationalism*, London: Verso Books.

Appadurai, A. (1996) *Modernity at Large: Cultural Dimensions of Globalization*, Minneapolis, MN: University of Minnesota Press.

Baudrillard, J. (1994) *Simulacra and Simulation*, Ann Arbor, MI: University of Michigan Press.

Blanchard, C. M. (2010) *Saudi Arabia: Background and US Relations*, Darby, PA: DIANE Publishing.

Burns, P. M. (2004) 'Six postcards from Arabia: A visual discourse of colonial travels in the Orient', *Tourist Studies*, 4(3): 255–275.

Crouch, D. (1999) *Leisure/Tourism Geographies: Practices and Geographical Knowledge*, London: Psychology Press, Routledge.

Daher, R. F. (2006) *Tourism in the Middle East*, Bristol: Multilingual Matters.

De Cleen, B. (2013) 'The stage as an arena of political struggle: the struggle between the Vlaams Blok/Belang and the Flemish City theaters', in R. Wodak, M. Khosravinil and B. Mral (eds) *Right-Wing Populism in Europe*, London: Bloomsbury, pp. 209–219.

Delong-Bas, N. J. (2004) *Wahhabi Islam: From Revival and Reform to Global Jihad*, Oxford: Oxford University Press.

Echtner, C. M. and Prasad, P. (2003) 'The context of third world tourism marketing', *Annals of Tourism Research*, 30(3): 660–682.

Eco, U. (1987) *Travels in Hyperreality*, London: Picador.

Exell, K. and Rico, T. (2013) '"There is no heritage in Qatar": Orientalism, colonialism and other problematic histories', *World Archaeology*, 45(4): 670–685.

Feighery, W. (2006). 'Reading tourism texts in context: A critical discourse analysis', *Tourism Analysis*, 11(1): 1–11.

Feighery, W. G. (2012) 'Tourism and self-Orientalism in Oman: a critical discourse analysis', *Critical Discourse Studies*, 9(3): 269–284.

Fibiger, T. (2011) 'Global display-local dismay: debating "globalized heritage" in Bahrain', *History and Anthropology*, 22(2): 187–202.

First, A. (2002) 'The fluid nature of representation: transformations in the representation of Arabs in Israeli television news', *Howard Journal of Communication*, 13(2): 173–190.

Foucault, M. (1980) *Power/Knowledge: Selected Interviews and Other Writings, 1972–1977*, New York: Pantheon.

Frew, E. and White, L. (2011) *Tourism and National Identity: An International Perspective*, London: Taylor & Francis.

Fromherz, A. J. (2012) *Qatar: A Modern History*, Washington, DC: Georgetown University Press.

Gaonkar, D. P. (2002) 'Toward new imaginaries: an introduction', *Public Culture*, 14(1): 1–19.

Geertz, C. (1977) *The Interpretation of Cultures Selected Essays*, New York: Basic Books.

Hall, S. (1996) 'Who needs identity?', in S. Hall and P. Du Gay (eds) *Questions of Cultural Identity*, London: Sage, pp. 1–17.

Hawker, R. W. (2002) *Imagining a Bedouin Past: Stereotypes and Cultural Representation in the Contemporary United Arab Emirates*, Beirut: Beirut Institute for Media Arts (BIMA).

Hazbun, W. (2004) 'Globalisation, reterritorialisation and the political economy of tourism development in the Middle East', *Geopolitics*, 9(2): 310–341.

Hill, C. A. and M. Helmers (2012) *Defining Visual Rhetorics*, London: Routledge.

Hull, D. (2000) 'Perceptions of the past: the role of archaeology in the United Arab Emirates', unpublished Master of Arts Dissertation, London: SOAS.

Khalaf, S. (1999) 'Camel racing in the Gulf: notes on the evolution of a traditional cultural sport', *Anthropos*, 94(1/3): 85–106.

Khalaf, S. (2000) 'Poetics and politics of newly invented traditions in the Gulf: camel racing in the United Arab Emirates', *Ethnology*, 39(3): 243–261.

Khoury, P. S. and J. Kostiner (1990) *Tribes and State Formation in the Middle East*, Oakland, CA: University of California Press.

Kirshenblatt-Gimblett, B. (1998) *Destination Culture, Tourism, Museums and Heritage*, Berkeley CA: University of California Press.

Layne, L. L. (1989) 'The dialogics of tribal self-representation in Jordan', *American Ethnologist*, 16(1): 24–39.

Lidchi, H. (1997) 'The poetics and the politics of exhibiting other cultures', in S. Hall (ed.) *Representation: Cultural Representations and Signifying Practices*, Thousand Oaks, CA: Sage and Open University, pp. 151–221.

Limbert, M. (2010) *In the Time of Oil: Piety, Memory, and Social Life in an Omani Town*, Redwood CA: Stanford University Press.

Maass, J., J. C. Massey, J. Thill and F. C. Williamson (1976) 'Heritage preservation and national mythology', *Monumentum*, 13(4): 36–44.

Mellinger, W. M. (1994) 'Toward a critical analysis of tourism representations', *Annals of Tourism Research*, 21(4): 756–779.

OECD (2013) *Gender Inequality and Entrepreneurship in the Middle East and North Africa: A Statistical Portrait*, Paris: OECD.

Partrick, N. (2009) 'Nationalism in the Gulf states: Kuwait programme on development, governance and globalisation in the Gulf States', Kuwait Programme on Development, Governance and Globalisation in the Gulf States, 5. London: London School of Economics and Political Science.

Pretes, M. (2003) 'Tourism and nationalism', *Annals of Tourism Research*, 30(1): 125–142.

Peterson, P. E. (2009) 'The Arabian Peninsula in modern times: a historiographical survey of recent publications', paper presented at the Gulf/2000 History Conference in Sharjah, United Arab Emirates.

Peutz, N. (2011) 'Bedouin "abjection": world heritage, worldliness, and worthiness at the margins of Arabia', *American Ethnologist*, 38(2): 338–360.

Qatar: Where Dreams Come to Life. Available online at www.you tube.com/watch?v=g4 Atnii-8hM).

Rabinow, P. (1991) *The Foucault Reader*, London: Penguin.

Rakić, T. and D. Chambers (2011) *An Introduction to Visual Research Methods in Tourism*, London: Routledge.

Rose, G. (2011) *Visual Methodologies: An Introduction to Researching with Visual Materials*, London: Sage.

Said, E. (1978) *Orientalism*, London: Vintage.

Said, E. W. (1985) 'Orientalism reconsidered', *Cultural Critique*, 1: 89–107.

Saudi Tourism: An Enriching Experience. Available online at www.youtube.com/watch?v=YKVKunwcGBM.

Sharara, W. (1981) *Kin and the Booty: The Foundation of Politics in Saudi Arabia*, Beirut: Dar al-Tali'a.

Small, J., C. Harris and E. Wilson (2008) 'A critical discourse analysis of in-flight magazine advertisements: the "social sorting" of airline travellers?', *Journal of Tourism and Cultural Change*, 6(1): 17–38.

Smith, A. D. (1991) *National Identity*, Reno, NV: University of Nevada Press.

Smith, A. D. (1994) 'The problem of national identity: ancient, medieval and modern?', *Ethnic and Racial Studies*, 17(3): 375–399.

Stamou, A. G. and S. Paraskevopoulos (2006) 'Representing protected areas: a critical discourse analysis of tourism destination building in a Greek travel magazine', *International Journal of Tourism Research*, 8(6): 431–449.

Valeri, M. (2009) *Oman: Politics and Society in the Qaboos State*, Hurst: London.

van Leeuwen, T. (2005) *Introducing Social Semiotics*, London: Psychology Press.

Wodak, R. (2011) *The Discourse of Politics in Action: Politics as Usual*, Basingstoke: Palgrave Macmillan.

Yan, G. and C. A. Santos (2009) '"China forever": tourism discourse and self-orientalism', *Annals of Tourism Research*, 36(2): 295–315.

4 Towards an integrated transport network in the GCC region

Fostering tourism and regional cooperation

Arnd N. Bätzner and Marcus L. Stephenson

The tourism industry has a dependable relationship with mobility infrastructure. The historical evolution of tourism is closely connected to, interlinked with and inseparable from the history of transportation and mobility. In order for the Gulf Cooperation Council (GCC) region to operate successfully as a global hub, it is important to acknowledge the fundamental importance of increased regional ties, infrastructural-based synergies and inter-territorial strategies. As this chapter will indicate, if tourism is to be a major part of the post-oil economic strategy of GCC states then it is essential that the region as a whole prioritizes coordinated, integrated, safe, sustainable, comfortable and rapid forms of transportation.

The use of the remaining oil reserves to finance infrastructural development for a post-oil future is an approach that virtually all GCC states recognize. The following four key industry areas have the capacity to reduce dependency on hydrocarbon oil in the GCC region: (1) energy-intensive manufacturing such as petrochemicals and aluminum processing, (2) mining and mineral-based industries, (3) trade and logistics and (4) tourism, hospitality and aviation (Kinninmont 2010). Moreover, these activities will rely on, or strongly benefit from, an integrated ground transport system.

To contextualize the present-day transportation needs of the region, the chapter provides a brief consideration of the rich history of transportation routes in the Middle East and implications for the Arabian Peninsula. The strategic ways forward for the advancement of a GCC railway network will be assessed, followed by a discussion identifying the challenges ahead for ground transportation systems. The work will then discuss the current issues facing the GCC airline industry, such as the need and capacity to maintain global dominance, hyper-competitiveness and resilience. This chapter draws caution to the argument, reflecting Western business interests, which emphasizes that GCC carriers are not competing fairly in the global aviation industry. It will also look at the significance of the rapid emergence of the low-cost carrier market, as well as the ramifications concerning increased airspace congestion. The latter section outlines the political and cultural implications for the advancement of an integrated and regional-based transportation network. The concluding comments will consider ways forward for future research in this field.

The development of a rail network in the Middle East

For the past 3,000 years, trade in the Arabian Peninsula was largely possible because of basic but endurable and natural forms of transportation. The domestication of camels and their use as 'beasts of burden' made the caravan trade possible. According to Ma (1998: 54):

> The greatest technological and institutional innovation in the means of transportation in the overland Silk Road was the adoption of camels and the subsequent rise of a camel-based caravan economy in Central Asia, North India, the Middle East and North Africa.

From the mid-1800s, British adventurers travelled to the region for economic, diplomatic and military purposes (see Bidwell 1994), as well as for reasons of curiosity and discovery. However, compared to Europe, leisure tourism in the Arabian Peninsula was not as institutionalized and was much less noticeably a social norm. In the late nineteenth century, the pace of socio-economic progress in Europe and the United States, precipitated by rapid industrialization and economic expansion, led to increased wealth generation and economic investment. Accordingly, infrastructural developments across Europe had been facilitated by a growing trans-European rail network, which eventually augmented the popularity of mass leisure travel (Tissot 2013). With the intent to modernize internal freight transport and accelerate military displacements, the Ottoman Empire was keen to maintain its control over the Arabian Peninsula. Accordingly, there was a need for a railway to be constructed, stretching from Constantinople (Istanbul) to the Persian Gulf (McMurray 2001). The first section of the route in Turkey was from Istanbul to Konya, known as the 'Anatolian Railway', which was financed by a consortium led by Deutsche Bank. A similar arrangement supported the development of subsequent sections of the railway from Konya to Baghdad, known as the 'Baghdad Railway', which started construction in 1903. These impressive developments advanced Germany's influence within a geographical region dominated by French and British interests (Barth and Whitehouse 1998: 115–121).

The railway was a competitor to Russian rail projects in Iran. Its ongoing construction contributed to a rapprochement between Britain, France and Russia while accentuating the tensions between Germany and neighbouring global powers (McMurray 2001). Conquering the Taurus Mountains in southern Turkey required some of the most advanced engineering capabilities. This factor, together with financial delays, meant that the project was not finished until 1940. Another objective of this railway was to establish a bridgehead to exploit mineral resources in the Near East (McMeekin 2012). In Baghdad, the railway allowed for a connection to the 'Basrah Mail' train, which utilized a railway connecting Baghdad to the Mesopotamian port of Basrah (Coke 1928), from where British steamships provided services to East India and the Asia-Pacific.

Importantly, another extension of the Ottoman railway network was from Istanbul to Damascus, which then paved the way for the development of the Hijaz

Railway. This network was originally intended to stretch from Damascus to the two holy cities, first to Madinah and then to Makkah. In addition to the wider political aspirations of the extended railway network, this particular route would ensure the safety of pilgrims travelling south to the holy cities. The railway construction began in 1900, and the station at Madinah was open to the public in 1908 (Orbaşli and Woodward 2008). However, the railway line did not reach further south to Makkah, as originally planned. Railway construction had ceased because of the advent of the First World War, and subsequently suffered severe destruction because of its geo-strategic significance. According to Anderson (2015: 1):

> For nearly two years, British demolition teams, working with their Arab rebel allies, methodically attacked its bridges and isolated depots, quite rightly perceiving the railroad as the Achilles' heel of the Ottoman enemy, the supply line linking its isolated garrisons to the Turkish heartland.

Political instability and the Six-Day War stopped attempts to rebuild the railway in the 1960s (*Spiegel* 1964). Nonetheless, like the Baghdad Railway, the Hijaz Railway was considered to be an 'extraordinary physical legacy' (McMeekin 2012: 341), built across difficult terrain. The full length of the original track is 1,300 km, which could be journeyed in less than 4 days – a camel caravan would travel this distance in 8 weeks (Assi 2005). The challenges experienced by such railway developments imply that supra-national governance over regional infrastructural developments is essential, especially if these developments are to be completed, maintained and protected. While neither the Baghdad Railway nor the Hijaz Railway were able to develop their full potential due to regional conflicts, long-distance rail links to the Arabian Peninsula could eventually gain new momentum in light of the planned GCC railway, which is crucial for fostering intra-regional travel, strengthening inter-state cooperation and leveraging mobility governance.

The emergence of a GCC rail network: strategic ways forward

The GCC rail network, involving the laying of 2,117 km of track from Kuwait City to Muscat (Oman), was originally scheduled for completion in 2018. However, given the scale of the project, and as some states are working at a different pace than others, this project could continue for a few more years to come. Oman, for instance, recently announced that it may not fully begin work until 2018 as it has, like the United Arab Emirates (UAE), initially prioritized the establishment of a freight network (Cornwell 2016). Nonetheless, if the passenger network is fully completed, a railway connection between Kuwait and Iraq could, in principle, lead to linking of the GCC region to the European network, though this is unlikely in the medium term given the ongoing conflict in Iraq. The GCC railway is an ambitious project, which also involves the construction of the King Hamad Causeway from Saudi Arabia to Bahrain. This project will involve 28 km of approach tracks, a 26 km causeway and a 10 km bridge, and is expected to cost

US$3 billion (Townsend 2015). The second intended causeway to contribute to the GCC network is the Qatar Bahrain Causeway. However, this initiative has not yet moved forward, since the initial announcement was made more than a decade and a half ago (see Chapter 5).

Given that Saudi Arabia is the only GCC country that connects to all the GCC states, its planned rail developments are indispensable if the region is to advance with an integrated rail network. One crucial rail development is the North-South Railway Line, involving the construction of a 2,750 km route stretching from Riyadh to Al Haditha, near the border with Jordan, and anticipated to cost US$8 billion (Briginshaw 2014). Another significant development concerns the Saudi Landbridge project, which involves the construction of a 950 km railway from Riyadh to Jeddah and Madinah. This project is scheduled for completion in 2020 and anticipated to cost US$7 billion (*Asian Cargo News* 2015). Another intended project in the eastern province concerns the 115 km track between Dammam and Jubail. The network will link with the 449 km Dammam-Riyadh Railway, which has been in operation since 1981 by the state-owned company Saudi Railways Organization. What is even more compelling for the wider connectivity of the GCC region is the proposed causeway linking Saudi Arabia to Egypt. The King Salman Bin Abdul Aziz Bridge will involve a 23 km track, helping to expedite the movement of people and goods between North Africa and the Arab Gulf, as well as strengthening trade between Saudi Arabia and Egypt, which already accumulated to US$4.9 billion in 2015 (Al Sherbini 2016). However, in light of the current low oil prices and an economic slowdown in Saudi Arabia (see Chapter 7), the extent to which the intended projects will be successfully completed is not yet guaranteed.

The GCC railway has significant possibilities in bringing together elements of commonality and unification. Accordingly, the GCC Assistant Secretary General emphasized that this development concerns 'a vision of 200 km/h trains cruising seamlessly across the borders within the planned common market and currency union' (*Railway Gazette* 2009). A focus on the requirements of tourism indicates that the connection of rail with other modes of transport can provide a real framework for transnational planning, which can only be effective in the context of the GCC region if there is an emphasis on safety, sustainability and cost efficiency. The GCC region has a track record of developing infrastructural-based projects, jointly planned between some states (e.g. oil pipeline projects and the King Fahd Causeway) (Shediac *et al.* 2011: 17–18). The railway could provide an infrastructural backbone for a future transnational and fully integrated network, strategically interconnected with light rail, metro and bus services. However, with no GCC-based regulatory authority yet in place to advance the network (Smith 2015), it is difficult to envisage the finer elements of integrative planning and how transnational governance will operate.

There may be some scope for the GCC region adopting the philosophy that underpins the highly successful travel system in Switzerland (Switzerland Tourism 2015), where specific design elements could be utilized. However, the following principles would need to drive this process: easy access, usability, comfort, good value, high productivity and full integration. Integration also concerns coordinated services and timetables, smooth connections and cross-modal ticketing – all contributing to ensuring that ground transport is an attractive user experience. Considering the Swiss practice, integration is not limited to ground transport but includes air travel and other options, where transportation components are included in hotel room bookings and major events. Ground transport in the final destination can be integrated as part of the flat fee when buying an air ticket to the destination. Travel offers can also be attractively priced and easy to book and purchase.

The three proposed levels of integration are (1) integration of functional planning: transport and tourism, (2) integration of modes: air, rail, coach and cruise and (3) integration of scales: urban, local and long-distance travel. Integration calls for a systematic and holistic approach to the planning of tourism across the GCC region, through a directive that is 'built on a comprehensive analysis of the urban fabric, land availability and its best use, environmental issues, mobility, infrastructure and urban services' (Alameri and Wagle 2011: 29–38). An interconnected multi-modal ground transport network, serving all destinations of interest, could encourage travel to create inimitable experiences linked to an appreciation of the distinct attributes of the region (e.g. desert, coastal and mountain landscapes, and Arabian architecture). Such a network would make individual tourist attractions part of something greater, linking them into one continuous experience instead of dissecting them into separate (disrupted) events. A well-designed transport system could help to showcase a GCC country, particularly in the context of an 'opened world', compliant with the customs of international tourism yet respectful of the region's strong social and religious heritage.

The popularity of leisure travel and luxury train journeys through Russia, East Asia, South Africa and Australia does illustrate that 'rail cruises' are a growing and often high-yield market (*Railway Gazette* 2007). In fact, the potentiality of the GCC rail route in terms of destination development, encouraged through regional place marketing, is significant. Accordingly, the railway, promoted along the lines of the 'Trans-Arabian Express', could evolve as part of a rail package incorporating culturally produced notions of the Arabian experience. An integrated ground transport system can help to personify the cultural dynamics of the region. 'Arabia', popularized by narratives of past European travellers whose depictions helped to construct popular images of the region (see Bidwell 1994), can be framed within touristic narratives associated with 'discovering Arabia' and the 'Arabian adventure'. In some way, this could help mitigate the negative popular perceptions and stereotypes associated with the 'Middle East' – as a land of 'sectarian conflict', 'terrorism' and 'fanaticism'. This framing would need to be sensitive to local representations and not based wholeheartedly on the Occidental script (see Chapter 3).

Blending the richness of the heritage, traditions and values of the GCC region with twenty-first-century technology is also key for local user acceptance of an integrative ground transportation system. This is a prerequisite for contemporary touristic use that also considers product and service quality, appearance, comfort and economic value as major inducements for long-term use. The opportunity to build transportation infrastructure from scratch allows for the systemic planning and design of interconnected tourism and transport structures, which should also aim for a sustainable, environmentally conscious and easy-to-use transportation system. Importantly, localized approaches to the greening of transportation in the region and to encouraging public transport consumption should be the utmost objectives of GCC states (see Bätzner 2015 and Chapter 12).

Identifying the challenges ahead for a ground transportation industry

The population in the GCC region is expected to reach 53.5 million by 2020, representing a 30 per cent increase from the year 2000 (*Economist* 2010a). This forecast, seemingly, considers the anticipated influx of foreign workers. Therefore, due to population increases and attempts by GCC states to diversify into tourism, high demand for additional infrastructure and transportation networks is likely to persist, especially in urban areas. GCC states are among the wealthiest countries in the world, with a car-dependent lifestyle influencing the spatial development of urban, semi-urban and non-urban places. Among the most visible problems associated with car dependency and its effect on daily life are traffic jams and lengthy gridlocks. The abundance of road accidents is such that they represent the 'fastest way to die in the region' (Ghazal 2012). In Saudi Arabia, for instance, there are around 526,000 road accidents annually and up to 17 deaths daily, with economic costs of around SR21 billion yearly (US$5.6 billion) (*Saudi Gazette* 2016). The photographic series 'Crashed Cars of Kuwait' artistically illustrates the gravity of accidents in the region (Milt 2005).

Time management and travel comfort represent other challenges relating to road travel. The scheduled intercity coach linking Dubai and Muscat makes no less than three consecutive stops at the UAE/Oman border. Passengers have to disembark on two of these occasions, involving the need to unload their luggage from the coach for an inspection check by the custom authorities. Such an inter-regional form of ground transport is more likely to remain a niche product for the budget-minded, unless a more efficient system can be established. Consequently, intercity coach services mainly cater for a budget-oriented local ridership. Nonetheless, non-GCC residents, having travelled along the Dubai-Muscat bus route as tourists, have actually praised this mode of travel for allowing them to gaze at the desert landscapes, considered as a special experience in itself (see Richardson 2013).

In Dubai, where road traffic density has reached saturation levels, the success of the Dubai Metro illustrates the feasibility and the acceptance of public sector approaches to transport in the region. Operating since 2009 and popular with both locals and tourists alike, the Dubai Metro doubled its passenger numbers to 138 million in 2013 compared to 2011 (Thomas 2014). Along with Dubai Tramway and the Road and Transport Authority (RTA) transit bus network, Dubai Metro proved that innovative and integrated solutions can encourage transformations in the behavioural patterns of tourists and mobile persons. In fact, in the first quarter of 2016, the Dubai Metro served 49,913,698 riders, and the Dubai Tram served 1,338,601 (*Khaleej Times* 2016). The Dubai Tram (see Figure 4.1) is the first tramway project in the region and outside Europe powered by a ground-based electric supply system. Operating from 2014 and involving 11 stations, the tramway encourages passengers to travel the full length of the 10.6 km route for only Dh3 (US$0.82) (Badam 2015). Dubai's urban transport network is seemingly an inspiration for other GCC states to follow. In Qatar, for instance, the first phase of the Doha Metro (Qatar) has been scheduled for completion in 2019, with two further phases scheduled for completion prior to the 2022 FIFA World Cup (*Railway Gazette* 2013). In Kuwait, although Kuwait City acknowledged the need to develop a metro system as early as 2006, the planned 160 km network, including 66 stations, should surpass the procurement stage by the end of 2016. Around 60 per cent of the network will be underground, with an anticipated cost of around US$7 billion (*Railway Gazette* 2015). Within the past 5 years, metro networks have also been announced in major cities in Saudi Arabia, notably Jeddah, Makkah, Medinah and Riyadh.

Light rail and highly flexible dial-a-ride systems can operate locally in inner-city areas and around major tourist attractions. It is essential that new destinations are designed to cater for efficient transportation networks. The chaos affecting Dubai's 2013 Sandance Festival on the Palm Island, illustrates how inadequate and unaccustomed transport infrastructure can be, where a surge in visitor demand can seriously compromise the tourist product (Trenwith 2014). Well-developed, scalable and expandable ground transport networks allow for easier accessibility to sites of interest, which can have an obvious impact on the customer's perception of the nature and quality of the transportation product and service. Consequently,

Figure 4.1   A new tram in Dubai (UAE).
Source: S-F, December 2015 (www.shutterstock.com/gallery-480532p1.html).

it is in the interests of GCC states to take heed of the need for a good internal transport network.

Identifying the challenges ahead for the airline industry

Gulf Air, initially launched in 1974 as the joint national airline of Bahrain, Qatar, Abu Dhabi and Oman, uniquely represented an act of cooperation between the four political entities. Gulf Air significantly contributed to linking the region to the world. However, the exiting of Qatar in 2003, Abu Dhabi in 2005 and Oman in 2007 from this arrangement illustrated a realignment to a more state-based approach to Gulf aviation, despite the fact that by 2007 the GCC operated as an entity for over a quarter of a century. Nonetheless, the fact that Gulf Air was a carrier that represented the interests of selected states and emirates was problematic for some of those not represented in this arrangement. For instance, Dubai raised concerns as early as 1984 over the significant reduction of Gulf Air's weekly flights from Dubai (Coates Ulrichsen 2016). Since going alone, Bahrain's ownership of Gulf Air continues to be confronted with a series of operational and financial challenges: unprofitability of long-haul flights; over-staffing of employees; increased debt concerns; the need for rationalization of aircraft fleet; and an intensified competitive environment in the region (Halligan 2016). Halligan (2016) notes that between 2008 and 2012 the company experienced deficits reaching US$560 million, though the subsequent endeavour to fully restructure the airline led to the reduction of the debt to US$166 million in 2014. Nonetheless, Gulf Air's regional supremacy and economic performance started to wane considerably at the turn of the twenty-first century, because of the rise of newer and stronger players in the field: Emirates (Dubai), founded in 1985; Qatar Airways (1993); Oman Air (1993); and Etihad Airways (Abu Dhabi) (2003).

Nevertheless, as the Gulf Air case illustrates, the region's increasing global aviation influence has not always been a success story. Bahrain Air in 2013 announced voluntary liquidity only after 5 years of operation, influenced, in part, by Bahrain's political circumstances. The airline claimed that it received no compensation because of financial losses experienced during the period of political discontent in 2011, when the airline had to suspend flights to several destinations (*Business Traveller* 2013). RAK Airways, the national airline of the emirate of Ras Al Khaimah (UAE), founded in 2006, announced in January 2014 that it had suspended operations because of such prevailing concerns as high operating costs, political instability in the region and general market conditions (Sophia 2014).

Nonetheless, the GCC airline industry started to become more resilient and hyper-competitive, placing significant emphasis on speed, time management and quality service standards. Emirates is of the opinion that there are three success factors to its operation: (1) well-managed and lean structures, (2) the ruling political conviction that highly liberal policies favourable to air transport issues will foster broad economic success and (3) a home base in Dubai, which ensures that the airline is in a strong strategic and geographic location (*Economist* 2010b). In fact, in the GCC region as a whole, there are around 4 billion potential passengers living within 7 hours' flight time from the Gulf. Based on this capacity, the CEO of Qatar Airways calls the Gulf carriers 'super-connectors' (de Fermor 2010).

However, the strength of presence of these airlines on the international scene has 'shaken global aviation markets to their core' (Coates Ulrichsen 2016: 159). One successful integrative strategy utilized by GCC carriers has been to secure direct routings to 'secondary airports', rather than having to stop in hub airports. For instance, it is possible to fly from the GCC region to Hamburg and Dusseldorf (Germany) without stopping in Frankfurt, and to fly to Nice and Lyon (France) without stopping in Charles de Gaulle Airport (Paris) (Coates Ulrichsen 2016: 156–157). American Airlines, Delta Air Lines and United Continental have claimed that the major Gulf carriers have received significant state subsidies, including interest-free loans, thus allowing the Gulf countries to compete in an inequitable way by including cheaper international connections through their hubs (*National* 2015). The European Commission has also indicated unease over Gulf carriers' increasing dominance of routes between GCC states and the EU states, where seats from scheduled flights between the GCC states and the European Union rose from 12 million in 2005 to 39 million in 2015 (Cronin 2015). One other concern relates to the ownership of other EU airlines, as seen in Etihad's acquisition of Air Berlin and Alitalia.

Nevertheless, there are counterarguments concerning the claim that GCC carriers receive heavy subsidies. Some GCC carriers, naturally, received substantial seed money from governments to help in the early stages of development, and this is not necessarily seen as the same as regular subsidies. Moreover, if any financial support is provided by the government, then the stakeholders (which can include government representation) have the right to provide financial support to airlines (*Economist* 2015). Furthermore, the unique role and function of state capitalism in the region (see Chapter 1) is something which Western interests fail to fully acknowledge as a viable source of economic development and financial aid, or as a regional norm, which in this case determines the political and socio-economic fabric of GCC states.

Current air traffic growth within the Middle East represents the largest increase in international traffic, at 10.5 per cent in 2015, ensuring that Middle East carriers have the largest share of the market – standing at 14.2 per cent (Rothman 2016). GCC's low-cost aviation sector is dominated by the following four airlines: Jazeera Airway, founded in 2004 and based in Kuwait; Flydubai, founded in 2009 and based in Dubai; Air Arabia, founded in 2003 and based in Sharjah; and Flynas, founded in 2013 and based in Saudi Arabia. Flydubai is seen as the principal player in the GCC region in terms of seat capacity, fleet size and destinations visited (Pivac 2015). The success of these carriers has been their ability to set new milestones in product and service development, especially by going beyond normative concepts associated with the low-cost ('no frills') service. Flydubai, for instance, introduced a new market segment by offering and developing a service for business-class passengers (Algethami 2013).

However, while load factors grow and the overall expansion of flight movements is fast-paced, there are increasing risks of serious airspace congestion. Deakin (2014) recognizes that there is a danger of spiralling delays and disintegrated connectivity, as well as a threat to the region's overall ability to act as a focal aviation hub. He also points out that no airport, however extended, can ever be more efficient than the airspace that serves it, calling for urgent action if the Gulf aviation industry wants to maintain competitiveness. Deakin (2014) suggests that parts of the military airspace could be made temporarily available, which would help relax demands on civil aviation. Nonetheless, a common GCC airspace will not successfully exist without further political integration and political will. The problem, however, is that every flight movement, be it short or long haul, blocks roughly the same fraction of airport and airspace capacity. The International Air Transportation Association also has identified crowded airspace in the GCC region as a serious threat to aviation growth. One source of information estimated that airspace congestion in the Middle East could cost up to US$16 billion over the next decade, especially considering such expenses as fuel and traffic delays (El Gazzar 2016). Congestion also potentially limits growth and investment in new carriers, and runs the risk of making carriers more vulnerable to collision. This is, perhaps, a good reason why GCC states need to think industriously about completing a fully integrated GCC railway network in the medium term, especially to encourage more people to make full use of inter-state rail trips in the future.

The political and cultural rationale for an integrated transport network

The nature of rail infrastructure makes it particularly vulnerable to crises, unrest and war. Obstructed or interrupted rail tracks are considerably more difficult to circumnavigate than roadblocks. The Beirut-Damascus Railway, for instance, was partially destroyed in the Lebanese civil war. Despite repeated requests from the Lebanese government to rebuild the line, the railway remains closed. In 1989, the Arab Union of Railways, representing the rail networks of Algeria, Iraq, Jordan, Lebanon, Libya, Saudi Arabia, Syria and Tunisia, produced a development plan for an inter-Arab rail network (AFAC-Liban 2008). In October 1991, after the end of the civil war in Lebanon, a 'train of peace' began to operate on the hastily repaired track between Beirut and Jbeil, receiving significant media coverage (AFAC-Liban 2008). However, due to the continued political problems experienced in Lebanon, trains ceased to operate. Meanwhile, Syria's comparably modern and well-functioning rail network suspended all operations in July 2012, as ongoing hostilities affected infrastructure and rolling stock (Barnard 2014). The current hostilities in the Levant and Iraq make it difficult to envisage an inter-Arab rail network. Nonetheless, the development of the GCC railway would be one positive step forward in working towards creating part of that vision. An integrated transport network across different states could help foster regional stability in times of political differences.

However, the threat of operating in a region affected by the war and conflict in the surrounding territories remains. It is of no surprise that the president of Emirates, in the wake of the downing of a Malaysian civil airliner over rebel territory in Ukraine in 2014, called for a global summit reviewing advisory issues on safe routing for airlines (Westcott 2014). The concern expressed by Emirates airline is not surprising. Accordingly, in January 2015, a Flydubai aircraft was hit with bullets as it landed in Baghdad International Airport, carrying 154 passengers, which led to the airline subsequently suspending UAE flights to the country's capital city (Hanif 2015).

Railways and roads not only create physical links between different spaces but also function in terms of fostering political ties. Social exchange and regular interaction can protect states against political radicalism. Lampugnani (2008) takes this argument even further and argues that urban density with good accessibility stimulates random and unplanned encounters between individuals from different cultural backgrounds, impeding social fragmentation and extremism. If tourism and travel can in some way contribute to international understanding and intercultural learning, and enhance transnational and global affinities (see Bianchi and Stephenson 2014), then transportation structures have a crucial role in transmitting and transferring cultural exchanges as well as helping to cement social ties and strengthen geo-political relations. Even redundant transportation structures have the potential to promote productive forms of cultural exchange. Orbaşli and Woodward (2008) present an illuminating evaluation of how the aforementioned Hijaz Railway could act as a 'cultural route' to attract heritage tourism in Saudi Arabia, especially as 'the physical remains of the railway can be used as an anchor for the preservation and interpretation of the Islamic and pre-Islamic cultural heritage of the route' (2008: 159).

A long-term planning approach to the development of sophisticated transportation systems and processes could encourage tourism attractions and destinations to flourish. The continual development of long-haul routes by GCC air carriers should also have a confirmatory impact on the long-term public perception of the region, helping to elevate the image of the country. Moreover, the position of Qatar Airways and Emirates in sponsoring internationally known sport teams and events exemplifies how an airline represents the country's ambition as a global and highly modernized destination. The role of transport, notably airlines, in the 'national building process' (see Raguraman 1997) could help strengthen the state's political confidence and regional and international status, and its role in (and contribution to) the global arena.

Conclusion and research implications

As this chapter has sought to demonstrate, the strength of an integrated and well-designed transport network in the GCC region would reside in the ability of the network to maximize efficiency and ensure effective coordination. These factors are essential if states intend to increase demand, pursue economic diversification and encourage regional integration. The discussion indicates that rail transportation in the region could be a good alternative to air travel, but needs to coordinate closely with the airline industry through a strategy of integrative connectivity. Given that many ground transport systems and networks in the region are quite new, others are emerging and some are yet to develop, the coordination of the level of integration will be a challenge in itself.

However, one important concern relating to airspace is the need to develop a more lean system and, at the same time, assure potential passengers that air travel in the GCC region is (and GCC carriers are) safe. This issue becomes of paramount importance in light of the fatal accident in March 2016, when Flydubai's Boeing 737-800 jet crashed trying to land at the airport in Russian's southern city of Rostov-on-Don, killing all 62 passengers (Walker 2016). Regional conflicts, along with the increased potential for accidents due to a congested airspace, will continue to represent challenges for Gulf carriers in the aviation industry. Nonetheless, their competitive attributes and financial strength ensure their resilience, and position and status in the global market.

As GCC states to some extent share familiar histories, colonialized encounters, cultural affinities and religious origins, interconnecting transportation networks, alliances and modes would be socially and politically useful to the GCC region. Integrated rail and bus travel need to be affordable though based on quality services and products, blending operational expertise from overseas with locally developed solutions catering to the GCC context. Reisz (2010) emphasizes the role of transportation infrastructure as a driver for cultural and social integration, observing that:

> the notion of a united Gulf finds its expression in infrastructure. Dubai's metro had its own stories, trials, and mistakes, and warnings that it would never work. All these different kinds of people would never step in the same train, rich and poor could never sit together, man and woman could never sit together. It quickly became part of what Dubai is: The metro became a place adapted to Dubai but, Dubai has also adapted to it. It becomes the public space that Dubai never had. Infrastructure, while often concrete and steel, lays the ground for social and cultural changes.

These reflections also point to the importance of future research in monitoring the use and value of new urban transport networks (e.g. Al Mashaaer Al Muqaddassah Metro in Mecca or the upcoming QRail in Doha). More research is required in the region concerning the needs of consumers/passengers and their degree of acceptance of and satisfaction with different modes of transport, as well as data relating to ethnic, social class and gender composition of users. It would be constructive to engage more with tourists' perspectives and perceptions of ground transport modes, looking at product and service experiences. As the GCC region looks towards more physical connections and infrastructural advancements, there is significant scope for industrial-based research. The effectiveness of interchanges (i.e. air-to-rail, rail-to-rail and rail-to-road) in the region is an area that need to be fully understood. Attention to considering energy saving devices and environmentally sustainable transport options is a useful way forward, especially as the cheap availability of oil in the region has meant that energy efficiency has not always been an immediate priority.

Within a decade, GCC states could make significant steps forward in moving away from a car-dependent lifestyle and start to establish a serious framework for reducing the carbon footprint. A well-designed pan-GCC network of rail and express buses, fully connected to local transportation (including light rail), could (1) move a significant amount of intra-GCC resident travel away from airlines, thus freeing up airport capacities for long-haul operations; (2) boost the trade and logistics sectors inside GCC states; (3) foster economic and political cooperation and integration; (4) encourage more sustainable use of transport; (5) help prevent long-term transport gridlocks; (6) contribute to pan-regional stability, which would be further affirmed if the region is linked to such countries as Egypt and Jordan in the medium term, and Iraq in the long term; and (7) enrich tourist experiences and perceptions of the Arabian Peninsula. Nonetheless, if a ground travel network within and across GGC states advances with the same eagerness and quality orientation observed in the GCC aviation industry, then the GCC region (like the European Union) will no doubt be able to boast an impressive travel and tourism mobility network.

References

AFAC-Liban (2008) 'Un bref aperçu des chemins de fer au liban', Association Française des Amis du Chemin de Fer Section du Liban. Available online at www.afacliban.org/AFAC-LIBAN/Histoire.html (accessed 28 July 2014, translation from French by author).

Alameri, A. and G. Wagle (2011) 'Abu Dhabi efforts in facing global warming challenges through urban planning', in C. A. Brebbia and E. Beriatos (eds), *Sustainable Development and Planning V,* Southampton: WIT Press, pp. 29–38.

Algethami, S. (2013) 'Flydubai introduces business class services', *Gulf News,* 19 June. Available online at http://gulfnews.com/business/sectors/general/flydubai-introduces-business-class-services-1.1199177 (accessed 12 June 2016).

Al Sherbini, R. (2016) 'Bridge linking Egypt, Saudi Arabia a "historic step"', *Gulf News,* 5 June. Available online at http://gulfnews.com/news/gulf/saudi-arabia/bridge-linking-egypt-saudi-arabia-a-historic-step-1.1708824 (accessed 6 June 2016).

Anderson, S. (2015) 'Lawrence's Arabia', in A. McCarthy, *The Best American Travel Writing 2015,* Boston, MA: Houghton Mifflin Harcourt, pp. 9–27.

Asian Cargo News (2015) 'Saudi Arabia's Land Bridge could be a game-changing plan', *Asian Cargo News,* 3 December. Available online at www.asiacargonews.com/en/news/detail?id=510 (accessed 7 May 2016).

Assi, E. (2005) *The Dynamic of Linear Settings: Hijaz Railroad,* ICOMOS 15th General Assembly and Symposium. Available online at www.icomos.org/xian2005/papers/4-3.pdf (accessed 26 December 2014).

Badam, R. T. (2015) 'Special report: Dubai tram's on the right track', *The National,* 13 February. Available online at www.thenational.ae/uae/dubai-tram/special-report-dubai-trams-on-the-right-track#full (accessed 17 August 2015).

Barnard, A. (2014) 'Once bustling, Syria's fractured railroad is a testament to shattered ambitions', *New York Times,* 25 May. Available online at www.nytimes.com/2014/05/26/world/middleeast/Damascus-syria-hejaz-railway-station.html (accessed 30 December 2014).

Barth, B. and J. C. Whitehouse (1998) 'The financial history of the Anatolian and Baghdad Railways, 1889–1914', *Financial History Review,* 5(2): 115–137.

Bätzner, A. (2015) 'Greening urban transport in the Gulf Cooperation countries: localized approaches to modal integration as key success factors', in M. A. Raouf and M. Luomi (eds) *The Green Economy in the Gulf*, London: Routledge, pp. 161–180.

Bianchi, R. V. and M. L. Stephenson (2014) *Tourism and Citizenship: Rights, Freedoms and Responsibilities in the Global Order*, Abingdon: Routledge.

Bidwell, R. (1994) *Travellers in Arabia*, London: Hamlyn.

Briginshaw, D. (2014) 'Opening up the desert: SAR pushes ahead with ambitious plans', *International Railway Journal, 3 June. Available online at* www.railjournal.com/index.php/middle-east/opening-up-the-desert-sar-pushes-ahead-with-ambitious-plans.html (accessed 7 June 2016).

Business Traveller (2013) 'Bahrain Air ceases operations', *Business Traveller*, 13 February. Available online at www.businesstraveller.com/news/bahrain-air-ceases-operations (accessed 2 June 2016).

Coates Ulrichsen, K. (2016) *The Gulf States in International Political Economy*, Basingstoke: Palgrave Macmillan.

Coke, R. (1928) 'The railways of Mesopotamia', *The Railway Magazine*, April. Available online at http://fuchs-online.com/iraq/images/files/TheRailwayMagazineApril1928.pdf (accessed 19 August 2015).

Cornwell, A. (2016) 'Oman targets 2018 to start building rail network', *Gulf News*, 10 March. Available online at http://gulfnews.com/business/sectors/shipping/oman-targets-2018-to-start-building-rail-network-1.1688161 (accessed 11 June 2016).

Cronin, S. (2015) 'New European Commission aviation strategy highlights concerns over Gulf airlines', *The National*, 7 December. Available online at www.thenational.ae/business/aviation/new-european-commission-aviation-strategy-highlights-concerns-over-gulf-airlines (accessed 2 June 2016).

Deakin, R. (2014) 'Time to Secure the Gulf's aviation future', Blog, Nats Limited, 7 April. Available online at http://nats.aero/blog/2014/04/time-secure-gulfs-aviation-future (accessed 31 July 2014).

de Fermor, P. (2010) 'Emirates: how one airline drives profit and passenger growth', *Forbes*, July. Available online at www.forbes.com/sites/wheelsup/2010/07/23/and-the-winner-is-emirates/ (accessed 12 June 2012).

Der Spiegel (1964) 'Hedschas-Bahn: Im Namen Allahs', *Der Spiegel*, 50. Available online at www.spiegel.de/spiegel/print/d-46176336 (accessed 9 April 2015).

Economist (2010a) *The GCC in 2020: Resources for the Future: A Report from the Economist Intelligence Unit Sponsored by the Qatar Financial Centre Authority*, London: Economist Intelligence Unit.

Economist (2010b) 'Aviation in the Gulf – rulers of the New Silk Road', *The Economist*, 3 June. Available online at www.economist.com/node/16271573 (accessed 9 July 2014).

Economist (2015) 'Airline subsidies in the Gulf: feeling the heat', *The Economist*, 6 March. Available online at www.economist.com/blogs/gulliver/2015/03/airline-subsidies-gulf (accessed 20 March 2015).

El Gazzar, S. (2016) 'Congested airspace could cost Middle East $16 billion over the next decade', *The National*, 7 March. Available online at www.thenational.ae/business/aviation/congested-airspace-could-cost-middle-east-16-billion-over-next-decade (accessed 2 June 2016).

Ghazal, R. (2012) 'Road accidents in the Gulf: fastest way to die in the region', *The National*, 10 September. Available online at www.thenational.ae/news/world/road-accidents-in-the-gulf-the-fastest-way-to-die-in-the-region (accessed 8 April 2015).

Halligan, N. (2016) 'Can Gulf Air become the fourth big player in the GCC', *Arabian Business*, 19 February. Available online at www.arabianbusiness.com/can-gulf-air-become-fourth-big-player-in-gcc-622203.html#.V09ugVV97IU (accessed 2 June 2016).

Hanif, N. (2015) 'UAE flights to Baghdad suspended after FlyDubai plane hit by gunfire', *The National*, 27 January. Available online at www.thenational.ae/uae/20150127/4432/ uae-flights-to-baghdad-suspended-after-flydubai-plane-hit-by-gunfire (accessed 2 June 2016).

Khaleej Times (2016) 'Al Rigga, Al Fahidi busiest metro stations in Dubai', 18 April, *Khaleej Times*. Available online at www.khaleejtimes.com/nation /transport/al-rigga-al-fahidi-busiest-metro-stations-in-dubai (accessed 25 May 2016).

Kinninmont, J. (2010) *The GCC in 2020: Broadening the Economy*, London: The Economist Intelligence Unit.

Lampugnani, V. M. (2008) 'Urban density as quintessence of the urban', *Swisspearl Architecture*, vol. 148, Niederurnen, Switzerland: Eternit AG, pp. 2–5.

Ma, D. (1998) *The Great Silk Exchange: How the World was Connected and Developed*, London: Routledge.

McMeekin, S. M. (2012) *The Berlin-Baghdad Express: The Ottoman Empire and Germany's Bid for World Power*, Cambridge, MA: Belknap Press, Harvard University Press.

McMurray, J.S. (2001) *Distant Ties: Germany, the Ottoman Empire, and the Construction of the Baghdad Railway*, Westport, CT: Greenwood.

Milt, P. (2005) 'Crashed cars of Kuwait', photoset, ongoing series. Available online at www.flickriver.com/photos/psycho_milt/sets/347706 (accessed 9 April 2015).

National (2015) 'Gulf and US airlines' open skies row "has reached impasse"', *The National*, 23 June 2015. Available online at www.thenational.ae/business/aviation/ gulf-and-us-airlines-open-skies-row-has-reached-impasse.

Orbaşli, A. and S. Woodward (2008) 'A railway "route" as a linear heritage attraction: the Hijaz railway in the Kingdom of Saudi Arabia', *Journal of Heritage Tourism*, 3(3): 159–175.

Pivac, D. Z. (2015) 'Turning the corner: what do the region's low-cost carriers bring to the market and what does this mean for their competitors?', *BQ Magazine*, 2 March. Available online at www.bq-magazine.com/industries/aviation-industries/2015/03/ low-cost-carriers-in-the-middle-east (accessed 7 June 2016).

Raguraman, K. (1997) 'Airlines as instruments for national building and national identity: case study of Malaysia and Singapore', *Journal of Transport Geography*, 5(4): 239–256.

Railway Gazette (2007) 'Growing niche market offers profitable opportunities', *Railway Gazette*, 1 August. Available online at www.railwaygazette.com/news/single-view/ view/growing-niche-market-offers-profitable-opportunities.html (accessed 16 December 2014).

Railway Gazette (2009) 'Gulf railway could start next year', *Railway Gazette*, 18 November. Available online at www.railwaygazette.com/news/single-view/view/gulf-railway-could-start-next-year.html (accessed 17 July 2014).

Railway Gazette (2013) 'More Doha metro constraints awarded', *Railway Gazette*, 11 June. Available online at www.railwaygazette.com/news/urban/single-view/view/ more-doha-metro-contracts-awarded.html (accessed 25 May 2016).

Railway Gazette (2015) 'Kuwait metro and rail procurement to begin next year', *Railway Gazette*, 9 October. Available online at www.railwaygazette.com/news/news/

middle-east/single-view/view/kuwait-metro-and-rail-procurement-to-begin-next-year. html (accessed 9 October 2015).

Reisz, T. (2010) *On Al Manakh 2*, video presentation, 24 September. New York: Graduate School of Architecture, Planning and Preservation at Columbia University. Available online at http://oma.eu/lectures/on-al-manakh-2 (accessed 23 July 2014).

Richardson, P. (2013) 'By bus from Muscat to Dubai', Travel with Pedro blog. Available online at www.travelwithpedro.com/by-bus-from-muscat-to-dubai (accessed18 July 2014).

Rothman, A. (2016) 'Gulf airlines led global air traffic growth in 2015', *Bloomberg*, 4 February. Available online at https://skift.com/2016/02/04/gulf-airlines-led-global-air-trafficgrowth-in-2015/ (accessed 6 June 2016).

Saudi Gazette (2016) 'Report: Saudi Arabia records road accidents annually', *Saudi Gazette,* 1 January. Available online at http://english.alarabiya.net/en/News/middle-east/2016/01/01/Report-Saudi-Arabia-records-526-000-road-accidents-annually.html (accessed 6 June 2016).

Shediac, R., P. Khanna, T. Rahim and H. A. Samman (2011) 'Integrating, not integrated – a scorecard of GCC economic integration', Abu Dhabi: Booz & Co. Available online at www.strategyand.pwc.com/me/home/strategic_foresight/sector_strategies/public_ sector_management/public_sector_reports (accessed 22 December 2014).

Smith, K. (2015) 'Delivering the GCC's integrated railway', *International Railway Journal*, 11 March. Available online at www.railjournal.com/index.php/middle-east/ delivering-the-gccs-integrated-railway.html (accessed 14 June 2015).

Sophia, M. (2014) 'RAK airways suspends operations', *Gulf Business*, 2 January. Available online at http://gulfbusiness.com/rak-airways-suspends-operations/#.V1OzwVV96Uk (accessed 5 June 2006).

Switzerland Tourism (2015) 'What is the Swiss Travel System?' Available online at www. swisstravelsystem.com/en/highlights-en/what-is-swiss-travel-system.html (accessed15 August 2015).

Thomas, B. (2014) 'Dubai Metro doubles number of users in 2 years', *Arabian Business*, 23 February. Available online at www.arabianbusiness.com/dubai-metro-doubles-number-of-yearly-users-in-2yrs-539894.html (accessed 2 July 2014).

Tissot, L. (2013) 'Tourism', in *Historic Encyclopedia of Switzerland*. Available online at www.hls-dhs-dss.ch/d/D14070.php (accessed 20 August 2014).

Townsend, S. (2015) 'Bahrain, Saudi Arabia escalate plans for $3 bn second causeway', *Arabian Business*, 7 October. Available online at www.arabianbusiness.com/bahrain-saudi-arabia-escalate-plans-for-3bn-second-causeway-608390.html#.V1NqqlV96Uk (accessed 25 January 2016).

Trenwith, C. (2014) 'Sandance organisers offer refunds amid traffic chaos', *Arabian Business*, 1 January. Available online at http://m.arabianbusiness.com/sandance-organisers-offer-refunds-amid-traffic-chaos-533065.html (accessed 20 August 2014).

Walker, S. (2016) 'FlyDubai passenger jet crash kills 62 in Russian city of Rostov-on-Don', *Guardian*, 19 March. Available online at www.theguardian.com/world/2016/ mar/19/passenger-jet-crashes-on-landing-in-russian-city-of-rostov-on-don (accessed 6 June 2016).

Westcott, R. (2014) 'Emirates to stop flying over Iraq after MH17 disaster', *BBC News,* Business, 28 July 2014. Available online at www.bbc.com/news/business-28524628 (accessed 1 August 2014).

Part Two

The challenges of international tourism development at a national level

5   Tourism development in Bahrain

Dealing with flux and transformation

Samer Bagaeen

In offering critical reflections on key themes driving and affecting tourism development in the Kingdom of Bahrain, particularly within the context of the Gulf Cooperation Council (GCC) region, this chapter takes a broader view by looking at the economic, social and political challenges concerning efforts to promote tourism. Harvey (2008: 30) draws attention to the socio-economic and environmental concerns and inequities over 'mega-urbanization' in the region, particularly a consequence of the 'surplus arising from oil wealth'. The chapter acknowledges that Bahrain is a tourism pioneer in the Arab world, being one of only three countries to have received a noteworthy amount of international visitors as early as 1990. Nevertheless, Bahrain still has a long way to go to reach global recognition as an international tourism destination.

The rationale behind a critical assessment of tourism development challenges in Bahrain reflects a similar intent supported by Stephenson and Ali-Knight's (2010: 279) observations of tourism development in the context of Dubai, suggesting that the social implications of rapid economic development through tourism have not yet been 'significantly deconstructed through a detailed and formal level of enquiry'. In framing tourism within the wider context of the Muslim world, the chapter builds on what Jafari and Scott (2014: 13) note is a 'relatively untapped theoretical field'. Although the chapter does not utilize primary data, the information contained within should go some way towards encouraging future research to develop.

The chapter also considers how Bahrain's approach to tourism development has been influenced by regional, domestic and political factors, and the need to engage in economic diversification and investment strategies. The work examines how culture and sport can be utilized to enhance Bahrain's destination brand, though it draws critical attention to one significant challenge: the need for more cosmopolitan and multicultural-based heritage representations. The chapter recognizes the underlying power relations in the region that impact tourism development, as manifested in the Arab Spring, especially the ramifications of Bahrain's political unrest upon the tourism industry. Finally, the work addresses the implications derived from the enquiry and future research possibilities.

The power, reach and limits of tourism

According to Matarrita-Cascante (2010: 1141), given the economic profits reaped from tourism, 'its promotion has become a popular economic strategy for many communities'. In China, for instance, Arlt (2006) and Richter (1983) suggest that the strategic deployment of tourism is part of the country's foreign policy apparatus, and Nyíri (2006) describes how China uses tourism and tourist sites to articulate claims about state authority beyond its borders. Saleh *et al.* (2015: 209), however, look at the links between tourism growth and economic growth in Saudi Arabia, Jordan and Bahrain, noting that tourism in these countries plays an important economic role, especially after experiencing rapid growth in the last few years. The Arab Spring presented these three countries and others across the Middle East with a difficult challenge, particularly in relation to degrees of concern over its impact on tourist numbers. Of the three countries indicated, Bahrain was worst affected when the state had a taste of the Arab Spring in 2011, rapidly affecting tourism. However, following China's approach to tourism development, Bahrain tried to deploy tourism strategically and to leverage its cultural heritage in order to entice tourists to return to the destination. Its capital, Manama, was named 'Arab Capital of Culture' in 2012, 'Capital of Arab Tourism' in 2013 and 'Capital of Asian Tourism' in 2014. Furthermore, GCC tourism ministers named this city as 'Capital of Gulf Tourism 2016' to help strengthen intra-regional tourism and confirm the state's tourism and cultural appeal (Oxford Business Group 2016).

Bahrain is, arguably, a tourism pioneer in the Arab World. United Nations World Tourism Organization (UNWTO) (2000: 21) data indicate that only three countries in the Middle East received a noteworthy amount of visitors in 1990: Egypt attracted a regional share of 26.9 per cent; Saudi Arabia a share of 24.7 per cent; and Bahrain a share of 15.4 per cent. Bahrain is, therefore, an old hand at playing the 'tourism game', and it is perhaps this maturity that has enabled the country to turn to tourism, especially to rebuild its image in the wake of the 2011 unrest that gripped the Kingdom. Nonetheless, Bahrain's tourism industry is still evolving, where structures for promoting and managing tourism are quite new. It was not until 2010 that a proposal for the formation of a tourism watchdog was developed. This initiative concerned a 10-member body operating as an independent entity under the Ministry of Culture, with the intention to regulate the tourism and hotel sectors (*Trade Arabia* 2010). 'Big brother' Saudi Arabia has more of a history in this respect, where the promotion of tourism development began with the creation of the Supreme Commission for Tourism (SCT) in the year 2000 (see Chapter 7). Nonetheless, Bahrain has since followed suit with the new Supreme Committee for Tourism formed in 2014 under the direction of HRH Prince Salman bin Hamad Al Khalifa, the crown prince. This committee is behind the 2015–18 tourism strategy, designed to boost visitor numbers over the same period. The Bahrain Tourism Strategy 2015–2018 was unveiled in July 2014 by the then culture minister, Shaikha Mai bint Mohammed Al Khalifa. Tactically, this strategy focuses on an 'experience-led' approach for tourists, involving the pre-packaging of Bahrain's main attractions and cultural heritage sites (Unnikrishnan 2014).

Nonetheless, despite Bahrain's recent attempts to strategize the tourism industry, its political instability has been challenging. Since early 2011, there have been protests at what the Shi'a Muslim population sees as discrimination by the Sunni Muslim ruling family. Random bomb attacks were still on the rise in 2014 (see Spong 2014a), following more than three years of protests demanding democratic reform and a constitutional monarchy in the Shi'a-majority country (see also Song Loong 2013). These protests cast a dark shadow over the Bahrain Formula One Grand Prix, which faced threats of a boycott from racing teams. As the Grand Prix was staged in Bahrain during times of political upheaval, a UK government panel in October 2014 upheld a complaint made by activists concerning the way in which human rights regulations were breached. It agreed that holding the Grand Prix events in 2012, 2013 and 2014 presented an international image of Bahrain that did not reflect the reality of ongoing human rights concerns (BBC 2014).

Bahrain's aviation sector also confronted difficulties since the onset of internal political upheaval in 2011. The country's airlines and airport had to contend with government restrictions on where passenger aircraft could fly to and from (see Spong 2013). There was a significant decrease in international tourism arrivals in 2011, hitting a low of 6,732,000 tourists. By 2014, however, inbound tourism started to show signs of a healthy return to normality, with 10,452,000 tourists recorded. Nonetheless, in terms of overall international tourist arrivals, numbers have not yet met the 2010 figures, when arrivals reached their peak at 11,952,000 (World Bank 2015).

Diversification and development strategy

Despite some ambitious construction projects such as Bahrain Bay and Bahrain Financial Harbour, the Kingdom did not experience the building frenzy that real estate developers and contractors became used to elsewhere in the region, especially during the building boom period of 2003–8 and particularly in Dubai. Moreover, Foreman (2009) notes that as the market had not been initially overinflated in the first place, the fall in property prices since their peak in the summer of 2008 was less dramatic in Bahrain than elsewhere.

King Hamad Al Khalifa's government sought to follow the lead of other Gulf states by using economic and fiscal initiatives to address the social roots of unrest. The latest 'residential' development, Diyar al-Muharraq, was designed to feature five-star hotels and a shopping mall close to Amwaj Islands off the coast of Muharraq (Florian 2014). The development, covering 12 square kilometres and with an investment value of BD1.2 billion (US$3.2 billion), is one of the biggest mixed-use urban developments ever undertaken by the private sector in Bahrain. Unlike other construction projects, such as the artificial island of Durrat Al Bahrain, Diyar al-Muharraq was conceived as an affordable housing project that was promoted by the government to address the fundamental problems of unrest amongst the country's poorer urban Shi'a population.

Florian (2014) points out that some of the more controversial elements of Bahrain's response to the 2011 unrest, such as the destruction of several Shi'a mosques, including the 400-year-old Amir Mohammed Barbagi Mosque, have been defused by a substantial investment in social infrastructure. He also points out that some of the strongest support for prioritizing economic development in Bahrain came from two GCC allies, Saudi Arabia and the United Arab Emirates (UAE), stepping in to shore up the security of the royal family at the start of the civil unrest. Florian (2014) reports that Riyadh is understood to have encouraged the Bahrain authorities to ensure an equitable use of the GCC Development Fund paid to Bahrain to mitigate the effects of the unrest and other state resources, so that such issues as housing shortages are properly addressed through concerted policy action. Saudi Arabia had also promised Bahrain US$1 billion a year in aid from the GCC over a 10-year period to help finance infrastructure projects, with potential implications for tourism development (Florian 2014). That said, with the slump in global oil prices late 2015 and early 2016, investors might be concerned about the impact of the decline on GCC's regional economies.

In Bahrain, policies of economic diversification were initially adopted in the mid-1950s and derived from directives influenced by the country's ruling family, emphasizing that 'in the long term, the limited oil revenues could not be used as the only source of economic development and governmental revenues' (Mansfeld and Winckler 2008: 239). As a result, and in the decades that followed, government planning in the Kingdom encouraged the development of local industries related to the petroleum sector, in addition to other forms of manufacturing. The author has shown elsewhere how the instability of the Lebanese civil war in the 1970s and 1980s gave impetus to Bahrain to emerge as a regional financial, communications and commercial centre, stimulating further business travel and investment in property and real estate (Bagaeen 2015).

Gavin (2014) points out that the relatively small size of Bahrain's oil endowment propelled the country to employ the most aggressive economic diversification strategy of any Gulf state. Spong (2014b) emphasizes that Bahrain's woes go much deeper than the size of the endowment, adding that the need to diversify coupled with outbreaks of violence make it difficult for the Kingdom to introduce the reforms needed to reduce the country's debt burden, which is the highest among the GCC states. Bahrain needs far higher oil prices than its richer neighbours to balance its budget. Although the energy sector is the largest contributor to Bahrain's GDP, its contribution is declining as Bahrain's non-oil sectors increase in significance, with the financial sector representing the second largest contribution (16.5 per cent in 2014) and manufacturing the third largest (14.4 per cent in 2014) (Oxford Business Group 2016).

Mansfeld and Winckler (2008: 247) noted that development in Bahrain consisted of three basic objectives: (1) The private rather than the public sector should take the lead on economic expansion through the promotion of private investments, both foreign and local; (2) a labour-intensive policy should be adopted to create new employment opportunities for the rapidly growing indigenous workforce; (3)

the knot between oil prices and economic growth should be broken, especially through the identification of key sectors as leading catalysts of future growth (i.e. banking, oil-related industries, education, infrastructure and tourism).

As part of Bahrain's diversification efforts, the Bahrain Airport Company invited firms in September 2014 to pre-qualify to work on the expansion of Bahrain International Airport. The project involves the construction of a 170,000-square-metre terminal building, together with associated buildings and such infrastructure as car parks and aircraft parking areas (Foreman 2014). At the time, there was an assumption on the part of the Kingdom's policymakers that the expansion of its tourism infrastructure will not only create new and varied employment opportunities, but in contrast to the UAE and Qatar, the view was that any new expansion could take place without a massive import of foreign workers. Nevertheless, when looking at official data the significant presence of foreign workers in Bahrain is clear, constituting 566,785 of the 725,113 total workforce in 2015 with Bahraini nationals constituting 158,328 (Labour Market Regulatory Authority 2016). Louër (2008) noted that Bahrain, like other GCC states, was subjected to mass labour in-migration. Additionally, Bahrain's large Shi'a majority have long complained of 'differential treatment and marginalisation' (Coates Ulrichsen, 2013: 8). In discussing the Bahraini labour market, Mansfeld and Winckler (2008) suggested that nationals, particularly the marginalized rural Shi'a, as a result of this marginalization, would be willing to accept lower-paid jobs, including those associated with building the country's infrastructure.

Big brother's presence

From the late 1990s, the infrastructure and regulatory framework conditions supporting tourism had improved in Bahrain, reflecting a general trend in the wider region as a whole (Peterson 2009). However, given that a significant proportion of Bahrain's tourists originate from neighbouring countries and that the nation has been a source of political conflict, its position as an internationally recognized tourism destination is tenuous. It is not possible to understand tourism development in Bahrain without comprehending its geographical and social relationship with Saudi Arabia. Both countries are physically connected by the King Fahd Causeway (Figure 5.1), which is a 26-kilometre bridge that was established in 1986 (www.kfca.com.sa). The causeway has arguably become the most prominent catalyst for Bahrain's tourism development. In fact, both the tourism and retail sectors in Bahrain owe much to the state's close ties with its self-nominated 'big brother', Saudi Arabia, one of the wealthiest Arab economies.

Saudis, significantly males, periodically cross the causeway to visit the more liberal island state of Bahrain. Official statistics from the causeway's website (www.kfca.com.sa) concerning the number of vehicles crossing the causeway show 6,207,938 vehicles crossing in 2011, 7,714,196 in 2012, 8,631,408 in 2013, 9,815,837 in 2014 and 10,427,541 in 2015. These figures reinforce the strong mobility component between the two nations. The King Fahd Causeway is a key facilitator of the nation's infrastructural developments and a crucial component

Figure 5.1   The King Fahd Causeway leading to Saudi Arabia.
Source: S. Bagaeen, April 2006

of Bahrain's economic growth strategy, acting as a vital artery for the flow of goods (and people) to and from the Kingdom. In addition to the economic impact, the causeway's role affirming the political affiliation between the two countries should not be underestimated. Matthiesen (2013: 30) notes that development assistance from Saudi Arabia was significant after the 1979 Iranian Revolution, as there was an apparent sense of nervousness that Bahrain may witness an uprising also. Accordingly, the causeway represents a 'vital lifeline' for both countries, where it can 'enable Saudi troops to roll over in the case of emergency'.

However, the development of a second crossing linking Bahrain with Qatar has been problematic. The Qatar Bahrain Causeway (or the Qatar Bahrain Friendship Bridge), connecting the village of Askar on the east coast of Bahrain to Ras Ashairij on the west coast of Qatar, was due for completion in 2009 (Construction Week Online 2013). This project was originally announced in 2001 and is estimated to cost around US$2.9 billion (*BQ Magazine* 2013). However, at the time of writing (June 2016), this project remains on hold. The plan, which intends to involve a road, bridges and a 40-kilometre railway, could bring significant benefits to tourism development and inter-regional cooperation.

In September 2014, Saudi Arabia's King Abdullah approved plans for another bridge linking Bahrain to Saudi Arabia – named the King Hamad Causeway. The business community in Bahrain welcomed the project announcement in September 2011, noting that it would offer a much-needed boost to the local and Gulf economies. This project, estimated to cost around US$3 billion and intended to be developed through private sector finance, is also a crucial section of the planned GCC rail network (Townsend 2015). This proposed development could be viewed as an attempt by Saudi Arabia to strengthen and consolidate its relationship with Bahrain, especially at a time when Bahrain remains politically vulnerable.

Looking further ahead, new initiatives and a growing infrastructure across the GCC states could be a game changer in terms of market diversification. Sea cruises to Bahrain, the UAE and Oman, for instance, have already featured on cruise line itineraries. The Cruise Arabia Alliance, which includes membership from Abu Dhabi, Bahrain, Dubai, Oman, Qatar and Sharjah, was established to coordinate region-wide standards of service (*Trade Arabia* 2015). According to Bains (2014), cruising is a US$100 billion global industry, and passenger numbers are growing at a rate of about 8.5 per cent annually. According to the Bahrain Economic Development Board (2014), the number of cruise ship arrivals in Bahrain grew by 143 per cent in the 2011–12 season and by 106 per cent in the 2012–13 season. By comparison, only 29 of the 50 port calls were scheduled when the political conflict was at its most intense period, that is, during the season of 2011–12 (Valdini 2012). Growth in cruise tourism has improved some aspects of the state's infrastructure, including the new Khalifa bin Salman port which contributed to the 600 per cent growth in the number of cruise ships docking in Bahrain between 2009 and 2013 (Bahrain Economic Development Board 2014: 128).

Leveraging culture and sport for tourism development

Bahrain has some significant cultural tourism sites, promoted to boost leisure tourism. The World Travel and Tourism Council (WTTC) (2015: 5) notes that leisure travel spending (inbound and domestic) in Bahrain produced 85.8 per cent of 'direct travel and tourism GDP' in 2014, in comparison to 14.2 per cent for business travel spending. Nonetheless, business tourism does play an increasingly important role in Bahrain's tourism development portfolio. The Bahrain Exhibition and Convention Authority (BECA), for instance, receives a number of industry events and international exhibitions. However, irrespective of the particular nature of the visit, cultural heritage can often have a generic appeal, particularly as it is often a crucial element of a destination's identity. Accordingly, Bahrain has several celebrated touristic-based heritage sites such as the Arad Fort, a fifteenth-century fort built in the typical style of Islamic forts and established prior to the Portuguese invasion of Bahrain in 1622 (Figure 5.2).

Rifaa Fort is another important cultural site in Bahrain. This sandstone structure was constructed in 1812 by Sheikh Salman Bin Ahmed Al Khalifa. The country hosts two significant United Nations Educational, Scientific and Cultural Organization (UNESCO) World Heritage Sites, Qal'at al-Bahrain (or Bahrain Fort – the former Portuguese Fort) and the 3.5-kilometre Bahrain Pearling Trail of Muharraq. Qal'at al-Bahrain's date of inscription for UNESCO recognition is 2005, with the trail following in 2012. The latter site includes 17 buildings embedded in the urban fabric of Muharraq city, three off-shore oyster beds and part of the seashore at the southern tip of Muharraq Island from where the boats set off to visit the oyster beds. The World Heritage List notes how 'the ensemble

Figure 5.2   Arad Fort.
Source: S. Bagaeen, April 2006.

of urban properties, fort, seashore and oyster beds is an exceptional testimony
to the final flourishing of the cultural tradition of pearling which dominated the
Persian Gulf between the 2nd and early 20th centuries'. Muharraq was the old
capital of Bahrain, boasting several traditionally restored houses. Another more
eclectic example and a haven for architectural connoisseurs is the La Fontaine
Centre of Contemporary Art. The building is a 150-year-old family mansion on
Hoora Avenue in the Ras Ruman district in Manama. It is located close to the old
Souq and is unique in that it captures the grand essence of a European chateau,
while retaining the charm of Gulf Islamic architecture.

In his assessment of urban heritage and architecture in Bahrain, Alraouf (2010)
indicates the need for more cosmopolitan and multi-ethnic cultural representations that reflect the distinctive traditions associated with 'two Islamic identities,
the Arabs and the Persians, the Sunni and the Shi'a' (2010: 56). This is in addition
to other key ethnic groups, such as the Indian community. He observes that in the
renovation and production of new spaces of heritage significance (e.g. Bab-Al-
Bahrain Souq), the spatial needs of the Shi'a community should be considered;
particularly in relation to their performance of the Ashouraa event. He further
informs that 'Urban heritage conservation does not necessarily mean preserving a
building but reviving its spirit and life' (2010: 65).

For the GCC states, including Bahrain, investing in sport is about building a
destination brand. Large international sporting events have been purposeful in
increasing visitor numbers, accelerating infrastructure spending and boosting a
nation's economy. After Dubai's early success in raising its international profile
through staging world-class tournaments, other GCC states have followed suit,

and the region now hosts many major sporting events. The trend began in Dubai in the 1980s with the launch of tennis and golf tournaments. In December 2010, Qatar made international headlines when it won the right to host the FIFA Football World Cup in 2022, as well as winning the bid for the 2019 World Athletics Championships. Dubai was successful in the bid to host Asia's premier football tournament, the 2019 Asian Football Confederation (AFC) Asian Cup.

Bahrain's proactive approach to sport development was clear when it secured the right to host the Grand Prix, an event that was part of the global expansion of the Fédération Internationale de l'Automobile (FIA) calendar of races in the early 2000s. The first Formula One Grand Prix held in the Middle East was premiered at the Bahrain International Circuit on 4 April 2004. The Bahrain government estimates that the event contributes around US$500 million to the economy, thus justifying paying US$40 million to host the event (Allison 2012). Although the race was cancelled in 2011 due to political unrest, the state continued to prioritize the event despite political pressure and significant opposition when it was re-scheduled the following year. According to Allison (2012), the intense media glare focused on whether the competition should have taken place while a 13-month uprising against the Bahrain government continued, with protestors promising 'days of rage' ahead of this event.

Other landmark events include the annual Bahrain Boat Show and the bi-annual Bahrain Air Show. However, when it comes to building an international brand, Allison (2012) argues that the rewards that sports events can bring to a destination far outweigh the risks. Few other marketing tools can ever achieve the depth of coverage that sport can offer. Writers have highlighted the increasing political importance of sport and the growing trend for states to actively seek to stage expensive and elaborate mega sporting events. Weed (2010: 187), for instance, notes how 'interest in the relationship between sport, tourism and image' is not new. He points to 'numerous examples of sport and tourism, and leisure and culture more generally, being used by politicians and policy-makers as part of deliberate attempts to change place imagery as a step towards the revitalisation of economies'. More recently, Grix (2012) also explains that in order to gain international prestige, states instrumentalize sport to promote a country's image or 'brand'.

The impact of political unrest on tourism

Morakabati (2013: 384) suggests that events in Tunisia in 2010 ignited ongoing turmoil in the Middle East, which had a 'profound effect on tourism activity in the region with many tourists seeking alternative destinations in the wake of the uprisings'. Morakabati (2013) points out that in the first half of 2011 there was a 10 per cent fall in the number of tourists in the Middle East, disguising more dramatic falls elsewhere, such as in Egypt. In the case of Bahrain, the state was looking to a rebound in tourism activities following the decline in tourism receipts, especially when civil unrest had an impact on Bahrain's tourism and financial sectors. Activists from the Shi'a majority launched protests against the Sunni-led government. Richter (2011) reported that Bahrain's hotel industry, which relied on a regular calendar of business conferences to ensure high occupancy, suffered initially due to the political turmoil. A close inspection of hotel guest data for the whole of 2011 shows a significant drop in numbers during what were the more turbulent months of the year, notably February, March and April (see Table 5.1). As a result of the competitive nature of GCC tourist destinations, other destinations benefitted from Bahrain's misfortunes. Evidence from Dubai, for example, shows that its hotel industry hosted 6.64 million guests in the first three-quarters of 2011, an 11 per cent increase compared with the corresponding period the previous year. Guest nights rose by 26 per cent to reach 23.68 million, while the average length of stay increased by 14 per cent during the same period (Dubai Tourism 2011).

Martin (2011) reported how demonstrations began on a small scale in several villages on the night of 13 February 2011 and continued into the morning of 14 February. By the evening of 14 February they had escalated, as protesters tried to converge on the Pearl Roundabout in Manama (Figure 5.3), where the Pearl Monument was erected in 1982 to mark the creation of the GCC. Its six dhow sails, all holding one single pearl, signified each GCC state. Coates Ulrichsen (2013) points out that 14 February was symbolic, marking the tenth anniversary of the referendum that had approved the Bahrain National Action Charter in 2001. A state of emergency was declared in Bahrain on 15 March 2011, lasting until 1 June 2011. However, the situation was quite volatile on 13 March, when anti-government demonstrators occupied the roundabout, and military reinforcements poured in from the UAE and Saudi Arabia as part of the Peninsula Shield Force, to help shore up the Bahraini government. It has

Table 5.1 Guest numbers for three-, four- and five-star hotels in Bahrain in 2010 and 2011

Month	Hotel guest numbers 2010	Hotel guest numbers 2011	% change
January	76,777	73,276	−4.6
February	90,302	66,625	−26.2
March	95,309	31,743	−66.7
April	89,304	38,214	−57.2
May	80,405	50,956	−36.6
June	74,432	64,086	−13.9
July	90,694	89,924	−0.09
August	59,766	46,719	−21.8
September	77,396	85,254	+10.2
October	90,032	80,870	−10.2
November	89,431	85,244	−4.7
December	81,213	69,422	−14.5

Source: Adapted from the 2010–11 data produced by the Bahrain Ministry of Culture – Tourism Sector (see www.cio.gov.bh/cio_eng/Stats_SubDetailed.aspx?subcatid=604).

Figure 5.3 Pearl Roundabout in Manama.
Source: S. Bagaeen, April 2006.

been suggested that its involvement was a response to a tweeted request from Bahrain's foreign minister for help to stabilize the uprising (Guzansky 2014). The GCC established the Peninsula Shield in 1986, which was composed of joint military forces with the mission to protect the security of member states from any external aggression.

The Pearl Roundabout remained the hub of Bahrain's rebellion until it was demolished on 18 March 2011 (Chulov 2011). The reasons for this could concern a desire for the site not to develop as a space of public commemoration representing the pro-democracy movement or values of religious plurality. Subsequently, the area was renamed 'Al Farooq Junction', which may be seen by some as a move towards reinforcing the government's claim over the territory. Accordingly, Farooq (meaning 'separator of truth from falsehood') is the epithet of Umar ibn Al-Khattāb (586–644), an influential caliph who is highly revered in the Sunni community (Virk 2014), though not necessarily so within the Shi'a community.

Conclusion and research implications

The total contribution of travel and tourism to Bahrain's GDP was Bahraini dinar (BHD) 1,336.2 million (10.3 per cent of GDP) in 2014, which increased to BHD 1, 133,7 million in 2015 (WTTC 2015, 2016). Given that oil revenues and government spending have been instrumental in driving growth for decades (Bahrain Economic Development Board 2016), the lower than expected oil revenues that have recently materialized could further underscore the importance of the long-standing strategic commitment to economic diversification, including investment in the tourism industry.

On the surface level, wooing tourists back to Bahrain following the uprisings does not seem to be a major challenge in the medium term, as there have been yearly increases since 2011. Accordingly, although tourist figures have not fully reached 2010 levels, the positive upturn has been shielded by the fact that the most significant national tourism segment is from Saudi Arabia. From an international marketing perspective, however, the challenge for Bahrain is its increasing reliance on regional tourism, especially tourists from Saudi Arabia. Another challenge highlighted concerns the serious consideration for Bahrain's tourism and heritage industry to foster more modern-day elements of plurality and cosmopolitanism.

Ethnographic research would be useful in looking primarily at the role of expatriate workers and transnational people flows, and their subsequent impacts on patterns of future economic and tourism growth. The parameters of this research could stretch to investigate the impact of the global political economy on Bahrain's tourism development agenda. It would be useful to examine how both brand image and destination identity can be constructively re-constructed. Several authors have outlined how destination branding can become an influential tool in tourism development (Leisen 2001; Marzano and Scott 2009). Moreover, the ability to create emotional appeal through the evolution, advancement and promotion of a unique brand image has been a fundamental component of the marketing strategies of various tourism regions and destinations. This has certainly been the case in the context of Dubai's effort to establish itself as a global brand (Bagaeen 2007). Particular attention could, thus, focus on how the country can try to pacify, in a symbolic manner, conflict within its borders by promoting cultural and event-based tourism through a sensitive but open approach, elevating a destination identity based on cultural plurality and cosmopolitan diversity as the emotive values of the brand. If the country ends up embracing its own cultural diversity because of such measures, then such a way forward can only be fruitful to the long-term social sustainability of Bahraini society.

Coates Ulrichsen (2013) examined the intersections between power and tourism in the context of Bahrain's development agenda, noting that ongoing unrest in Bahrain forms part of a cycle of recurrent periods of strife that predate the Arab Spring revolutions in Tunisia and Egypt and observing how Bahrain is caught 'between powerful geopolitical cross-currents that give domestic developments a regional and international dimension' (2013: 7). Therefore, regional geopolitical manoeuvring, oil, infrastructure, sport and power may yet determine the relationship between tourism and economic growth in Bahrain. What is also necessary is a more detailed treatment of power for a 'vital to a fuller understanding of tourism' (Church and Coles 2007: xii).

References

Alraouf, A. A. (2010) 'Regenerating urban traditions in Bahrain. Learning from Bab-Al-Bahrain: the authentic fake', *Journal of Tourism and Cultural Change*, 8(1–2): 50–68.

Allison, A. (2012) 'Gulf uses sport to build brands', *Middle East Business Intelligence (MEED)*, 27 April–3 May. Available online at www.meed.com/sectors/economy/tourism/gulf-usessport-to-build-brands/3135141.article (accessed 23 October 2014).

Arlt, W. G. (2006) *China's Outbound Tourism*, Oxford: Routledge.

Bagaeen, S. (2007) 'Brand Dubai: the instant city; or, the instantly recognisable city', *International Planning Studies*, 12(2): 173–197.

Bagaeen, S. (2015) 'Saudi Arabia, Bahrain, United Arab Emirates and Qatar: Middle Eastern complexity and contradiction', in G. Squires and E. Heurkens (eds) *International Approaches to Real Estate Development*, London: Routledge, pp. 100–121.

Bahrain Economic Development Board (2014) Economic Yearbook 2013. Available online at www.bahrainedb.com/en/EDBDocuments/Bahrain-Economic-Yearbook.pdf (accessed 31 March 2015).

Bahrain Economic Development Board (2016) *Bahrain Economic Quarterly*, March 2016. Available online at www.bahrainedb.com/en/EDBDocuments/BEQ-March-2016.pdf (accessed 1 May 2016).

Bains, E. (2014) 'Transport plans to drive tourism', *Middle East Business Intelligence (MEED)*, 24 April. Available online at www.meed.com/sectors/economy/tourism/transport-plans-to-drive-tourism/3191446.article (accessed 23 October 2014).

BBC (2014) 'Bahrain F1 Grand Prix rights complaint "merits examination"', 24 October. Available online at www.bbc.co.uk/news/uk-politics-29762156 (accessed 3 November 2014).

BQ Magazine (2013) 'Redesign of Qatar-Bahrain causeway almost ready', *BQ Magazine*, 15 April. Available online at www.bq-magazine.com/industries/2013/04/redesign-of-qatar-bahrain-causeway-almost-ready_a (accessed 16 April 2016).

Chulov, M. (2011) 'Bahrain destroys Pearl roundabout', *Guardian*, 18 March. Available online at www.theguardian.com/world/2011/mar/18/bahrain-destroys-pearl-roundabout (accessed 28 February 2015).

Church, A. and T. Coles (2007) *Tourism, Power and Space*, New York: Routledge.

Coates Ulrichsen, K. (2013) 'Bahrain's uprising: regional dimensions and international consequences', *Stability: International Journal of Security and Development*, 2(1): 1–12.

Construction Week Online (2013) 'Bahrain and Qatar hold talks on delayed causeway', 30 October. Available online at www.constructionweekonline.com/article-24861-bahrain-and-qatar-hold-talks-on-delayed-causeway/ (accessed 15 August 2015).

Dubai Tourism (2011) 'DTCM host Dubai tourism GCC conference to boost visitors number from Arabian Gulf states'. Available online at http://pr.dubaitourism.ae/2011/12/19/dtcm-host-dubai-tourism-gcc-conference-to-boost-visitors-number-from-arabian-gulf-states/ (accessed 15 August 2015).

Foreman, C. (2009) 'A steady approach benefits Bahraini property and tourism sectors', *Middle East Business Intelligence (MEED)*, 29 October. Available online at www.meed.com/supplements/2009/bahrain-report-2009/a-steady-approach-benefits-bahraini-property-and-tourism-sectors/3001754.article (accessed 23 October 2014).

Foreman, C. (2014) 'Bahrain starts airport prequalification', *Middle East Business Intelligence (MEED)*, 1 September. Available online at www.meed.com/sectors/

transport/aviation-and-airports/bahrain-starts-airport-prequalification/3194988.article (accessed 23 October 2014).

Florian, J. (2014) 'Al-Hedaya wins deal for affordable housing project in Bahrain', *Middle East Business Intelligence (MEED)*, 14 May. Available online at www.meed.com/sectors/construction/real-estate/al-hedaya-wins-deal-for-affordable-housing-project-in-bahrain/3192009.article (accessed 23 October 2014).

Gavin, J. (2014) 'Manama's future energy challenge', *Middle East Business Intelligence (MEED)*, 15 April. Available online at www.meed.com/sectors/oil-and-gas/oil-upstream/manamas-future-energy-challenge/3191182.article (accessed 23 October 2014).

Grix, J. (2012) '"Image" leveraging and sports megaevents: Germany and the 2006 FIFA World Cup', *Journal of Sport and Tourism*, 17(4): 289–312.

Guzansky, Y. (2014) 'Defence cooperation in the Arabian Gulf: the Peninsula Shield Force put to the test', *Middle Eastern Studies*, 50(4): 640–654.

Harvey, D. (2008) 'The right to the city', *New Left Review*, 53 (September/October), 23–40.

Jafari, J. and N. Scott (2014) 'Muslim world and its tourisms', *Annals of Tourism Research*, 44(1): 1–19.

Labour Market Regulatory Authority (2016) 'Total employment at 725,113 workers by end of Q4 2015'. Available online at http://blmi.lmra.bh/2015/12/mi_dashboard.xml#key-messages-box (accessed 16 April 2016).

Leisen, B. (2001) 'Image segmentation: the case of a tourism destination', *The Journal of Services Marketing*, 15(1): 9–66.

Louër, L. (2008) 'The political impact of labour migration in Bahrain', *City and Society*, 20(1): 32–53.

Mansfeld, Y. and O. Winckler (2008) 'The role of the tourism industry in transforming a *rentier* to a long-term viable economy: the case of Bahrain', *Current Issues in Tourism*, 11(3): 237–267.

Martin, M. (2011) 'Protests escalate in Bahrain', *Middle East Economic Digest (MEED)*, February. Available online at www.meed.com/countries/bahrain/protests-escalate-in-bahrain/3087411.article (accessed 23 October 2014).

Marzano, G. and Scott, N. (2009) 'Power in destination branding', *Annals of Tourism Research*, 36(2): 247–267.

Matarrita-Cascante, D. (2010) 'Beyond growth: reaching tourism-led development', *Annals of Tourism Research*, 37(4): 1141–1163.

Matthiesen, T. (2013) *Sectarian Gulf: Bahrain, Saudi Arabia, and the Arab Spring that Wasn't*, Standford, CA: Standford University Press.

Morakabati, Y. (2013) 'Tourism in the Middle East: conflicts, crises and economic diversification, some critical issues', *International Journal of Tourism Research*, 15(4): 375–387.

Nyíri, P. (2006) *Scenic Spots: Chinese Tourism, the State, and Cultural Authority*, Seattle, WA: University of Washington Press.

Oxford Business Group (2016) 'Bahrain capitalises on tourism title', 24 February. Available online at www.oxfordbusinessgroup.com/news/bahrain-capitalises-tourism-title (accessed16 April 2016).

Peterson, J. E. (2009) 'Life after oil: economic alternatives for the Arab Gulf states', *Mediterranean Quarterly*, 20(3): 1–18.

Richter, F. (2011) 'Bahrain's tourism, financial sectors hit by unrest'. Available online at http://uk.reuters.com/article/2011/03/01/uk-bahrain-economy-idUKLNE72005H 20110301 (accessed 23 October 2014).

Richter, L. K. (1983) 'Political implications of Chinese tourism policy', *Annals of Tourism Research*, 10(3): 395–413.

Saleh, A. S., A. G. Assaf, R. Ihalanayake and S. Lung (2015) 'A panel cointegration analysis of the impact of tourism on economic growth: evidence from the Middle East region', *International Journal of Tourism Research*, 17(3): 209–220.

Song Loong, M. (2013) 'Bahrain police puts end to opposition protests', *Middle East Economic Digest (MEED)*, 15 August. Available online at www.meed.com/sectors/economy/government/bahrain-police-puts-end-to-opposition-protests/3184134.article (accessed 23 October 2014).

Spong, R. (2013) 'Financial bids submitted for Bahrain airport expansion', *Middle East Economic Digest (MEED)*, 18 August. Available online at www.meed.com/sectors/transport/aviation-and-airports/financial-bids-submitted-for-bahrain-airportexpansion/3184164.article (accessed 23 October 2014).

Spong, R. (2014a) 'Further bomb explosions in Bahrain', *Middle East Economic Digest (MEED)*, 13 March. Available online at www.meed.com/sectors/economy/government/further-bomb-explosions-in-bahrain/3190199.article (accessed 23 October 2014).

Spong, R. (2014b) 'Bahrain's debt problem', *Middle East Economic Digest*, 22 June. Available online at www.meed.com/supplements/2014/middle-east-economic-review/bahrains-debt-problem/3192947.article (accessed 23 October 2014).

Stephenson, M. and J. Ali-Knight (2010) 'Dubai's tourism industry and its societal impact: social implications and sustainable challenges', *Journal of Tourism and Cultural Change*, 8(4): 278–292.

Townsend, S. (2015) 'Bahrain, Saudi Arabia escalate plans for $3bn second causeway', *Arabian Business*, 7 October. Available online at www.arabianbusiness.com/bahrain-saudi-arabia-escalate-plans-for-3bn-second-causeway-608390.html (accessed 16 April 2016).

Trade Arabia (2010) 'Bahrain to set up tourism watchdog', *Trade Arabia*, 14 August. Available online at www.tradearabia.com/news/ttn_184510.html (accessed 30 June 2015).

Trade Arabia (2015) 'Bahrain joins Cruise Arabia Alliance', *Trade Arabia*, 9 December. Available online at www.tradearabia.com/news/TTN_296385.html (accessed 2 June 2016).

Unnikrishnan, R. (2014) 'Bahrain's four-year strategy to focus on an "experience-led" approach', *Gulf Daily News*, 3 August. Available online at www.gulf-daily-news.com/source/XXXVII/136/pdf/ page06.pdf (accessed 15 April 2016).

UNWTO (United Nations World Tourism Organization) (2000) *Tourism Highlights 2000* (2nd edn, August), Madrid: UNWTO.

Valdini, C. (2012) 'Cruise operators mull restarting Bahrain routes', *Arabian Business.com*, 18 July. Available online at http://m.arabianbusiness.com/cruise-operators-mull-restarting-bahrain-routes-466360.html (accessed 16 April 2016).

Virk, Z. (2014) 'Hadrat Umar ibn al-Khattab – his generous treatment of non-Muslims', *The Muslim Times*, 19 March. Available online at https://themuslimtimes.info/2014/03/19/hadrat-umar-ibn-al-khattab-his-generous-treatment-of-non-muslims/ (accessed 17 April 2016).

Weed, M. (2010) 'Sports, tourism and image', *Journal of Sport and Tourism*, 15(3): 187–189.

World Bank (2015) 'International tourism, number of arrivals'. Available online at http://databank.worldbank.org/data/reports.aspx?source=2&series=ST.INT.ARVL&country= (accessed 16 April 2015).

WTTC (World Travel and Tourism Council) (2015) 'Travel and tourism economic impact 2015: Bahrain'. Available online at www.wttc.org//media/files/reports/economic%20 impact%20 research/countries%202015/bahrain2015.pdf (accessed 31 March 2015).

WTTC (World Travel and Tourism Council) (2016) 'Travel and tourism economic impact 2016: Bahrain'. Available online at www.wttc.org/-/media/files/reports/economic%20 impact %20research/ countries%202016/bahrain2016.pdf (accessed 27 May 2016).

6 (No) tourism in Kuwait

Why Kuwaitis are ambivalent about developing tourism

Marjorie Kelly

The World Economic Forum published its Travel and Tourism Competitiveness Report: Growth Through Shocks in 2015. This edition of the biennial report ranks 141 countries in terms of their overall travel and tourism competitiveness, with the aim of building strong and sustainable industries that can contribute to international economic development (World Economic Forum 2015: 7). Of the 141 countries, Kuwait ranked 103, based on the following four indices: (1) the enabling environment (e.g. security, health, business and labour), (2) travel and tourism policy, (3) infrastructure and (4) natural and cultural resources. Kuwait ranks 54, 141, 77 and 137, respectively, in the four categories. Of the 16 Middle Eastern and North African nations included in the report, Kuwait ranks thirteenth in competitiveness (World Economic Forum 2015). Despite the apparent lack of competitiveness, Kuwait had developed a National Tourism Master Plan (submitted in 2005) which cited tourism to be the means of (1) diversifying the economy, (2) creating 30,000 much-needed jobs by 2025 and (3) enhancing the government's goal of becoming a commercial and financial centre in the region. With 15 consecutive years of budget surpluses totalling US$92.5 billion (*Arab News* 2014), funding the plan would not have been an obstacle. Why, then, has it not been implemented?

Starting with the strengths and weaknesses in Kuwait's tourism industry as detailed in the World Economic Forum report, this chapter explains why the country's ranking is as low as it is and continues by describing what the obstacles to developing tourism are. The work proceeds to question whether tourism is the best strategy for advancing national development, and then examines the social norms that underlie Kuwaiti ambivalence towards the industry. After a discussion of the National Tourism Master Plan and its strategy for achieving implementation, future avenues for tourism research are suggested.

Kuwait's rankings in the 2015 World Economic Forum report

Kuwait ranks 135 in terms of prioritization of travel and tourism, though in terms of government policy and support it is at the bottom position, 141. It also ranks very low, at 138, in terms of marketing tourism. However, when looking at the indices of the first component – enabling environment – Kuwait scores much higher, with a rank of 43 for safety and security, 62 for health and hygiene and 46 for the business environment. But, in terms of human resources and its labour market, Kuwait held the lowest position of the GCC states at 93 (World Economic Forum 2015).

Longva (1997: 63–64) notes that when Kuwait became independent in 1961, the government pledged to 'provide citizens with employment in the public sector if they wished to work'. As a result, Kuwaiti employees are so heavily concentrated in this sector that, Longva continues, one could argue that the public sector's main function is to serve as a channel for distributing oil revenues to citizens. Kuwaitis have, seemingly, come to regard their government salaries as an entitlement rather than the product of meaningful work and/or a measure of job performance. As a consequence of this heavy concentration of Kuwaiti employees in the public sector, around 84 per cent (*Arab Times* 2015), the country scores a relatively low 96 in the World Economic Forum report for employee training. This may be due to the private sector preference for hiring already well-trained expatriate workers who command lower wages and receive fewer benefits than do Kuwaiti citizens. It is also easier to hire and fire non-citizens, who can be deported within 24 hours for criminal causes such as theft. Finding citizens with the appropriate job credentials can be difficult. The quota system, requiring the private sector to hire one Kuwaiti for every eight expatriate workers, can be burdensome for employers, as the following example illustrates. A graduate of the American University of Kuwait, who fully intended to utilize his skills, informed the author that an employer offered him a job but asked that he not come into the office because his presumed lack of work ethic would demoralize the other (foreign) workers.

Out of a population of 4.3 million, 2.9 million residents are foreign workers (*Arab Times* 2015). Most are Asians working in the construction and service sectors, or employed as domestic helpers – jobs that Kuwaitis do not want. Even so, there is a plan to (1) cut expatriate numbers by 100,000 workers every year for the next decade, (2) impose a limit on the number of workers for each nationality and (3) limit the length of time an expatriate can remain in Kuwait (*Gulf News* 2013; Sajjad 2013). An additional plan calls for expatriates aged 50 and over to relinquish their jobs to unemployed Kuwaitis in their field (*Arab Times* 2015). Underlying these sweeping proposals is the sense of vulnerability and unease that Kuwaitis feel at being a minority in their own country. The perception exists that a massive influx of foreigners represents 'a threat to national heritage and cultural values, and even a latent threat to political stability' – a reaction not unique to Kuwait (Kamrava and Babar 2012: 10–11).

Turning to the second set of indices in the World Economic Forum (2015) report, infrastructure, Kuwait is in the mid-range at 77. As the first Gulf nation to modernize, Kuwait has an adequate, if somewhat outdated, infrastructure. This is especially apparent when compared to the facilities in other Gulf Cooperation Council (GCC) states, such as the recently completed airports in Dubai and Doha. Kuwait has a range of hotels and guest residences as well as numerous car rental companies, most often utilized by expatriates working on short-term contracts.

Even so, the country's almost 7,000 hotel rooms have an occupancy rate that averages only about 50 per cent (*Kuwait Times* 2015).

In the last set of indices, natural and cultural resources, Kuwait's overall rank is 137, five places from the bottom of the list (World Economic Forum 2015). The score is, arguably, due in part to the devastation wrought during the Iraqi occupation of Kuwait (2 August 1990–25 February 1991). Retreating Iraqi forces used explosives on over 700 oil wells and set another 600 on fire, creating lakes of oil and considerable pollution (Cordesman 1997: 32). An oil slick of 4 million barrels covered 750 square miles of sea, and 25 million barrels of oil spilled on Kuwaiti soil. It took eight months to extinguish the oil fires that blackened the skies. Unfortunately, the chemical foam used to extinguish the flames caused further damage by seeping into the ground to poison the earth.

While few signs of war damage remain visible in urban areas today, there has been a failure to implement and/or enforce zoning regulations, as well as a lack of environmental protection. The result is crowded conditions, very little green space and poor air quality. It is not unusual to see people wearing surgical-type masks during windy periods when the sand and dust in the air make breathing difficult. The problem of air quality is compounded by Kuwait's high level of energy consumption. On a per capita basis, Kuwait has the fourth highest rate of energy consumption in the world (Fineren 2013), no doubt encouraged by the fact that the government subsidizes the cost of energy. In fact, Kuwait ranked 136 in terms of environmental sustainability in the World Economic Forum (2015) report.

Kuwait ranks 125 for cultural resources and business travel. While its sports facilities and international fairs and exhibitions are recognized, Kuwait has not hosted the international sporting events, film festivals or concerts that its Gulf neighbours have (though local events do exist). Kuwait also lacks any World Heritage Cultural Sites (World Economic Forum 2015). In sum, Kuwait does not possess the scenic landscape of Oman, the heritage sites of Bahrain or the nightlife and artificial beaches of Dubai. Environmentally, it is perhaps closest to Qatar, although it lacks one thing that Qatar has in abundance: the political will to reinvent itself to attract international visitors (see Chapter 8). To use the terminology of the 2013 World Economic Forum (2013: 221) report, Kuwait lacks an 'affinity for travel and tourism'.

Reasons for the lack of tourism investment in Kuwait

Due to the requirement that all financial enterprises be majority-owned by Kuwaiti citizens, foreign investment is generally discouraged. In situations where investment occurs, it is not uncommon for an expatriate partner to provide the capital for an enterprise in addition to expertise, labour and management, while the Kuwaiti partner provides sponsorship in return for a share of the profits. The percentage is negotiated between the partners and does not necessarily remain fixed. By law, only a Kuwaiti's signature is valid on all legal documents, rental leases, banking deals and so forth. As a result, the expatriate partner has little choice but to see his or her Kuwaiti counterpart's share of the profit as 'a tax collected on foreigners' profit-making activities carried out on Kuwaiti territory' (Longva 1997: 65).

Although Kuwaitis may be happy to partake in the wealth generated in their country, they were not eager to invest within Kuwait themselves for well over a decade after the Iraqi occupation ended (United Nations official, pers. comm. November 2012). As long as Saddam Hussein remained in power in Iraq, Kuwait felt threatened – and with good reason. For example, in October 1994, Iraqi troops moved to within 20 kilometres of the Kuwaiti border and deployed there until they were forced back by international pressure (Cordesman 1997: 12). Apprehensive about triggering fresh clashes with Iraq, Kuwait delayed plans to increase foreign involvement in the development of oil fields near the Iraqi border in June of 1995 (1997: 34). Until Saddam Hussein was removed from power in 2003, Kuwait did not experience the kind of development one might otherwise have expected to occur after its liberation.

During their enforced stay outside the country while it was occupied, many Kuwaitis realized the value of having foreign investments for access to funds, second (or third) homes abroad for long-term residence and dual citizenship for indefinite stays. An estimated 120,000 Kuwaitis are also citizens of other GCC countries, and 50,000 hold US passports, even though Kuwait does not recognize dual citizenship (Calderwood 2010). Given the last quarter-century of Kuwaiti history, it is hardly surprising that attracting visitors to Kuwait has not been a priority at a time when Kuwaitis themselves were investing in safe havens abroad. After the regime change in Iraq, internal investment in Kuwait picked up as huge shopping malls opened and lucrative franchises were purchased. Well-known European and North American brands, stores and restaurants became accessible for the first time in Kuwait. However, although these establishments became highly popular with Kuwaitis and expatriates alike, they are hardly an incentive for Western tourists to visit Kuwait.

Other obstacles to tourism development

In addition to the factors cited in the World Economic Forum report, other obstacles to the development of a tourism industry in Kuwait exist. These include the perception (accuracy aside) of the region as being unsafe at worst and unwelcoming at best, limited airline connections, high hotel prices, congested highways and insufficient tourist attractions. Moreover, Kuwait is a conservative society where the sale of alcohol is illegal, films are censored, Western-style nightlife is considered culturally inappropriate and the dress code (garments reaching below knees and elbows) requires that tourist cover up in a hot climate. Finally, since many jobs in tourism are low-level service positions (e.g. bus drivers, travel and car rental agents, airport and hotel workers and wait staff), which are relatively poorly paid and are currently held almost exclusively by expatriates, the wisdom of making tourism a national priority can be questioned.

Longva's (1997) study, *Walls Built on Sand*, supports the questioning of whether Kuwaitis would accept most tourism-related jobs. She argues that because Kuwaitis perceive 'migrant workers first and foremost as a threat against their own stability, security, and cultural identity [*their*] dominant concern [*is*] with the ways and means of protecting themselves' (1997: 103). The result is what Longva calls the 'politics of exclusion', maintained by restricting citizenship and differentiating labour, that is, segregated job categories. If Kuwaitis were to work in service positions, then the legal, political, economic and behavioural distinctions between nationals and non-Kuwaitis would become blurred, breaching the carefully maintained social wall dividing the two groups and thereby threatening the identity of any Kuwaiti holding such a position. Indeed, one analysis found that about 44 per cent of unemployed Kuwaitis do not accept private sector jobs if offered to them (*Arab Times* 2015). Thus, creating service jobs in tourism could well result in increasing the need for foreign workers rather than the intended goal of producing private sector employment for Kuwaitis.

Other reasons for concern about developing a tourism industry in Kuwait include the carrying capacity of the land and environmental sustainability issues, particularly in a country that already has pollution and refuse collection problems, imports much of its food and relies on desalinization plants for its water supply. Financially, while the amount of leakage of tourist revenues to foreign entities may be reduced by Kuwaiti laws requiring local ownership and participation, it should be noted that profit transfers, foreign managers' remittances, and food and furnishings for international hotels remain an issue (Daher 2007: 24). In terms of non-material considerations, given the 'tourist bubble' that surrounds most short-term visitors, AlSayyad (2001: 19) indicates that such visits can 'often function as little more than instruments of stigmatization and stereotyping' – the reverse of the Kuwait National Tourism Master Plan's stated goal of enhancing the country's image. Focusing on tourism also ignores the fact that a good number of Kuwaitis might have other ideas about what their country's priorities should be, and thus are not shy about saying so in private conversation and at social gatherings.

The likelihood of cultural misunderstanding compounds the problem of a foreign presence in Kuwait, since tourists cannot be expected to know the rules for maintaining social distance that migrant workers have learned, or may simply choose to ignore the rules in order to get that 'perfect photo', for instance. As Robinson (2001: 48) expresses, although the tourist's visit may be of short duration, the 'experience for the host community is quite different, consisting of a constant stream of undifferentiated tourists, united by their transitoriness, anonymity, and propensity to "gaze"'.

The 'tourist gaze'

As John Urry (2002) observed in *The Tourist Gaze*, tourist sites attract the visitor's gaze because they differ from his or her everyday experience. On the one hand, tourists seek out that which is unusual for them. On the other hand, they search for the stereotypical aspects of the foreign culture in question – in this case, whatever is regarded as quintessentially 'Kuwaiti'. Urry (2002: 3) further notes that these aspects or signs are visually objectified or captured through such mediums as photographs, postcards and films, so that the gaze can be 'endlessly reproduced and recaptured'. If his description is applied to Kuwait, one finds little in the way of internationally recognizable images. Indeed, there are less than a dozen different postcard images for sale in the country. These can be summarized as buildings, boats and bedouin artefacts, in addition to the omnipresent Kuwait Towers (see Figure 6.1). Urry (2002: 127) further observes that in photographing an object or person, one appropriates it and has power over it. Does such an act of appropriation lie behind the taboo on public photographs of private individuals in Kuwait?

Echoing Susan Sontag's (1973: 14) belief that photography turns people into objects that can be symbolically possessed, Kuwaitis explain their attitude by saying that having someone's photograph gives one symbolic control of – if not the person – that person's reputation, especially in the case of females. Young women fear what their parents' or brothers' reactions would be if they were to learn that a young man possessed their picture, even if the photo was taken against their will or without their knowledge. In the age of digital photography and sophisticated photo alteration, women also fear having their faces 'pasted' on immodestly dressed bodies and placed on the Internet to the detriment of their reputations. The spontaneous point-and-shoot style of photography typical of tourists on the lookout for the exotic 'other', whether male or female, is

Figure 6.1   Kuwait Towers.

Source: N. Scharfenort, March 2016.

deemed unacceptable for the simple reason that the subject does not control how the image is to be used or, indeed, understand why someone would want it in the first place.

Sometimes foreigners need not even possess a camera to trigger a negative response. An observer at a shopping mall described the following interaction involving a Kuwaiti male (accompanied by his veiled wife) and two American males. The latter were in all likelihood US military or military contractors with a rudimentary understanding of the rules, given the immediate attempt by one of the men to defuse the situation. The Kuwaiti man 'caught' the two Americans looking at his wife and made no distinction between their staring at her as a person (she was completely covered so as to be more or less invisible) and their observing what was to them exotic garb. His heated protests led to one of the Americans leaping up from his seat to profusely apologise for the situation (pers. comm. March 2013).

Although Kuwaitis often overlook foreigners' faux pas in recognition of their ignorance of local customs and etiquette, there are some missteps that are not so easily dismissed; particularly if they involve interaction between genders. In focusing on this red line of behaviour, it should not be assumed that these incidents occur all the time or that foreigners are constantly fearful of making mistakes. Nonetheless, looking fixedly at someone can often be perceived as being sexually provocative or challenging and can elicit a response, even if that response is just looking away or moving away, as is the usual female reaction (cf. Bristol-Rhys [2012: 79–80] on staring and eye contact in the United Arab Emirates and, similarly, Burns [2007: 230] on Saudi Arabia). Therefore, the tourist gaze, much less verbal comments and picture-taking, would be regarded as an unwelcome intrusion by many citizens at the most personal level and could well give rise to unpleasant exchanges (like the one described in the previous paragraph), and/or engender greater hostility towards the presence of foreigners.

The issue of 'gazing' is particularly sensitive at hotel swimming pools and beach resorts, where patrons are wearing swimsuits. Photography is generally prohibited at these locations, and security personnel are quick to enforce the ban. While provisions for privacy in pool areas vary from hotel to hotel, the following observations by the writer while at a hotel in 2013 illustrate the social rules for poolside behaviour. The Kuwaiti-owned hotel had no separate pool hours for men and women, thus (unlike in neighbouring Saudi Arabia) the entire family could swim at the same time. Signs stated that all those seated around the pool must be in bathing suits. In other words, one cannot watch swimmers if one is fully clothed oneself, so that all are equally exposed and hence vulnerable (cf. Bristol-Rhys 2012: 78 on the visibility of beachgoers in Abu Dhabi). None of the hotel guest rooms overlook the pool, so no one can gaze down from his or her room or take unwanted photographs. At some hotels, a private pool is designated exclusively for female use. Thus, even in commercial establishments with international clientele, such as hotels, privacy and gender gazing are strictly regulated. With these cultural sensitivities in mind, how does Kuwait plan to develop tourism?

Kuwait's National Tourism Master Plan

Though submitted over a decade ago, in 2005, much of Kuwait's National Tourism Master Plan has yet to be implemented (tourism consultant, pers. comm. April 2013). The plan is thorough and thoughtful, recognizing problem areas and cognizant of missed opportunities. It realizes that tourism has been neglected in Kuwait and that competition for tourists is high in the Gulf. The plan also acknowledges that tourism development will have to be carefully presented to Kuwaitis if it is to be accepted, with close attention paid to comprehending societal norms. The plan's goals consist of five key objectives: (1) development of tourism to diversify the Kuwaiti economy, (2) provision of new (private sector) jobs, (3) improvement of the quality of life for Kuwaitis, (4) enhancement of the country's image to encourage foreign investment and (5) development of Kuwait as a commercial gateway to the region (Kuwait National Tourism Master Plan 2005: 2). It proposes that a Kuwait Tourism Authority (KTA) be established with responsibility for marketing tourism, developing human resources for the industry and creating the tourism product.

The Kuwait National Tourism Master Plan (2005: 6) proposes expansion in three already existing markets: the domestic market, regional market (Gulf citizens) and foreign market, which is limited to discretionary business/special interest tourism. By focusing on domestic and regional markets, problems are avoided vis-à-vis tourists from outside the region who lack familiarity with the social and cultural norms of the Gulf. For example, fellow Muslims will not question why alcohol is not available for purchase. Since GCC citizens may freely visit each other's countries, the barrier to travel represented by visas is also not an issue.

While cognizant of the fact that Kuwaitis believe their country lacks tourist assets compared to those of neighbouring states, the formulators of the plan think otherwise. They list them as follows: quality hotels, heritage and archaeological sites, civic buildings, shopping malls, sports facilities, desert camping and seaside chalets (Kuwait National Tourism Master Plan 2005: 4–5). These are clearly not world-class attractions but recreational venues, for the most part. However, according to the National Tourism Master Plan, this is what Kuwaitis said they wanted when surveyed on the subject: new forms of shopping, large festivals, island development and new coastal resorts. Such facilities already exist in Kuwait, though not in the quantity or of the quality that cosmopolitan Kuwaitis would like. In addition to asking Kuwaitis what they wanted, the survey might have elicited more novel responses had it also inquired what factors draw Kuwaitis to foreign destinations and which attractions they visit while there. This would have helped to gauge the tourism and travel habits of Kuwaitis, which in some way would be productive in understanding the opportunities associated with the domestic tourism market for this particular segment.

As for the third market, visitors from outside the region (most often business travellers, conference attendees or military personnel) find it difficult to know what sites exist, where they are located and when they are open. Among the most visited sites are museums, some of which have websites, while others do not. Few of the websites are up to date. The tourism plan seeks to remedy this situation by working to improve ground transportation and/or providing tours. Currently, one often needs to possess the phone number of a reputable taxi company and have a good idea of what the fare is before setting out, as few taxis use meters. Taxi drivers are almost entirely expatriates with a limited knowledge of locations and of English. Consequently, passengers are often at a loss or feel frustrated at having to direct drivers to their intended destination.

Having recognized what is missing from Kuwait's tourism product, identified what Kuwaitis want to see developed, and determined what would enhance visits for international travellers, the plan goes on to consider the challenge of gaining acceptance for tourism from the local populace. As Aziz (2002: 154) noted:

> When it is recognized that no Islamic country has yet managed to accommodate the needs of Western tourists without compromising the religious and cultural expectations of most of its own people, it is evident that tourism development for much of the region is still some distance away.

According to a survey conducted for the Tourism Master Plan, the Kuwaiti aversion to tourism development stems from the belief that multinational corporations will design and manage projects solely with Western tourists in mind. The feared outcome is that these tourist activities and attractions will lead to the disappearance of Kuwaiti culture (National Tourism Master Plan 2005: 29–30). The plan thus argues that by focusing on domestic tourism, Kuwaitis will realize that development is occurring on their behalf and for their enjoyment, rather than being based on foreign concepts aimed at indulging outsider preferences. Further, by training young Kuwaitis (both genders, the plan emphasizes) for tourism jobs, the industry will literally have a Kuwaiti face and represent Kuwaiti sensibilities. To ensure that nationals are active participants, the plan envisions a grant incentive scheme for young Kuwaiti entrepreneurs. To facilitate the public's acceptance of tourism, an action plan proposes the use of media, the utilization of prominent figures as spokespersons in favour of tourism and the establishment of a community relations unit within the KTA.

The National Tourism Master Plan appears realistic, hence doable – if one is willing to disregard the employment distinctions that exist between Kuwaitis and non-Kuwaitis. However, if the plan was executed, would the KTA become just another segment of the government bureaucracy, a means of employment for Kuwaitis? Further, could it change public attitudes regarding tourism and train young Kuwaitis to provide 'service with a smile'? At this point, there are no firm answers to these questions, because no appreciable progress has taken place. Like the tourism development plans in other Arab countries that go unimplemented, only to be reworked some years later (Fahmi 2008; Kelly 1998), the effort almost seems to be an end in itself. Indeed, the chairman of Kuwait's Supreme Tourism Committee has called for drawing up and activating a strategy for developing tourism, with no reported mention of the already existing Kuwait National Tourism Master Plan (*Times* 2015).

Conclusion and research implications

Based on the findings of the World Economic Forum's 2013 and 2015 reports on travel and tourism, the Kuwait National Tourism Master Plan and research conducted during the author's eight-year residency in Kuwait, this chapter has examined the reasons why tourism development is not significant in Kuwait. The obstacles can be summarized as follows: lack of attractive scenery, harsh climate and polluted environment, congested highways and poor airline connections, no nightlife or live entertainment, prohibition of alcohol, expensive hotels, inaccessible cultural sites and perceived regional instability. The main subjective obstacle is the Kuwaiti view that tourism is a threat to local culture and values. Additionally, one is hard pressed to imagine Kuwaitis being eager to replace expatriates in the low-paying service jobs characteristic of the tourism industry.

Thus, despite the recognized need to diversify the economy, create jobs and improve the quality of life for Kuwaitis, there is apparently no sense of urgency to meet these challenges on the part of decision makers. Nor is there a demand for tourism development on the part of cosmopolitan Kuwaitis, as long as they have the means to leave their country at will to enjoy recreation abroad. For less cosmopolitan or less affluent citizens, holding the line against the encroachment of alien cultures is far more important than making Kuwait more hospitable to outsiders. In terms of attracting foreign visitors, it may be sufficient for Kuwait to be a safe haven where fellow Arabs seek temporary respite from their home country's political upheavals, or to be a family-centred vacation destination for Saudis who come to visit relatives, shop and enjoy the relative openness of Kuwaiti society.

Since there is currently no formalized tourism industry in Kuwait or any prospect of a tourism boom in the immediate future, perhaps the most beneficial focus of further research would be to examine Kuwaiti attitudes towards tourism, but as guests rather than hosts. It would be useful to have hard data on such basic information as why Kuwaitis travel for leisure, how they choose their destinations and which attractions they visit while spending $5 billion annually on foreign tourism (*Kuwait Times* 2013a). Wynn (2007) sheds some light on the general subject in her comparison of the behaviour of Western and Saudi tourists in Egypt. Nonetheless, further research is called for. For example, one might ask whether (or how) Kuwaitis fit into MacCannell's (1987) theory of the 'new leisure class' in search of authentic experiences. With more leisure time than is available in many societies, especially given early retirement packages and extended holidays, as well as considerable discretionary income and good language skills, many Kuwaitis travel abroad frequently and in relative comfort; yet, little is known of how deeply they experience foreign cultures.

In conclusion, Kuwait could be characterized as a gated community whose citizens, already threatened once with political extinction, are determined to maintain dominance despite a numerically superior expatriate community. Consequently, establishing an industry aimed at attracting more foreigners is not an attractive prospect to many Kuwaitis. Further, even if tourism in Kuwait was developed exclusively for citizens and fellow GCC residents, it is not regarded as a significant means of economic diversification compared to the level of income provided by oil. So, what should Kuwaitis do to guarantee their financial future? In July 2013, the Leaders Group, which holds the government contract for developing tourism in Kuwait, issued a report noting that Kuwaiti individuals and corporations invested US$37 billion abroad in 2012 (mostly in the United States and Europe), of which US$7 billion was, somewhat ironically, for tourism projects (*Kuwait Times* 2013b). Thus, forward-looking Kuwaitis are doing as their peripatetic ancestors did, whether merchants, seafarers or bedouin: they are insuring their future by expanding their base of operation beyond their borders – financially, residentially and recreationally.

References

AlSayyad, N. (2001) 'Global norms and urban forms in the age of tourism: manufacturing heritage, consuming tradition', in N. AlSayyad (ed.) *Consuming Tradition, Manufacturing Heritage: Global Norms and Urban Forms in the Age of Tourism*, London: Routledge, pp. 1–33.

Arab News (2014) 'Kuwait posts $45 billion budget surplus but warned of risks', *Arab News,* 2 October. Available online at www.arabnews.com/economy/news/638381 (accessed 20 January 2015).

Arab Times (2015) 'Kuwait government's descision to cut number of expatriates may backfire', *Arab Times*, 25 December. Available online at www.arabtimesonline. com/news/kuwait-govts-descision-to-cut-number-of-expats-may-backfire-analysis-considers-decision-controversial/ (accessed 25 January 2015).

Aziz, H. (2002) 'The journey: an overview of tourism and travel in the Arab/Islamic context', in D. Harrison (ed.) *Tourism and the Less Developed World: Issues and Case Studies*, Cambridge, MA: CABI Publishing, pp. 151–159.

Bristol-Rhys, J. (2012) 'Socio-spatial boundaries in Abu Dhabi', in M. Kamrava and Z. Babar (eds) *Migrant Labor in the Persian Gulf*, London: Hurst, pp. 59–84.

Burns, P. (2007) 'From hajj to hedonism? Paradoxes of developing tourism in Saudi Arabia', in R. Daher (ed.) *Tourism in the Middle East: Continuity, Change, and Transformation*, Clevedon: Channel View, pp. 215–236.

Calderwood, J. (2010) 'Tribal MPs in Kuwait protest at threat to take citizenship from dual passport holders', *The National*, 12 March. Available online at www.thenational. ae/news/world/middle-east/tribal-mps-in-kuwait-protest-at-threat-to-take-citizenship-from-dual-passport-holders (accessed15 April 2014).

Cordesman, A. (1997) *Kuwait: Recovery and Security after the Gulf War*, Boulder, CO: Westview Press.

Daher, R. (2007) 'Reconceptualizing tourism in the Middle East: Place, heritage, mobility, and competitiveness', in R. Daher (ed.) *Tourism in the Middle East: Continuity, Change, and Transformation*, Clevedon: Channel View, pp. 1–69.

Fahmi, W. S. (2008) 'Global tourism and the urban poor's right to the city: spatial contestation within Cairo's historical districts', in P. M. Burns and M. Novelli (eds) *Tourism Development: Growths, Myths, and Inequalities*, Wallingford: CAB International Publishing, pp. 159–191.

Fineren, D. (2013) 'Gulf states take baby steps in energy efficiency', *International Herald Tribune*, 11 April.

Gulf News (2013) 'Kuwait plans quotas and limits for expatriates', *Gulf News*, 28 March. Available online at http://gulfnews.com/news/gulf/kuwait/kuwait-plans-quotas-and-limits-for-expatriates-1.1164103 (accessed 14 April 2014).

Kamrava, M. and Z. Babar (2012) 'Situating labor migration in the Persian Gulf', in M. Kamrava and Z. Babar (eds) *Migrant Labor in the Persian Gulf*, London: Hurst, pp. 1–20.

Kelly, M. (1998) 'Jordan's potential tourism development', *Annals of Tourism Research*, 25(4): 904–918.

Kuwait National Tourism Master Plan (2005), Kuwait: Kuwait Ministry of Planning and Kuwait Ministry of Information.

Kuwait Times (2013a) 'Kuwait placed last in GCC tourism, 101 worldwide: Al-Anjari', 23 September. Available online at http://news.kuwaittimes.net/kuwait-placed-last-gcc-tourism-101-worldwide-al-anjeri/ (accessed 14 April 2014).

Kuwait Times (2013b) 'Kuwaitis invested $37 billion abroad in 2012', 23 July. Available online at http://news.kuwaittimes.net/kuwaitis-invested-37-billion-abroad-in-2012/ (accessed 14 April 2014).

Kuwait Times (2015) 'Kuwait lacks professional hotel apartments: report'. Available online at http://news.kuwaittimes.net/website/kuwait-lacks-professional-hotel-apartments-report/ (accessed 4 April 2016).

Longva, A. (1997) *Walls Built on Sand: Migration, Exclusion, and Society in Kuwait*, Boulder, CO: Westview Press.

MacCannell, D. (1987) *The Tourist: A New Theory of the Leisure Class*, 2nd edn, Berkeley, CA: University of California Press.

Robinson, M. (2001) 'Tourism encounters: Inter- and intra-cultural conflicts and the world's largest industry', in N. AlSayyad (ed.) *Consuming Tradition, Manufacturing Heritage: Global Norms and Urban Forms in the Age of Tourism*, London: Routledge, pp. 34–67.

Sajjad, V. S. (2013) 'Cut in expats to loss of valuable experience', *Arab Times*, 14 April. Available online at www.arabtimesonline.com/NewsDetails/tabid/96/smid/414/ArticleID%20/194308/reftab/73/t/Cut-in-expats-to-loss-of-valuable-experience/Default.aspx (accessed 14 April 2014).

Sontag, S. (1973) *On Photography*, New York: Picador.

Times (2015) 'Kuwait looking to set up tourism authority', *Times*, 1–7 November. Available online at www.google.com/search?q=kuwaits+looking+to+set+up+tourism%2C+times&ie=utf-8&oe=utf8#q=kuwait%27s+looking+to+set+up+tourism+authority%2C+times (accessed 4 April 2016).

Urry, J. (2002) *The Tourist Gaze: Leisure and Travel in Contemporary Societies*, 2nd edn, London: Sage.

World Economic Forum (2013) *The Travel and Tourism Competitiveness Report: Reducing Barriers to Economic Growth and Job Creation*, Geneva: World Economic Forum.

World Economic Forum (2015) *The Travel and Tourism Competitiveness Report: Growth Through Shocks in 2015*, Geneva: World Economic Forum. Available online at www3.

weforum.org/docs/TT15/WEF_Global_Travel&Tourism_Report_2015.pdf (accessed 22 March 2016).

Wynn, L. (2007) *Pyramids and Nightclubs: A Travel Ethnography of Arab and Western Imaginations of Egypt, from King Tut and a Colony of Atlantis to Rumors of Sex Orgies, Urban Legends about a Marauding Prince, and Blonde Belly Dancers*, Austin, TX: University of Texas Press.

7 Tourism development in the Kingdom of Saudi Arabia

Determining the problems and resolving the challenges

Erdogan Ekiz, Zafer Öter and Marcus L. Stephenson

The Kingdom of Saudi Arabia comprises the majority of the Arabian Peninsula and is the second largest country in the Arab world. Despite political tensions in the Middle East, the Kingdom continues to attract tourists, albeit of a particular type. Being the unique destination for Hajj and Umrah, the country possesses a range of prominent pilgrimage sites. Stereotypical perceptions of the country prevail, notably 'wells spurting oil, kings as rich as Croesus' (Shearer 2010: 291).

In 2014, the president of the Saudi Commission for Tourism and National Heritage (SCTNH), formerly known as the Saudi Commission for Tourism and Antiquities (SCTA), praised two resolutions made by the Council of Ministers on 13 January 2014. One of these resolutions approved the King Abdullah Project for Care of Cultural Heritage of the Kingdom, and the other resolution approved financial and administrative support to SCTNH to enable it to carry out its mandate (SCTNH 2014). There is an emerging awareness at government level of a vision of tourism that reaches beyond the country's popular image as a holy destination. The challenge, however, concerns the extent to which this vision is achievable.

This chapter deals with comprehending tourism development pathways in Saudi Arabia. It initially presents an overview of tourism demand and discusses the key facilitators of tourism development. The chapter then evaluates the challenges that the country faces in developing tourism, particularly the rigidity of the tourist visa regime, limited public transportation systems, over-reliance on foreign workers, political turmoil in the Middle East, safety issues in pilgrimage sites and zones and economic concerns pertaining to low oil prices. The discussion also contextualizes the effect of modernization projects on tangible heritage and culture, and the physical environment. Understanding the challenges to tourism development in Saudi Arabia helps to provide a background for identifying feasible ways forward for the Kingdom to become an internationally recognized tourism destination.

Therefore, the work will discuss a range of opportunities for resolving ongoing concerns and challenges in diverting tourism away from an over-reliance on pilgrimage, notably the differentiation of tourism markets as well as the advancement of new products and niche markets. Particular focus thus concerns how Saudi Arabia can develop leisure tourism by attracting a range of leisure-related market segments. The discussion also indicates the mechanisms for encouraging nationals to work in the tourism and hospitality industry, and the need for Saudi Arabia to develop international and domestic transportation structures. Importantly, the chapter demonstrates that the future success of Saudi Arabia as a tourism destination will inevitably depend on the extent to which it can proactively deal with the challenges it faces.

Tourism in the Kingdom of Saudi Arabia

At the end of 2015 there were around 31.5 million people living in the Kingdom, representing an annual growth rate of 2.4 per cent. Saudi Arabian nationals comprise 67 per cent of the population, that is, 21.1 million in total, and expatriates comprise 33 per cent, that is, 10.5 million in total (Al Arabiya 2016). Saudi Arabia significantly represents a young and urban population. Estimated figures for 2014 indicate that 46.9 per cent of the population are between 0 and 24 years of age. Data for 2011 indicate that 82.3 per cent of the total population live in urban areas (Index Mundi 2015).

Saudi Arabia received 15,098 million international tourist arrivals in 2014 (UNWTO 2015). It is currently forecasted that tourist arrivals will increase to 32,273,000 in 2026, generating Saudi Arabian riyal (SAR) 55.9 billion (US$14.9 billion) in expenditure and representing an average annual increase of 5.2 per cent (WTTC 2016). Nonetheless, the direct contribution of tourism and travel to GDP was around SAR 59.6 billion (US$15.9 billion) in 2015, representing just 2.5 per cent of the total GDP. It is anticipated that by 2026 the direct contribution will be SAR 93.9 billion (US$25 billion), representing 2.8 per cent of the total GDP (WTTC 2016). In 2014, around 65 per cent of visitors originated from countries in the Middle East, 22 per cent from South Asia and 8 per cent from Africa. The top four source countries visiting the Kingdom were from the Middle East, Kuwait being the most popular, followed by Egypt, United Arab Emirates (UAE) and then Qatar (MAS and SCTNH 2015a). Religious motivation is certainly the most popular reason as to why international tourists travel to Saudi Arabia. In 2014, around 65 per cent of tourists visited Saudi Arabia for religious reasons (Umrah and Hajj), and 26 per cent of them visited for family reasons. Around 71 per cent of inbound tourists prefer to visit holy sites, 22 per cent wish to engage in shopping and the remainder travel to engage in other activities, notably recreational and/or environmental based activities (MAS and SCTNH 2015a).

There were around 48 million domestic tourist trips in 2015, compared to 37.1 million in 2014. Nonetheless, Saudis have been travelling out of the country in ever-increasing numbers. There were 20.9 million outbound trips in 2015, compared to 19.8 million in 2014. The total night trips for domestic tourism was 247.2 million in 2015 compared to 165.3 in 2014, and the total nights for outbound tourist trips was 251.7 million in 2015, compared to 174.3 million in 2014 (figures for 2015 incorporate estimates only for the month of December) (MAS and SCTNH 2015b). Despite the potential for the advancement of the domestic tourism industry, encouraged by the vastness of the country, nationals do place significant emphasis on outbound travel. High levels of per capita income have strengthened the outbound travel market for the mobile elite, who have become fixated on frequent visits abroad. Nonetheless, the popularity of domestic tourism for nationals is pilgrimage, where they benefit from being able to travel to the holy sites without the same amount of advance planning and resource allocation as international tourists. In 2014, more than 45 per cent of nationals visited Makkah, and 28 per cent visited Madinah. However, only 15 per cent of nationals actually visited the Eastern Province. During their travel, 42 per cent of Saudis preferred to stay in private houses, 36 per cent wished to stay in hotels and 12 per cent favoured furnished apartments (MAS and SCTNH 2015a). Rimmawi and Ibrahim (1992) note that Saudi Arabian nationals generally prefer their own privacy, and large hotels have a tendency to accommodate this preference rather than small-size hotel rooms, where privacy is relatively limited. There is potential to strengthen the premium hotel market, especially the quality of service and facilities. The quality of the Kingdom's four-star hotels, as rated by customers on Trip Advisor, is low in comparison to competing destinations (McKinsey Global Institute 2015).

In 2015, travel and tourism produced around 727,500 jobs directly, representing 6.4 per cent of total employment. It is forecasted that by 2026, travel and tourism will account for 1,085,000 jobs directly, an annual increase of 3.9 per cent over the next 10 years (WTTC 2015). From 2005 to 2014, the number of nationals working in the tourism and hospitality sector quadrupled to more than 200,000, representing 27 per cent of direct employment. Nationals commonly work in transportation, notably in the airline, railway and car rental industries (McKinsey Global Institute 2015).

Identifying tourism development's key facilitators

Saudi Arabia is home to Islam's two holiest shrines, Al-Masjid Al Nabawi (Prophet's Mosque) in Medinah and Al-Masjid Al-Haram (Holy Kaaba) in Makkah. As these two cities are central destinations for pilgrims, they are often visited within the same package tour (Henderson 2010). As pilgrimage to Makkah (Hajj) is one of the five pillars of Islam, it should be performed at least once in a person's lifetime. Hajj is a mega event that takes place once a year following the lunar calendar, which means there is no specific season of the year for Hajj. Accordingly, the special concentration of Hajj pilgrims varies over time (see Chapter 13).

The country's religious heritage facilitates a positive destination image for first-time visitors (Eid 2012; Henderson 2010). This attribute should ensure that the destination maintains continual visitation and interest, if indeed the country does not endure a major disaster or crisis. Nonetheless, the genesis of Islam in Saudi Arabia and its auspicious religious attractions provide a rather unique platform for marketing itself as a tourism destination, beyond the pilgrimage dimension. Although non-Muslims cannot enter the holy cities, as these places are designated sacred spaces rather than touristic spaces, the religious foundations and culture of the country ensure that it embodies an authentic appeal.

The economic strength of the country has been another primary facilitator of tourism development and the advancement of the industry. Saudi Arabia is a leading oil producer that enables strong commercial and political relationships to exist, not only with Arab and/or Muslim countries but also with the rest of the world (Mansfeld and Winckler 2004). The Kingdom's oil wealth is a key facilitating factor strengthening its potential to expand its tourism and hospitality industry. Saudi Arabia's proximity to emerging markets like India, China, Turkey and other GCC states strengthens its economic viability. Moreover, Saudi Arabia has favourable tax regulations, and cheap fuel and energy supplies for foreign investors. The state's past budgetary surplus encouraged the development of new mega-project investments, especially in relation to the transportation industry and infrastructure (see Chapter 4). The financial strength and competitiveness of its economy has logically facilitated tourism (pilgrimage) development, simply because of the degree to which the economy has been able to invest and reinvest in infrastructure, accommodation and mega-developments. However, as will be discussed in the next section, due to the recent plummeting of oil prices there are some concerning signs that the economy is weakening, which could be considered as a potential threat to future tourism development.

Political stability has been a major facilitator of tourism development, where political relationships with global policy-makers and key states have facilitated degrees of stability in the Kingdom. Accordingly, the Kingdom is a member of several international organizations including the Global Cooperation Council (GCC), Organization of the Petroleum Exporting Countries (OPEC) and Organization of Islamic Cooperation (OIC) (Daniels *et al.* 2012). Additionally, the country had the third highest military budget expenditure in the world, spending around US$80.8 billion in 2014, an amount which quadrupled in the past decade (Kaplan 2015). However, the contribution decreased to US$46 billion in 2015 (Carey and Fatta 2016). Nonetheless, as discussed in the next section, such stability is becoming tenuous because of changing political circumstances in the region.

One important asset that Saudi Arabia possesses concerns a strong 'knowledge economy' based on the production and reproduction of relevant sources of knowledge and expertise, crucial in facilitating tourism development. The mobility of expatriates, both blue- and white-collar workers, is also helping to advance knowledge exchange in the country. As a result, large transportation and hospitality-based investments are emerging. Years of experience and knowledge in organizing a mega-event, notably Hajj, is certainly a confidence factor for Saudi Arabia to deliver tourism events on a large scale (Alsini and Ekiz 2013). Furthermore, this GCC state is starting to develop significant knowledge and understanding of the tourism and hospitality industries, particularly in relation to operational astuteness, strategic foresight and investment intelligence. Accordingly, since the early 2000s, Saudi Arabia started to pay significant attention to the tourism industry, assisted by the work of the Tourist Information and Research Centre (MAS) of SCTNH. Furthermore, large hospitality investments have taken place.

Such global hospitality brands as InterContinental, Crowne Plaza, Hilton and Mövenpick encourage expatriates to work in the Kingdom, having the experience and know-how as well as the capacity for knowledge transfer (Zamani-Farahani and Henderson 2010). Hence, given that nationals have not been significant role models in the tourism and hospitality industry, imported knowledge can be crucial, especially in the medium term. Nonetheless, such knowledge can be productively utilized, reproduced and advanced within a localized context, thereby broadening and enriching a nationalized approach to tourism and hospitality employment.

Identifying key inhibitors and challenges to tourism development

One significant inhibitor that Saudi Arabia faces in expanding the tourism industry concerns its strict visa regime, making it difficult to obtain visas for tourism reasons and thus limiting its potential to diversify its visitor base. Visa applications have to be processed several weeks prior to travel, and applicants need to secure local Saudi Arabian sponsors. Female travellers under 30 years of age cannot travel alone without the company of their husband or brother, and unmarried couples cannot travel together. However, the state has started to recognize that visa restrictions could ease with time, especially as there is an emerging realization that a more liberalized visa regime would equate to increased tourism numbers. India, for instance, changed its visa processes so that nationals from such countries as Australia, Finland, Germany, Japan and New Zealand could receive visas on arrival rather than applying for them in their home country (Paris 2015). The Kingdom recognized the need to encourage more inbound tourism and develop the tourism industry to facilitate flexible forms of inward mobility. In 2014, the Umrah Plus Programme was launched, where Umrah pilgrims from 65 countries were permitted to reside in the country for one month, with the intention of visiting archaeological, heritage and religious sites (*Gulf Business* 2014). At the time of writing (May 2016) this development has yet to come into full effect, though it is scheduled to commence in the coming months. Nevertheless, the current visa restrictions that are in place inevitably inhibit tourism development beyond pilgrimage and, therefore, limit the advancement of Saudi Arabia's tourism industry.

One important challenge for the tourism industry is to ensure that tourists have access to public transportation. Car and fuel prices are cheaper in Saudi Arabia, which entices nationals and residents to be vehicle dependent. In Jeddah, for instance, only 2 per cent of journeys made within the city are by public transport, whereas 89 per cent are by private transport and 9 per cent by walking (Elledge 2014). Getting people to use public transportation and move away from a reliance on automobiles is also paramount in a region notable for a high carbon footprint. Nonetheless, given an automobile-dependent culture, there is a significant need to advance the development of public transportation.

The fact that the Kingdom is over-dependent on foreign workers represents a significant challenge for the tourism and hospitality industry. Although external expertise is necessary and enables knowledge exchange (as indicated earlier), the downside is that the industry could misrepresent the national and cultural particularities of the country itself if it does not encourage substantial local involvement and representation, as, arguably, is the case in the UAE (cf. Stephenson *et al.* 2010). Nonetheless, however, there is a fundamental gap between the labour market and available national human resources (Hazbun 2006). The Kingdom's aura of conservativeness may obstruct nationals from working within the tourism industry (Al-Hamarneh 2013). However, the limited role of nationals in the industry, especially the hospitality sector, could decrease the authenticity of 'Saudi Arabia' as a tourism destination.

The political turmoil in the Middle East potentially affects people's positive perceptions of, and their confidence in travelling to, the region as a whole. Any disorder in the region can indeed pose some risks for tourism development. Although political turmoil in the Middle East has not directly affected the Kingdom's tourism industry, especially as the preference for pilgrimage relates to religious needs and obligations rather than touristic choice (Zamani-Farahani and Henderson 2010), plans for future tourism developments could make Saudi Arabia more vulnerable to political disruptions. Political tensions are starting to represent a threat to Saudi Arabia's potential to develop a buoyant tourism industry. The Saudi Arabia military intervention in Yemen and the Kingdom's internal concerns relating to sectarian allegiances could raise some concerns regarding safety issues. The Risk Advisory Group and Anon have now classified Saudi Arabia along with Kazakhstan, Zimbabwe and Angola as having a risk rating for political turmoil (Anderson 2016).

Nevertheless, one area affecting positive perceptions of personal safety concerns the Kingdom's pilgrimage industry. The death of around 769 pilgrims in 2015, caught in a stampede during the final major rite of Hajj in the city of Mina, could have an impact on pilgrimage participation in the medium term, particularly as there was strong criticism of the tragedy from Iran, Indonesia, Nigeria and Syria. Accordingly, Iran has continued with this concern and recently declared that Iranian pilgrims will not attend Hajj because of the lack of safety assurance. This decision may be reflective of the ongoing political disputes between the two countries (*Guardian* 2016). The stampede, however, was not an isolated incident. One week prior to the tragedy, a crane collapsed at Makkah's Grand Mosque, killing more than 100 pilgrims. Furthermore, a stampede at a bridge in Mina in 2006 resulted in the death of 364 pilgrims (Whitman 2015). Travelling to pilgrimage sites from other countries could also become a safety concern for groups travelling via ground transportation, especially in light of several recent road accidents. Accordingly, in March 2016, 19 Egyptians died when a bus overturned on the road between Madinah and Makkah. In the same month, 16 Palestinian pilgrims died in another road incident when their bus crashed in the southern region of Jordan while travelling to Saudi Arabia (Smith 2016).

Despite the fact that Saudi Arabia has a strong economy, recent economic volatilities associated with global oil price fluctuations are questioning the extent to which the country and region will be able to fully maintain economically sustainability. Although the country had benefitted from soaring oil prices in the past, leading to a budget surplus, constant fluctuations and a significant downturn in oil prices could affect ongoing investments and the economic stability of the country. Although the country has an estimated US$757.2 billion sovereign wealth funds, and where oil and gas comprise around 50 per cent of the country's GDP, this GCC state arguably needs to pursue tourism development as oil recently lost half of its market value. By late 2015, a barrel of Brent crude, for instance, traded at US$48.87 compared to US$114 in June 2014 (Ellyatt 2015). Also in 2015, the country has a budget deficit of around US$98 billion (Al Maeena 2016). Nonetheless, the 'Vision 2030', announced in April 2016, emphasized the government's intention for the country to undergo social and economic reform to break away from oil dependency. The plan points to the need for the financial reform of major institutions (e.g. Aramco and the Public Investment Fund) and for a system to be established encouraging residents to live and work longer in the Kingdom. Furthermore, objectives were set concerning an increase in the use of renewable energy, more capacity to cater for pilgrims and a doubling of the number of United Nations Educational, Scientific and Cultural (UNESCO) archaeological sites (*National* 2016). The plan also emphasized the need to develop tourism projects over large coastal areas (Taylor 2016).

However, new challenges could emerge concerning market competition in the Gulf region, making it even more of a necessity to pursue a diversification strategy based significantly on the advancement of the service sector industries. The decision in January 2016 to halt international sanctions against Iran could represent a challenge to the markets and economies of GCC states (Gardner 2016), if it is upheld and Iran is successful in opening up old and new markets.

Modernization brings with it sustainable challenges and environmental concerns in Saudi Arabia and, indeed, in other GCC states (see Chapter 12). Taher and Hajjar (2014) acknowledge that Saudi Arabia's rapid economic development and growth has encouraged over-consumption, leading to the drainage of natural resources and long-term deterioration of the natural environment. The authors draw attention to the problems associated with the cheap availability of oil and gas, stating:

> Noteworthy are non-targeted subsidies (i.e., subsidies being provided to all people, regardless of their income level and status), which has contributed to encouraging the current high domestic consumption of oil in transportation, utilities and other sectors of the local economy (2014: 1).

They thus point to shoreline damage, hotel waste dumped in the sea, excessive carbon dioxide emissions and irreversible damage to coral reefs as key indicators of environmental degradation. The challenge is to ensure that the environmental impacts of tourism development are formally monitored and analyzed. Indeed, lack of sustainable tourism development, without clear environmental impact assessments in place, can adversely affect tourism development (Seddon and Khoja 2003; Seddon 2000).

Modernization is also transforming heritage sites in the Kingdom. In Makkah, for instance, various sites associated with Prophet Muhammad have been redeveloped or earmarked for development. There have been plans to build an underground car park and a metro line on the site of the House of Mawlid where the Prophet was purportedly born. There have also been significant redevelopments taking place at the Grand Mosque itself, where a large extension has replaced historic stone columns and vaults (*Guardian* 2013).

The ethnic origins, lifestyle patterns and religious traditions of international tourists (not pilgrims) would represent a challenge to Saudi Arabia's tourism industry. It is a well-established contention that tourism brings with it concerns relating to the acculturation and cultural dependency of local destinations and societies (Turner and Ash 1975). The political impact that the tourism industry can have on local values, beliefs and traditions is a notable concern in a society that pursues a deeply conservative approach to everyday life, aligned to the traditions and principles of Shari'a law. This impact could indeed lead to intensified social tensions between the hosts and guests, and have a profound impact on cultural norms.

Identifying productive ways forward

In comparison to the competitive threat of other key tourism destination players in the region, especially UAE, Saudi Arabia should, arguably, advance its tourism development strategy in terms of considering its unique features and selling points. Therefore, the country needs to look towards ways to differentiate its tourism markets. The current 160 tour operators that do exist in the Kingdom cater mainly for religious tourists (Sahoo 2014), so there are opportunities for the industry to branch out to wider markets. Tourism policy-makers, destination marketers and tourism operators ought to understand the changing global profile of traveller needs. Accordingly, it is important to come to terms with the increased independent mobility of new travellers, as well as the rise of metasearch and information technology-based travel behaviour, which loosens the control of operators and destinations over tourism products (Ali *et al.* 2014).

As clarified, one major challenge Saudi Arabia faces is the one-dimensional nature of tourism development, exemplified through the dominance of religious tourism. Nevertheless, to ensure that Saudi Arabia's tourism industry moves towards a multidimensional approach to tourism development, the advancement of new products and niche markets would be necessary. Accordingly, meetings, incentives, conventions and exhibitions (MICE) tourism would be one productive way forward. To this end, King Abdulaziz University, supported by SCTNH and the Ministry of Education, is launching an event management programme to educate young Saudis in managing MICE tourism (Ekiz and Ekiz 2015). The development of the new city, King Abdullah Economic City, is one such illustration of how the tourism industry can develop this sector (Johnson 2010). However, the challenge is a crucial one as business travel spending only generated 9.6 per cent of direct travel and tourism GDP in 2015, that is, around

SAR 7.4 billion (US$1.9 billion). Leisure travel spending, however, generated 90.4 per cent, that is, SAR 69.3 billion, in the same year (US$18.5 billion) (WTTC 2016).

However, the greatest potential concerns the development and expansion of the leisure market and related sub-markets. Retail tourism, for instance, would be a positive response to the prospects of a growing retail sector in Saudi Arabia. Large-scale developments are taking place in the region to attract new brands, exemplified through increased investment in the construction of hypermarkets and shopping malls (Oxford Business Group 2014). Nonetheless, the Kingdom has substantial natural and archaeological resources that could appeal to both domestic and international tourists. There are over 3,000 kilometres of coastline and 1,300 islands in total, of which 1,150 islands are located in the Red Sea and 150 in the Persian Gulf. The Red Sea's Farasan Islands are attractive to the diving tourism industry but also have significant archaeological sites associated with Roman settlements (Cooper and Zazzaro 2014). The southwest part of the Kingdom, notably the Al Bahah region, has an abundance of natural resources (e.g. mountains, forests and wildlife areas) and archaeological sites (Som and Al-Shqiarat 2013). The UNESCO World Heritage Site of Mada'in Saleh, located in the northwest of the country, comprises 140 tombs carved out of a hillside and covering 175 hectares of land. The site originates from the first-century Nabataean kingdom and is situated at an intersection of trading routes leading to Greece, Egypt, Persia and India (Elvin 2010). Consequently, there are opportunities for the Saudi Arabia to promote a range of destination attributes and local assets. Accordingly, there is considerable scope for marine/diving tourism, nature/wellness tourism, activity tourism, eco-tourism and cultural heritage tourism – all positioned under the wider leisure market.

There is potential for nationals to work more in the hotel industry, and some promising initiatives are already in place. Several international hotel chains developed specific training programmes to ensure that nationals occupy 30 per cent of available positions within the hotel sector (Sahoo 2015). The Saudi Arabian government is also addressing this concern, where SCTNH has dedicated considerable resources to work towards a nationalization of employment programme. The movement towards the 'Saudization' of tourism and hospitality institutions is paramount (cf. Abu Tayeh and Mustafa 2011). According to Sadi and Henderson (2005: 251), Saudization involves 'finding local workers to perform specific jobs that only immigrants have been willing to handle, particularly at the prevailing wage rates. It also means training citizens for top-level management jobs'. Despite the economic benefits to accrue from tourism, the country's over-reliance on imported labour is problematic given the increasing unemployment rates among nationals. The opportunities for nationals working in the tourism industry are immense. In 2014, for instance, there were around 17,135 rooms under construction, exceeding the amount of rooms under construction in the UAE (16,627) and Qatar (5,633) (Sahoo 2014).

As tourists can, arguably, aspire for authentic quests (cf. MacCannell 1976), the role of nationals as tourism and hospitality employees (and employers) is crucial, as they can act as cultural ambassadors of their country, enriching the tourism experience and increasing the value of tourism products. For visitors, attractions not only concern cultural heritage assets and natural beauty but also the human element (Burns 2007). Therefore, one useful way forward would be for nationals to undergo formal training as cultural brokers, such as tour guides, helping to represent their society and culture to the visitors. This initiative could have a knock-on effect by strengthening the brand personality of the destination (Hosany *et al.* 2006). Nonetheless, education has a crucial role in ensuring that nationals are familiar with the opportunities associated with working in the tourism and hospitality industries. Despite significant knowledge exchange in the country (as illustrated earlier), however, there is still a need for improvement of the education sector. The concept of tourism education is a recently established one in Saudi Arabia, and thus the number of colleges and higher educational institutions offering diplomas and degrees in this field is negligible. Therefore, great potential exists in investing more in educational units to encourage people to consider career opportunities in the tourism and hospitality sectors, as well as helping employees and employers attain the necessary professional skills and competencies to make a successful contribution to the advancement of the industry.

One niche market that would help to strengthen the cultural representations of the industry is that of Islamic tourism. The world population of Muslims totalled around 1.6 billion in 2010, forecasted to rise to 2.8 billion in 2050. Based on the predicted number of adherents, Islam will overtake Christianity as the world's largest religion by the end of the century (Lipka and Hackett 2015). There is scope for the advancement of a range of Islamic products, notably Shari'a-compliant hotels and restaurants, halal modified food products, halal accredited food outlets, Islamic festivals and events, halal-friendly airports, Islamic cruises and Islamic heritage villages (Stephenson 2014a). Stephenson (2014a) indicates that the Islamic dimension has considerable potential for not only the Muslim market but also non-Muslims, especially those interested in cultural appreciation, well-being and health-conscious lifestyles. Thus, it is of no surprise that Saudi Arabia could be the region's top Islamic tourism destination, especially in terms of visitor numbers. Travel is strongly evoked in the Qu'ran, where several sura motivate Muslims to travel and discover the world, notably Al-Ankabut, Al-Anam and Mohammed (Jafari and Scott 2014). In addition to pilgrimage, there are also spiritual journeys associated with 'Rihla', which concern quests for knowledge, business and health (Haq and Wong 2010). In many ways, the Kingdom has the Islamic resources and infrastructure already in place. The objective, however, is to adapt, formalize and strategically position these resources through a destination brand which embraces and celebrates Islamic tourism and hospitality. Nonetheless, being located close to North Africa, which has a significant Muslim population, ensures that there are considerable opportunities for market expansion.

However, Saudi Arabia's future as an internationally recognized tourism destination depends on long-term investments in transportation infrastructure. Investments in the aviation industry, for instance, would help to bring more tourists to Saudi Arabia, encouraging the Kingdom to become a potential central hub for international flights (Medawar 2014). The development of tourism in the Middle East is a prime example of how tourism and aviation can act together as drivers of tourism growth. One pertinent illustration concerns the expansion of Dubai's tourism industry in conjunction with the evolution of Emirates airline and the intensification of its new international routes from the mid-1990s, as well as the competitive rise of low-cost airlines (LCAs) thereafter (Stephenson 2014b). There are some promising signs that LCAs are developing in Saudi Arabia, exemplified by the establishment of Flynas in 2007. Saudi Arabian Airlines recently announced the establishment of a new LCA in 2017, known as Flyadeal (*Arab News* 2016). With an expanding LCA market, low-cost airstrips and smaller airports (e.g. Taif Regional Airport) in less centralized locations are, arguably, crucial for a wider tourism development plan that spreads tourism development throughout the nation. As LCAs are a recent phenomenon in the Kingdom, they should help encourage the expansion of the domestic market.

Ongoing domestic speed train projects are likely to have a positive effect on the advancement of the tourism industry by boosting domestic tourism and facilitating transportation priorities for Hajj and Umrah. Nevertheless, tourism development should be fully integrated with transportation networks, especially those located in such major destinations as Makkah, Medinah and Jeddah. In Jeddah, for instance, given the realization that the city has an inadequate transportation system, there are plans to establish an integrated public transport network that involves metro lines, a commuter rail line, a waterfront tramway and a network of boat services. It is anticipated that the network will open in 2022, with an estimated cost of around SAR 45 billion (US$12 billion) (Elledge 2014). The Haramain High Speed Rail Network (HHR) is anticipated to open in 2018 and will involve a 450 km line from Makkah to Jeddah and Madinah (*Railway Gazette* 2016). The network should be able to transport more than 50 million passengers per year and have a daily carrying capacity of 160,000 passengers (Briginshaw 2015).

Conclusion and research implications

Through pilgrimage, Saudi Arabia attracts a reliable tourism segment. However, the dominance of pilgrimage tourism has meant that the country has monopolized the inbound tourism market, which has been counter-effective to the equitable spreading of tourism development throughout the country. If other segments of the tourist market are to grow, it is crucial to understand the changing profiles in the global travel market. Nonetheless, what is fundamental is that any movement towards more diversified forms of tourism would require a social transformation of the national psyche.

As the chapter highlighted, there is a real need for increased investments in integrated public transportation systems and a concerted movement towards localized human resource systems and structures, as well as a liberalized visa regime. Accordingly, this chapter discussed in detail the various challenges Saudi Arabia faces, especially in the context of its potential to become an international tourism destination. One notable challenge identified is the country's modernization agenda, which is already having a considerable cultural and environmental impact. This is certainly another crucial area that requires more critical investigation in relation to developing planning directives to consider sustainable alternatives.

Another major challenge concerns the Kingdom's dependency on oil income, which is vulnerable to price fluctuations. Therefore, diversification of economic activities is of great importance to the government's '2030 Vision'. Accordingly, there will be a need to track the objectives of this plan and assess the extent to which economic and social reform will positively have an impact on tourism development. As also indicated, diversification of tourism types is crucial, and Saudi Arabia has great potential for the development of various types of tourism, notably domestic tourism, business tourism and leisure tourism. Such markets would help spread tourism across diverse regions of the country and thus challenge the extant pattern of pilgrimage tourism, which concentrates only on specific places and spaces. There is, thus, substantial scope for considering the expansion of other Islamic forms of tourism and hospitality, attracting both Muslim and non-Muslim tourists. Given that the Islamic dimension embodies an emphasis on well-being and lifestyle, it would partly enrich the leisure tourism market. Moreover, such a development would reflect the Kingdom's religious and cultural traditions but, at the same time, encourage tourism development beyond pilgrimage tourism. Given these attributes, it would be useful for market research to ascertain the market potentiality and investment prospects of Islamic tourism and hospitality.

Although product diversification can be positive, new types of tourism would necessitate a paradigmatic change in the different layers of Saudi society, and thus there would need to be transformations in the social attitudes of destination societies. Accordingly, key concerns relate to the degree to which the Kingdom can embrace socio-cultural transformations associated with tourism development, but at the same time uphold its heritage and traditions. Anthropological enquiry and ethnographic-based research would be appropriate to forecast the readiness of culture and the potential of destination societies to embrace transformations in the tourism market. Research concerning local perceptions of tourism development would need to be developed, taking into consideration dimensions of age, social class, gender and ethnicity. This multidimensional approach to understanding local (and national) perceptions is crucial in ascertaining the degree to which particular population sets embrace specific forms of tourism and travel behaviour. Such an approach is vital if the diversification the tourism industry is to move beyond its religious element.

References

Abu Tayeh, S. N. and M. H. Mustafa (2011) 'Toward empowering the labor Saudization of tourism sector in Saudi Arabia', *International Journal of Humanities and Social Science*, 1(3): 80–84.

Al Arabiya (2016) 'Saudi Arabia's population grows buy 2.4 per cent', *Al Arabiya*, 4 February. Available at http://english.alarabiya.net/en/News/middle-east/2016/02/04/ Saudi-Arabia-s-population-grows-by-2-4-percent.html (accessed 5 May 2016).

Al-Hamarneh, A. (2013) 'International tourism and political crisis in the Arab world – from 9/11 to the "Arab Spring"', *e-Review of Tourism Research (eRTR)*, 10(5/6): 100–109.

Ali, R., J. Clampet, J. Schaal and S. Shankman (2014) 'The 14 trends that will define travel in 2014', Skift. Available online at http://skift.com/travel-trends/14-global-trends-that-will-define-travel-in-2014/ (accessed 20 June 2014).

Al Maeena, T. A. (2016) 'Air of confidence over vision 2030', *Gulf News*, 28 May. Available online at http://gulfnews.com/opinion/thinkers/air-of-confidence-over-vision-2030-1.1836278 (accessed 29 May 2016).

Alsini, I. and H. E. Ekiz (2013) 'Saudi Arabia: a great potential for Chinese hoteliers', *China Tourism and China Hotel-Branding Forum 2013*, 16–18 May, UNWTO, Hong Kong Polytechnic University, Hong Kong.

Anderson, R. (2016) 'Saudi Arabia risks coup or insurrection – global study', *Gulf Business*, 14 April. Available online at www.gulfbusiness.com/articles/country/ saudi-arabia/saudi-arabia-placed-at-risk-of-coup-or-insurrection-inglobalstudy/?utm_ medium=email&utm_campaign (accessed 2 May 2016).

Arab News (2016) 'Saudi creates new low cost airline', *Arab News*, 18 April. Available online at www.arabnews.com/saudi-arabia/news/912146 (accessed 29 May 2016).

Briginshaw, D. (2015) 'Saudi HS line "on schedule" for 2017 opening', *International Railway Journal*, 7 July. Available online at www.railjournal.com/index.php/middle-east/saudi-hs-line-on-schedule-for-2017-opening.html (accessed 6 June 2016).

Burns, P. (2007) 'From Hajj to Hedonism? Paradoxes of developing tourism in Saudi Arabia', in R. F. Daher (ed.) *Tourism in the Middle East: Continuity, Change, Transformation*, Clevedon: Channel View Publications, pp. 215–236.

Carey, G. and Z. Fatta (2016) 'Saudi Arabia to overhaul military in plan for life after oil', *Chicago Tribune*, 25 April. Available online at www.chicagotribune.com/news/ sns-wp-blm-saudi-60838adc-0afe-11e6-bc53-db634ca94a2a-20160425-story.html (accessed 7 May 2016).

Cooper J. P. and C. Zazzaro (2014) 'The Farasan Islands, Saudi Arabia: towards a chronology of settlement', *Arabian Archaeology and Epigraphy*, 25: 147–174.

Daniels, J. D., L. H. Radebaugh and D. P. Sullivan (2012) *International Business: Environments and Operations*, 10th edn, New York: Prentice Hall.

Eid, R. (2012) 'Towards a high-quality religious tourism marketing: the case of Hajj service in Saudi Arabia', *Tourism Analysis*, 17(4): 509–522.

Ekiz, K. and Ekiz, H. E. (2015) 'Preparing tomorrow's tourism leaders', *Saudi Voyager*, 18: 17–21.

Elledge, J. (2014) 'Saudi Arabia's second city is building an entire public transport system from scratch', *City Metrics*, 14 August. Available online at www.citymetric. com/politics/saudi-arabia-s-second-city-building-entire-public-transport-system-scratch(accessed 29 January 2016).

Ellyatt, H. (2015) 'Tourism to replace oil in Saudi Arabia?', *CNBC*, 1 October. Available online at www.cnbc.com/2015/10/01/tourism-to-replace-oil-economy-in-saudi-arabia. html (accessed 29 January 2016).

Elvin, F. (2010) 'Saudi Arabia's pre-Islamic treasures come to the Louvre', *Guardian*, 10 August. Available online at www.theguardian.com/culture/2010/aug/10/louvre-saudi-arabia-exhibition (accessed 29 January 2016).

Gardner, D. (2016) 'Iran poses an economic challenge to Saudi Arabia', *Financial Times*, 26 January. Available online at www.ft.com/intl/cms/s/0/427186b0-c419-11e5-b3b1-7b2481276e45.html (accessed 4 February 2016).

Guardian (2013) 'As the Hajj begins, the destruction of Mecca's heritage continues', *Guardian*, 14 October. Available online at www.theguardian.com/artanddesign/2013/oct/14/as-the-hajj-begins-the-destruction-of-meccas-heritage-continues (accessed 27 May 2014).

Guardian (2016) 'Iranian pilgrims won't attend hajj amid row with Saudi Arabia', *Guardian*, 29 May. Available at www.theguardian.com/world/2016/may/29/iran-pilgrims-will-not-attend-hajj-amid-row-with-saudi-arabia (1 June 2016).

Gulf Business (2014) 'Saudi Arabia mulls lifting visa restrictions', *Gulf Business*, 5 May. Available online at www.gulfbusiness.com/articles/industry/tourism/saudi-arabia-mulls-lifting-visa restrictions/ (accessed 21 June 2014).

Haq, F. and H. Y. Wong (2010) 'Is spiritual tourism a new strategy for marketing Islam?', *Journal of Islamic Marketing*, 1(2): 136–148.

Hazbun, W. (2006) 'Explaining the Arab Middle East tourism paradox', *The Arab World Geographer/Le Géographe du monde arabe*, 9(3): 201–214.

Henderson, J. C. (2010) 'Religious tourism and its management: The Hajj in Saudi Arabia', *International Journal of Tourism Research*, 13(6): 541–552.

Hosany, S., Y. Ekinci and M. Uysal (2006) 'Destination image and destination personality: An application of branding theories to tourism places', *Journal of Business Research*, 59(5): 638–642.

Index Mundi (2015) *Saudi Arabia Demographics Profile 2014*, 30 June. Available online at www.indexmundi.com/saudi_arabia/demographics_profile.html (accessed28 November 2015).

Jafari, J. and N. Scott (2014) 'Muslim world and its tourisms', *Annals of Tourism Research*, 44(1): 1–19.

Johnson, D. J. (2010) 'Tourism in Saudi Arabia', in N. Scott and J. Jafari (eds) *Tourism in the Muslim World* (*Bridging Tourism Theory and Practice, Volume 2*), Cambridge: Emerald Group Publishing Limited, pp. 91–106.

Kaplan, M. (2015) 'Saudi Arabia White House visit: growing military, regional security concerns could mean boom for US weapons industry', *International Business Times*. Available online at www.ibtimes.com/saudi-arabia-white-house-visit-growing-military-regional-security-concerns-could-mean-2082028 (accessed 9 March 2015).

Lipka, M. and C. Hackett (2015) 'Why Muslims are the world's fastest-growing religious group', Factank, 23 April, Pew Research Centre. Available online at www.pewresearchorg/fact-tank/2015/04/23/why-muslims-are-the-worlds-fastest-growing-religious-group/ (accessed 8 September 2015).

MacCannell, D. (1976) *The Tourist: A New Theory of the Leisure Class*, London: Macmillan.

Mansfeld, Y. and O. Winckler (2004) 'Options for viable economic development through tourism among the non-oil Arab countries: the Egyptian case', *Tourism Economics*, 10(4): 365–388.

MAS and SCTNH (2015a) *Tourism Statistics 2014*, Tourism Information and Research Centre (MAS) of the Saudi Commission for Tourism and National Heritage, Riyadh, Kingdom of Saudi Arabia.

MAS and SCTNH (2015b) *Tourism Statistics 2015*, Tourism Information and Research Centre (MAS) of the Saudi Commission for Tourism and National Heritage, Riyadh, Kingdom of Saudi Arabia.

McKinsey Global Institute (2015) *Saudi Arabia Beyond Oil: The Investment and Productivity Transformation*, McKinsey and Company, December.

Medawar, A. (2014) 'Shaping the future of travel in the Gulf Cooperation Council: big travel effects', Amadeus, 5 June. Available online at www.amadeus.com/blog/05/06/ middle-east-report/ (accessed 10 October 2014).

National (2016) 'Saudi Arabia Vision 2030: eight things you need to know about the reform plan', *The National, 26 April. Available online at* www.thenational.ae/business/ economy/saudi-arabia-vision-2030-eight-things-you-need-to-know-about-the-reform-plan (accessed 2 May 2016).

Oxford Business Group (2014) *Saudi Retail Set for Growth*, 4 February. Available online at www.oxfordbusinessgroup.com/news/saudi-retail-set-growth (accessed 15 June 2015).

Paris, N. (2015) 'New Indian visa rules require British tourists to provide fingerprints', *Telegraph*, 20 February. Available online at www.telegraph.co.uk/travel/destinations /asia/india/11426221/New-Indian-visa-rules-require-British-tourists-to-provide-fingerprints.html (accessed 12 August 2015).

Railway Gazette (2016) 'Haramain High Speed Rail opening delayed', *Railway Gazette,* 12 May. Available online at www.railwaygazette.com/news/high-speed/single-view/ view/haramain-high-speed-line-opening-delayed.html (accessed 7 June 206).

Rimmawi, H. S. and A. A. Ibrahim (1992) 'Culture and tourism in Saudi Arabia'. *Journal of Cultural Geography*, 12(2): 93–98.

Sadi, M. A. and J. Henderson (2005) 'Tourism in Saudi Arabia and its future development', *Cornell Hospitality Quarterly*, 46(3): 247–257.

Sahoo, S. (2014) 'Saudi Arabia opens its doors to tourism', *The National*, 2 April. Available online at www.thenational.ae/business/industry-insights/tourism/saudi-arabia-opens-its-doors-to-tourism (accessed 10 January 2016).

Sahoo, S. (2015) 'Hotel groups in Saudi Arabia set up training for nationals', *The National*, 7 September. Available online at www.thenational.ac/business/travel-tourism/hotel-groups-in-saudi-arabia-step-up-training-of-nationals (accessed 10 January 2016).

SCTNH (2014) *King Abdullah Project for Care of Cultural Heritage of the Kingdom*, Riyadh, Kingdom of Saudi Arabia. Available online at www.scta.gov.sa/en/Antiquities-Museums/CulturalDimension/Pages/KingAbdullahProjectCulturalHeritageCare.aspx (accessed 11 June 2014).

Seddon, P. J. (2000) 'Trends in Saudi Arabia: increasing community involvement and a potential role for ecotourism', *Parks*, 10(1): 11–24.

Seddon, P. J. and A. R. Khoja (2003) 'Saudi Arabian tourism patterns and attitudes', *Annals of Tourism Research*, 30(4): 957–959.

Shearer, I. (2010) *Saudi Arabia, Oman, UAE, and Arabian Peninsula*, London: Lonely Planet Publications.

Smith, D. (2016) 'Many Egyptian pilgrims killed in Saudi Arabia bus crash', *Guardian*, 19 March. Available online at www.theguardian.com/world/2016/mar/19/many-egyptian-pilgrims-killed-in-saudi-arabia-bus-crash (accessed 29 May 2016).

Som, A. P. M and M. Al-Shqiarat (2013) 'Effects of tourism seasonality to a highland destination: evidence from Al Bahah Province', Saudi Arabia, *International Journal of Innovations in Business*, 2(6): 630–644.

Stephenson, M. L. (2014a) 'Deciphering "Islamic Hospitality": developments, challenges and opportunities', *Tourism Management*, 40: 155–164.

Stephenson, M. L. (2014b) 'Tourism, development and destination Dubai: cultural dilemmas and future challenges', *Current Issues in Tourism*, 17(8): 723–738.

Stephenson, M. L., K. A. Russell and D. Edgar (2010) 'Islamic hospitality in the UAE: indigenization of products and human capital', *Journal of Islamic Marketing*, 1(1): 9–24.

Taher, N. and B. Hajjar (2014) *Energy and Environment in Saudi Arabia: Concerns and Opportunities*, London: Springer International Publishing.

Taylor, A. (2016) 'Holidays in Saudi Arabia? The Kingdom's ambitious post-oil tourism plan', *Washington Post*, 27 April. Available online at www.washingtonpost.com/news/worldviews/wp/2016/04/27/holidays-in-saudi-arabia-the-kingdoms-ambitious-post-oil-tourism-plan/ (accessed 2 May 2016).

Turner, L. and J. Ash (1975) *The Golden Hordes: International Tourism and the Pleasure Periphery*, London: Constable.

UNWTO (2015) UNWTO Tourism Highlights, 2015 edn, United Nations World Tourism Organization. Available at www.e-unwto.org/doi/pdf/10.18111/9789284416899 (accessed 29 November 2015).

Whitman, E. (2015) 'Saudi Arabia Hajj tourism crisis 2015: after deadly stampede, will royal family improve security?' *International Business Times*, 30 September. Available online at www.ibtimes.com/saudi-arabia-hajj-tourism-crisis-2015-after-deadly-stampede-will-royal-family-improve-2121059 (accessed 27 January 2016).

WTTC (2016) *Travel and Tourism, Economic Impact 2016*, Saudi Arabia, World Travel and Tourism Council. Available online at www.wttc.org/-/media/files/reports/economic%20impact%20research/countries%202016/saudiarabia2016.pdf (accessed 5 May 2016).

Zamani-Farahani, H. and J. C. Henderson (2010) 'Islamic tourism and managing tourism development in Islamic societies: the cases of Iran and Saudi Arabia', *International Journal of Tourism Research*, 12(1): 79–89.

8 Tourism development challenges in Qatar

Diversification and growth

Nadine Scharfenort

Although Qatar has modernized rapidly, it has not yet developed into an internationally renowned tourism destination. Nonetheless, the hosting of the 2022 FIFA World Cup is ensuring that Qatar is receiving worldwide visibility. Hosting such prestigious events can act as a catalyst for urban and economic development, especially if planned well and with strategic foresight. Generally, flagship events are viewed not just as 'cash cows' but also as opportunities for advertising destinations and signifying a country's hospitality, which can transform perceptions of destinations and challenge national stereotypes (Gold and Gold 2009: 3–4).

The country's economic wealth has generously funded the rapid expansion of its infrastructure, especially the transportation and hospitality industries. Along with strategic planning and destination brand initiatives, Qatar intends to invest around US$20 billion in tourism infrastructure in preparation for the 2022 FIFA World Cup (Oxford Business Group 2013). An additional US$65 billion is targeted for new transportation projects, for instance, the expansion of Doha Port and a new cruise terminal, a metro line in Doha and a railway network in Qatar (Zawya 2012). Around US$11.5 billion is planned for investment until 2030, including the development of a diverse range of projects, for instance, tourism-related sport and cultural infrastructure, beach and wellness resorts and investments in training facilities and educational programmes (QNTSS 2030 2014: 23). Although investments tend to be associated with World Cup-related activities, they provide new opportunities for the expansion of tourism and the long-term development of the service sector industries.

Qatar has established ambitious tourism development goals. According to the Qatar National Tourism Sector Strategy 2030 (QNTSS 2030 2014), released in February 2014, the country aims to position itself as a 'world-class hub with deep cultural roots' (QTA 2014). The intention is to attract around 7 million annual arrivals by 2030 (*DTZ* 2016). Travel and tourism contributed to 2.8 per cent of the GDP directly in 2015, equating to Qatari riyal (QAR) 18.8 billion (US$5.16 billion) and projected to increase by 4.4 per cent in 2016 (World Travel and Tourism Council 2016). Qatar experienced around 2.93 million tourist visits in 2015, representing a 3.7 per cent increase from the previous year (Walker 2016).

This chapter will provide a general outline of the historical and contemporary context of tourism development in Qatar and then will present an analysis of the country's tourism potential and performance. Importantly, the subsequent discussions identify the challenges affecting tourism development and the difficulties the country faces in its attempts to become an international tourism destination, especially in relation to dealing with modern infrastructural needs and limited tourism facilities. The work also indicates ways forward to move beyond such challenges, especially through the development of forms of tourism associated with culture, sport and the meetings, incentives, conventions and exhibitions (MICE) market, comprehending the degree to which Qatar can fully modernize and successfully cater for increased tourism numbers.

Tourism sector development and strategy in Qatar

Qatar's hospitality industry evolved from the mid-twentieth century, when basic accommodation facilities catered for oil workers and experts visiting or working in Qatar. The Bismillah Hotel, located close to Souq Waqif and built in the 1960s, was the first main hotel in Doha. However, the first internationally branded hotel to open in 1982 was the Sheraton Doha Hotel and Conference Center, designed by William L. Pereira Associates and located in the West Bay (Kultermann 1984: 54). Due to its pyramid shape, it has been a significant landmark for over three decades. In the 1980s, Doha had 18 hotels, including four luxury hotels: Gulf, Ramada, Sheraton and Sofitel. The number of rooms and apartments in Doha in 1983 totaled around 1,878, comprising 2,753 beds (Ritter 1985: 140).

More rapid forms of development, however, occurred after Sheikh Hamad bin Khalifa Al Thani, father of the ruling Emir Sheikh Tamim bin Hamad Al Thani, took leadership in 1995. During his reign, Sheikh Hamad introduced measures to improve the overall infrastructure, and encouraged cultural and educational development. Such developments stimulated a process of liberalization (albeit slow) of the economy, with economic investments focused on favourable sectors, especially liquefied natural gas (Fromherz 2012: 83). It is only recently, however, that urban studies have begun to pay specific attention to the social, economic and cultural fabric of Doha (cf. Adham 2008; Rizzo 2013; Salama and Wiedmann 2013; Scharfenort 2013). Indeed, the city escaped academic discussion for a number of crucial years (Elsheshtawy 2008).

The foundations for strategic tourism development were laid in the early 2000s, when the state-owned Qatar Tourism Authority (QTA) was established and Qatar renewed its membership of the United Nations World Tourism Organization (UNWTO) in 2002. QTA's prime objectives were to organize and enable tourism industry development in the country. A US$15 billion Tourism Master Plan was unveiled in 2004 to establish Qatar as a premier destination (Sherwood 2006). Its main goals concern the intention to build and develop local infrastructure, attract international hotel chains and develop museums, theme parks and entertainment facilities. Other key goals concern the expansion of the national airline (i.e. Qatar Airways) and the strategic improvement of transportation services for passengers and freight. The Emiri Decree (no. 46) in 2009 ensured that QTA would undergo restructuring and that one of its central functions would concern marketing activities and destination branding, especially to positively strengthen Qatar's overall image. To develop new target groups and markets, Qatar promotes itself as an outstanding yet evolving tourism destination based primarily on leisure, business, culture and sport. QTA participates in international roadshows and premier business-to-business trade shows and conventions, with an intention to establish potential customer contacts and create new business engagements through networking opportunities. Recent activities have taken place through marketing events held in Asia Pacific, Europe and the Middle East, such as the Arabian Travel Market, World Travel Market and International Tourism Bourse (*The Peninsula* 2011a). In 2014, QTA opened satellite offices in Germany, Saudi Arabia and Singapore (Marhaba 2015).

In late 2013, QTA released the Qatar National Tourism Sector Strategy 2030 (QNTSS 2030 2014), serving as a road map for the country's tourism growth. The QNTSS 2030 was developed in conjunction with the objectives and guiding principles of the Qatar National Vision 2030 (GSDP 2008), as well as the country's first National Development Strategy 2011–2016 (GSDP 2011), emphasizing the need to reduce Qatar's reliance on the energy sector and diversify its economic activities. QTA attempts to play a key role in the diversification process, helping to promote tourism development as well as coordinate and foster consultation between all key tourism stakeholders (Rivera 2013; Scott 2013), thereby acting as an interface between those private and public actors who are concerned with the development and expansion of tourism activities. In an endeavour to promote Qatar as an attractive destination for business, leisure and cultural activities, QTA intends to continue to expand its network of branches in core markets outside the Arab world, particularly in Europe and Asia. Therefore, according to the QNTSS 2030 (2014), the most effective way forward is to strive towards attaining the optimal market mix and ensuring social sustainability. Emphasis should be placed on the development of a strategy focusing on attracting Arab tourists and families seeking leisure, entertainment, comfort and well-being, as well as prioritizing the attraction of high-income travellers looking for 'unique and authentic' destinations, and 'experienced travellers' pursuing 'new destinations and cultures' (QNTSS 2030 2014: 24). Despite implying that Qatar is an inimitable destination, which can actually be contested because of its association as a 'dull' destination (see the following discussion), the strategy acknowledged that the market mix should include 'budget conscious' Arab travellers (2014: 24).

The Qatar Museum Authority (QMA), a state institution formed in 2005 with a mission to contribute to Qatar's international profile in arts and culture, is involved with the management of all historical and archaeological sites in Qatar, along with the supervision of all museums. It also organizes and sponsors related events and is involved in the development of a number of new museums scheduled to open by 2020 (www.qm.org.qa/en). The new National Museum of Qatar, due to open in 2016 and designed by Jean Nouvel, will exist within the design framework of the original National Museum building. This particular museum, which opened in 1975 within the build of the old Amiri Palace, achieved the Aga

Khan Award for Architecture due to the way in which it was restored (Excell and Rico 2013).

Members of the Al Thani royal family are known art collectors, and the QMA has been involved in important and expensive art acquisitions, notably Cézanne's *The Card Players* and Munch's *The Scream* (Jordan 2012). In late 2008, the Museum of Islamic Art, designed by architect I. M. Pei, had already opened its doors to the public. The museum promotes itself as possessing one of the world's most complete collections of Islamic artifacts, with items originating in Central Asia, India, Mesopotamia, Egypt and Spain (www.qm.org.qa/en). The emphasis on cultural capital feeds into national strategic objectives to establish Qatar as a cultural and educational hub. The focus on education, along with a drive towards being perceived as a knowledge-based economy, has been demonstrated through the instrumental establishment of Doha's Education City along with the work of the Qatar Foundation, which is a non-profit organization supported by the government to help sustain education, science, research and community development. The city incorporates a range of educational and research based institutions, including US and European university campuses (Henderson 2015).

Trends in the tourism and hospitality sector

Qatar received 2.93 million tourists in 2015, of which 44 per cent originated from Gulf Cooperation Council (GCC) countries, an increase of 4 per cent from the previous year. While tourist numbers from Asia, including Oceania (including Australia and New Zealand), recorded a fall of 6 per cent to 735,841, visitors from China had actually increased by 15 per cent from the previous year. Tourists from Europe also increased 4 per cent from the previous year, representing around 437,122 visitors (Walker 2015). Unfortunately, statistical data do not provide sufficient information to assess domestic tourism mobility flows in Qatar, but this market has potential. Doing business in the capital can be combined with overnight stays. The decision to extend the city visit may be for business purposes, or related to an increased supply of suitable and attractive accommodation and entertainment facilities. With the rise in the hotel resort stock, Qatari families could be increasingly tempted to take 'staycations' within their home country, residing in local hotel resorts. Most of the international hotels and chains (e.g. Grand Hyatt Doha, Intercontinental, Sheraton and Ritz Carlton) offer special weekend and 'Eid' holiday rates, as well as special summer packages for whole families during the off-peak season. Such deals can attract both nationals and residents to take full advantage of the available discounts.

Due to the growing demand and capacity expansion in the convention sector, Qatar expects a further rise in the number of visitors in the coming years, especially given the anticipated increase in new hotels and apartments. The opening of the 317-room Melia Doha, located inside the Bin Samikh Tower in West Bay, is one notable development. Furthermore, around 57 new hotels and 13 hotel apartments are due for completion over the next five years, especially as the country expands its hospitality offerings in advance of the surge of visitors expected during the 2022 World Cup. However, occupancy rates for 2015 stood at around an average of 71 per cent (Walker 2016), despite the fact that in the first quarter of that year occupancy rates reached an average rate of 82 per cent (*Gulf Times* 2015). Notwithstanding Qatar's need to anticipate intensified numbers in 2022, the key challenge will be the extent to which the country can rapidly accelerate tourism demand.

In 2014, the tourism sector directly contributes around QAR 13.6 billion (US$3.74 billion) to the country's GDP, representing 4 per cent of the non-extraction economy. However, tourism indirectly contributes QAR 28 billion (US$7.69 billion) to GDP, consisting of 8.3 per cent of the total non-extraction GDP; with around 61,000 jobs directly sustained by the industry (Marhaba 2015). There has been a remarkable increase of the number of hotels, from 18 in 2000 (MDPS 2015: 36) to 97 hotels in 2015 (and 22 hotel apartments) (Aguilar 2015). Although this equated to 119 hotels and apartments, along with more than 20,000 rooms (Walker 2016), FIFA's minimum requirement of 60,000 rooms by 2022 (FIFA 2010: 5) seems to be a very ambitious target. Rooms in the non-luxury sector will be in high demand for the tournament, especially as around 84 per cent of the current supply of hotels concern four- and five-star establishments (*DTZ* 2016). Until recently, Qatar has placed much emphasis on developing hotels in the luxury segment (Oxford Business Group 2013).

A noteworthy demographic indicator is the male-to-female ratio of hotel guests, illustrating the gendered composition of tourists. From the data available in 2011, only 35.1 per cent of all occupants in Qatar were female, and 28.2 per cent of all female visitors were GCC nationals, 9.5 per cent were Arab nationality and 62.3 per cent were of 'foreign' origin (MDPS 2012). Qatar is, thus, significantly frequented by male travellers, which is not surprising as the state is evolving as a MICE destination based on a market segment overrepresented by male professionals. Moreover, a range of facilities and activities in public spaces target male visitors in particular, and are less attractive to female travellers. Reasons for this could be a lack of leisure activities and shopping options, and limited transportation services, gender sensitive hotels and family facilities. Accordingly, the cultural norms of Qatari society may be one indication of the fact that public spaces and places are not effectively developed, nor prioritized, for female consumers. Hence, it is not always socially acceptable for women to venture outside of the home domain without an accompanying male relative, that is, the 'mahram'.

Limitations to tourism development

Qatar still has limited tourism infrastructure and does not offer the variety of urban landscapes and places of interest that, perhaps, other GCC states do, notably the United Arab Emirates (UAE). In contrast to the shopping destination of Dubai, for instance, Doha generally lacks leisurely indoor attractions, which are imperative for tourism destinations suffering from unfavourable climate conditions for a significant proportion of the year. Accordingly, outdoor recreation is normally only possible during the winter months from November to April. Therefore, a strong and varied supply of air-conditioned indoor facilities is, arguably, necessary to cater successfully for locals, residents and visitors. Although there were no fewer than 14 malls and shopping centres of different sizes in 2013, there is still a significant opportunity for Doha to develop modern shopping facilities and leisure-based infrastructure. Such shopping venues as City Center, Landmark, Centrepoint and Villaggio are starting to respond to increased demand in retail products. Nonetheless, changing lifestyle habits and increasing expatriate populations are having a significant effect on customer expectations. There is, thus, a need to expand specialized shopping activities and respond to specific entertainment preferences, as well as develop a range of gastronomic experiences which cater for international (i.e. cosmopolitan) and localized (i.e. cultural) tastes. Nevertheless, the lack of sufficient shopping facilities and a limited number of international brands encourages individuals, especially female citizens, to head for Dubai (Harrison 2014). This concern is starting to be addressed through a focus on the construction of such new shopping malls as the Mall of Qatar and Doha Festival City Mall, both scheduled to open in the latter part of 2016, as well as the Doha Marina Mall that is scheduled to open in 2017. Following the Dubai model concerning the purpose of developing shopping malls as an integral part of the tourism experience (cf. Stephenson and Ali-Knight 2010), the Mall of Qatar will not only focus on the retail of consumer products and dining experiences, but also embrace various forms of family entertainment and hospitality-based activities (*Gulf Times* 2016).

The absence of an abundance of entertainment and leisure facilities, as well as insufficient public space, are the main reasons to consider Doha as a non-touristic and unattractive city, despite the fact that there are increased attempts to transform the city through various urban developments and targeted events. Moreover, Doha has faced the problem of trying to counteract negative perceptions of the city as a non-vibrant tourism destination. At the turn of the twenty-first century, the *Lonely Planet* (2000: 175) noted: 'Around the Gulf, Doha […] has earned the unenviable reputation of being the dullest place on earth, and you'll be hard-pressed to find anyone who'll claim the place is exciting'.

Even in relation to developing localized forms of cultural-based tourism development, Qatar has much to do. There are only a few places in Qatar that attract significant archaeological interest, despite the fact that the country owns more than 200 estimated archaeological sites, largely located outside of Doha (GSDP 2011: 206). Qatar's heritage sites date from the seventeenth century and include ruins of fishing villages, forts, houses and towers. Many of these sites are deteriorating and in a poor state of repair. Nonetheless, Qatar received its first United Nations Educational, Scientific and Cultural Organization (UNESCO) World Heritage Site designation in 2013, when Al Zubarah Archaeological Site, an abandoned walled coastal town around 150 kilometres northeast of Doha, with trading links across Arabia, the Indian Ocean and Western Asia, was added to UNESCO's World Heritage List (UNESCO 2013).

Given that the production of a positive image can be seen as an intangible asset of a tourism-led growth strategy (Morakabati *et al.* 2014), Qatar is certainly eager to move away from past associations of being perceived as being boring, unambitious and uncultured. The rapid construction of a strong destination image and the desire to become a high-profile luxury destination, offering a range of entertainment facilities and leisure-based opportunities, are mechanisms by which this GCC state aims to develop a new global image as an international tourism destination. However, regardless of such potentiality, and despite a general acknowledgement that tourism development can be important, tourism may indeed clash with the region's conservative traditions and culture.

Consequently, while Dubai is commonly accepted as a comparatively liberal and trendy metropolis with little threat of civil unrest and low crime rates (Henderson 2006: 91), Qatar remains concerned about its regional standing in the Islamic community and being perceived to be too liberal. While the state is predominantly Wahhabi, it is less conservative than Saudi Arabia and, to some degree, influenced by Westernized lifestyles. After Qatar won the FIFA World Cup 2022 bid in 2010, matters such as alcohol consumption, dress codes and human rights have been the subject of considerable debate, both inside and outside of the state. Nonetheless, there has also been a sense of unease about attracting (mass) tourism within the context of a conservative society (Scharfenort 2012: 221–222).

The development of culture, sport and MICE tourism

In 2011, QTA released a brochure entitled '48 Hours in Qatar', which was distributed at most hotels and tourism sites. It recommends a two-day itinerary involving the main attractions in Doha, notably Souq Waqif, Museum of Islamic Art, the Corniche, Katara and The Pearl, as well as other parts of the country including Al Zubarah Fort and the Pearl Merchant's House. The itinerary recommends participation in such recreational activities as golfing, dune bashing, quad biking, dhow cruise dining, shopping and camel racing. One of the main attractions for both visitors and residents within Doha is Souq Waqif (Figure 8.1), where the structure and style of the original buildings were fully restored in 2008. The development of a wide range of recreation and leisure activities is fundamental to the long-term cultural development of Doha as an accommodating and livable city, which is integral to Qatar's wider aspirations to exploit and utilize its potential as well as present itself as a global tourism destination (Scharfenort 2014).

A steady rise in business- and family-based events has been crucial for the hospitality industry. The holy month of Ramadan and Muslim-based holidays encourage family-based consumption patterns to develop (MDPS 2014a, 2014b). Furthermore, music festivals, theatrical performances, sporting contests, cultural shows and artistic events are increasingly presented at different sites. The Katara Amphitheatre, Opera House, Drama Theatre, National Theatre, Aspire Dome and Khalifa Stadium (Figure 8.2) are major examples of such sites. Doha became 'Arab Capital of Culture' for 2010, a UNESCO-based initiative since 1996, to promote Arab culture and encourage cultural development in the Arab region. A diverse range of entertainment activities accompanied the cultural year,

Figure 8.1   Souq Waqif.
Source: N. Scharfenort, May 2015.

Figure 8.2   Khalifa Stadium.
Source: N. Scharfenort, May 2015.

which also represented the inauguration of such cultural institutions as the Katara Cultural Village and Mathaf, which is the Arab Museum of Modern Art.

Qatar aims to brand itself globally as a premier location for hosting and enjoying sports. Although GCC states are not traditionally associated with possessing a sporting culture as such, sport has become a major component in the diversification plans of some of these states, notably Bahrain, Qatar and the UAE. Indeed, sport can act as an important tool to help redefine national and place identities. In 2006, Qatar was one of the first GCC countries to host a major international multi-sport event, the Asian Games, investing US$2.8 billion in sport-related infrastructure to ensure that sport becomes a key component of Qatar's drive to create a strong destination brand identity (Baabood 2008: 100–101). Foley, McGillivray and McPherson (2012: 109) indicate that this event really set the scene for locating Qatar within 'the global market of staging events'. These authors further claim that the event 'demonstrated to international media that it could deliver a spectacular opening ceremony on a scale never witnessed before and a cost never previously encountered' (2012: 109).

Doha is now developing itself as a centre for sports, accommodating institutions like the Aspire Zone Foundation, also known as Doha Sports City, incorporating sports stadia, medical facilities and the Aspire Dome – the world's biggest convertible indoor sporting hall (Scharfenort 2012: 215). Due to mild weather conditions in the winter season, visits from high-profile sport teams have placed Qatar firmly in the spotlight as a destination for mid-season workouts, training camps, rejuvenation programmes and rehabilitation schemes. Over the past few years, Qatar has also grown in popularity as the host for both annual and one-off sporting events. There are annual sporting events for tennis (e.g. Qatar ExxonMobil Open and WTA Tour Championships) and golf (e.g. the Commercial Bank of Qatar Masters), plus the Motor Bike Grand Prix, Cycling Tour of Qatar, Powerboat Grand Prix and Diving World Series. Qatar has also been the host for the AFC Asian Cup (2011) and the Arab Olympics (2011). These events all attract international attention, facilitating overall development and encouraging investment in tourist infrastructure (Scharfenort 2012: 214), as well as enhancing the hospitality industry.

However, the rationale behind these tourism-related developments relates to the planning tradition of 'boosterism', popular during the 1960s and 1970s and concerned with boosting tourism infrastructural developments through capital injection. This planning approach has been subject to significant criticism for excluding tourism destination residents from the decision-making and planning processes, and for the uncontrolled exploitation of resources for short-term economic gain (Sharpley 2008). Boosterism can actually be considered as a form of non-planning in that it has a significant effect on the economic, social and physical setting. Moreover, the hosting of mega-events in many ways exemplifies boosterism in that such initiatives are considered as 'inherently good and of automatic benefit to the host' (Hall 2008: 21), despite that fact that they may not always economically penetrate communities or lead to community betterment in the long term.

One potential profitable niche concerns the MICE market. According to QTA, a significant number of visitors are entering the country for commercial reasons, and the subsequent expansion of this domain should be encouraged (Zawya 2014). Thus, there have been some positive developments. The Doha Exhibition Centre, for instance, launched in 2007 under the supervision of the QTA, has been a major facility for exhibitions and events (*The Peninsula* 2011b). The Qatar National Convention Centre (QNCC), opened in December 2011 in the grounds of the Qatar Foundation and designed by Arata Isozaki, is able to host up to 4,000 delegates (*Qataridiar* 2014). Consequently, there is a real intent to attract international events and indeed business tourism.

Comprehending tourism development challenges for the future

As indicated earlier, interregional tourism is strong, reflected in the high proportion of well over 40 per cent of visitors coming from other GCC countries. Muslim consumers in general are one of the fastest growing market segments in the world, potentially demanding a range of Islamic hospitality products and services (Stephenson 2014). Qatar's appeal as an Islamic tourism destination could intensify for the wider Muslim market. Like Dubai, Qatar could also introduce several themed festivals and entertainment events to nationals, expatriates and visitors alike, especially to encourage both inbound and domestic tourism (QTA 2010). Some event-based developments have taken place. The 2013 Eid Al-Adha Festival, for example, built on the success of the Eid Al-Fitr Festival, was launched by QTA to promote the country regionally as a family tourist destination (Pratap 2013).

In terms of offering easy access to the country, Qatar has at least turned into a major airline hub with the capacity to compete with other globally operating Gulf airports, such as Dubai and Abu Dhabi, along with their local airlines: Emirates, FlyDubai, and Etihad Airways. The quantity of passenger throughput at its international airport has more than trebled within a 9-year period, from 9.5 million in 2007 (DOH 2011, 2014) to over 30 million passengers in 2015, with an estimated 28 million passengers utilizing its facilities. This increase has partly been possible because of airport expansion developments. The Hamad International Airport (HIA), formerly known as Doha International Airport (DOH), became fully functional in May 2014 with the intention to continue its expansion to handle at least 50 million passengers and adopt a more integrated transport network in the run-up to the 2022 World Cup. Accordingly, this network involves developing stronger connecting infrastructure between HIA and Doha Metro, for instance (Walker 2015). Doha, with the support of Qatar Airways, is building a reputation for connectivity, albeit a significant number of passengers are transiting. Accordingly, one key government objective would be to encourage transit passengers to stopover within the destination itself.

Strong regional competition should not be underestimated, since destinations in neighbouring countries are already well developed (especially Dubai and

Manama), or have similar ambitious endeavours (especially Abu Dhabi). Within the Middle East, the oil-rich GCC states have built their economies primarily on the hydrocarbons industry. Dubai was one of the first destinations to develop its tourism infrastructure as an alternative source of revenue, especially through developing a clear brand strategy to attract visitors and position itself as a newly globalized economy (Govers and Go 2009: 81–82). Qatar will not find it easy to discover a niche, compete and defend its position.

Conclusion and research implications

Although Qatar modernized rapidly in the last 10 to 15 years, it has not yet developed into a renowned tourism destination. In late 2013, QTA launched its QNTSS 2030, which will serve as a road map for the country's tourism growth. Qatar's long-term objectives are concerned with establishing the country as a destination for culture and business, as well as a destination for sport, education and wellness. While benefitting from interregional tourism movement, Qatar needs to develop into a destination that encourages repeat tourism by offering easy access to the country and a strong hospitality and tourism infrastructure. Despite the launch of QNTSS 2030, Qatar has not fully developed a clear strategy for tourism development or even a distinctive identity necessary for destination branding. Qatar needs to significantly increase visitor numbers and hotel capacity, especially if it is to host the 2022 World Cup, and effectively respond to meet the ambitions of the state. It will need to broaden its market segments and establish hotels that cater to the middle-income markets.

Qatar is still in the early phase of development and yet to be discovered by the global tourism market. Accordingly, further research is required to monitor and evaluate the political, economic, social and environmental consequences for Qatar as a tourism destination. Research should be attentive to the overall organization and structure of the tourism sector, the influence of stakeholders and decision makers and the potential of certain forms of tourism to contribute significantly to the economy – notably domestic tourism and Islamic tourism. Not much is known about employment opportunities for locals in the tourism sector, particularly the crucial nature of nationalization objectives and targets (i.e. 'Qatarization') to the socio-cultural development of the tourism and hospitality sector. While attention to the economic impacts of tourism development often predominates over socio-cultural impacts, there may be a need to draw caution to some rapid forms of development that Qatar wishes to pursue. Accordingly, if visitor numbers continue to increase, there may well be a need to monitor the socio-cultural impacts of tourism over time and space. It would also be pertinent to focus on the gendered dimension of the destination, including market research dealing with ways in which the destination could be attractive to women tourists, not just as a separate entity but also in terms of family tourism and women's role as decision makers.

On the supply side, further investigation must build on areas and recommendations explicitly mentioned in the QNTSS 2030, especially to benchmark future developments and realities on the ground. Therefore, one key recommendation concerns the desire to attract a contrasting range of market segments, especially Arab visitors and families, high-income earners and budget-conscious Arab travellers. Nevertheless, the current tourism and leisure infrastructure focuses on higher-end market segments with higher prices, directed mainly to the more affluent groups. The supply of possible new product categories to cater for wider segments would be useful to research, especially to ensure that the destination is more socially and economically accessible. Although infrastructural developments are being prioritized, Qatar has not yet fully overcome its inactive image as an unexciting place to stay. It would be useful to conduct a longitudinal-based image analysis of people's perception of Qatar as a tourist destination, taking into consideration the background of the subjects and accounting for nationality, religion, gender, age and social class. Such data sets could help in forming a systematic understanding of the core factors that constitute Qatar's destination personality and appeal.

From a planning point of view, it would be insightful to have a closer look at the degree and quality of participation of the local population in the planning and decision-making processes involved in tourism development. Although the QNTSS 2030 developed following a nation-wide consultative process, through which QTA was able to gather the input and feedback of a wide range of stakeholders from the public and private sector, the local population apparently had no voice to express their opinion. Therefore, it would be pertinent to look at the potential relationship between civil society and tourism development and, indeed, to monitor the problems associated with the boosterist approach to tourism development and its impact upon Qatari society and culture.

One major challenge concerns the need for more tourism data and related official data concerning tourism development, as they are not always systematically forthcoming, nor is the government data-collection process always thoroughly clear. One major concern is the lack of access to data pertaining to the nature and purpose of domestic tourism, including places and venue selected and experienced.

From the Qatar National Vision 2030, the National Development Strategy 2011–2016 and the Qatar National Tourism Sector Strategy 2030, it can be concurred that World Cup-related activities have the capacity to enhance Qatar's perception and international image as a premier host for mega (sporting) events. Such developments should, thus, ensure a steady flow of visitors. Nonetheless, given the anticipation of a large number of visitors entering this small GCC state, it is essential to account for a form of development that considers local traditions and values in a sensitive manner, as well as economic and environmental sustainability. Therefore, there is a need for continued academic discussion and community-based research concerning Qatar's highly ambitious tourism development objectives. It is, arguably, important that a destination seeking an international tourism profile is able to develop a strategy based on feasible rather than simply desirable change, particularly if the destination is to achieve the respect of the wider public.

References

Adham, K. (2008) 'Rediscovering the island: Doha's urbanity from pearls to spectacle', in Y. Elsheshtawy (ed.) *The Evolving Arab City: Tradition, Modernity and Urban Development*, London: Routledge, pp. 218–257.

Aguilar, J. (2015) 'Hotel occupancy rates in Qatar steady at 71% – Qatar Tourism Authority', *Gulf Times*, 20 September. Available online at www.gulf-times.com/story/455825/Hotel-occupancy-rates-in-Qatar-steady-at-71 (accessed 9 April 2016).

Baabood, A. (2008) 'Sport and identity in the Gulf', in A. Alsharekh and R. Springborg (eds) *Popular Culture and Political Identity in the Arab Gulf States*, London: Saqi, pp. 97–120.

DOH (Doha International Airport) (2011) 'Statistical figures 2007 and 2008', 8 May. Available online at www.dohaairport.com/pdfs/2007-2008_DIA_Statistics.pdf (accessed 9 May 2012).

DOH (Doha International Airport) (2014) 'Passenger movements 2012-2013', 23 January. Available online at www.dohaairport.com/iwov-resources/DIA/en/PDFs/Stats/2007-2013_DIAStatistics.pdf (accessed 21 February 2014).

DTZ (2016) 'Q4 2015 Qatar market report: hospitality market overview', *DTZ*, 21 January. Available online at http://dtzqatar.com/press_releases/q4-2015-qatar-market-report-hospitality-market-overview/ (accessed 9 April 2016).

Elsheshtawy, Y. (2008) 'The great divide: struggling and emerging cities in the Arab world', in Y. Elsheshtawy (ed.) *The Evolving Arab City: Tradition, Modernity and Urban Development*, London: Routledge, pp. 2–26.

Excell, K. and Rico, T. (2013) '"There is no heritage in Qatar": orientalism, colonialism and other problematic histories', *World Archaeology*, 45(4): 670–685.

FIFA (Fédération Internationale de Football Association) (2010) *2022 FIFA World Cup. Bid Evaluation Report 2010*, FIFA, 17 November. Available online at www.fifa.com /mm/document/tournament/competition/01/33/74/56/b9qate.pdf (accessed 17 February 2014).

Foley, M., M. McGillivray and G. McPherson (2012) 'Policy pragmatism: Qatar and the global events circuit', *International Journal of Event and Festival Management*, 3(1): 101–115.

Fromherz, A. (2012) *Qatar. A Modern History*, London: Tauris.

Gold, J. R. and M. M. Gold (eds) (2009) *Olympic Cities. City Agendas, Planning, and the World Games, 1896-2012*, Abingdon: Routledge.

Govers, R. and F. Go (2009) *Place Branding: Glocal, Virtual and Physical Identities, Constructed, Imagined and Experienced*, Basingstoke: Palgrave Macmillan.

GSDP (General Secretariat for Development and Planning) (2008) *Qatar National Vision 2030*. Available online at www.gsdp.gov.qa/portal/page/portal/gsdp_en/qatar_national_vision/qnv_2030_document/QNV2030_English_v2.pdf (accessed 2 March 2015).

GSDP (General Secretariat for Development and Planning) (2011) *Qatar National Development Strategy 2011-2016. Towards Qatar National Vision*. Available online at www.gsdp.gov.qa/portal/page/portal/gsdp_en/knowledge_center/Tab/Qatar_NDS_reprint_complete_lowres_16May.pdf (accessed 2 March 2015).

Gulf Times (2015) 'Tourist inflow to Qatar rises 11%', 21 April. Available online at www.gulf-times.com/Mobile/Qatar/178/details/435892/Tourist-inflow-to-Qatar-rises-11%25 (accessed 31 August 2015).

Gulf Times (2016) 'Mall of Qatar to open in the third quarter of 2016', 18 February. Available online at www.gulf-times.com/story/480504/Mall-of-Qatar-to-open-in-third-quarter-of-2016 (accessed 10 April 2016).

Hall, C. M. (2008) *Tourism Planning: Policies, Processes and Relationships*, Harlow: Pearson Education Limited.

Harrison, R. (2014) 'Mall wars: Doha vs Dubai', *Gulf Business*, 4 January. Available online at http://gulfbusiness.com/2014/01/mall-wars-doha-vs-dubai/#.UwXf5oW3AqI (accessed 20 February 2014).

Henderson, J. C. (2006) 'Tourism in Dubai: overcoming barriers to destination development', *International Journal of Tourism Research*, 8(2): 87–99.

Henderson, J. C. (2015) 'The development of tourist destinations in the Gulf: Oman and Qatar compared', *Tourism Planning and Development*, 2(3): 350–361.

Jordan, W. (2012) 'Qatar shakes up the art world', *Al Jazeera*, 11 February. Available online at www.aljazeera.com/video/middleeast/2012/02/20122116551320898.html (accessed 19 February 2014).

Kultermann, U. (1984) 'The architects of the Gulf states: Kuwait, Bahrain, Qatar, the United Arab Emirates, Yemen and Oman', *MIMAR 14: Architecture in Development*. Available online at https://archnet.org/system/publications/contents/3938/original/DPT0460.pdf?1384777593 (accessed 27 February 2017).

Lonely Planet (2000) *Bahrain, Kuwait and Qatar*, London: Lonely Planet Publications.

Marhaba (2015) 'QTA releases 2014 annual tourism statistics revealing over 2 million visitors in 2014', 4 February. Available online as http://marhaba.qa/qta-releases-2014-annual-tourism-statistics-revealing-over-2-million-visitors-in-2014/ (accessed 7 August 2015).

MDPS (Ministry of Development Planning and Statistics) (2012) *Annual Statistical Abstract 2011. Media, Culture and Tourism Chapter*. Available online at www.qix.gov.qa/portal/page/portal/QIXPOC/Documents/QIX%20Knowledge%20Base/Publication/General%20Statistics/Annual%20Abstract/Source_QSA/Annual_Abstract_QSA_AnBu_AE_2011.pdf (accessed 2 March 2015).

MDPS (Ministry of Development Planning and Statistics) (2014a) *The Annual Bulletin of Hotels and Restaurant Statistics 2013*. Available online at www.qsa.gov.qa/Eng/Last_Statistics.htm (accessed on18 December 2014).

MDPS (Ministry of Development Planning and Statistics) (2014b) *The Annual Bulletin of Hotels and Restaurant Statistics 2012*. Available online at www.qsa.gov.qa/Eng/Last_Statistics.htm (accessed on18 December 2014).

MDPS (Ministry of Development Planning and Statistics) (2015) 'Qatar in Figures 2014'. Available online at www.qsa.gov.qa/eng/publication%5Cqif%5C2014%5CQatar_in_Figures _2014_En.pdf (accessed on 2 March 2015).

Morakabati, Y., J. Beavis and J. Fletcher (2014) 'Planning for a Qatar without oil: tourism and economic diversification, a battle of perceptions', *Tourism Planning and Development*, 11(4): 415–435.

Museum of Islamic Art (2017) Available online at https://www.qm.org.qa/en (accessed 27 February 2017).

Oxford Business Group (2013) Qatar: developing tourism. Available online at www.oxfordbusinessgroup.com/economic_updates/qatar-developing-tourism (accessed 19 February 2014).

Pratap, J. (2013) 'Tourism growth boosts Qatar hotel revenue', *Gulf Times*, 11 November. Available online at www.gulf-times.com/qatar/178/details/371251/tourism-growth-boosts-qatar-hotel-revenue (accessed 20 February 2014).

Qataridiar (2014) 'The Doha Exhibition and Convention Centre', *Qataridiar*. Available online at www.qataridiar.com/English/OurProjects/Pages/DohaExhibitionandConventionCentre.aspx (accessed 19 February 2014).

Qatar Museums Authority (2017) Available online at https://www.qm.org.qa/en (accessed 27 February 2017).

QNTSS 2030 (Qatar National Tourism Sector Strategy 2030) (2014) *Qatar National Tourism Sector Strategy 2030. A World-Class Hub with Deep Cultural Roots*. Available online at http://corporate.qatartourism.gov.qa/Portals/0/English%20Strategy.pdf (accessed 14 November 2014).

QTA (Qatar Tourism Authority) (2010) 'Doha Summer Amusement Park promises fun, family entertainment during the summer months', *QTA Media Centre*, 5 July. Available online at www.qatartourism.gov.qa/press/index/1/100 (accessed 12 May 2012).

QTA (Qatar Tourism Authority) (2014) 'Qatar Tourism Authority unveils the Qatar National Tourism Sector Strategy 2030', *QTA Media Centre*, 24 February. Available online at http://corporate.qatartourism.gov.qa/en-us/mediacenter/news/details.aspx?ID=2057 (accessed 14 November 2014).

Ritter, W. (1985) Qatar. Ein arabisches Erdölemirat', *Nürnberger Wirtschafts- und Sozialgeographische Arbeiten* (38). Nurenberg: Friedrich-Alexander-Universität.

Rivera, R. C. (2013) 'Tourism sector to create 127,000 jobs by 2030', *The Peninsula*, 23 October. Available online at http://thepeninsulaqatar.com/news/qatar/258097/tourism-sector-to-create-127000-jobs-by-2030 (accessed 17 February 2014).

Rizzo, A. (2013) 'Metro Doha', *Cities*, (31): 533-543.

Salama, A. M. and F. Wiedmann (2013) *Demystifying Doha: On Architecture and Urbanism in an Emerging City*, Farnham: Ashgate.

Scharfenort, N. (2012) 'Urban development and social change in Qatar: the Qatar National Vision 2030 and the 2022 FIFA World Cup', *Journal of Arabian Studies: Arabia, the Gulf, and the Red Sea*, 2(2): 209–230.

Scharfenort, N. (2013) 'Large-scale urban regeneration: a new "heart" for Doha', *Arabian Humanities*, (2). Available online at http://cy.revues.org/2532 (accessed 17 February 2014).

Scharfenort, N. (2014) 'The Msheireb Project in Doha: the heritage of new urban design in Qatar', in K. Exell and T. Rico (eds) *Cultural Heritage in the Arabian Pensinsula: Debates, Discourses and Practices*, Farnham: Ashgate, pp. 189–204.

Scott, V. (2013) 'To diversify economy, Qatar strives to attract more tourists', *Doha News*, 23 October. Available online at http://dohanews.co/to-diversify-economy-qatar-strives-to-attract-more-tourists/ (accessed 17 February 2014).

Sharpley, R. (2008) 'Planning for tourism: the case of Dubai', *Tourism and Hospitality Planning and Development*, 5(1): 13–30.

Sherwood, S. (2006) 'Is Qatar the next Dubai?' *New York Times*, 4 June. Available online at www.nytimes.com/2006/06/04/travel/04qatar.html?pagewanted=all&_r=0 (accessed 15 February 2014).

Stephenson, M. L. (2014) 'Deciphering "Islamic hospitality": developments, challenges and opportunities', *Tourism Management*, 40: 155–164.

Stephenson, M. and J. Ali-Knight (2010) 'Dubai's tourism industry and its societal impact: social implications and sustainable challenges, the "Middle East and North Africa special issue"', *Journal of Tourism and Cultural Change*, 8(4): 278–292.

The Peninsula (2011a) 'Qatar Tourism Authority participates in ITB Asia', *The Peninsula*, 22 October. Available online at http://thepeninsulaqatar.com/news/qatar/170092/qatar-tourism-authority-participates-in-itb-asia (accessed 2 May 2012).

The Peninsula (2011b) 'QTA to modernise Doha Exhibition Centre', *The Peninsula*, 10 July. Available online at www.zawya.com/story/ZAWYA20110710041513/QTA_to_modernise_Doha_Exhibition_Centre/ (accessed 2 May 2012).

UNESCO (United Nations Educational, Scientific and Cultural Organization) (2013) 'Qatar and Fiji get their first World Heritage sites as World Heritage Committee makes six additions to UNESCO List', UNESCO press release, 22 June. Available online at http://whc.unesco.org/en/news/1045 (accessed 19 February 2014).

Walker, L. (2015) 'Hamad airport welcomes more than 30 million passengers in 2015', *Doha News*, 31 December. Available online at http://dohanews.co/hamad-airport-welcomes-30-million-passengers-2015/ (accessed 10 October 2015).

Walker, L. (2016) 'Despite global challenges, Qatar saw 100,000 more tourist visits in 2015', *Doha News*, 24 January. Available online at http://dohanews.co/despite-global-challenges-qatar-welcomes-100000-more-visitors-in-2015/ (accessed 10 April 2016).

World Travel and Tourism Council (2016) *Travel & Tourism Economic Impact 2016 – Qatar*. Available online at www.wttc.org/-/media/files/reports/economic%20impact%20research/countries%202016/qatar2016.pdf (accessed 22 April 2016).

Zawya (2012) 'Tourism to contribute $1.1 billion to Qatar economy in 2012', *Zawya*, 12 March. Available online at www.zawya.com/story/ZAWYA20120314113311/ (accessed 19 February 2014).

Zawya (2014) 'Qatar Tourism Authority promotes Qatar's MICE expertise at GIBTM', *Zawya*, 25 March. Available online at www.zawya.com/story/Qatar_Tourism_Authority_promotesQatars_MICE_expertise_at_GIBTM-ZAWYA20140325130830/ (accessed 22 April 2016).

9   Evaluating ecotourism challenges in Oman

Hafidh AlRiyami, Noel Scott, Ahmad M. Ragab and Jafar Jafari

Of the different forms of tourism studied under the theme of sustainable tourism, ecotourism has received the most attention. Ecotourism is considered as a preferable economic activity to promote sustainability and is often discussed in the same context as sustainable livelihoods (Funnell and Bynoe 2007). Ecotourism, understood as sustainable tourism in natural areas, has the potential to assist in the development of a workable approach to achieving sustainability objectives through tourism. Ecotourism contributes not only to sustainable development but also to the long and difficult process of its implementation in the tourism system (Pforr 2001; Thurau *et al.* 2007).

A number of different individual ecotourism components or tenets have been discussed. The most common components that have been addressed in the ecotourism literature in the last decade are nature-based activities, improvements in preservation and conservation, environmental and cultural education, distribution of benefits, ethics and responsibility, and sustainability (cf. Braden and Prudnikova 2008; Buckley 2009; Butcher 2006; Buultjens and White 2010; Cusick *et al.* 2010; Higgins-Desbiolles 2009; Higham and Lück 2002; Holden and Sparrowhawk 2002; Jones *et al.* 2009; Manuel and Robertico 2010; Lai and Shafer 2005; Powell and Ham 2008). These six main tenets, which are widely agreed upon as basic components of sustainable ecotourism (Zambrano *et al.* 2010), need to be addressed to provide successful sustainable ecotourism destinations (Lai and Shafer 2005). To date, no research has used these six tenets as criteria to evaluate ecotourism in a destination. Previous evaluation frameworks have used some, but not all, of them. Bhattacharya and Kumari (2004) focused on conservation and preservation, distribution of benefits and cultural education. Lee and Snepenger (1992) did not use sustainability and ethics as criteria to evaluate how ecotourism is being practiced, because these components were not seen as main tenets of ecotourism at that time.

Evaluation of the practice of ecotourism in different ecotourism destinations, such as Kenya, South Africa, Tanzania, Zambia and Zimbabwe by Dieke (2001); North America by Fennell (2001); East Asia, Southeast Asia and South Asia by Lew (2001); Australia, New Zealand and the South Pacific by Dowling (2001); Europe by Blangy and Vautier (2001); and Latin America and the Caribbean by Weaver and Schuelter (2001), have found that only some aspects and tenets of ecotourism were well adopted. Good practice was found in the contribution of economic and social benefits to local communities, though principles such as conservation, education, resource protection and local resident involvement were poorly practiced. The net result was that although there were some successful cases, the majority failed to implement all the tenets of ecotourism.

This chapter will focus on the Sultanate of Oman and will initially provide a brief overview of the tourism industry. The work will then examine the main aim of this chapter, which is to evaluate the performance of ecotourism in Oman based on the six separately identified components of ecotourism, namely (1) nature-based activities (2) preservation and conservation (3) environmental and cultural education (4) distribution of benefits (5) ethics and responsibility, and (6) sustainability. In doing so, the following discussions address the challenges facing the development and advancement of ecotourism in Oman.

Oman and tourism

Oman is located at the eastern corner of the Arabian Peninsula, south of the Strait of Hormuz. The Sultanate enjoys a varied climate ranging from hot and humid on the coast, to mild in the mountains, to monsoonal around the southern city of Salalah. Oman combines rich culture with diverse nature. Its history spans at least 5,000 years when it traded with the ancient world, accepted Islam in ce 630 and ruled lands in the northern Arabian Peninsula and eastern Africa (Al-Haddad 2006). Footprints of this long history are evident in unique attractions such as four United Nations Educational, Scientific and Cultural Organization (UNESCO) World Heritage Sites: (1) the 5,000-year-old Bat tombs, (2) the Aflaj traditional irrigation system, (3) the Land of Frankincense and (4) the Bahla Fort (Walsh 2013).

An important component of Oman is its diverse natural landscape. The country's long coast embraces clean beaches, numerous diving sites such as the Daymaniyat Islands, and turtle nesting locations like the Ras Al-Jinz reserve (Sur). The country's Hajar Mountains rise to 3,000 metres at Al Jabal Al Akhdar and encompass Majlis al-Jinn, one of the largest cave chambers in the world. Oman is home to many varieties of wildlife, including over 400 species of birds across the different seasons of the year and 20 species of whales and dolphins. Natural reserves for species such as leopards, hyenas, oryx, gazelle, tahr, ibex, desert fox, antelope and wild cats are already established (Kabasci and Franzisky 2005).

The Sultanate of Oman has taken great care in protecting and promoting wildlife as a part of its tourism strategy, where strict laws are in place to prohibit hunting of animals and birds. Oman's ecotourism resources are no doubt a significant pull factor (O'Hanlon 2008; Winckler 2007). Indeed, Altaameer (2011) considered Oman as the main ecotourism destination of the Middle East region. Ahmed and Choudri (2012) emphasized Oman's strong record for the conservation of diversity, becoming a ratifying country of the Convention of Biological Diversity (CBD) in 1994.

While oil is an important component of Oman's economy, tourism is playing a key role in the country's economic diversification strategy. Tourism in Oman was encouraged to develop in the 1990s as a means to diversify its economy from over-dependence on oil, to conserve the natural environment and culture and to develop local communities (Winckler 2007). Since then, the tourism industry has grown rapidly, becoming one of its most crucial non-oil sectors. In 1999, Oman received 380,000 tourists, who spent about US$110 million. Shortly after, in 2001, the country adopted a strategic plan to develop the tourism sector. Due to Oman's focus on tourism development, more than 2,065,414 tourists visited Oman during the first 10 months of 2015 (*Oman Daily Observer* 2016). The Oman Airports Management Company recorded over 10 million passengers travelling through Muscat International Airport in 2015, representing an 18 per cent increase, and over 1 million passengers passing through Salalah International Airport, a 22 per cent increase (*Times of Oman* 2016). Furthermore, numbers of hotels and hotel apartments have significantly increased from 30 units in 1990 to 287 in 2014, representing a 10 per cent annual increase (ONCSI 2015). The destination is not following the luxury tourism path, where the search for sustainable alternatives to high levels of touristic consumption is, arguably, a pertinent way forward for the country. In fact, there are around 47 two-star licensed hotels in 2015, an increase of 27 per cent from 2014 (*Oman Daily Observer* 2016).

The National Tourism Development Agency's mission statement notes, 'Tourism will facilitate economic diversification, preservation of cultural integrity and protection of the environment of the Sultanate of Oman' (Ministry of Tourism 2014a: 1). Hence, the Omani government is following the principles of 'sustainable tourism' to have a lower impact on the natural environment and less negative effects on the local community, culture and religion. Mershen (2007) considers that Oman is seeking to avoid the negative impacts of mass tourism. It does not want to make the same mistakes as other destinations in the Middle East, which have become synonymous with mass tourism. Oman is targeting tourists who are interested in admiring and maintaining its natural environment, culture, heritage, history and archaeology (Ministry of Information 2009). An important feature of tourism in Oman is that tourism development started relatively late compared to neighbouring countries. Because of this, Oman was able to evaluate the implications of tourism development in other countries and avoid their problems.

The Omani government and the private sector have attempted to promote Oman as a destination for high quality ecotourism experiences. The state's main objectives concerning ecotourism relate to economic diversification, bringing economic benefits to local communities and conserving and protecting the environment, culture and heritage (Winckler 2007).

Characteristics of ecotourism in Oman

The following section examines the six main elements of sustainable ecotourism.

1 Nature-based activities

Oman boasts several natural ecotourism attractions in different governorates including Muscat, Dhofar Al-Batinah, Al-Sharqia and Al-Dakhlia. These attractions are promoted as offering high quality ecotourism experiences supported by a rich natural heritage. The attractions include whale, dolphin and bird watching, and appreciating sand dune deserts, wadis (dry rivers), natural oases, unspoiled beaches and unique mountainous areas. In addition, there are endangered wild animals such as leopards, oryx, gazelle and tahr (Kabasci and Franzisky 2005). However, some sites and resources are not managed well, nor are they properly interpreted. There are some natural attractions in different regions suffering from lack of basic facilities such as signage and toilets, and lack of local tour guides and administrators to control the sites. Moreover, sand dunes and some areas in the Dhofar Governorate are suffering from random off-road driving, causing destruction to vegetation and affecting the wild animal population (Al-Rasbi 2013). In some respects, Oman is still at its experimental stage when it comes to ecotourism development. Accordingly, in May 2015 the government indicated that the Bandar al Khayran Reserve in the Muscat Governorate will be piloted for sustainable tourism development (Muscatdaily.com 2015).

2 Preservation and conservation

The Omani government has introduced laws to protect and conserve the environment. It has more than 15 natural reserves and protected areas stretching over an approximate area of 30,000 square kilometres, including the Arabian Oryx Sanctuary, Wadi A'Sareen Nature Reserve, Dymaniyat Islands Nature Reserve, Al Saleel National Park and Ras Al-Jinz Turtle Reserve. These protected areas and natural reserves represent assets for the ecotourism market (Mershen 2007). The government claims that the reserves and protected areas help to provide jobs for local people, as well as contribute to conservation and ecotourism development (Ministry of Information 2009). Some of these protected areas are well resourced and managed (e.g. Turtle Reserve), while others are relatively untapped and, thus, are not generating reasonable revenues for local communities (e.g. the Dymaniyat Islands Nature Reserve).

Oman also has many historical, archeological and heritage sites which have been renovated for preservation and for tourism purposes. There are four key sites listed in the UNESCO World Heritage List: (1) Bat Tombs and Settlement, (2) Five Aflaj Irrigation Systems (Falaj Al-Khatmeen, Falaj Al-Malki, Falaj Daris, Falaj Al-Mayassar and Falaj Al-Jeela), (3) Land of Frankincense and (4) the Bahla Fort. The Ministry of National Heritage and Culture renovated many forts and castles, and 26 of these were developed as museums. Oman's forts and castles received more than 308,000 visitors in 2014, compared to around 176,000 visitors in 2005 and 119,000 visitors in 2002 (ONCSI 2015)

3 Environmental and cultural education

The Oman Ministry of Tourism published a number of guidebooks concerning forts and castles in Oman, and specialized touristic-based information concerning specific cities (e.g. Muscat) and governorates (e.g. Dhofar), with the purpose of notifying tourists and the local community about attractions concerning the environment, ecology, heritage and culture. In addition, some of the natural reserves and protected areas, such as the Al-Hoota Cave (Nizwa) and Ras Al-Jinz Turtle Reserve, have an information centre and available guides to educate tourists. Furthermore, tour operators offer ecotourism programmes and tours educating tourists about the flora and fauna of Oman and its heritage and cultural attractions. However, many tour guides accompanying these tourists are not from Oman, hence they might not have sufficient information and facts about the country's history and nature. Although the Ministry of Tourism provided on-site interpretations of the history and characteristics of some forts and castles (such as Nizwa Fort, Jabreen Castle, Taqa Castle and Khasab Castle), tour guides are still in need for more on-site information and interpretation. Such attractions as wadis, mountains and old villages lack tourism interpretation. Prominent archeological sites, such as the Tower Tombs of Wadi Al Ain in the governorate of Al-Dhahira, lack site signage and interpretation.

4 Distribution of benefits

There has been a significant attempt in Oman to ensure that local people are involved and working in the tourism and hospitality sector. Tourism's economic benefits are ensuring that some infrastructural improvements have taken place and that some villages have become more accessible. However, Mershen (2007) claims that the majority of local people who live in villages in Oman do not obtain feasible benefits from the activities of visitors, due to the lack of tourism facilities. For example, many villages have no accommodation units, no local guides and not even coffee shops or small shops that sell postcards or handicrafts. Community forms of ecotourism in Oman arguably face the challenge of overcoming the conflicts that often exist within small villages (Buerkert *et al.* 2010). For instance, a project concerning Ain Al Kasfa, a hot water spring in the governorate of Al Batinah South, was stopped because of conflicts occurring between local people and government representatives in the area. There were disagreements concerning the water source (i.e. the hot water springs) and how it will be shared and distributed between the local people and the project (Alshabiba 2014; *Oman Daily* 2014).

However, there are projects that have been more successful in involving local people in the decision-making, planning and development regarding tourism services. For example, Khasab Castle in the governorate of Musandam received a UK-based 'Museums and Heritage Awards for Excellence', under the international category of awards concerning best practice in developing such places for tourism purposes (E Turbo News 2010). In this project, the local Khasab community and the governorate of Musandam, with the support of the Ministry of Tourism, worked together to rehabilitate and develop the castle. Local people were responsible for the interpretation of the castle's history and distribution of Omani traditional handicrafts to visitors. Similar projects have taken place in Taqa Castle and Mirbat Castle in the governorate of Dhofar. These projects raise local awareness of the importance of heritage and culture, involving the local community in tourism and supporting traditional handicrafts. Anecdotal evidence suggests that the earnings that locals receive from tourism activities are still quite low, with limited career pathways available. Additionally, locals see jobs in the tourism and hospitality sectors as inferior, a reflection of the low salaries and job security in tourism. There appears to be a cultural stigma associated with tourism employment, insofar as conservative families frown on family members working in tourism. For example, they may consider that the work environment in hotels and other tourism-related jobs is not suitable for women. Nonetheless, more research assessment concerning local perceptions of tourism employment is required, especially to examine the challenges associated with the nationalization of the tourism workforce.

The Omani government aims to offer job opportunities to local people through developing tourism and ecotourism. According to the Director of Statistics at the Ministry of Tourism (pers. comm. January 2013), more than 60 per cent of the workers employed in tourism and ecotourism attractions are foreigners. Many of the jobs offered to local people are vocational occupations (e.g. drivers, guards and waiters), while foreigners significantly occupy managerial positions. It is also worth mentioning that the government offers free training and education opportunities for local people, though few are trained for managerial positions. In 1988, the Omani government developed an Omanization Policy Programme to provide more jobs for local Omanis and replace expatriates with well-educated and trained Omani personnel (Omanuna 2015). Based on the five-year national plan 2005–10, one of the main objectives of the Ministry of Tourism was to decrease the percentage of expatriates working in the tourism industry from 63 per cent to 10 per cent while increasing the percentage of Omani nationals from 37 per cent to 90 per cent by 2010 (Ministry of Tourism 2013). This objective was overly ambitious and, thus, was not achievable. According to recent available data, the percentage of Omanis working in the tourism industry is still less than 50 per cent (ONCSI 2015). Indeed, many locals seemingly do not aspire to work in tourism and hospitality-related jobs because they consider them as short-term or temporary jobs, often preferring to take up employment opportunities in the public sector.

Another factor that decreases the distributive benefits of tourism to locals concerns the limited local ownership or management of tourism projects. While the government has set legislation to facilitate and encourage investment by locals as well as foreigners in the various tourism activities, most funds and investments have gone into establishing hotels and hotel apartments. There is a clear shortage of localized tourism services, for example, the governorates of South Al-Batinah and North Al-Batinah have limited souvenirs or traditional handicrafts shops. Consequently, only a small amount of local people within these governorates are in receipt of direct benefits from visitors. The government shows concern, however, in supporting small and medium-scale enterprises and offering loans to locals to operate their own businesses as a way of supporting entrepreneurship activities in tourism. Nevertheless, very few people have been willing to invest in tourism industry-related projects. This has led to the government reducing the deposit paid by new investors in the tourism sector. Accordingly, in order to open a travel agency or tour operating business the investor needed to deposit Omani rial (OMR) 5,000, though this has since been reduced to OMR 1,000 (around US$2,600). Another challenge comes from the existing legislative framework, which may restrict small-scale tourism investments. For example, legislation states that any person must have a minimum experience of five years working in the tourism sector to be a manager or an owner of a tourism business, thereby limiting tourism as a career route for fresh graduates or young locals (Ministry of Tourism 2016).

5 Ethics and responsibility

The Ministry of Tourism organized several national and international conferences, workshops and seminars to share environmental and cultural knowledge and information with key stakeholders, as well as promote sustainable tourism and ecotourism – such as the Built Environment for Sustainable Tourism Conference in 2005 and the Geotourism Conference in 2011. In addition, it has also organized the 4th International Conference on Responsible Tourism which was held in Muscat in 2010. Moreover, it has invited tour operators in Oman to discuss the topics and issues, and to focus on ways to stimulate tourists visiting Oman to respect its heritage, environment and culture. In order to inform and educate local people about the positive and negative impacts of tourism on Oman, the Ministry of Tourism also developed a tourism awareness campaign, entitled 'Tourism Enriches' (Islamic Tourism Media 2005). Other more recent workshops have continued to deal with the sustainable tourism theme, one of which was organized by the Ministry of Tourism in 2015 in cooperation with the United Nations World Tourism Organization (UNWTO) (Muscatdaily.com 2015).

According to Oman's Ministry of Tourism (2014b), it has adopted the sustainable tourism principles developed by UNWTO. The Ministry of Tourism is thus encouraging tourism businesses to apply UNWTO's guidelines and related standards of sustainability, notably performance standards on environmental and social sustainability. The Ministry of Tourism has also developed a framework for controlling tourism developments to guide tourism organizations in embracing sustainability practices in their tourism activities. However, some ecotourism activities need more attention. There have been no standards and guidelines, so far, for managing dolphin and whale watching trips in Muscat (Ponnampalam 2011).

6 Sustainability

Ecotourism in Oman has remarkable potential. Some ecotourism attractions, such as the Arabian Oryx Sanctuary, did achieve desired sustainable outcomes in term of providing economic benefits to local people, and protecting and conserving the wild animals and the environment (Kabasci and Franzisky 2005; GSCAO 2016). However, the Arabian Oryx Sanctuary was delisted from the UNESCO World Heritage List because the size of the sanctuary was reduced by 90 per cent due to the expansion of hydrocarbon exploration in the region where it was located. Accordingly, the number of oryx declined from 450 in 1996 to 65 in 2007 (UNESCO 2007). The government, however, claimed that the initiative would be managed more effectively given its size reduction. Nonetheless, oil exploration was prioritized more than wildlife conservation, and this is one of the central dilemmas of ecotourism development: where economic development takes absolute precedence over sustainable development (and environmental appreciation) (see Chapter 12). Henderson's (2015: 358) observations of this particular case are noteworthy, especially given the implication that ecotourism demand can be a potential risk. She states: 'Ecosystems are thereby exposed to strain from natural and human agents and ecotourism, identified as a commercial opportunity, constitutes a further threat' (Henderson 2015).

Some natural reserves, such as the Ras Al-Jinz Turtle Reserve, have applied carrying capacity directives to manage visitors' trips (Ras Al-Jinz Turtle Reserve 2016). Through managing these natural reserves in a sustainable manner, local community members are presented with employment opportunities. However, ecotourism resources and attractions in remote old oasis settlements, such as Wadi Bani Khlaid and Wadi Shab in the governorate of Ash-Sharqiyah, and Misfat Al Abreyeen in the governorate of Ad Dakhiliyah, are not well managed. This is despite their potential in attracting tourists interested in nature and unique ecosystems (Mershen 2007).

Preserving the Omani architecture style is another objective for achieving sustainability and protecting the environment, heritage and culture. Oman is striving to keep its culture and heritage intact, and the government is developing regulations and laws to ensure that local people, businesses and investors abide by formal guidelines concerning the building and the architectural design of new projects. To ensure that sustainable standards are being instituted, any such construction must be approved by the Ministry of Housing, Ministry of Regional Municipalities and Water Resources, Ministry of Tourism and Ministry of Environment and Climate Affairs. Buildings should follow the traditional Omani style and reflect local environment peculiarities in terms of colours, designs and constructing materials. This has certainly been the case in the Al-Qurm region, where there are very stringent regulations concerning the colour of houses. Accordingly, such directives help regions to avoid being castigated as visually or aesthetically polluting. Also, most of the government and non-governmental buildings in Oman follow Islamic, Arabic or Omani architectural styles. Since 2010, the Ministry of Tourism established a 'Development Control Plan Framework' (DCPF) for tourism projects.

This initiative concerns a desire to maintain Omani authenticity and retain elements of Arabian culture. Importantly, DCPF also monitors the natural environment and conservation (Prabhu 2013).

Conclusion and research implications

Oman generally appears to be developing its tourism industry in a careful manner. The country has a wide range of natural and human-made tourism resources, as well as various protected and natural reserve areas. These attraction factors allow Oman to target many tourism niche markets as types of ecotourism: cultural tourism, bird watching, adventure tourism, desert tourism and geo-tourism. These developments can encourage Oman to focus on educated tourists with higher incomes and responsible lifestyles. Yet, Oman has not made full use of all its natural and human-made resources for tourism development. There are many potential areas of development for Oman to pursue to enrich its ecotourism product portfolio.

This chapter has evaluated the performance of ecotourism in Oman based on six main tenets: nature-based activities, preservation and conservation, environmental and cultural education, distribution of benefits, ethics and responsibility, and sustainability. On one hand, the assessment indicated that Oman has applied all these tenets, though to varying extents. On the other hand, some areas are points of weakness and should be addressed by the tourism authorities in Oman. Particular challenges concern the need for improvement in the management of tourism resources and attractions; additional core infrastructure and superstructure for the development of specific areas (for example, the Arabian Oryx Sanctuary and Misfat Al Abreyeen); more site information and interpretation required for natural areas and old villages; and locals encouraged to become more engaged in tourism activities.

This chapter is a first attempt to evaluate how ecotourism principles are being practiced in Oman, using the six most common tenets found in the ecotourism literature over the last decade. The findings in this chapter are consistent with the previous literature inferring that some principles of ecotourism are well practiced, and others are poorly implemented. It also confirms that achieving sustainability through ecotourism is not an easy task, particularly as many destinations failed to implement all the tenets.

Future studies may expand the deductions raised in this chapter, especially by comparing the situation in Oman with other Gulf countries such as the UAE and the Kingdom of Saudi Arabia. This comparative undertaking may address whether the approach to ecotourism development in Oman and other Gulf countries is sensitive to cultural and religious sensitivities (cf. Saniotis 2012). In addition, future research in the Gulf area might consider examining and comparing the sustainability of ecotourism in natural attractions (e.g. Ras Al-Jinz Turtle Natural Reserve in Oman) in contrast to human-made ecotourism projects (Al Maha Desert Resort and Spa in the UAE). Future studies might also conduct market research of ecotourism in Oman and other countries in the GCC region, comparing these with other international ecotourism destinations in terms of ecotourism activities, products and type of tourists.

References

Ahmed, M. and B. S. Choudri (2012) 'Climate change in Oman: current knowledge and way forward', *Education, Business and Society: Contemporary Middle Eastern Issues*, 5(4): 228–236.

Al-Haddad, F. (2006) *'A'siyaha fi sultanat Uman'* [Tourism in the Sultanate of Oman], Muscat: Al-Dharmi Publishing.

Al-Rasbi, A. (2013) 'Vegetation destruction and hunting of wild animals', *Oman Observer*, 8 December. Available online at http://2016.omanobserver.om/vegetation-destruction-and-hunting-of-wild-animals/ (accessed 12 September 2014).

Alshabiba (2014) *'A'siyaha: tahafudhat alahali tuacher tatweer ain alkasfah'* [Tourism: local concerns delay the devlopment of Ain Alkasfah], Alshabiba.com, 18 December. Avaliable online at www.shabiba.com/News/Article-66120.aspx. (accessed 1 February 2015).

Altaameer (2011) 'Mena hospitality update report', *AlTaameer Real Estate*, April. Available online at www.altaameer.com.kw/newletter/April2011.pdf (accessed 12 January 2014).

Bhattacharya, P. and S. Kumari (2004) 'Application of criteria and indicator for sustainable ecotourism: scenario under globalization'. Paper submitted for the IASCP Bi-Annual Conference on The Commons in an Age of Global Transition: Challenges, Risk and Opportunities at Oaxaca, Mexico, 9–14 August.

Blangy, S. and S. Vautier (2001) 'A regional survey by continent: Europe', in D. B. Weaver (ed.) *The Encyclopaedia of Ecotourism*, Wallingford: CABI Publishing, pp. 155–172.

Braden, K. and N. Prudnikova (2008) 'The challenge of ecotourism development in the Altay region of Russia', *Tourism Geographies*, 10(1): 1–21.

Buckley, R. (2009) 'Evaluating the net effects of ecotourism on the environment: a framework, first assessment and future research', *Journal of Sustainable Tourism*, 17(6): 643–672.

Buerkert, A., E. Luedeling, U. Dickhoefer, K. Lohrer, B. Mershen, W. Schaeper and E. Schlecht (2010) 'Prospects of mountain ecotourism in Oman: the example of As Sawjarah on Al Jabal al Akhdar', *Journal of Ecotourism*, 9(2): 104–116.

Butcher, J. (2006) 'Natural capital and the advocacy of ecotourism as sustainable development', *Journal of Sustainable Tourism*, 14(6): 529–544.

Buultjens, J. G. D. and N. E. White (2010) 'Synergies between Australian indigenous tourism and ecotourism: possibilities and problems for future development', *Journal of Sustainable Tourism*, 18(4): 497–513.

Cusick, J., B. McClure and L. Cox (2010) 'Representations of ecotourism in the Hawaiian Islands: a content analysis of local media', *Journal of Ecotourism*, 9(1): 21–35.

Dieke, P. U. C. (2001) 'A regional survey by continent: Kenya and South Africa', in D. B. Weaver (ed.) *The Encyclopaedia of Ecotourism*, Wallingford: CABI Publishing, pp. 89–106.

Dowling, R. K. (2001) 'A regional survey by continent: Oceania (Australia, New Zealand and South Pacific)', in D. B. Weaver (ed.) *The Encyclopaedia of Ecotourism*, Wallingford: CABI Publishing, pp. 139–154.

eTurboNews (2010) 'Khasab Castle in Oman bags international award', eTurboNews.com, 18 May. Available online at hwww.eturbonews.com/16213/khasab-castle-oman-bags-international-award (accessed 1 February 2015).

Funnell, D. C. and P. E. Bynoe (2007) 'Ecotourism and institutional structures: the case of North Rupununi, Guyana', *Journal of Ecotourism*, 6(3): 163–183.

Fennell, D. A. (2001) 'A regional survey by continent: Anglo-America', in D. B. Weaver (ed.) *The Encyclopaedia of Ecotourism*, Wallingford: CABI Publishing, pp. 107–122.

GSCAO (General Secretariat for the Conservation of the Arabian Oryx) (2016), Oman. Available online at www.arabianoryx.org/En/Oman/Pages/default.aspx (accessed 26 April, 2016).

Henderson, J. C. (2015) 'The developement of tourist destinations in the Gulf: Oman and Qatar compared', *Tourism Planning and Development*, 12(3): 350–361.

Higgins-Desbiolles, F. (2009) 'Indigenous ecotourism's role in transforming ecological consciousness', *Journal of Ecotourism*, 8(2): 144–160.

Higham, J. and M. Lück (2002) 'Urban ecotourism: a contradiction in terms?', *Journal of Ecotourism*, 1(1): 36–51.

Holden, A. and J. Sparrowhawk (2002) 'Understanding the motivations of ecotourists: the case of trekkers in Annapurna, Nepal', *International Journal of Tourism Research*, 4(6): 435–446.

Islamic Tourism Media (2005) 'Tourist caravan launched in Salalah', Islamictourism.com, 11 August. Available online at www.islamictourism.com/country_E.php?country= 32&nid=1435 (accessed 1 February 2015).

Jones, T., D. Wood, J. Catlin and B. Norman (2009) 'Expenditure and ecotourism: predictors of expenditure for whale shark tour participants', *Journal of Ecotourism*, 8(1): 32–50.

Kabasci, K. and P. Franzisky (2005) *Oman2005: Gheminesvolles Sultanat Zwischen Gestern und Uebermorgen*, 4th edn, Bielefeld: Reise KNOW-HOW.

Lai, P-H. and S. Shafer (2005) 'Marketing ecotourism through the internet: an evaluation of selected ecolodges in Latin America and the Caribbean', *Journal of Ecotourism*, 4(3): 143–160.

Lee, D. N. B. and D. J. Snepenger (1992) 'An ecotourism assessment of Tortuguero, Costa Rica', *Annals of Tourism Research*, 19(2): 367–370.

Lew, A. A. (2001) 'A regional survey by continent: Asia', in D. B. Weaver (ed.) *The Encyclopaedia of Ecotourism*, Wallingford: CABI Publishing, pp. 123–138.

Manuel, A. R. and C. Robertico (2010) 'Ecotourists' loyalty: will they tell about the destination or will they return?', *Journal of Ecotourism*, 9(2): 85–103.

Mershen, B. (2007) 'Development of community-based tourism in Oman: challenges and opportunities', in R. Daher (ed.) *Tourism in the Middle East*, Clevedon: Channel View, pp. 188–214.

Ministry of Information (2009) *Oman 2008–2009*, Muscat: Alnahda Printing.

Ministry of Tourism (2013) 'Objectives'. Available online at www.omantourism. gov.om/ wps/portal/ mot/tourism/oman/home/ministry/about/objectve/ (accessed 1 February 2015).

Ministry of Tourism (2014a) Vision and Mission. Available online at www.omantourism. gov.om/wps/portal/mot/tourism/oman/home/ministry/about/vision (accessed 10 September 2014).

Ministry of Tourism, (2014b) '4th International Conference on Responsible Tourism in Destinations, Muscat 10–12 October 2010'. Available online at www.omantourism. gov.om/rtd/environmental%20statment.html (accessed 12 September 2014).

Ministry of Tourism (2016) *Tourism Law*. Available online at www.omantourism.gov.om/ wps/wcm/connect/77bdfb0042b56c4a89e7a9e161b1c19a/%D9%82%D8%A7%D9%8

6%D9%88%D9%86+%D8%A7%D9%84%D8%B3%D9%8A%D8%A7%D8%AD%
D8%A9.pdf?MOD=AJPERES (accessed 26 April 2016).

Muscatdaily.com (2015) 'Bandar Al Khairan reserve chosen for pilot project in sustainable development', *Muscat Daily*, 12 May. Available at www.muscatdaily.com/ Archive/Oman/Bandar-al-Khairan-reserve-chosen-for-pilot-project-on-sustainable-development-41j4 (accessed 22 April 2016).

O'Hanlon, R. (2008) 'Oman's challenge: hospitality vision Middle East performance review, Deloitte'. Available online at www.omantourism.gov.om/wps/wcm/connect/39c2b800435 cd07fb139fbac65cfb36c/Hospitality.pdf?MOD=AJPERES&CONVERT_TO=url&CA CHEID=39c2b800435cd07fb139fbac65cfb36c (accessed 13 January 2014).

Oman Daily (2014) 'AlMuhrezi: la masas bemiah ain alkasfah wa la mashroaat siyahia ella bemowafaqat alahali' [AlMuhrezi: nothing will happen to the water source in Ain Alkasfa water spring and no tourism projects without permission from the local community], Omandaily.com, 24 October. Available online at http://omandaily. om/?p=38410 (accessed 1 February 2015).

Oman Daily Observer (2016) 'Over 2 million tourists visted Oman', 8 February. Available online at http://omanobserver.om/over-2-million-tourists-visited-oman/ (accessed 22 April 2016).

Omanuna (2015) 'Omanization policy'. Available online at www.oman.om/wps/portal/!ut/p/ a0/04_Sj9CPykssy0xPLMnMz0vMAfGjzOKDvbydgj1NjAwszELNDDxDv QND3NwMDA0MzPWDU_P0C7IdFQHJ46k0/?WCM_GLOBAL_CONTEXT=/wps/ wcm/connect/EN/site/home/gov/gov2/gov22omanisationpolicy (accessed 1 February 2015).

ONCSI (Oman's National Centre for Statistics and Information) (2015) *Statistics Year Book 2014*, Muscat: National Centre for Statistics and Information.

Pforr, C. (2001) 'Concepts of sustainable development, sustainable tourism, and ecotourism: definitions, principles, and linkages', *Scandinavian Journal of Hospitality and Tourism*, 1(1): 68–71.

Ponnampalam, L. S. (2011) 'Dolphin watching in Muscat, Sultanate of Oman: tourist perceptions and actual current practice', *Tourism in Marine Environments*, 7(2): 81–93.

Powell, R. B. and S. H. Ham (2008) 'Can ecotourism interpretation really lead to pro-conservation knowledge, attitudes and behaviour? Evidence from the Galapagos Islands', *Journal of Sustainable Tourism*, 16(4): 467–489.

Prabhu, C. (2013) 'International firms eye tourism ministry's consultancy contract', *Oman Daily Observer*, 3 August. Available online at http://omanobserver.om/international-firms-eye-tourism-ministrys-consultancy-contract/ (accessed 22 April 2016).

Ras Al-Jinz Turtle Reserve (2016) 'Turtle viewing'. Available online at www.rasaljinz-turtlereserve.com/pages/92/turtle-viewing (accessed 26 April 2016).

Saniotis, A. (2012) 'Muslims and ecology: fostering Islamic environmental ethics', *Contemporary Islam*, 6(2): 155–171.

Thurau, B. B., A. D. Carver, J. C. Mangun, C. M. Basman and G. Bauer (2007) 'A market segmentation analysis of cruise ship tourists visiting the Panama Canal Watershed: opportunities for ecotourism development', *Journal of Ecotourism*, 6(1): 1–18.

Times of Oman (2016) 'Muscat, Salalah airports' passenger traffic exceeds expectations', *Times of Oman*, 31 January. Available online at http://timesofoman.com/article/76579/Oman/ Government/Muscat Salalah-airports'-passenger-traffic-exceeds-expectations (accessed 23 April 2016).

UNESCO (United Nations Educational, Scientific and Cultural Organization) (2007) 'Oman's Arabian Oryx Sanctuary: first site ever to be deleted from UNESCO's World

Heritage List'. Available online at http://whc.unesco.org/en/news/362 (accessed 12 September 2014).

Walsh, T. (2013) *Walking Through History: Oman's World Heritage Sites*, Muscat: Al Roya Press and Publishing House.

Weaver, D. B. and R. Schuelter (2001) 'A regional survey by continent: Latin America and the Caribbean', in D. B. Weaver (ed.) *The Encyclopaedia of Ecotourism*, Wallingford: CABI Publishing, pp. 173–188.

Winckler, O. (2007) 'The birth of Oman's tourism industry', *Tourism: An International Interdisciplinary Journal*, 55(2): 221–234.

Zambrano, A. M. A., E. N. Broadbent and W. H. Durham (2010) 'The economic promise of ecotourism for conservation', *Journal of Ecotourism*, 9(1): 62–83.

Part Three

Destinations and opportunities

10 Examining the marketing opportunities of Sharjah as an Islamic tourism destination

Nicholas J. Ashill, Paul Williams and Prakash Chathoth

There are more Muslim tourists today than ever before who seek specific Islamic products and services during their travels. The Muslim population is growing rapidly, with such tourists in 2011 generating US$126 billion worldwide in tourism expenditure (Stephenson 2014). The potential growth in Islamic tourism worldwide is only going to increase given that the Middle East and North Africa (MENA) Arab region comprises around 315 million people who are Muslim, and this population base is rapidly growing (Jafari and Scott 2014). The Gulf Cooperation Council (GCC) offers many significant competitive advantages for attracting tourists, including those looking for specific tourism-related products and services that have cultural and religious connotations (Mansfeld and Winckler 2007). As a result, several destinations have invested in tourism development in the region aiming to serve such growing markets, including the heritage tourism market. Notable GCC destinations that deal with the religious and/ or the cultural heritage element of Islam are the Emirate of Sharjah, Saudi Arabia and Oman. Sharjah has attempted to monopolize on regional growth in tourism as a prime factor to position itself and define its specific identity as an Islamic tourism destination.

This paper highlights some of the opportunities and challenges that Sharjah faces when marketing itself to the world as an attractive Islamic tourism destination. The case of Sharjah is unique in that the destination, specifically over the past two decades, has focused on the creation of an identity largely based on its Islamic culture and heritage. This is in contrast to the strategies adopted by Dubai and Abu Dhabi (though Abu Dhabi does celebrate to tourists the prestigious attraction of the Sheikh Zayed Grand Mosque). Nonetheless, these emirates have received more international attention in recent times due to their enormous investment in tourism attractions and infrastructure, tending to attract a broader base of tourists from overseas (Henderson 2006; Sharpley 2002).

This paper first identifies the background as well as historic and emerging factors that underlie tourism development within Sharjah. Following this, it identifies specific tourism-related opportunities and challenges, which need to be considered for the Emirate to create an economically sustainable niche for itself within the United Arab Emirates (UAE) and the GCC region as a whole.

Background to Sharjah and its tourism development

Sharjah, which in Arabic literally means 'rising sun', is one of the seven emirates of the UAE. The city of Sharjah is located on the shores of the Arabian Gulf and is the capital of the Emirate of Sharjah, which spreads across the Arabian Peninsula to the east coast (i.e. Gulf of Oman) and includes Dibba Al Hisn, Khor Fakkan and Kalba. His Highness Sheikh Dr Sultan Bin Mohammed Al Qasimi, member of the UAE Supreme Council and ruler of Sharjah, has been at the helm since 1972, a year after the establishment of the Federation of the UAE. Sharjah was an important port for coastal trading, fishing and pearling in the early nineteenth century. It was one of the wealthiest towns in the region (SCTDA 2014).

Sharjah is the third largest economy within the UAE, with economic growth at 5.5 per cent in 2014 (Saadi 2015). Sharjah's per capita GDP grew by 50 per cent from 2000 to 2009. In fact, Sharjah's economy has one of the highest levels of diversification in the region and is the only economy in the Middle East with no single sector contributing to more than one-fifth of GDP (*Khaleej Times* 2012). Major sectors of the economy include manufacturing, real estate, business services and trading, as well as the fastest growing sectors being transportation, tourism, logistics and healthcare. Sharjah is also an established re-export and education hub within the region.

The growth of the Emirate has resulted in an increase in the number of residents who call Sharjah home. Approximately 19 per cent (946,000) of the UAE population (both Emiratis and expatriates) live in the Emirate, of which 85 per cent live within the city of Sharjah. Historically, affordable housing and subsistence as compared to Dubai led to a spillover effect on Sharjah, as residents have moved to the Emirate to manage escalating real estate costs. However, in recent times, this has had a detrimental effect in that the rentals have also increased in Sharjah (Kakande 2013a), thereby affecting its position as an affordable destination. Despite this, accommodation and subsistence related costs are far below the nearby emirates of Dubai and Abu Dhabi.

Sharjah has had a significant tourism history since 1932 when its airport opened, the first of its kind in the region. Sharjah International Airport handled a record number of 10 million passengers in 2015 (Sharjah Update 2016). The government is also planning to invest in a new and extended Sharjah Airport terminal, especially to improve access around the terminal (Cornwell 2015). Sharjah is home to Air Arabia, which began business in 2003 and claims to be the first and largest low-cost carrier in the MENA. It has since increased the level of connectivity, with more than 101 destinations across the MENA, Asia and Europe (Air Arabia 2016). The airline carried more than 7.6 million passengers in 2015, representing a 12 per cent increase from 2014 (El Gazzar 2016).

Sharjah's cruise ship industry is also a positive development, where around 238,000 international cruise tourists visited the Emirate in 2015 (Zriqat 2015), and a new cruise ship terminal on Sharjah's Indian Ocean coastline in Khorfakkan is being built. Such developments illustrate the Emirate's aspiration to strengthen this industry and increase the numbers further (Sharjah Update 2015a).

Although Sharjah does not directly compete with its neighbouring emirates, specifically Dubai and Abu Dhabi, it provides a basis for travellers to connect with a wider array of mid-priced and economy related travel products and services including a select few upscale hotels. The tourism development strategy of the Sharjah Commerce and Tourism Development Authority (SCTDA) intends to attract 10 million tourists to Sharjah by 2021 (Sharjah Update 2016). Although there were around 53 hotels and 52 hotel apartments, as well as 1.79 million hotel guests in 2015, the number of guests fell by 13 per cent from 2.06 million in 2014 (Algethami 2016). Overall, however, the hotel sector represented a significant improvement over the past decade. In 2007, for instance, there were just around 5,000 rooms divided among 22 hotels and 30 hotel apartment buildings (Jeffreys 2007).

Europe is a key feeder market for Sharjah, which witnessed around 409,578 European tourists in the first half of 2014, representing around 37 per cent of the total number of tourists. Sharjah also proved popular with tourists from the GCC region, receiving 369,485 visitors (34 per cent of the total). About 13 per cent of tourists were from Asia, 12 per cent from other Arab countries and 5 per cent from the Americas, Africa and the Pacific (Sharjah Update 2014). Although there is no direct intention to mirror Dubai's legacy of attracting the luxury market segment, Sharjah opened Starwoods' five-star Sheraton Sharjah Beach Resort and Spa in 2015. On the east coast, the Sharjah Investment and Development Authority (Shurooq) is developing a luxury villa resort in the name of Al Jabal Resort – the Chedi Khorfakkan. The construction of a further luxury hotel resort was announced in 2015, the Majlis Grand Mercure Sharjah, which is to be managed by Accor. The intention of this development is to incorporate contemporary art and cultural forms of the region, especially to align itself to the wider tourism strategy of the Emirate, that is, to develop tourism through its culture, heritage and history (Sharjah Update 2015b).

Sharjah has opted for a focused approach, building on its reputation as a centre of Islamic culture to take advantage of the burgeoning field of Islamic tourism. The emphasis on Islamic tourism is both an intelligent choice and an obvious one, providing a clear point of difference relative to the other emirates. Such positioning is founded upon a long-term tourist development strategy that aims, on the one hand, to increase the number of tourists and revenues, and on the other hand to maintain the Islamic and Arabic character of the Emirate. Sharjah boasts of its origins in Islamic traditions and Arabian heritage, encompassing art, architecture, culture, tradition and history. The United Nations Educational, Scientific and Cultural Organization (UNESCO) selected Sharjah as the Arab Cultural Capital in 1998 and the Organization of Islamic Countries designated it as the Islamic Culture Capital for 2014. This designation was achieved on the basis that the Emirate is sustainably proactive in 'preserving, promoting and disseminating culture at local, Arab and Islamic levels' (*Hamriyah Times* 2014). At the Arab Tourism Ministers Summit, the Emirate was selected as the Tourism Capital of the Arab World for 2015 (Zriqat 2015).

The focus for the Islamic Cultural Capital celebrations involves over 4,000 projects based partly on existing attractions, such as the Sharjah Museum of

Islamic Civilization, and partly on new attractions such as Al Majaz Island. The latter attraction is a Dh140 million (US$38.1 million) artificial island, built in Khalid Lagoon and intended to be the centrepiece of the Emirate's celebrations. The island includes an open-air amphitheatre capable of seating 4,500 people (*National* 2013). Also, the entire Al Majaz Waterfront has been transformed, currently featuring tourist attractions such as a musical fountain, fine-dining restaurants, recreational facilities and venues for diverse events.

Therefore, what distinguishes Sharjah is its commitment to art, culture and the preservation of local heritage. The commitment has been evident in the Heart of Sharjah mega-project, involving the restoration of traditional historical sites within the Emirate and scheduled for completion in 2025 (Khamis 2013). The overall intention is to work towards the preservation of national historic landmarks in Sharjah and the UAE, including archaeological sites and museums. According to Fox, Mourtada-Sabbah and al-Mutawa (2006: 285), 'We note that the government of Sharjah has revitalized a historical/cultural identity that will provide a degree of distinction within the ultramodern cityscapes that have come to characterize the Gulf'.

Sharjah boasts a number of unique heritage and cultural tourism events and attractions, including the Sharjah Biennial, the Sharjah International Book Fair, Sharjah Heritage Days, the Sharjah Water Festival, the UIM Formula One H20 Grand Prix and the Sharjah Light Festival (Dubai PR Network 2015). Sharjah has been a pioneer in developing culture and education in the region, and educational tourism has emerged as a tourism product. The University City, built in 1997, covers over 1,600 acres of land and showcases Islamic architecture. It houses three universities, among other educational institutions, which include the American University of Sharjah (AUS), ranked as one of the leading universities within the GCC and one among the top 400 universities in the world (see AUS 2014); the University of Sharjah; and the Higher Colleges of Technology. Domestic (UAE-based) and international students travel to Sharjah from other GCC countries and adjoining regions such as Central and South Asia. Sharjah aims to further emphasize and build its cultural identity under the auspices of the Department of Culture and Information.

Another pull factor is that the Emirate is geographically close to other Gulf countries and benefits from its unique geographic location on two coastlines: the Persian Gulf on the east and the Gulf of Oman on the west. The Emirate has firmly established itself as a family tourism destination due to its high-quality cultural attractions and tourist landmarks. For instance, the Sharjah Museums Department has developed programmes marketed to target families, particularly children, including finger print workshops at the Sharjah Art Museum as well as aircraft and automobile projects at the Al Mahatta and Vintage Car museums. Another event that focuses on families is 'Art through the Ages' at the Sharjah Archaeology Museum, which is also part of the Family Amusement Day programme exposing families to the museum's collections and statues (www.sharjahmuseums.ae).

Many Islamic cultural attractions within the Emirate have appeal because Muslim tourists, arguably, prefer to remain within a familiar culture while travelling (Kalesar 2010). There are more tourists travelling to Sharjah from GCC countries than ever before. The Emirate received 42,150 guests from Saudi Arabia during January and February 2015, compared with 37,941 during the same period in 2014. To strengthen its GCC market, and especially the Saudi Arabian segment, SCTDA annually attends the Riyadh Travel Fair, which is the largest exhibition for travel and tourism in Saudi Arabia (SCTDA 2015). Alcohol, bars, nightclubs and public beaches do not exist, and thus maintaining sensitivity towards Muslim travellers is not a major concern as the destination naturally appeals to those immersed in, or who have an appreciation of, Islamic culture and heritage. To accommodate increased numbers of Muslim tourists, the industry has learnt to abide by fundamental precepts such as the serving of halal food and beverages, adherence to prayer time and the provision of gender separate facilities. According to the director general of SCTDA:

> visitors from Saudi Arabia and other Gulf and Arab countries feel themselves totally at home and welcome in the Emirate. With its celebration of Arab and Islamic culture, heritage and values and complete with safe and friendly environment and incredible diversity, Sharjah is an ideal holiday destination for the Saudi and Arab families.
>
> (*Gulf Today* 2014)

Tourism development challenges

The potential growth of tourism arrivals is likely to be moderated by a number of challenges that will need to be managed carefully by Sharjah tourism operators and the government authorities. While these challenges are both numerous and complex, tourism industry leaders in the private and public sectors can develop strategies to strengthen the tourism industry and related infrastructure. The objective is to ensure that tourism development generates economic benefits for Sharjah, without compromising the host community.

Accessibility and mobility are critical issues for Sharjah's development as a tourism destination. With limited public transportation options, the city of Sharjah has been known for its heavy traffic congestion on the roads (Kakande 2013b). The large resident population, attracted to the Emirate because it offers better value real estate, has intensified the congestion problems as many residents commute to Dubai for work. Subsequently, the road infrastructure has struggled to cope with the high volumes of traffic. To its enormous credit, the Sharjah government has invested heavily in several large-scale infrastructure projects in recent years. This has been evident through the construction of new roads, bridges and tunnels to improve road accessibility around the Emirate (Ali 2011). Nonetheless, Sharjah's roads cannot cope effectively in the short to medium term, due to the rapid growth of the resident population and higher accommodation prices in Dubai. As the road infrastructure improves, paradoxically, it becomes more accessible to a wider resident population of commuters. In effect, the extra demand from road users quickly exceeds the capacity of the newly built roads, and the traffic congestion continues, only now on newer and wider roads. Excess traffic is also impacting car parking space in the Emirate (Francis 2013).

Movement of tourists on roads between the key attractions is thus a core challenge for tour operators who run their businesses in Sharjah and manage tourists staying in the Emirate. Similarly, tourists visiting the Sharjah attractions from other emirates such as Dubai and Abu Dhabi also fear becoming snarled up in traffic congestion (Xpress 2013). This situation can dissuade them from visiting the Emirate, even for a day trip to visit the souks and bazaars. A coordinated public transportation system both within and between each emirate would appear to be the only realistic solution in the long term, with the intention of diverting residents away from using their cars and thus freeing up the roads for tourist traffic to flow easily. A combination of buses, taxis, metro-link transport (similar to the one in Dubai), passenger trains and even ferries between emirates are likely to help alleviate the road infrastructure problems in the long term.

In addition to the road infrastructure, Sharjah has some other challenges with specific markets. One notable segment that has been strong in the past is the Russian market, which declined by 75 per cent in 2015 from the previous year. This was probably the result of the weakening of the Russian ruble compared to the US dollar, to which the UAE dirham is pegged (Algethami 2016). It may well be the case that the Emirate needs to look towards new markets as well as strengthen established and more reliable markets in the GGC region, especially given the government's intention to attract 10 million tourists by 2021, that is, to almost double its current figures in the next six years. The way forward would be to follow a more proactive approach in pursuing established and new markets. In fact, the Sharjah Commerce and Development Authority (SCTD) is intending to persist with encouraging Russian tourists to travel to the Emirate, as acknowledged in the plan to open an overseas office in Russia as well as establish offices in China, Germany, India and Saudi Arabia (Sharjah Update 2016). These regions involve major markets, which are arguably very lucrative.

Russia was a major tourist market for the Emirate, especially as Sharjah's flagship airline, Air Arabia, had been expanding its network in Russia and the Commonwealth of Independent States (CIS) region. A dedicated Russian-language website profiling Sharjah's tourism landscape, leisure opportunities and international festivals and events caters to this particular segment (Basyrova 2011). The main destination attributes that Russian tourists seek are the sun, sand and sea. Sharjah offers Russian tourists attractions in the form of some excellent beaches on both sides of the country. From a tourism context, however, Sharjah is also strategically located in close proximity to the emirates of Ajman and Dubai, offering a broad array of shopping and nightlife opportunities. In 2012, Sharjah earned the Most Active Destination Award at the Leisure Moscow Fair (*Middle East Online* 2013). Therefore, there is a considerable need for Sharjah to re-position itself more towards this particular segment to regain strong visitor numbers. As the Russian market is price sensitive and volatile, then there is a strong argument for the Emirate to present itself as a value-for-money destination, though holding the same core values that appealed to these tourists in the first place. The increasing hotel stock and emerging events and festivals in the Emirate are destination attributes which offer such tourists more flexible and suitable offerings.

Destination image concerns

Sharjah has a number of Islamic and cultural attractions, which focus on the history and heritage of the Arab world. These museums, events, arts and heritage areas serve as potential 'honeypot' attractions (Fyall *et al.* 2001) to bring tourists who are from the region and interested in their own heritage, as well as tourists from outside the region who are interested in Islamic culture and heritage. The awards Sharjah received for Islamic Culture and Arab Tourism reinforce the strength of its regional tourism presence, conveying positive tourism destination images.

Unfortunately, the Arab region has received negative images from foreign media, which distort the potential attractiveness of Sharjah as a tourism destination. For example, the 'neighbourhood effect' from other countries in the Middle East where there is civil unrest or security issues such as in Syria, Egypt and Iraq (Hazbun 2006) can create negative perceptions in the minds of prospective tourists, particularly from outside the Arab world. The perception that the region is not safe is common, and this could mitigate the desire to travel to Sharjah. Similarly, Al Hamarneh and Steiner (2004) also highlight the anti-Islamic sentiments present after 9/11, which immediately reduced Western travel around the world, especially to the Middle East, due to over-reaction, ignorance and xenophobia. The perceived danger in the Middle East created after the 9/11 terrorist attacks led to a significant drop in tourist arrivals from outside the region, but tourist arrivals increased significantly within the region as Arab travellers were sceptical of travelling overseas (Kalesar 2010).

Destination awareness challenges

In a study of international travellers, TCI Research (2013) reported that in comparison to other destinations from the Arabian Peninsula, Dubai achieves the highest scores in both awareness and positive brand image. With 93 per cent of prompted awareness and three in four travellers having a positive image of Dubai, the Emirate surpasses all if its regional competitors. In contrast, 'emerging destinations' in the region such as Sharjah are known, but normally by name only. Accordingly, Sharjah only has a prompted awareness of 26 per cent, with only around one in four travellers having a positive image of this destination. These findings clearly indicate that this emirate has a major opportunity to build a stronger awareness and consolidate its destination brand image.

Promotion of the Emirate as a tourist destination is the responsibility of SCTDA. This is a public authority, with a corporate body operating an independent budget, together with finance and administration systems in place. The authority participates in top local exhibitions in the region, including the Arabian Travel Market in Dubai and the Gulf Incentive Business Travel and Meetings

Exhibition in Abu Dhabi. On the international stage, the authority promotes the Emirate at all key international exhibitions and forums to bolster Sharjah's position on the world tourism map. Two of the world's leading travel trade shows are the World Travel Market (WTM) in London, which hosts around 5,000 exhibitors each year, along with 3,000 representatives of the international media (www.wtmlondon.com/en/visit/why-visit/), and Internationale-Tourismus-Börse Berlin (ITB Berlin), where more than 10,000 exhibitors participate each year (www.itb-berlin.de/en/Exhibitors/). When participating in such events, Sharjah concentrates on its tourism strengths, particularly its rich heritage and culture. As an example, it includes its culture of henna drawings and performances by folk artistes that are unique worldwide. Additionally, visitors also see traditional outfits and drawings made with calligraphic letters that arouse their interest in Sharjah's cultural offerings. Past involvement at this event has provided significant outcomes for the Emirate. The participation of SCTDA at ITB Berlin saw the number of tourists from Germany increase from 134,000 in 2009 to 140,000 in 2010 (Rizvi 2011).

The SCDTA is Sharjah's destination marketing organization (DMO), responsible for coordinating and integrating all elements of the destination mix (Pike 2008). This includes tourism attractions, events, facilities, operators and hospitality establishments (Mill and Morrison 2012). In particular, the SCDTA is responsible for planning, organizing and integrating all tourism-related activities in the Emirate to improve visitor flows and hotel occupancies. In addition, Sharjah has a distinct Islamic, cultural, heritage and family destination image. Like other DMOs, it is responsible for promoting its unique destination image and brand values to potential visitors (Morgan *et al.* 2011). Other trade shows more recently attended by SCTDA include the USA Roadshow and the UAE-South Korea Partnership Summit, reflecting the recognition that other opportunities exist to build bridges with new tourism and investment markets. In 2013, SCTDA also implemented a weeklong promotion in Singapore with the objective of familiarizing Singaporean tourists with Sharjah's heritage, traditions and cultural diversity (Schwab 2013).

SCTDA has also launched an interactive map of the Emirate offering residents and visitors a smart, convenient and interactive way to visit and know Sharjah. The interactive map highlights all the major tourist attractions, historical sites and business centres across the Emirate of Sharjah, including the city of Sharjah and the towns of Khor Fakkan, Kalba and Dibba Al-Hisn. The landmarks in these destinations have been classified into such categories as cultural, tourism and recreational. The authorities' endeavour is to strengthen smart, e-governance solutions in the tourism sector. Therefore, new initiatives have been launched, such as a Sharjah tourism portal, a Sharjah tourism mobile app, an event ticketing system and interactive touchscreen (*Khaleej Times* 2014).

Mixed-market challenges and opportunities

In marketing Sharjah as an international tourism destination, there are several marketing challenges faced by the tourism authorities. The first challenge concerns customer compatibility issues, particularly when representing different ethnic and religious backgrounds. Henderson (2008) noted that the marketing of Islamic destinations is not an easy task, especially given the significant variance between the demands of Western tourists and Islamic teachings. Interestingly, tourism demand from ex-Soviet Islamic countries has started to grow, partly due to Air Arabia's strategic presence in these emerging economies but also, possibly, as a consequence of the religious associations. Accordingly, tourists from the Islamic states of Azerbaijan, Uzbekistan and Kazakhstan are showing an interest in Sharjah. SCTDA has participated in promotional road shows, which recently included two other ex-Soviet (non-Islamic) countries, Georgia and Armenia (UAE Interact 2015).

As Dubai holidays can generally be viewed to be more expensive than holidays in Sharjah, tourists can fly to and from and stay in Sharjah while visiting both emirates. Many leisure visitors from these markets expect to go to mixed-gender pools and beaches, strip down to swimwear that is not respectful to the local culture and drink alcohol, which is not available in Sharjah. Many markets look for this as part of their way of relaxing (for example in China, Russia and many Western countries). In Sharjah there are no nightclubs, bars or restaurants selling alcohol, which may inhibit some potential tourist markets to Sharjah. For example, Sharpley (2002: 227) noted that 'a ban on the sale of alcoholic beverages towards the end of the decade severely reduced hotel occupancies in Sharjah'. Such restrictions are not evident in the more liberal Emirate of Dubai, which promotes these 'hedonistic' images (Henderson 2008) and, arguably, attracts a larger proportion of the lucrative Western tourist dollar as a result.

Moreover, Islamic restrictions may not be compatible with some leisure tourist segments, viewed as excessive and a limitation on people's freedom to dress, consume, act and communicate (Zamani-Farahani and Henderson 2010). With Muslim tourists and non-Muslim tourists staying in the same hotels, there is potential for confusion and disrespect. On the other hand, however, the lack of such non-Islamic experiences may indeed appeal to family markets from multiple national and religious segments, as well as appeal to the health-conscious markets (Stephenson 2014).

Getting the balance right between liberalism and conservatism is the likely challenge for the tourism authorities, who want to attract as broad a tourism base of travellers as possible. The solution may be a reasonable balance of tolerance, education and respect from the different tourist groups. Alternatively, the Sharjah tourism authorities may focus their destination marketing efforts on segments that are familiar with Muslim societies and those who follow the Islamic religion. Although this approach may be viewed as a missed opportunity for monopolizing on some tourist revenues, it could be viewed as an opportunity for countering negative images of Muslim nations (Zamani-Farahani and Henderson 2010).

Conclusions and research implications

This paper has highlighted issues and challenges that Sharjah needs to address to develop its tourism market potential. The emergence of tourism as a major focus of adjoining emirates and countries within the region has raised several questions related to sustaining the value of tourism related products and services within the Emirate. This paper delves into some of these challenges with the objective of underscoring their importance in order for Sharjah to benefit from leveraging tourism related resources for future growth and development.

While the tourism and hospitality industry in Sharjah has seen significant investments in the past few years, the Emirate's goal to attract tourists faces an obvious and profound challenge: it sits right next to one of the most famous cities in the world which is home to the world's tallest building, the biggest mall and the boldest land reclamations (Williams and Ashill 2011). Dubai deliberately targets a very broad demographic, as demonstrated most markedly by its successful bid to host World Expo 2020. Nonetheless, Sharjah benefits from the outflow of tourists from Dubai who extend their stay in the UAE by visiting Sharjah and commuting back to Dubai. In other cases, visitors go to Sharjah as their first stop in the UAE before heading to Dubai. In this regard, it would be worthwhile for future research to delve more into the impact of the emergence of Dubai as a global tourism hub and its potential impact on Sharjah as a tourism destination. For instance, one such research topic could include whether or not Sharjah's attractions, facilities and activities individually or collectively complement (including synergistic effects), cannibalize or compete with Dubai's tourism-related products and services. In this context, at present, not many studies exist which could be used to inform strategic decision making at the destination level.

In addition to Sharjah's own positioning as an Islamic cultural capital, the momentum behind increasing tourism numbers in the Emirate is helped by the large number of tourists already visiting Dubai and Abu Dhabi. Sharjah's emphasis on the family segment would enable it to enhance its stature as a family-friendly destination, especially for the target markets within the Middle East. The challenge that Sharjah faces is for the culture and heritage based attractions to create a profound impact such that the positioning of the Emirate becomes the unique selling proposition that draws travellers to the destination from within the region and globally. At present, however, such an impact has not yet materialized. Hence, it would be worthwhile for tourism and marketing researchers to study the potential impact of Sharjah's positioning strategy on the market and the competition within the immediate neighbouring environment as well as the GCC at large; including potential target audiences from both developed and developing countries alike would also benefit such research. Methods could include primary research capturing the perceptions of travellers using survey methods. The findings emanating from such research would influence future tourism policy formulation and implementation.

The budget airline Air Arabia, formed by the Sharjah government, facilitates the movement of tourists and business travellers within the UAE and from neighbouring countries. If Sharjah's positioning has a greater impact on travellers, and if it gets more exposure given Dubai's growing importance as a tourism destination, this would further influence travel to the region and, perhaps, direct inbound travel to the destination. This needs to be further explored through research that entails perception-based studies using primary data as well as *ex post* analysis using secondary data to reveal trends, both past and emerging.

Despite the threats that Dubai and other destinations within the region pose, there is much to benefit for Sharjah if it focuses on sustainable tourism. Such an approach would enable the Emirate to exploit its unique position as a centre for Islamic culture and heritage while attracting tourists who visit other prominent neighbouring destinations within the region. To tap into this already emerging opportunity would require the Emirate to address the challenges in terms of infrastructure and access, as well as tourism product development. At the same time, Sharjah would need to focus on developing its destination image with tourism promotion as the basis. Such campaigns should focus on the destination's uniqueness while using pull factors to sustain tourism growth. Sharjah would need to develop further the tourism product as a family-oriented destination, which would enhance its identity and uniqueness. This, in combination with its position as an Islamic cultural capital, would reduce its reliance on neighbouring emirates while generating and sustaining tourism demand. Marketing challenges related to image development and positioning would need to be addressed in the short term, whereas resource development in terms of attractions, facilities and activities that underlie Sharjah's positioning need to be at the crux of its long-term strategy. This would further deemphasize the Emirate's reliance on the success factors of its neighbours.

Finally, there is also potential for the destination to create tourism networks with its neighbours (co-opetition) to address the challenges. There has been a strong call for more collaborative marketing and regional marketing alliances for tourism DMOs (Fyall, Garrod and Wang 2012), but to date there has been little empirical application towards Islamic tourism destinations such as Sharjah. Although SCTDA is devoted to developing and promoting the tourism and hospitality sectors, and showcasing the Emirate of Sharjah as a distinct global destination with authentic Islamic heritage and culture, cross-emirate collaboration is the key to ensuring long-term sustainable growth. Low regional collaboration between different emirates remains a weakness of the UAE tourism sector. The Emirate of Sharjah has a great deal to gain from exchanging experience and expertise with other emirates. Case-study research using focus groups and personal interview methods could address this through strategic analysis of tourism networks and their short-term and long-term economic, social, cultural and political impacts. Such studies could form the basis for decision-making at the Emirate and country levels. Needless to say, addressing the challenges through such research would determine if Sharjah is able to build and sustain value associated with tourism in the long term. Accordingly, a holistic approach is required for the sustainable development of Sharjah as a tourism destination.

References

Air Arabia (2016) 'About us'. Available online at www.airarabia.com/en/about-us (accessed 24 February 2016).

Algethami, S. (2016) 'Sharjah eyes 3–5% growth in hotel guests in 2016', *Gulf News*, 13 January. Available online at http://gulfnews.com/business/sectors/tourism/sharjah-eyes-3-5-growth-in-hotel-guests-in-2016-1.1653386 (accessed 26 February 2016).

Al-Hamarneh, A. and C. Steiner (2004) 'Islamic tourism: rethinking the strategies of tourism development in the Arab world after September 11, 2001', *Comparative Studies of South Asia, Africa and the Middle East*, 24(1): 173–182.

Ali, A. (2011) 'Sharjah traffic congestion to continue for two years', *Gulf News*, 7 October. Available online at http://gulfnews.com/news/gulf/uae/traffic-transport/sharjah-traffic-congestion-to-continue-for-two-years-1.886991 (accessed 8 February 2014).

AUS (American University of Sharjah) (2014) 'AUS jumps to 390 in world university rankings', 22 September. Available online at www.aus.edu/news/article/771/aus_jumps_ to_390_in_world_university_rankings (accessed 20 October 2014).

Basyrova, N. (2011) 'Sharjah woos German, Russian tourists with new website', *Rus Tourism News*, 21 March. Available online at www.rustourismnews.com/2011/03/21/sharjah-woos-german-russian-tourists-with-new-websites/ (accessed 3 March 2016).

Cornwell, A. (2015) 'Sharjah international airport expansion to get a new masterplan', *Gulf News*, 20 April. Available online at http://gulfnews.com/business/aviation/sharjah-international-airport-expansion-to-get-new-master-plan-1.1495702 (accessed 24 January 2016).

Dubai PR Network (2015) 'Sharjah's acclaimed festivals and events draw huge interest at ITB Berlin', 7 March. Available online at www.google.com/search?q=Sharjah+Has+Always+Been+A+Pioneer%E2%80%99%2C+2010&ie=utf-8&oe=utf-8 (accessed 24 January 2016).

TCI (Tourism Competitive Intelligence) (2013) 'Dubai ranked 1st in awareness and image in the Arabian Peninsula', TCI Research Traveller Panel, July. Available online at http://tci-research.com/dubai-nb-1-in-awareness-and-positive-image-in-the-arabian-peninsula/ (accessed 21 February 2014).

El Gazzar, S. (2016) 'Air Arabia profit falls as competition squeezes margins', *The National*, 7 February. Available online at www.thenational.ae/business/aviation/air-arabia-profit-falls-as-competition-squeezes-margins (accessed 26 February 201).

Francis, S. (2013) 'Al Nahda community watch: rent vs traffic… what's driving Sharjah tenants back to Dubai'. *Emirates 24/7*, 19 November. Available online at www.Emirates247.com/news/Emirates/al-nahda-community-watch-rent-vs-traffic-what-s-driving-sharjah-tenants-back-to-dubai-2013-11-19-1.528498 (accessed 11 February 2014).

Fox, J. W., N. Mourtada-Sabbah and M. al-Mutawa (2006) 'Heritage revivalism in Sharjah', in J. W. Fox, N. Mourtada-Sabbah and M. al-Mutawa (eds) *Globalization and the Gulf*, London: Routledge, pp. 266–287.

Fyall, A., A. Leask and B. Garrod (2001) 'Scottish visitor attractions: a collaborative future?', *International Journal of Tourism Research*, 3(4): 211–228.

Fyall, A., B. Garrod and Y. Wang (2012) 'Destination collaboration: a critical review of theoretical approaches to multi-dimensional phenomenon', *Journal of Destination Marketing and Management*, 1: 10–26.

Gulf Today (2014) 'GCC visitors show interest in Sharjah's tourism offering', *Gulf Today*, 21 April. Available online at http://gulftoday.ae/portal/ad7d121c-c87a-4335-b6d55c7d064a1e7d.aspx (accessed 25 May 2014).

Hamriyah Times (2014) 'Sharjah is capital of Islamic culture for 2014', *Hamriyah Times*, January–March, 1: 1. Available online at www.hfza.ae/Portals/0/pdf/HamriyahTimes/Hamriyah_Times_issue_28.pdf (accessed 24 February 2016).

Hazbun, W. (2006) 'Explaining the Arab Middle East tourism paradox', *The Arab World Geographer/Le Géographe du monde arabe*, 9(3): 201–214.

Henderson, J. C. (2008) 'Representations of Islam in official tourism promotion', *Tourism Culture and Communication*, 8(3): 135–145.

Henderson, J. (2006) 'Tourism in Dubai: overcoming barriers to destination development', *International Journal of Tourism Research*, 8(2): 87–99.

ITB Berlin – International Travel Trade Show Berlin (2014). Available online at www. berlin.de/en/events/2101408-2842498-itb-berlin-international-travel-trade-sh.en. html (accessed 20 October 2014).

Jafari, J. and N. Scott (2014) 'Muslim world and its tourism', *Annals of Tourism Research*, 44: 1–19.

Jeffreys, A. (ed.) (2007) *Emerging Sharjah*, Istanbul: Oxford Business Group.

Kakande, Y. (2013a) 'Sharjah residents feel effect of rising Dubai rents', *The National*, 15 December. Available online at www.thenational.ae/uae/sharjah-residents-feel-effect-of-rising-dubai-rents (accessed 11 February 2014).

Kakande, Y. (2013b) 'Public transport survey part of plan to beat Sharjah traffic woes', *The National*, 18 September. Available online at www.thenational. ae/uae/transport/public-transport-survey-part-of-plan-to-beat-sharjah-traffic-woes (accessed 11 February 2014).

Khaleej Times (2012) 'Sharjah's economy has highest level of diversification', *Khaleej Times*, 2 May. Available online at www.khaleejtimes.com/article/20120502/ARTICLE/305029812/1002 (accessed 11 February 2014).

Khaleej Times (2014) Sharjah tourism launches interactive map of the emirate, *Khaleej Times*, 6 January. Available online at www.khaleejtimes.com/article/20140106/ARTICLE/3010 698 60/1037 (accessed 15 February 2014).

Kalesar, M. (2010) 'Developing Arab-Islamic tourism in the Middle East: an economic benefit or a cultural seclusion?', *International Politics*, 33(5): 105–136.

Khamis, J. (2013) 'Heart of Sharjah project under way', *Gulf News*, 10 March. Available online at http://m.gulfnews.com/news/uae/tourism/heart-of-sharjah-project-under-way-1.1156359 (accessed 15 February 2014).

Mansfeld, Y. and O. Winckler (2007) 'The tourism industry as an alternative for the GCC oil-based rentier economies', *Tourism Economics*, 13(3): 333–360.

Middle East Online (2013) 'Sharjah earns itself prominent position in tourism and travel market', *Middle East Online*, 19 September. Available online at www.middle-east-online.com/english/?id=61459 (accessed 14 February 2014).

Mill, R. C. and A. M. Morrison (2012) *The Tourism System*, 7th edn, Dubuque, IA: Kendall/Hunt Publishing.

Morgan, N., A. Pritchard and R. Pride (2011) *Destination Brands: Managing Place Reputation*, 3rd edn, Abingdon: Butterworth-Heinemann, Elsevier.

National (2013) 'Sharjah's tourism focus is all about Islamic culture', *The National*, 17 December. Available online at www.thenational.ae/thenationalconversation/ editorial/sharjahs-tourism-focus-is-all-about-islamic-culture#ixzz2tPVuRwPo (accessed 21 February 2014).

Pike, S. (2008) *Destination Marketing: An Integrated Marketing Communication Approach*, Abingdon: Butterworth-Heinemann, Elsevier.

Rizvi, M. (2011) 'Sharjah tourism is special', *Khaleej Times*, 13 March. Available online at www.khaleejtimes.combiz/inside.asp?xfile=/data/business/2011/March/business_March249.xmlandsection=businessandcol (accessed 22 February 2014).

Saadi, D. (2015) 'S&P reaffirms positive sovereign credit rating for Sharjah', *The National*, 9 May. Available online at www.thenational.ae/business/economy/sp-reaffirms-positive-sovereign-credit-rating-for-sharjah (accessed 3 March 2016).

Schwab, K. (2013) *The Global Competitiveness Report 2013–2014*, Geneva: World Economic Forum.

SCTDA (2014) Sharjah Commerce and Tourism Development Authority, Government of Sharjah. Available online at www.sharjahtourism.ae (accessed 11 February 2014).

SCTDA (2015) 'Sharjah tourism aims to strengthen position in Saudi market with participation in "Riyadh Travel Fair 2015"'. Available online at http://sharjahmydestination.ae/en-us/About-Sharjah/News/ArtMID/681/ArticleID/139/Sharjah-tourism-aims-to-strengthen-position-in-Saudimarket-with-participation-in-%E2%80%98Riyadh-Travel-Fair-2015%E2%80%99 (accessed 24 February 2016).

Sharjah Archaeology Museum (2014). Available online at www.sharjahmuseums.ae.

Sharjah Update (2014) 'Sharjah welcomes 15 per cent more tourists', 30 September. Available online at www.sharjahupdate.com/2014/09/sharjah-tourists-15-percent-more-in-h1-2014/ (accessed 24 February 2016).

Sharjah Update (2015a) 'Sharjah's busy cruise season begins', 9 December. Available online at www.sharjahupdate.com/2015/12/sharjahs-busy-cruise-season-begins/ (accessed 26 February 2016).

Sharjah Update (2015b) 'New US$100m Sharjah luxury resort planned', 6 May. Available online at www.sharjahupdate.com/2015/05/new-us100m-sharjah-luxury-resort-planned/ (accessed 26 February 2016).

Sharjah Update (2016) 'Sharjah top open five global offices', 17 February. Available online at www.sharjahupdate.com/2016/02/sharjah-tourism-to-open-five-global-offices/ (accessed 24 February 2016)

Sharpley, R. (2002) 'The challenges of economic diversification through tourism: the case of Abu Dhabi', *International Journal of Tourism Research*, 4(3): 221–235.

Stephenson, M. (2014) 'Deciphering "Islamic hospitality": developments, challenges and opportunities', *Tourism Management*, 40: 155–164.

UAE Interact (2015) 'Sharjah set to promote tourism landmarks in Russia, Armenia, Georgia and Kazakhstan', *UAE Interact*, 30 September. Available online at www.Uaeinteract.com/docs/Sharjahset_topromote_tourism_landmarks_in_Russia,_Armenia_Georgia_and_Kazakhstan/71338.htm (accessed 26 February 2016).

Williams, P. and N. Ashill (2011) 'Definitely Dubai: destination branding in action', in A. Fyall and B. Garrod (eds) *Contemporary Cases Online*. Oxford: Goodfellow Publishers, pp. 57–77.

World Travel Market. Available online at www.wtmlondon.com/en/visit/why-visit/.

Xpress (2013) 'Why has Sharjah traffic gone from bad to worse?', *Xpress*, 25 December. Available online at http://gulfnews.com/xpress/why-has-sharjah-traffic-gone-from-bad-toworse-1.1270905 (accessed 22 September 2014).

Zamani-Farahani, H. and J. C. Henderson (2010) 'Islamic tourism and managing tourism development in Islamic societies: the cases of Iran and Saudi Arabia', *International Journal of Tourism Research*, 12(1): 79–89.

Zriqat, T. (2015) 'Sharjah pulling in the crowds as a tourist destination', *The National*, 29 January. Available online at www.thenational.ae/business/travel-tourism/sharjah-pulling-in-the-crowds-as-a-tourist-destination (accessed 24 February 2015).

11 Kuwait

Why tourism?

Peter Burns and Lyn Bibbings

The primary purpose of this chapter is to provide insight into the background and rationale behind the development of tourism in an oil-rich state that has no obvious economic imperative driving tourism's case for development investment. Underpinning this purpose is the identification of obstacles to the development of tourism. Tourism development in Kuwait has been slow paced, with some emphasis on business tourism (Euromonitor International 2013) that has enabled society to absorb the impacts without causing any noticeable negative effects. Tourism development, according to the marketing strategy relating to the implementation stage of the Tourism Master Plan (in 2012–13), is to focus on an upmarket clientele attracted by well-developed family tourism products which respect traditional values, as well as the development of world-class mega-attractions to distinguish the destination from the regional competition. Overall, the authorities wish to encourage more Kuwaitis to holiday at home as a form of affirming national identity in a somewhat homogenizing world (Fairweather and Rogerson 2003).

More specifically, the Tourism Master Plan created a vision for tourism in Kuwait based around being a 'culturally rich and interesting society' contextualized within an 'Islam-friendly setting', that is, more relaxed in markedly different ways than, say, Dubai. Such a product is thought by the authorities to be of particular interest to Saudi Arabians (Euromonitor International 2013), for whom Kuwait, which does not have the excesses of Dubai, is a simple drive across the border. Key tourism products targeted by the Tourism Master Plan for development include the following: beach resorts, the sea and islands; comfort, good restaurants and wellness; shopping (traditional and modern); family-friendly facilities; and Kuwaiti culture (contemporary culture, Islam and maritime and desert heritage).

The chapter presents an exploratory case study that examines Kuwait's decision to engage with international tourism in its real-life context from multiple perspectives. Even though Kuwait has a huge oil income, the vagaries of international markets and the risk associated with relying on a single source of income provide one central rationale for the development and promotion of tourism in Kuwait. However, this is something of a normative view. For Kuwait, the development of tourism seems like an enigma, as it holds the fifth-largest oil reserves in the world in 2014, which represents 6.8 per cent of such reserves, and ranks fourth among Arab countries according to the World Economic Forum's Global Competitiveness Report 2015–16 (GCC-Stat 2016).

Despite the usual starting position of economic necessity, Kuwait's approach to instigating tourism is based on two important premises: (1) the development of a bedrock for national pride (and thus unity) and (2) the widening of an employment base, which is currently over-reliant on a 'functional but bloated state bureaucracy' (BTI 2014: 6). Additionally, however, the role of tourism in communicating a positive image of Kuwait overseas is also, arguably, vital to this Gulf Cooperation Council (GCC) state.

The case study focuses on complex social conditions surrounding Kuwait's hesitant attempts to enter the international tourism arena, rather than identifying the more prosaic matters such as marketing and product development. In taking this approach, particular emphasis is placed on two areas: first, a tourism awareness programme aimed at a number of stakeholders and second, employment opportunities for Kuwaiti nationals, especially youth and graduates. Unemployment among Kuwaitis was 5 per cent in 2014. However, an estimated 54.3 per cent of those eligible to work are not part of the workforce (*Arab Times* 2016). In an earlier 2012 report from Saudi Arabia's National Commercial Bank, it was estimated that 36.3 per cent of the unemployed in Kuwait were in the politically and culturally critical 20–24 age bracket (*Emirates 24/7* 2012).

There is an ongoing issue in Kuwait over private (dominated by foreign labour at all levels) versus public sector employment (the traditional graduate employment destination), with the government taking a range of actions and incentives to shift reliance away from public sector employment for Kuwaiti nationals (Hertog 2013). The BTI report (2014: 23), which examines progress towards democracy in market economies, highlights the problem:

> Growing unemployment among young Kuwaitis … continued to rise, while at the same time, hundreds of thousands of foreign workers are hired each year. A policy to nationalize the workforce has not yielded the expected results as the government is unable to enforce its own laws on the matter.

Moreover, BTI (2014: 20) also draws attention to another problem common to a number of GCC countries, 'the continued presence of informal patronage networks'. In other words, 'who you know' is often more important than 'what you know'. Such patronage has powerful impacts on equality of opportunity. The debate over employment and the role of government is only one strand of a wider discussion about the future of Kuwait. The seventh edition of *Kuwait: Facts and Figures* (Ministry of Information circa 2001: 11) has a preface that provides considerable insight into how Kuwait was thinking about its future at that time: 'living in a world that is prepared to meet the third millennium of modern man [sic] in an age of information and revolution in technology'; and 'Kuwait … making strides to stay abreast of these developments … in the global arena'. This arena is framed by international tourism and mobility, especially as there were over 1 billion international arrivals recorded for the first time in 2012 (UNWTO 2012).

The forthcoming discussion focuses on the rationale behind the development of tourism in Kuwait as a single unit of analysis. Qualitative data in the form of fieldwork, archival records, verbal reports and participant observations are highlighted as evidence. The methods chosen to collect data from multiple sources were designed to unfold an understanding of the facts and a consideration of alternative explanations, as well as provide an evaluation leading to a single most congruent explanation (Yin 2012). The research instruments were deployed by the first author of this chapter, who was proactively involved in the development and implementation of Kuwait's Tourism Master Plan between 2009 and 2013, which was subsequently submitted to government in 2015.

The secondary research element of this chapter utilizes official reports from both public and private sector institutions, which establishes a clear background to the study. The work then reflects on general issues emerging from interviews with 32 key stakeholders, including senior government officials, business leaders, media commentators, opinion leaders and academics. These interviews laid the groundwork for six focus group studies held with teachers, employers, tourism business federations, youth organizations and the investment sector, which helped to strengthen the ideas presented. The focus group topics concentrated on issues concerning youth, employment, society, social identity, conservatism and Kuwait's image abroad. Focus group results are distilled into two mind maps (see Figures 11.2 and 11.3 later in this chapter). The main purpose of these activities is to understand the rationale behind tourism development from a range of different perspectives. In all cases, access to the field was through the 'gatekeeping' facilitation of Kuwait's Ministry of Commerce and Industry.

Kuwait's planning and vision

The dominant public discourses and commissioned visioning reports seem to indicate that the government cares about its national achievements and its image and role in the wider, global sphere. In a sense, this provides a clear rationale for using tourism as part of a global strategy to promote an image of Kuwait overseas. More recently, these thoughts have been developed further. The Supreme Council for Planning and Development (SCPD), for instance, adopted a vision for Kuwait 2035 (T. Aldowaisan, pers. comm. July 2012) that talks of Kuwait becoming a 'financial and commercial centre that is attractive to investors' and where the private sector 'leads economic activity, inspiring competition, and enhancing efficient production'. The SCPD even talks about being a 'supportive state that instils values, maintains social identity, and achieves human development and balanced development'. Kuwait hopes that its plans for tourism will strengthen social identity and values. In 2011, the National Assembly approved the SCDP's National Development Plan (NDP). The SCPD offered several strategic objectives to realize the 2035 Vision, attempting to incentivize more private sector-led businesses, thus shifting the burden away from the government. The intention is that the private sector leads development according to specific incentives.

The Blair Vision (see Aldowaisan 2010), commissioned by the Kuwaiti government and published in 2009, developed a vision for the government's 'Kuwait 2030' project suggesting that by that date, Kuwait 'should be the main international trade, energy and services hub for the Northern Gulf'. Moreover, Kuwait's strength should be based on 'its uniquely open, tolerant and diverse society, a strong and well-diversified economy led by the private sector'. The Blair Vision went on to suggest five dimensions for future change within a wider pan-Arabian Gulf context that links Kuwait's trading past with its entrepreneurial future: (1) an outward-looking, entrepreneurial trading economy, (2) open and capable people, (3) tolerance, (4) free expression and (5) a rich cultural heritage. Tourism fits quite well with this vision, which provides a rationale for tourism development beyond the usual motivation of providing foreign income and employment generation.

The rationale for tourism in Kuwait

These reports and 'visions' provide a background for the rationale supporting tourism development in an oil-rich country. First, it seems that tourism can deliver a message that Kuwait is, as in the words of the tourism plan, 'an attractive place to live, work and visit' – a message inward investors would no doubt welcome. Second, the visions offer a cohesive approach to tourism development that facilitates a friendly welcome and provides soft infrastructure (i.e. good hotels, restaurants and leisure and retail facilities) for sustainable and productive business and enterprise. Third, a successful and effective tourism industry, in its widest sense, is an essential pillar supporting Kuwait's broader societal ambitions for the future and its sense of place in the world (Bhandary 2014). Drawing together purposeful forms of leisure, recreation and retail, good hotels and other support infrastructure can act as the foundation for social stability and a pillar to support sustainable growth.

Table 11.1 plots changes in the socio-cultural characteristics of Kuwait and provides a snapshot of the country's stages of development. It illustrates the extent to which levels of co-presence with outsiders have increased and population mobility has changed, that is, the extent to which people have physical and virtual exposure to other cultural experiences and society.

Tourism development and society

This section outlines ideas about tourism, culture and society and, thus, sets the theoretical scene to the chapter. This background enables the reader to locate or contextualize the problems and challenges of Kuwait with what is generally known about tourism and its social impacts. Societal development can be framed by a number of factors: transnational mobility; political relations with neighbours near and far; access to resources; and creativity, political innovations and the

Table 11.1 Kuwait: stages of development and mobility

Stage of development	Mobility and co-presence with outsiders	Effects on society and mobility
1930–1955 Pre-oil 'naïve' era	Some mobility among pearl and maritime traders.	Relatively little exposure except to Asia and Africa.
1950s–1970s Early oil era	Increased sphere of travel for Kuwaiti merchants. Significant immigration of Arab labour to Kuwait.	Rapid population increase but within the context of homogenous Arab communities.
1980s–1991 Modern Kuwait (Iraq invasion and subsequent liberation)	Rise in Kuwaiti travel, especially younger generation for education and leisure. Significant immigration of 'contract labour', largely comprising of single males to service the construction industry and other projects.	Heterogeneous society emerging with cultural tolerance but based on hierarchical social structures. Emerging fears of being overwhelmed by single migrant workers, especially from South East Asia and poor Arab countries.
Post-1991 The postmodern era	Change of emphasis from Arab immigration to more labour from Philippines and South Asia. Education and relative wealth leads to Kuwait nationals being frequent flyers and global travellers. Increase of virtual mobility via satellite TV and the Internet.	The co-presence of a Kuwaiti minority alongside an Asian majority, resulting in a society composed of a series of parallel but unequal co-existing groups. Emergence of a consumer and connected society, rise of the MTV generation, and the recognition of a cultural turn (such as more power to women and attention to the needs of the younger generations).

Source: Developed by the authors in discussion with Dr Lubna Al-Kazi (pers. comm. September 2009).

grasping of new opportunities that arise from various forms of tension, especially the tensions that shape society (see Keesing 1971).

The presence of visiting tourists brings a special complication to the lives of people strongly following Islamic custom and Arabic tradition, which demands that acts of hospitality and courtesy are communicated to strangers and visitors alike – a tradition that is framed by reciprocal relations and strict rules of etiquette (Keesing and Strathern 1997). Tradition stipulates, for instance, that a person should not enter another person's house before the first call to prayer in the morning or after *isha*, the last call to prayer of the day. In times gone by, these strict conditions on the giving and receiving of hospitality in private houses were adhered to. In more recent times, this problem has effectively been circumvented by entertaining in public restaurants. Traditions and social fabric are inevitably weakened when consuming strangers, who take hospitality but do not give it in return, enter the scene without due respect to religion and tradition; and when modernity takes its toll by altering and influencing the tensions that shape modern society.

There are policy and other social measures that can be taken to ameliorate perceived negative effects of tourism development in Kuwait. Prime among these are the development and implementation of creative and honest public awareness and communication programmes designed to build trust and allay fears, and integration of stakeholder and community consultation about co-presence and its implications within tourism planning. Moreover, while Kuwaitis know full well that changes to lifestyle patterns are an inevitability of oil wealth, measures can be put in place that enable such changes to be assimilated by the existing culture at an acceptable pace that will not create generational anxiety or other family tensions (Ohaeri *et al.* 2009). Kuwaiti people have a strong sense of culture, religion, family values and community spirit. These attributes will go a long way in helping individuals, communities and society at large cope with the impacts of tourism, as has been shown in some other countries in the GCC region.

Theoretical developments

From the literature and fieldwork (observations, interviews and focus groups), a model is developed (Figure 11.1) that helps theorize the links between tourism, co-presence (i.e. the meeting of cultures at a destination) and potential conflicts. The model comprises three main elements:

1 Extent of economic and employment dependency on tourism, in the sense that cases of high dependence on tourism places countries and regions at risk from (a) various slowdowns in the general (global) tourism economy, (b) natural/political shocks and (c) vulnerability to transnational tourism corporations (e.g. hotel groups, major airlines and online booking agencies) exerting business conformity pressure.

2 Strength of political and cultural identity, especially conservative versus liberal views (for Kuwait, see Abdel-Khalek 2006), and existing experiences of tourism as a host and as a tourist, and the cultural and socio-economic propensity for population mobility. Although digital co-presence is one mechanism of such exposure, this discussion mainly concerns the effects of physical mobility.

3 Extent and nature of co-presence between nationals and tourists, that is, nationals sharing space with tourists leading to potential competition for leisure resources (Crouch *et al.* 2001). This is especially vexatious for Kuwait and other GCC countries, given the numerical minority of nationals. It was

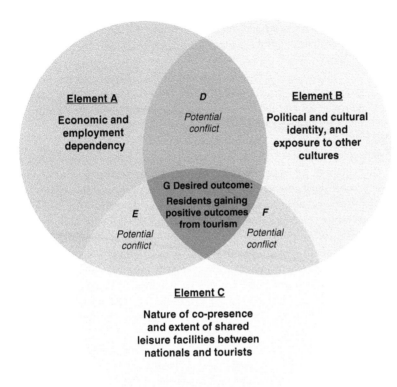

Figure 11.1 Theoretical model for tourism, co-presence and potential conflicts.

Source: Developed by the authors.

estimated that only 32.8 per cent of the population were Kuwaitis in 2014 (*Arab Times* 2016). However, the socio-economic superiority of indigenous populations in the region could ensure that local populations do not become marginalized in the co-presence relationship, as can be the case in less developed countries (see Turner and Ash 1975).

Where the three main elements of the model overlap (parts 'D', 'E' and 'F'), potential for conflict exists. When the model is tested in the context of Kuwait, a number of conclusions may be inferred. Where straightforward economic dependence is low (element A), and cultural identity is high and attitudes are conservative (element B), then there is potential conflict in that the population at large might think, 'Why do we need tourism?' and 'Why are these tourists here?'. While the economic impacts of tourism will always be overwhelmed by oil revenue, there are limits to the number and type of jobs generated in this extractive industry. The need is for employment opportunities generated by the private sector (including entrepreneurial activities), which are of increasing importance as the government struggles with the social issues caused by youth unemployment and underemployment.

The two most important factors to arise from the aforementioned views outlined in Figure 11.1 concern the extent to which development brings about changes to local lifestyles and the impact of the physical co-presence of tourists and locals through the sharing of leisure pursuits with local communities and populations.

In the particular case of Kuwait, employment and economic dependency could, at first glance, be separated. However, through tourism these new employment opportunities contribute to social harmony, societal satisfaction and personal fulfilment, not simply income generation. Likewise, the situation for Kuwait in relation to co-presence, the intersection of elements A (low economic dependence on tourism) and C (where domestic use of public leisure facilities is high) might create conflict through competition for leisure resources (especially seaboard). However, high levels of quality control and sophisticated resource management will help reduce any such potential conflicts. Finally, where competition for space (element C) intersects with element B conflict may arise, especially where the nature of the public leisure facilities is changed through domination by other cultures and foreigners, leaving Kuwaitis feeling 'uncomfortable' in their leisure pursuits. Nonetheless, this is a situation already common in a society that has a massive presence of migrant labour in service positions. It is noteworthy that a Kuwaiti is highly unlikely to be served in a shop or other commercial encounter by another Kuwaiti, where the service worker is likely to be foreign.

The potential conflicts identified are not inevitable (see Gibson 2010) but simply highlight areas to focus on in a public awareness campaign for Kuwait. If the areas noted in Figure 11.1 are adequately addressed and managed, then the desired outcome outlined in 'G', that is, nationals being positive about tourism, will be reached. Note the use of the word 'positive' rather than its alternative, 'acceptance', which does not imply a positive socio-cultural environment but could actually indicate passive resentment.

Concerns of Kuwaiti society and key stakeholders

Over time, tourism in Kuwait, including domestic leisure facilities and attractions, has developed at a relatively slow pace. This has enabled society to attune to the impacts without causing any overtly noticeable effects. Observations at the local level reveal that Kuwaitis and foreign leisure activities do not always share common space, with some notable exceptions such as at luxury shopping malls. However, even in Kuwait's largest shopping mall, 'The Avenues', there is a separate section which houses high-end brands distinct from the middle and lower consumer brands. In order to gain specific perceptions about further tourism development, focus group discussions were held with Kuwaiti academics and officials. The results are summarized in Figure 11.2, providing a snapshot of attitudes towards tourism in Kuwait.

The range of present attractions, including desert, seashore and museums, forms a reasonable and realistic starting point for this vision and its accompanying ambitions. Figure 11.3, developed from fieldwork and focus group meetings, illustrates the level of awareness about tourism issues and their implications. The main categories to think about (not in any order of priority) are religion, careers, culture, national pride, business, community and social capital.

Each of the seven categories in Figure 11.3 has sub-branches that further identify concerns and priorities that can help shape sensitive tourism planning. In addition to the information illustrated in Figures 11.1 and Figure 11.2, a series of themes emerged from the fieldwork (see Table 11.2), which included interviews with key players, including officials from various government agencies and the investment community, as well as a number of senior managers in the tourism and hospitality industries. Focus group discussions also took place with social stakeholders and special interest groups for women, conservation and youth. This process has helped to shape some questions about tourism, society and culture, which in turn enabled the production of a summary assessment of the wider situation in Kuwait.

Tourism and employment in Kuwait

The structural difficulties in employment caused by a strong reliance on migrant labour and expatriate management are significant in Kuwait. The latest data available, at the time of writing, come from Kuwait's Central Statistical Bureau, which indicates that only 19 per cent of the workforce (i.e. 342,417) consists of Kuwaitis, compared to 81 per cent from overseas (i.e. 1,463,090 foreigners) (Toumi 2016). Evidence seems to suggest that a long-term structural problem of Kuwaitis being reluctant to take up private sector jobs exists, and this is not necessarily restricted to the tourism industry. The 2014 (October–December) data indicate that around 77.2 per cent of public sector employees and only 5.2 per cent private sector employees are Kuwaitis (*Arab Times* 2016). These structural employment issues are not unique to Kuwait and are often found in other GCC countries, notably Saudi Arabia, which is experiencing high rates of unemployment coupled with cultural resistance to many private sector jobs, despite efforts by the government to encourage private sector employment. The long-standing government programme of 'Kuwaitization' (Hertog 2013) is attempting, to some extent at least, to tackle some of the challenges that Kuwait nationals face. There are five significant observations concerning tourism employment:

1. Local recruitment challenges

Although some Kuwaitis have been recruited into the tourism workforce, local employment is not significant. In 2006, for example, only 85 Kuwaitis were

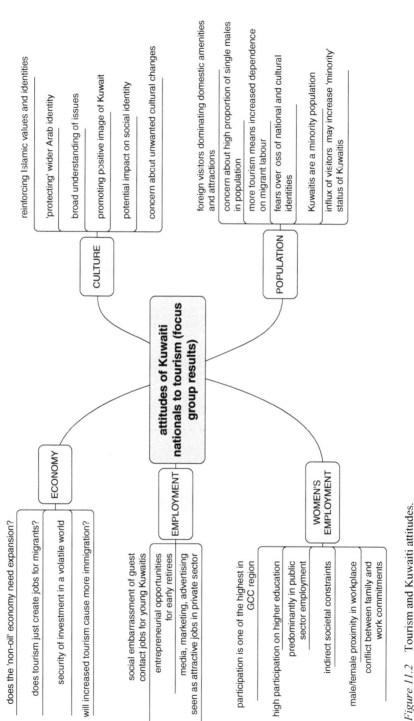

Figure 11.2 Tourism and Kuwaiti attitudes.

Source: Developed from the authors' fieldwork.

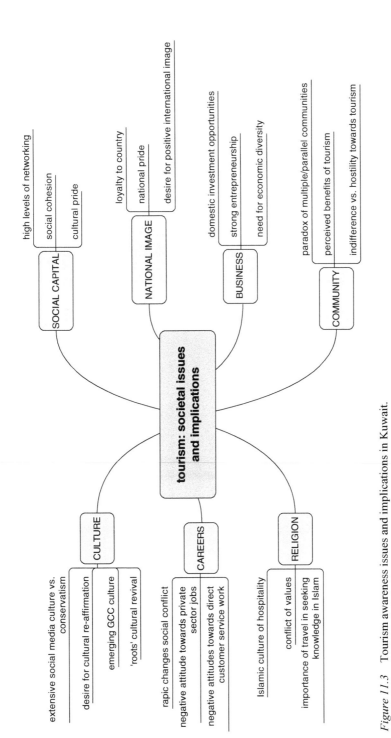

Figure 11.3 Tourism awareness issues and implications in Kuwait.

Source: Developed from the authors' fieldwork.

Table 11.2 Key questions for tourism and the situation in Kuwait

Framework element	Key questions the framework element seeks to answer	Overview of situation in Kuwait
T1. Co-presence: hosts and the tourist	Is mutual respect and understanding between 'host' and 'guest' possible?	Yes, it is possible, given that Kuwaitis themselves are self-confident, experienced tourists, and the class/wealth gap between Kuwaitis and potential tourists is not going to be a problem as it is in some poor countries.
	Is the potential relationship flawed by uncertainty and competition for leisure resources (e.g. beaches and malls)?	Yes, this could be a problem. If the amenities become overused with tourists to the extent where Kuwaitis feel crowded out, resentment might build.
T2. Historical development of the industry	When and how did it start?	If the term 'mobility' replaces 'tourism', then it has been a factor for centuries (albeit without the leisure aspect). However, business tourism is well established, along with supporting soft and hard infrastructure.
	What were the stages of development?	The stages are as described in Table 11.1.
T3. Structure and organization of the industry	What are the ownership patterns?	Ownership is in local hands and the problem of profit repatriation, as happens in poor countries, is not an issue for Kuwait.
	What is the level of development of local tour operators?	Local tour operators have local ownership and investment but are run by foreigners.
	How many airlines fly into Kuwait?	26 airlines fly into Kuwait, the majority based in Asia and Middle East. BA and Kuwait Airlines tend towards business, others towards flying workers.
T4. Workforce profile	Is the expansion of the industry likely to benefit Kuwaitis, or simply expand an already large migrant workforce?	This is a difficult question, and the answer depends on planning and awareness. The main purpose of developing more tourism for Kuwait is to develop more jobs for Kuwaitis, so the answer is linked to sufficient training supply and Kuwaitis' willingness to participate.
	Can the paradox of the co-presence of a majority migrant workforce and minority Kuwaiti employees be resolved?	Yes, it can be resolved by awareness and the rapidly changing nature of post-1991 Kuwait, together with imaginative ways of recruiting, inducting and retaining Kuwaitis.

T5. *Tourism and the national economy*	What is the level of investments?	The particular situation of Kuwait is unusual for an advanced capitalist country in that much reliance is placed on government investment through, inter alia, Kuwait Airlines, Directorate General of Civil Aviation, Kuwait Touristic Enterprises Company and the Partnership Technical Bureau (which is investing heavily in sports and leisure).
	What are the benefits and the costs?	Benefits and costs differ from countries with greater distance between investment and government policy.
	Overall, how does tourism benefit Kuwait?	The main message is being focused around solving the employment/underemployment issues for Kuwaiti youth rather than simplistic data on contribution to GDP (which will always be overwhelmed by the oil economy).
T6. *Economic development*	What are the policies, procedures and prospects, and how could these benefits be improved?	The economic development links between growing demand for increased leisure, sport, retail opportunities and job creation/economic diversification have been realised at a late stage in Kuwait.
T7. *Impact on the cultural environment*	Are the changes to society caused by tourism beneficial?	Generally, tourism is likely to be positive for Kuwait and its image in the world, and the development of pride in the country. These benefits can exceed counting the oil revenues.
	What is the likelihood of tourism being 'blamed' for changes in society?	However, it is possible for tourism to be 'blamed' as Kuwait modernizes following global trends. Conservatives might think that increased tourism is the cause.
T8. *Impact on the natural and built environment*	What are the costs and benefits of changes to the environment caused by tourism?	Building and development notwithstanding, tourism is likely to make common cause for thinking far more carefully about the environment, so attitudes and behaviours are likely to improve. Public consultation repeatedly reveals the desire not to follow the Dubai model of touristic and leisure development.

Source: Developed from the authors' fieldwork.

employed out of a workforce of 4,200 (Department of Tourism 2011). However, the investigation found that far from there being a cultural barrier to employment, as might have been supposed, there was a complex economic issue at hand going far beyond tourism, which is dealt with in point 2 next, 'retention'. Other GCC countries share these complexities in arranging private sector jobs for their nationals. A government public awareness campaign is required if national targets for Kuwaiti participation in the workforce are to become a reality.

2. Levels of retention of locals

Evidence suggests that the salary structure in Kuwait is distorted; it does not operate as a classic unfettered employment market, even though there is government intervention in the form of private sector salary subsidies. The expectations of private sector employers have been governed by a wage structure catering to workers from the developing world, notably the Philippines and the Indian subcontinent. Here, low salaries, long working hours, (in some cases) poor working conditions and health and safety concerns are often deemed acceptable. The expectations of Kuwaiti employees, however, are influenced by the amount of waged money that can be earned in the government sector and the oil industry. This dichotomy will not be resolved simply through an awareness campaign aimed at targeting national employees to consider working in the hospitality and tourism sector. These distorted salaries, a reflection of the distorted labour market, are a major cause of difficulties in retaining Kuwaitis in the industry, even with government salary subsidies in place.

Another factor concerns the dominance of migrant contract labour, where the work visa directly relates to the job, and labour turnover is thus limited. Employers use the employment visa system as a tool for damping wage and employee benefits. Accordingly, while Kuwaiti employees are able to seek employment wherever they can strike a reasonable deal, the structural employment issue (i.e. competition from foreign workers) makes this somewhat problematic. The government has schemes to encourage the employment of nationals (Hertog 2013; Salih 2010), but these feed an already distorted labour market, and the situation is not a sustainable proposition for the future.

3. The range of available training

There is a surprising amount of activity in tourism sector training, where a variety of organizations are active in developing employment opportunities for Kuwaitis, such as Kuwait Airways, University of Kuwait Centre for Community Services and Continuing Education, the Skills Institute (run by the Public Authority for Applied Education and Training), Australian College of Kuwait, Kuwait Foundation for the Advancement of Science and Development, Kuwait College of Education, Skyline Institute, the Lothan Youth Achievement Centre and the 'Proud to be Kuwaiti' (P2BK) youth movement. However, these institutions tend to work alone with no umbrella organization to pull or shape them into a creative and effective network that would provide the value-added elements, especially those associated with a critical and coordinated approach to ameliorate employment and skills problems.

4. Role of women in the workforce

Women do take an active part in social, commercial and political spheres, especially in the public sector (the Kuwait Tourism Department is an excellent example) but do not enjoy full equality (Al Mughni 1993). A report by the *Financial Times* (2013) notes that 'compared with other Gulf states, Kuwaiti women are more emancipated'. In another report by the United Nations Children's Emergency Fund (UNICEF), concerning gender equality in the Middle East and North Africa (UNICEF 2011), Kuwait is ranked 105 in the 2010 Gender Equality Gap. This report cites a Freedom House (2010) report, which emphasizes that 'advocacy for women's rights has been strong in recent years, particularly with regard to political participation' (UNICEF 2011: 3). In fact, the most recent data released confirm that Kuwaiti women outnumber Kuwaiti men in employment, with 188,141 women in the labour market compared to 154,276 men. However, in terms of expatriate employment, there are 1,311,076 men in the workforce compared to only 152,014 women (Toumi 2016).

Nevertheless, given positive signs concerning Kuwaiti women participating significantly in the national workforce, tourism, with its necessity for co-presence and civility as well as its role in cultural brokerage, can play a pivotal role in promoting gender equality and communicating the diverse career opportunities for women.

5. Structural and societal disparities

There are other employment and societal issues that require due consideration. For instance, commercial tourism in Kuwait faces some suspicion as foreign expatriate managers and migrant workers dominate employment patterns, where Kuwaitis would be joining what is essentially a foreign workforce. There is also the problem of the co-presence of women and men who are not related. There is some evidence to suggest that employers may discriminate against Kuwaitis whom they may stereotype as less committed to the business and more expensive to hire. Finally, foreign workers may not cooperate in assimilating Kuwaitis into the workforce because they feel threatened by job losses through the Kuwaitization of employment. There are deep structural problems in employment patterns for all sectors in Kuwait, exacerbated by poor salaries in large parts of the private sector caused by internal labour market distortion. South Asian workers' salaries, the most predominant foreign labour pool, are the norm. This creates difficulties for Kuwaitis in joining and assimilating in what is essentially a foreign labour force. Hence, the company culture might be more reflective of South Asian values than those associated with Kuwaiti culture. These issues militate against Kuwaitis, which is not helped by a lack of imagination in tackling the issue: young Kuwaitis join a company, get fed up and leave, and are then 'blamed' as being 'feckless' or having a lack of motivation. While the government is making some efforts to tackle the employment issue, the tourism sector is but one small part of a wider structural concern that affects all GCC states.

Opportunities and ways forward

The main opportunity for tourism is not only economic but its potential to contribute to social cohesion and national identity. Business opportunities for Kuwaitis are most likely to be through start-up enterprises in fast food, health food, drink products, specialist tours and personalized tourist services. This approach promises to be far more attractive to Kuwaitis looking for employment and business opportunities, particularly as the traditional supply of government employment falters in the face of a bloated and frustratingly slow civil service (Al Zumai 2013). The government's intention to stop the increase of government jobs to soak up unemployed nationals is quite clear. Relying on the private sector is very complex as the shape and nature of Kuwait's economic and employment structures are entirely embedded in a system that privileges Kuwaitis over the majority workforce, comprised largely of Asians rather than the Palestinians and Arabs from North Africa that dominated prior to Iraq's invasion and occupation. When Kuwait was freed from Iraqi occupation, there was a moment of national self-sufficiency and a realization that too much reliance was placed on foreigners (Metz 1993). One of the first acts of the newly formed government after the invasion was to make legislation to significantly limit the percentage of foreigners and work permits. However, even with calls for further reducing foreign labour, as well as efforts to incentivize Kuwaitis into the private sector, the moment seems to be lost. The question remains: who would undertake the physical and technical work needed to fulfil infrastructural and construction needs?

Despite significant changes to the education system, vocational training institutes and school-to-work programmes, as inferred earlier, there is a need to ensure that a synchronized strategy to tourism and hospitality education and training is firmly in place. Therefore, building localized institutional capacity is a paramount objective, especially in establishing a professionalized workforce and industry. Strengthening a skills acquisition framework for future tourism and hospitality employers and employees can further help raise the public perception of the industry, as well as the working environment.

With Kuwait's determinism not to be like Dubai or Abu Dhabi, the best way forward seems to be with high-end retail in purpose-built luxury malls, as well as through the expansion of the well-being industry and family leisure; including water-based activities. The question of Failaka Island, an extremely important site of Mesopotamian and Greek antiquity, has yet to be reconciled (see Chapter 15). The best-case scenario would for the island to be set up as a site of special antiquarian and archaeological interest to stop further damage to its tangible history, but such arguments are likely to lose out in favour of resort development. The other area of future tourism might be the development of a high quality theme park, perhaps carrying a global brand to attract tourists from GCC countries to a fun but controlled environment.

Conclusion and research implications

Kuwait has a minority indigenous population: a large, controversial and even fractious co-presence of foreign workers, and an oil-based economy and society characterized by conspicuous consumption. At first glance, it is difficult to understand why a country like Kuwait, rich in oil revenues, would want to encourage tourism. However, with a growing population and recognition that the government cannot go on supplying public sector jobs, a diversified private sector is the only solution to the socially debilitating problem of youth unemployment. Accordingly, tourism is an obvious candidate for inclusion in the diversification approach. Moreover, tourism, in its wider context of recreation and leisure, can provide the soft infrastructure needed to support the delivery of a vision of Kuwait as a desirable and interesting place to live, work, play and invest. The intention of this approach would be to work towards a balance between the extremes of conservatism (as seen in Saudi Arabia) and hedonism (as seen in Dubai).

However, the chapter has identified certain conflicts in the internal environment that may militate against the development of Kuwait's tourism. For example, while there is a cultural and commercial tradition that encourages Kuwaitis to be outward looking and at ease with foreigners, and a society that fundamentally understands the 'spirit of hospitality' and travel, this is not translated into any appetite for being employed in the tourism sector. There are still conservative elements that remain suspicious of tourism and its purpose. One essential way forward is for both the public and private sectors to develop an overarching approach to training, education and capacity building in the country, with a focus on encouraging Kuwaitis to have a crucial role to play in the national development and advancement of the tourism (and hospitality) industry.

The confluence of tourism, society and culture engenders complex issues, complicated further by Kuwait's population mix and economic strategy. Nonetheless, there is still a need to understand tourism in Kuwait and comprehend the government's approach to development. First, particular research implications can be found in the relationship between various aspects of tourism and religion, careers, culture, national pride, business, community and social capital. Each of these areas requires empirical enquiry that would lead to greater insight into the complex relationship between tourism, society and culture, encouraging a better understanding of Kuwaiti society as it continues in its transitional state. Second, on a more pragmatic front, monitoring and measuring Kuwait's tourism industry would be fruitful. Thus, a quantitative approach could help the government understand the economic realities of tourism development, especially the employment contribution that tourism could make in reducing the country's reliance on oil and its dependence on government jobs. Third, it would be productive to engage Kuwaitis in a research programme concerning the examination of their perceptions of tourism and desired co-presence scenarios, linked to ascertaining preferred forms of tourism and tourist types. The results could subsequently feed into future tourism planning directives, which would be sensitive to the needs of culture, religion and society.

Acknowledgements

Grateful thanks for the courtesy shown and facilitation provided by Ms Huda Al-Enzini, Director of Tourism, Ministry of Commerce and Industry, during the various field visits. Thanks also to Dr Lubna Al-Kazi, Professor of Sociology and the Director of the Women's Studies Unit at Kuwait University, who provided invaluable insights on the history of Kuwait. The final edit and responsibility lies with the authors.

References

Abdel-Khalek, A. (2006) 'Happiness, health, and religiosity: significant relations', *Mental Health, Religion and Culture*, 9(1): 89–97.

Aldowaisan, T. A. (2010) *A Reconciled Country Vision*, Kuwait University and Gulf Lead Consultants. Available online at http://glcim.com/wpcontent/uploads/2012/12/Reconciled. Kuwait.Vision.E.pdf (accessed 6 March 2014).

Al Mughni, H. (1993) *Women in Kuwait: The Politics of Gender*, Wallingford: CABI Publishing.

Al-Zumai, F. (2013) 'Kuwait's political impasse and rent-seeking behaviour: a call for institutional reform'. *Research Paper*, Kuwait Programme on Development, Governance and Globalization in the Gulf States, London: London School of Economics.

Arab Times (2016) '54.3 pct of Kuwaitis "eligible" to work are not part of labor market', *Arab Times*, 16 January. Available online at www.arabtimesonline.com/news/54-3-pct-of-kuwaitis-eligible-to-work-are-not-part-of-labor-market/ (accessed 6 March 2014).

Bhandary, K. (2014) *Tourism and National Identity: Heritage and Nationhood in Scotland*, Bristol: Channel View Publications.

BTI (Bertelsmann Stiftung's Transformation Index) (2014) *Kuwait Country Report*. Available online at www.btiproject.de/uploads/tx_itao_download/BTI_2014_Kuwait. pdf (accessed 22 March 2015).

Crouch, D., L. Aronsson and L. Wahlstrom (2001) 'Tourist encounters', *Tourist Studies*, 1(3): 253–270.

Department of Tourism (2011) Internal Report, as empirical evidence presented to the Tourism Master Plan, Kuwait City, Kuwait.

Emirates 24/7 (2012) 'GCC hit by high youth unemployment', *Emirates 24/7*, 26 July. Available online at www.emirates247.com/business/gcc-hit-by-high-youth-unemployment-2012-07-251.468856 (accessed 6 March 2014).

Euromonitor International (2013) *Country Report: Travel and Tourism in Kuwait*, London: Euromonitor. Available online at www.euromonitor.com/travel-and-tourism-in-kuwait/report (accessed 2 November 2014).

Fairweather, N. and S. Rogerson (2003) 'The problems of global cultural homogenization in a technologically dependent world', *Journal of Information, Communication and Ethics in Society*, 1(1): 7–12.

Financial Times (2013) 'Kuwait 2013: gender equality: women blaze a difficult trail', *Financial Times*, 24 April. Available online at www.ft.com/cms/s/0/e689daa2-a86c-11e2-b03100144feabdc0.html#axzz3G6Lepg8R (accessed 2 October 2014).

Freedom House (2010) 'Women's rights in the Middle East and North Africa 2010', Washington, DC: Freedom House. Available online at www.freedomhouse.org/report/ women039s-rights-middle-east-andnorthafrica/womensrights-middle-east-and-north-africa-2010#.VDzTdktyjWU (accessed 2 October 2014).

GCC-Stat (2016) 'The GCC-Stat congratulates State of Kuwait on the National Day and Liberation Day on 25th and 26th of February 2016', GCC-Stat, 24 February. Available online at https://gccstat.org/en/about/news/kwt-national-day-2016 (accessed 15 March 2016).

Gibson, C. (2010) 'Geographies of tourism (un)ethical encounters', *Progress in Human Geography*, 34(4): 521–527.

Hertog, S. (2013) *The Private Sector and Reform in the Gulf Cooperation Council*, Research Paper, Kuwait Programme on Development, Governance and Globalization in the Gulf States, London: London School of Economics.

Keesing, R. (1971) *New Perspectives in Cultural Anthropology*, New York: Henry Holt.

Keesing, R. and A. Strathern (1997) *Cultural Anthropology: A Contemporary Perspective*, 3rd edn, Belmont, CA: Wandsworth.

Ministry of Information (*c.* 2001) *Kuwait: Facts and Figures*, Kuwait City: Ministry of Information.

Metz, H. (ed.) (1993) *Reconstruction after the Persian Gulf War: Country Studies* (Kuwait), Washington, DC: US Library of Congress. Available online at http://countrystudies.us/ persian-gulf-states/#Kuwait (accessed 22 March 2015).

Ohaeri, J., A. Awadalla and O. Gado (2009) 'Subjective quality of life in a nationwide sample of Kuwaiti subjects using the short version of the WHO quality of life instrument', *Social Psychiatry and Psychiatric Epidemiology*, 44(8): 693–701.

Salih, A. (2010) 'Localizing the private sector workforce in the Gulf Cooperation Countries: a study of Kuwait', *International Journal of Public Administration*, 33(4): 69–181.

Toumi, H. (2016) 'Kuwait women outnumber men in workforce', *Gulf News*, 4 March. Available online at http://gulfnews.com/news/gulf/kuwait/kuwaiti-women-outnumber-men-inworkforce-1.1684159 (accessed 16 March 2016).

Turner, L. and J. Ash (1975) *The Golden Hordes: International Tourism and the Pleasure Periphery*, London: Constable.

UNICEF (United Nations Children's Emergency Fund) (2011) *Kuwait. MENA Gender Equality Profile: Status of Girls and Women in the Middle East and North Africa*, Regional Office for the Middle East and North Africa: UNICEF. Available online at www.unicef.org/gender/files/Kuwait-GenderEqaulityProfile2011.pdf (accessed 2 October 2014).

UNWTO (United Nations World Tourism Organization) (2012) *International Tourism Hits One Billion*, Madrid: UNWTO. Available online at http://media.unwto.org/en/press-release/2012-12-12/international-tourism-hits-one-billion (accessed 12 August 2015).

Yin, R. (2012) *Applications of Case Study Research*, 3rd edn, London: Sage.

12 Deciphering the environmental impact of tourism development in Dubai

Developing sustainable directives and a citizenship agenda

Marcus L. Stephenson Anuradha Vyas

Dubai-based tourism research has started to focus on the issues and concerns associated with tourism development and modernization, notably social impacts (Stephenson and Ali-Knight 2010); physical access to hotels and related ethical concerns (Morris and Kazi 2016); semiotic and ideological implications of tourism and development (Gottdiener 2011; Steiner 2010); political economy challenges (Meethan 2011; Schmid 2009); and cultural implications (Stephenson 2014; Stephenson *et al.* 2010). However, an evaluation of the impact of tourism and development on Dubai's physical and natural environment has not been significantly forthcoming. Nonetheless, Ryan and Stewart's (2009) case study concerning Al Maha resort, located within the Dubai Desert Conservation Zone, does provide some useful insights into the ambiguous relationship between luxury modern developments and eco-tourism initiatives. Given limited awareness of the profundity of environmental impacts of tourism in Dubai, the paper will conceptually decipher the main impacts and identify the threats and challenges. The work will examine impacts associated with construction activities, desalination plants, the hotel industry, land reclamation schemes, transportation infrastructure and, indeed, tourists themselves. Dubai's mega-development objectives and grandiose ambitions have a significant role to play in terms of the mounting environmental challenges.

The chapter will seek to identify tourism development's impact upon such natural resources as water, marine life, the atmosphere and the desert environment, with the intention of indicating the sustainable challenges that the city faces in its resolute quest to become an ultra-popular tourism destination. Gladstone, Curley and Shokri (2013: 384) note that 'environmental impacts of tourism arise from both the direct activities of tourists and from the provision of the facilities and services that support tourism'. Therefore, this paper will implicitly recognize tourism's close relationship with other related developments and their impact on the physical environment.

Development and urbanization physically encroach upon desert terrain, requiring additional resources to be able to cater for the diverse needs of human populations – residents, nationals and tourists alike. One elemental concern is that the desert environment is hardly replete with an abundance of natural resources in the first place, so its subsequent transformation is an environmental challenge in itself. The dearth of arable land and water thwart the development of carbon sinks, forests and green areas, leading to an over-reliance on fossil fuels and a subsequent increase in carbon dioxide emissions (see Bhutto *et al.* 2014). Nonetheless, the desert landscape has undergone radical transformation, and the city has become a destination of superlatives. Pretes (1995: 4) notes:

> Regions lacking spectacular attractions must create them by some other means. The spectacle can be formed by attaching signifiers to an otherwise ordinary sight. Regions proclaim themselves unique, as seen by the plethora of modifiers (e.g., 'world's largest …', 'world's only …', and 'world's northernmost …') used in tourism marketing.

The artificialization of the physical and natural environment through tourism and development serves the purpose of 'commodifying the spectacle'. Such terminology evolved from Debord's (1994 [1967]: 2) work on 'The Society of the Spectacle', where he claimed that 'the spectacle corresponds to the historical moment at which the commodity completes its colonization of social life'. Given that the physical environment can be economically consumed for touristic use, its long-term sustainability is seriously threatened, irrespective of its capacity to act as a human habitat for populations from diverse backgrounds, cultures and regions. As will be asserted, the ecological environment commonly occupies a low ranking in terms of development priorities. Nonetheless, as the latter part of this paper will acknowledge, although some environmentally friendly planning initiatives and policy directives have started to evolve, it is essential that Dubai re-looks at its development priorities and approaches a sustainable agenda through fostering a responsibility-based approach embedded within a discourse of environmental citizenship. Here, attention will focus on the responsibilities and obligations of key stakeholders who can help drive forward a sustainable agenda.

The development of 'destination Dubai' and the transformation of the physical environment

Dubai emerged as a mercantile city from the late 1800s, importing goods from its trading ties with the British and exporting pearls. In the early 1900s, Dubai was a major distribution centre in the region, also supplying the interior of Oman. The Creek, a saltwater inlet, divided the city into two districts: 'Bur Dubai', which was dominated by government buildings; and 'Deira', dominated by mercantile activities. However, the pearl trade witnessed a drastic downfall in the 1930s, and the economy suffered until the discovery of oil in the 1950s. Increased trade was encouraged by the dredging of the Creek in the late 1950s, enabling ships of around 800 tonnes to enter its waters (Sampler and Eigner 2008: 69) and facilitating the rapid development of the port facilities and international trade. Along with the electrification of Dubai in 1961 (Kazim 2000), these projects helped to advance Dubai's profile as a regional centre of trade in the Gulf region. This advancement was encouraged by Dubai's rapid construction of roads, development of its international airport in the early 1960s and its position as a free port. Dubai's population growth is notable, which increased from 3,000 people at the turn of the twentieth century (Sampler and Eigner 2008) to a current amount of 2.46 million (Nagraj 2016).

Dubai witnessed the development of grandiose projects that have received world acclaim, such as the world's first so-called seven-star hotel (Burj Al Arab), the world's largest shopping mall (Dubai Mall) and the tallest building in the world (Burj Khalifa) (Stephenson 2014). Dubai's spectacle is purposeful, devised in a strategic way to serve the economy. Utilizing Dubai and Las Vegas as case exemplars, Schmid (2009) indicates the capitalistic significance of such places in relation to the principle of the 'economy of fascination'. Fascination is embodied within the 'enchanting and spellbound attraction' (2009: 64) and, thus, is operationally crucial to the commercialization of the attraction/destination, ensuring that the urban landscape is predominantly utilized for economic means. For Dubai to be economically sustainable, long-term investment in the production and consumption of fascination is thus necessary. The gradual depletion of oil forced the Emirate to consider an economic diversification pathway, involving heavy investment in the tourism and hospitality industries.

Tourism data illustrate an ever-increasing inflow of tourists since the early 1990s. Dubai received 944,350 overnight visitors in 1992 (Laws 1995), 6.9 million in 2007 (*TTN* 2008) and 14.2 million in 2015 (Anderson 2016). In 1990, there were around 70 hotels in Dubai (Laws 1995), rapidly increasing to around 676 hotel establishments in the city at the end of the first quarter of 2016 (Thomson 2016). The Dubai Tourism Vision for 2020 aims for Dubai to receive 20 million visitors by the end of the decade (Neuhof 2013). Though this target may appear overly ambitious, Dubai will host the World Expo in the same year.

The creation of cities within a city has transformed Dubai's physical environment, examples being Maritime City, Festival City, Sport City, Logistics City, Motor City, Academic City, Internet City and Health Care City. In 2012, the Dubai government announced the development of Mohammed Bin Rashid City. The project will incorporate the largest mall in the world, aptly known as 'Mall of the World', with a capacity of 80 million visitors a year. The city will also encompass over 100 hotels, a number of golf courses and a park – planned to be 30 per cent larger than London's Hyde Park (Croucher 2012). An extensive transport infrastructure comprising two international airports, a cruise ship terminal, a metro system, a tramway and six-lane highways led to further transformations of the environment. There are also plans to connect the city to other Gulf Cooperation Council (GCC) countries, initially through Etihad Rail and then via the GCC rail network (see Chapter 4).

Given the rapid growth of tourist numbers and tourism infrastructure, the intensity of interaction between human beings and the environment will, inevitably, exacerbate tourism's impact on the physical environment. Shaw and Williams (2002: 296) note that, regardless of the type of tourism a destination attracts, there is 'a point beyond which deterioration in the environment becomes a critical factor, even outweighing price economies'. As implied earlier, studying the environmental impact of tourism represents a challenge, as it is often difficult to differentiate tourism from development itself and from other forms of economic activity.

Excessive water consumption in the hospitality and tourism sectors

Hotels in Dubai, on average, use between 650 and 1,250 litres of water per guest and consume between 275 and 325 kilowatt-hours of power per square metre. In stark contrast, similar hotels in Germany use around 350 litres of water per guest and around 100 kilowatt-hours of power (*Gulf News* 2007). Hot climate conditions in the United Arab Emirates (UAE) increase the need for more air conditioning, bathing and water consumption. Air conditioning contributes to approximately 60 per cent of the total electricity bill in any large building or hotel, especially during the summer months when temperatures can reach 50 degrees Celsius (Golden 2007). In spite of being more ozone friendly due to legal regulations, some of the gases that run air conditioners continue to have a global warming effect, claimed to be up to 2,100 times higher than the effect produced by carbon dioxide – the standard greenhouse gas (Rosenthal and Lehren 2012). Increased development and hotter temperatures will continue to increase the demand for air conditioning products.

Water consumption is omnipresent in the accommodation sector, with high levels of usage taking place in guests' rooms. Water is required in the production of food, where average water use for food per person over a 2-week period can surpass 70 cubic metres. Apart from water consumption for drinking, bathing, cooking and laundry purposes, swimming pools can account for around 15 per cent of the water demand of hotels (Gössling *et al.* 2012). Large amounts of water evaporate from hotel swimming pools, where a typical unoccupied pool of a regular size (9.3 x 4.5 metres) can lose approximately 37,260 litres of water each year during an average air temperature of around 78 degrees Fahrenheit (Shah 2011). However, this is anticipated to be much higher in Dubai, especially during the hot summer months.

Disturbingly, many destination tourism products in Dubai utilize water as a central theme, for instance water parks (e.g. Aqua-Venture and Wild Wadi); the Dubai Fountain, a musical fountain set on the 30-acre Burj Khalifa Lake; and aquaria (e.g. the Atlantis Hotel Aquarium, and the Aquarium and Underwater Zoo at Dubai Mall). Legoland is also planning to develop a theme park involving a half-million gallon wave pool, with the intention of targeting 6.7 million ticketed visits by 2017 (*Emirates 24/7* 2015). Water is also highly utilized for the beautification and greening of the desert, ensuring that many grass lawns and water-guzzling species continue to thrive. Ignatieva (2011) observes how Dubai adopted Western styles of landscaping by pursuing a more 'picturesque' and 'gardenesque' approach, noting that the popular Safa Park comprises over 70 per cent lawn, various non-native plants (e.g. bougainvillea) and only one native tree: the date palm. One serious issue relates to excessive water use associated with Dubai's 19 golf courses, of which 14 are 18-hole courses. Much emphasis in and around golf courses concerns aesthetics, involving the utilization of extensive landscaping features (e.g. ponds, lakes and fountains) and creating a touristic atmosphere. While golf tourism may well contribute significantly to Dubai's tourism revenue and economy, and especially considering that it hosts such major golfing events as Dubai Desert Classic and DP World Tour Championship, the high level of water and energy consumption involved in the development and maintenance of extensive infrastructure and grass landscapes will inevitably have environmental ramifications. Although the Yas Links Golf Course in the neighbouring Emirate of Abu Dhabi is utilizing a blend of recycled and potable water, it consumes a daily average of 5,000 cubic metres in winter and 7,000 cubic metres in summer, where water represents one-fifth of the business operating costs (Todorova 2011).

Desalination, land reclamation and marine damage

Essex, Kent and Newnham (2004: 3–4) also note that the 'sustainability of tourism is dependent on an adequate water supply of sufficient quality and quantity'. Like most Gulf countries, the UAE has a limited supply of fresh renewable ground water, leaving it heavily dependent on seawater desalination. The UAE has witnessed drastic ground water withdrawal rates over the last 30 years, causing the fresh water table to decrease by one metre. According to one observation, if this continues, complete depletion could occur within the next half-century (Elgendy 2015). The UAE has the second highest desalination capacity in the world, desalinating more than 1.7 billion cubic metres of water annually (*Emirates 24/7* 2012). The Water Resources Institute noted that by 2020, GCC states will require a 40 per cent increase in the total of seawater desalination capacity, and by 2040 water resources in the UAE are likely to be classified as 'extremely highly stressed' (Water Technology 2015). The traditional method to desalinate water in the region is through energy-intensive thermal desalination methods, notably the 'multistage flash' (MSF) method, where steam from power plant turbines is used as a heat source to isolate the saline to between 90 and 110 degrees Celsius (Carlise 2009). Much of the leftover, known as brine, is often distributed back into the sea. Due to its high temperature, it often floats on the seawater, increasing the salinity levels as well as affecting water quality and marine life. Alderman (2010) notes that the salinity levels in the Persian Gulf rose by over 40 per cent in the previous 30 years, a period during which Dubai emerged as a serious tourist destination. Due to its narrow design and limited circulation of water, the Persian Gulf is subject to rising salinity along its shoreline. More recently, however, the 'reverse osmosis' method is starting to be embraced as a more sustainable technique because it uses chemical methods rather than the heating process to desalinate the water, though considerable energy is still used to pump seawater into the plant (Water Technology 2015). Seawater desalination generally requires around 10 times more energy than pumping water from wells (Hamdan 2013). About 4 tonnes of carbon are emitted per million gallons of fresh water produced, whereas the energy required to pump fresh water from underground would normally produce just over 1.5 tonnes of carbon dioxide per million gallons (Glass and Webster 2012). Desalination activity would have contributed to UAE's status in 2010 as having the highest carbon footprint in the world.

Despite the fact that scientific advancement in the efficiency of the desalination process has increased significantly over the past decade, Darwoud and Al Mulla (2012) observe that there have been limited developments in the management of by-product waste. The desalination process can release chlorine, algae-harming antiscalants and copper into the sea, affecting the marine ecosystem, coral reefs and seagrass beds. These beds play an important role in marine ecology, being the sole food for some endangered Gulf marine species and the main food source for all turtle species. Apart from being home to many fish species and pearl oysters, seagrass beds help to stabilize shorelines by holding the mobile sands (Dawoud and Al Mulla 2012).

The construction of Dubai's artificial islands, such as the Deira Islands, World and Palm Jumeirah (Figure 12.1), serves the purpose of producing more tourism destination resources and much-needed land and beach expansion. In fact, by 2010 the Dubai coastline increased from its natural coastline of 70 kilometres to 1,500 kilometres (Sale *et al.* 2011). The irony, of course, is that these developments, together with the suction dredging techniques utilized to construct the islands, have exacerbated beach erosion on Dubai's main coastline. Beach nourishment projects and the construction of groynes are common activities (Saseendran 2014).

Palm Jumeirah began construction in 2001, where 3 billion cubic feet of sand were dredged from the seafloor to formulate a 17-fronded palm tree, and around 7

Figure 12.1   Aerial view of Palm Jumeirah on the left and on the right, The World/The World Islands.

Source: Mario Hagen (www.shutterstock.com/pic.mhtml? id=365501231&src=id).

million tonnes of rock were placed around the island to protect it from waves and storms (Jennings 2015). Marine life in the area was distressed; for instance, turtle nesting sites were destroyed (*Economist* 2008), and coral habitats were damaged (Sale *et al.* 2011). However, Gladstone *et al.* (2013) draw attention to one common perspective that views the formation of artificial environments as 'replacement' habitats, simply modifying marine environments rather than destroying them. Such a defensive approach rationalizes the function and purpose of environmental change and, thus, does not consider the mechanisms of physical development and advanced modernization to be directly causal towards the degradation of the natural environment. Although there have been attempts to improve the quality of seawater in the region (Nakheel 2013), many tourist activities occur in and around fragile ecosystems. Gladstone *et al.* (2013: 377) summarize the outcomes of tourism-related developments in Dubai, stating:

> Construction of artificial waterways, marinas, lagoons, and breakwaters has indirectly caused loss of intertidal and shallow subtidal habitats by altering local circulation leading to inadequate flushing, sedimentation and smothering.

The authors note that tourist activities also cause damage to coral beds, notably through tourists trampling in intertidal areas and from anchor damage from boats. However, tourism and development affect the marine environment in other ways. One concern relates to the way in which individuals (especially tourists) over-consume resources, which then places direct pressure on the local environment and the availability of indigenous resources. The Environmental Agency – Abu Dhabi, for instance, draws attention to the significant decline of fish stock in UAE waters over the past three decades. The organization found that hammour and kingfish have been fished seven times more than sustainable levels. Hammour declined by 87–92 per cent between 1978 and 2003, despite the fact that 50 per cent of UAE fish consumers order hammour when eating at restaurants (Sethi 2013: 5). It is also worth mentioning that the fish species the hata goby, once indigenous to the wadi areas in the Hata district of the Dubai Emirate, is now extinct, partly due to overfishing (Feulner 2006).

Marine life is further threatened due to the dumping of litter on public beaches and coastal areas. The digestion of garbage by green turtles and endangered hawksbill turtles has had fatal consequences in Dubai (Shahbandari 2014). In 2014, Dubai Municipality retrieved around 1,160 tonnes of debris along the 7-kilometre Dubai Creek (Townsend 2015), a popular hotspot for tourists given its heritage and historical roots. To illustrate the concerns of littering in popular tourism areas, in a 1-hour cleanup of the Umm Suqeim Beach, 350 volunteers collected around 48,000 cigarette stubs (*Filipino Times* 2014). Prior to opening the second sewerage plant in Dubai, the Jebel Ali sewerage plant received twice its capacity, subsequently leading to concerns over the improper disposal of waste, some of which flowed into the sea adjacent to one of Dubai's most popular hotspots, the Jumeirah coastline (Alderman 2010).

Air pollution impacts and challenges

Rapid development, intense building construction and increased motorization are key contributors to air pollution in Dubai. The emission of significant amounts of greenhouse gases from automobiles, particularly carbon monoxide, hydrocarbons and oxides of nitrogen, affects the atmosphere. The UAE Environmental Agency estimates that around 850 deaths per year in the UAE are through air pollution, causing high levels of asthmatic cases and affecting approximately 15 per cent of the population. Vehicular growth has increased around 12 per cent annually, and it is more than likely that the continuing effect of diesel emission will intensify as the population increases (Ali *et al.* 2012: 37).

Nonetheless, the ever-expansion of Dubai's transportation infrastructure will no doubt mean a continuous increase in the emission of carbon dioxide into the environment, exacerbated through intensified automobile use. In March 2014, Dubai announced a further Dh700 million (US$190.6 million) for the development of two major road projects (*Gulf News* 2014: 4). Euromonitor International reported that the car rental market in the UAE is increasing yearly at a compound annual growth rate of 10 per cent (*Gulf Business* 2015). Additionally, there are nearly 8,100 taxis normally operating at the same time (Dhal 2013), and the Roads and Transport Authority noted that in the first 6 months of 2015, taxis made around 52 million trips (*Gulf News* 2015).

Despite Dubai's rapidly developing public transportation network, including popular metro and tramway networks (see Chapter 4), there is still a long way to go to challenge people's over-reliance on automobiles in the Emirate. Public transport practices in particular urban areas abroad illustrate how progressive measures are challenging car usage. In Tallinn (Estonia), for instance, from 1 January 2013 around 400,000 residents were eligible for free transportation on buses, trams and trolleybuses, all subsidized by Tallinn City Government (Davis 2013). Although other European cities, notably Templin (Germany), Châteauroux and Aubagne (France), have adopted similar free transit systems, there are other effective mechanisms for reducing automobile use, such as increasing the price of parking and petrol (Vedler 2014).

Although the environmental problems associated with airports and air traffic have been widely noted and researched (see Unal *et al.* 2005), Dubai's aviation objectives have been indomitable. Dubai International Airport became the world's busiest airport in 2015. Passenger traffic flying outside Dubai increased to 69.9 million, overtaking Heathrow's 68.1 million (*Telegraph* 2015). By 2020, Emirates airline intends to carry 70 million passengers a year with a fleet of 250 aircraft operating from Dubai (Critchlow 2014). However, the airline claims to have lower carbon dioxide emissions than other major airlines, because of its energy efficient fuel systems (Emirates Group 2011). Nonetheless, the scale of emissions overall could intensify, as the airline is significantly expanding its fleet.

Not only is the air quality of the environment affected through tourism development, but other inter-dependable environments are also adversely impacted. Dubai's large-scale land reclamation schemes and major construction activities have increased the demand for rocks and cement brought from mountainous parts of the country. Quarrying activities in the northern part of the UAE have been excessive and have caused air pollution concerns for the Emirates of Ras Al Khaimah and Fujairah. Villagers in areas adjacent to quarrying facilities have experienced respiratory problems (Zacharias 2013). Subsequently, the production of one (unnatural) destination is contributing to the destruction of another (natural) destination. Moreover, quarrying activities lessen the potential for developing geo-tourism activities and affect natural biodiversity, hampering sustainable (and conservational) options for tourism development in the country as a whole.

Urbanism, environmental citizenship and sustainable alternatives

Capital and its accumulation have taken precedent over Dubai's natural environment and ecosystem, transforming and disturbing the physical environment. Debord's (1994: 169) comments are pertinent:

> Urbanism is the mode of appropriation of the natural and human environment by capitalism, which, true to its logical development toward absolute domination, can (and now must) refashion the totality of space into its own peculiar decor.

Debord's (1994) work also implies that modern capitalism partly develops commodities to produce obsessive and submissive patterns of consumption. Consequently, the physical environment becomes a commodity for the consumptive needs of individuals who participate dutifully and abundantly in leisure, recreation and mobility, as well as for the productive requirements of the tourism industry to capitalize on such needs through interfering with, and transforming, such places and spaces. Dubai's 'self-styled role as the apotheosis of luxury consumer production and consumption' (Bianchi and Stephenson 2014: 52) represents the economic priorities of capitalistic intentions and values over priorities towards sustaining a trouble-free natural environment and ecosystem. In fact, a number of analysts have observed that the commodification of the natural environment and the consequent increase in human activity will inevitably mean that any productive vision of sustainable development is simply unfeasible (Cock and Hopwood 1996; Mellor 1992; Shiva 1998). However, societies that are resolutely intent on commoditizing socially produced pleasure often face a significant dilemma, where the physical environment struggles to cater for ways of life that are not symbiotically synchronized to the natural environment.

As the concentration of tourist activities and the expansion of tourist infrastructure intensify, destination attractiveness is at risk. Dubai, however, limits such risks through its aesthetic management of tourist places and spaces. This is strategically important in creating a sense of false consciousness that negative environmental impacts are negligible (see previous section for the modification/replacement perspective), ensuring that the expectations of tourists are prioritized and that the destination is perceived to be managed well. On the surface level, a green and colourful (non-arid) environment commonly symbolizes vitality, durability and lushness. Beautification conceals the truth of the matter concerning the fragile nature of desert land. It is difficult, however, for tourists and the public to contemplate the fact that the synthetic appearance of the environment is having a long-term impact. Ryan and Stewart (2009: 292) observe that the 'greening' of the desert in the context of the UAE is underpinned by a national philosophy emphasizing that '"goodness" is associated with "greenness"' and is expressed through values of improvement, progress and modernization.

Tourists often have sovereign rights in contemporary tourism destinations and societies, primarily the economic right to consume a whole variety of tourist activities, products and experiences (Bianchi and Stephenson 2014). Macnaghten and Urry (1998: 25) appropriately note that tourists:

> are increasingly consumers of environments outside their own national territory, and as such develop systematic expectations of such environments and of the quality of air, water, scenery, and so on. Indeed part of the imposition of such expectations about a non-polluted environment is a contemporary form of economic and cultural imperialism.

Nonetheless, it is fundamentally necessary to balance the rights of tourists (to travel/consume) with the rights of destination communities (to a clean and non-polluting environment), and harmonize the responsibilities of tourists (to think more critically about the effects of their consumption patterns) with the responsibilities of the destination/state authority (to prioritize development activities for the good of the environment). Bianchi and Stephenson (2014: 180) state, 'Environmental citizenship emphasizes an ethic of care towards nature, demanding a new paradigm of thinking about the relationship between the individual and the planet's natural environment'. The authors also indicate that part of the debate is about 'rights beyond the sphere of human relations altogether' (2014: 180), or what Steward (1991: 65) coins, 'citizens of planet earth'. Although there is a need for governments to systematically pursue sustainable initiatives and encourage the corporate sector to contribute to a sustainable future, the problem Dubai faces relates to the need for a more holistic-based approach involving all key stakeholders.

Importantly, however, sustainable tourism development needs to involve the community at a grassroots level. One way to drive this agenda forward is to reach out to communities through the role of non-government organizations. However, as Sale *et al.* (2011) note, the wealth of the Gulf region has meant that there has been little need for significant support from such organizations as United Nations agencies. On the positive side, however, the authors do note that support can be easier to attain at higher levels, stating that 'Building awareness among the leaders may be surprisingly easy if access can be gained, because there does appear to be support for the concept of environmental sustainability' (Sale *et al.* 2011: 13). Ryan and Stewart (2009: 291) acknowledge that although an 'environmental movement' in the UAE has been initiated through such organizations as Emirates Environmental Research and the Wildlife Development Agency, public representation and individual membership are not the norm. However, some areas of the corporate sector have started to become active in the support of environmental initiatives. For instance, Sheraton Dubai Mall of the Emirates Hotel claimed a 17.5 per cent decrease in water usage, 50 per reduction in excessive waste and 5 per cent reduction in energy (Walsh 2016). Other companies have set ambitious targets, for instance, Dubai-based Hospitality Management Holdings aims to reduce consumption of water and energy by 20 per cent (Sambridge 2014). Nonetheless, the pace of development and the continued production of more hotels and tourism-based projects will simply militate against lower reductions While there were 65,000 rooms available in 2015, 100,000 rooms are anticipated for the World Expo 2020 (Bhatia 2015). Bianchi and Stephenson (2014: 184) assert that 'corporations should balance their freedom to trade and responsibility to stakeholders with a set of wider social and environmental obligations to communities in which they operate'.

Since the economic recession hit Dubai in 2008, the Emirate has had to re-think its approach to development on a more long-term basis. As environmental concerns have partly evolved because of rapid modernization, a sustainable agenda needs to draw the full attention of private and public sector organizations. There are some notable green initiatives in place. In January 2009, the government introduced a decree that new buildings launched in Dubai need to comply by the basic Leadership in Energy and Environmental Design (LEED) standards (Crane 2009). LEED is an internationally recognized green building certification programme established by the non-profit organization US Green Building Council, and concerns ratings relating to the adoption of strategies to reduce resource consumption (e.g. energy and water) and decrease carbon dioxide emissions (Mahdavinejad *et al.* 2014).

There is an 'accreditation culture' evolving in the tourism and hospitality industry in Dubai concerning environmental standards and performance. Since 2010, numerous beaches have been allocated a Blue Flag Award, which is internationally recognized and established by the Foundation for Environmental Education. The criteria involve standards for environmental education and management, water quality and other services (Kader 2014). Another internationally recognized initiative that is becoming popular in the Emirate concerns sustainable performance standards associated with the Green Globe Certificate. Such luxury hotels as Radisson Blu Hotel, Jumeirah Beach Hotel and Burj Al Arab have been certified. Interestingly, Wild Wadi Waterpark was awarded a Green Globe Certificate in 2016 because of its 'environmental efforts and sustainability management', especially in the reduction of energy and water consumption. However, as Balbo (2015) argues, although such businesses recognize sustainable practices and performances, the objective should be to engrain sustainability in the planning process at the start of the development:

> resulting in facilities that are maximally efficient from day one, and not leave them to aspire for incremental improvements over a lifetime. … Making

minor improvements to an operation that is, at its core, unsustainable, is positive action. It reduces operational costs and may result in measurable ecological benefits, but it doesn't change that the operation is inherently environmentally negative.

Dubai is also developing a large solar park, especially as the extensive manufacturing capacity of solar panels in China has meant that their price has fallen significantly. Solar energy is becoming a more viable option as a purposeful and abundant energy source (Yee 2013). The intention is that the development of new recreational parks in Dubai will use solar power, which already heats 140,000 litres of water daily at the Burj Khalifa (Alnaser and Alnaser 2011: 3086). There is an emerging realization that the development and utilization of clean energy should be taken seriously. Kazim (2010) emphasizes UAE's potential to use hydrogen energy as an environmentally clean, transportable and storable source, especially in the commercial, power generation and transportation sectors. Dubai's objective is to cut energy consumption by 20 per cent by 2020 (El Gazzar 2014). Given the hosting of the Expo in the same year, the Emirate is targeting a carbon-neutral event, and sustainability is a central theme in the design and planning of this mega-initiative (see Bitar 2014).

One prevailing problem is the extent to which tourism development not only takes priority over the environment, but dictates transformations within it. An initial step is to embrace environmental citizenship discourse within the context of the tourism environment and comprehend the degree to which individuals as well as public and private sector organizations are inherently responsible for the environment and its long-term sustainability. However, the movement towards a sustainable agenda could be an implausible task, particularly when 'destination Dubai' is intent on continuing to increase tourism demand and set new development targets.

Conclusion and research implications

Although tourism development has raised Dubai's global profile, it has created a set of environmental challenges strongly questioning the extent to which tourism can ever produce a sustainable environment for all concerned. The impact of tourism and development on Dubai's physical environment should not be underestimated. It has already started to present challenges in terms of rising sea temperatures, loss of marine life, greenhouse effects, biosphere damage and various pollution problems. Dubai's tourism planning approach ought to consider water supply in relation to appropriate tourist and resident carrying capacity levels, as well as exploring more sustainable and eco-friendly alternatives for securing useable water. One other concern identified in this paper relates to the over-use of energy. As energy production comes at a high environmental cost, there is a real need to develop alternative sources.

Consequently, the fundamental question concerns the extent to which Dubai can sustain a rapid increase in tourists and tourism development over the coming years. The evidence already points to a deep concern that the physical environment is not coping well. Yet, Dubai's aesthetic appeal and 'wow factor' detract attention away from the environmental realities of rapid modernization, development and touristification. The discussion implies that Dubai needs to reconsider its strategic approach to tourism development and the long-term effects that current development scenarios are having on the environment. In advocating the importance of the 'precautionary principle' concerning the calculated anticipation of environmental harm, Fennel and Ebert (2010: 477) state:

> When it comes to the well-being of tourism destinations, and the people and natural resources that comprise these areas, the adage: 'an ounce of prevention is worth a pound of cure' has perhaps never been so meaningful.

Further research is necessary to identify the strategic options, driving forces and challenges towards ensuring that Dubai adopts a sustainable agenda, with clear and comprehensive planning directives. This approach ought to take into consideration the perspectives and positions of all key stakeholders associated with tourism development in the Emirate. Representation at 'grassroots' community level is imperative, but for this to happen a redirection in environmental governance would be necessary. One important future enquiry concerns the identification of new ways in which Dubai's tourism industry can achieve a balance between economic growth and environmental sustainability. A strategically informed agenda could, thus, help in some way to consider more innovative solutions and alternative approaches (and technologies) to tourism development, especially within the context of recognizing the fragilities of the desert environment. Such ways forward certainly sound hopeful. Indeed, we are actively encouraged in the study of tourism to be optimistic in our enquiries (see Pritchard *et al.* 2011). Nevertheless, unless the challenges faced by the increased commodification of the environment are to be fully addressed, then the development of a sustainable environment will be difficult to achieve. Ideals concerning an environmental citizenship agenda, supported by acts of corporate citizenship, are imperative in that the right to enjoy and utilize the environment should be met with certain responsibilities and obligations. Critical evaluation and strategic foresight concerning the mechanisms to achieve a sustainable tourism environment should scrutinize the rudimental causes of environmental impact and degradation, that is, capitalism, market enterprise and the market economy.

References

Alderman, L. (2010) 'Dubai faces environmental problems after growth', *New York Times*, 27 October. Available online at www.nytimes.com/2010/10/28/business/energy-environment/28dubai.html?_r=0 (accessed 19 September 2013).

Ali, Y. A., M. Hrairi and I. K. Kattan (2012) 'Comparison of diesel experiments in view of the environment: a case study of Dubai', *International Journal of Management Science and Engineering Management*, 7(1): 36–42.

Alnaser, W. E. and N. W. Alnaser (2011) 'The status of renewable energy in the GCC countries', *Renewable and Sustainable Energy Reviews,* 15: 3074–3098.

Anderson, R. (2016) 'Dubai world's fourth most visited city in 2015, tourists up 7.5%', *Gulf Business,* 28 January. Available online at http://gulfbusiness.com/dubai-receives-7-5-per-cent-more-tourists-in-2015/#.V11YPlV95hE (accessed 11 June 2016).

Balbo, L. (2015) 'Green Global certifies Dubai's Wild Wadi Waterpark', Green Prophet: Sustainable News for the Middle East, 23 February. Available online at www.greenprophet.com/2015/02/dubais-wild-wadi-waterpark-is-green-globe-certified/ (accessed 17 June 2016).

Bhatia, N. (2015) 'Dubai set for 100,000 hotel rooms by Expo 2020', *Construction Week Online,* 28 June. Available online at www.constructionweekonline.com/article-34205-dubai-set-for-100000-hotel-rooms-by-expo-2020/ (accessed 15 June 2016).

Bhutto, A. W., A. A. Bazmi, G. Zahedi and J. J. Klemes (2014) 'A review of progress in renewable energy implementation in Gulf Cooperation Council countries', *Journal of Cleaner Production,* 71: 168–180.

Bianchi, R. V. and M. L. Stephenson (2014) *Tourism and Citizenship: Rights, Freedoms and Responsibilities in the Global Order,* London: Routledge.

Bitar, Z. (2014) 'Sustainability to take central role in greenest-ever expo', *Gulf News,* 14 April, p. B4.

Carlise, T. (2009) 'Reverse osmosis gains ground on "flash" process', *The National,* 31 August. Available online at www.thenational.ae/news/uae-news/environment/reverse-osmosis-gains-ground-on-flash-process (accessed 17 November 2014).

Cock, M. and B. Hopwood (1996) *Global Warming: Socialism and the Environment,* London: Militant Labour.

Crane, J. (2009) *Dubai: The Story of the World's Fastest City,* London: Atlantic Books.

Critchlow, A. (2014) 'Dubai mulling Emirates airline float', *Telegraph,* 1 March. Available online at www.telegraph.co.uk/finance/newsbysector/transport/10670605/Dubai-mulling-Emirates-airline-float.html (accessed 10 September 2014).

Croucher, M. (2012) 'Dubai to build world's biggest mall … again', *The National,* 25 November. Available online at www.thenational.ae/news/uae-news/dubai-to-build-worlds-biggest-mall-again/ (accessed 5 December 2014).

Davis, A. (2013) 'Estonia's capital made public transit free to make people give up driving', *Business Insider,* 3 January. Available online at www.businessinsider.com/tallin-estoniamakes-public-transit-free-2013–1 (accessed 27 April 27).

Dawoud, M. A. and M. M. Al Mulla (2012) 'Environmental impacts of seawater desalination: Arabian Gulf case study', *International Journal of Environment and Sustainability,* 1(3): 22–37.

Debord, G. (1994) *The Society of the Spectacle,* New York: Zone Books.

Dhal, S. (2013) 'Taxi shortage hits Dubai commuters during evenings', *Gulf News,* 4 June. Available online at http://gulfnews.com/news/gulf/uae/general/taxi-shortage-hits-dubaicommuters-during-evenings-1.1343089 (accessed 29 June 2013).

Economist (2008) 'How green is the world? Evaluating Dubai's island-reclamation project', *Economist,* 17 March. Available online at www.economist.com/node/10870938 (accessed 14 June 2016).

El Gazzar, S. (2014) 'Dubai plans to go greener with 20% reduction in energy consumption', *The National,* 11 February. Available online at www.thenational.ae/business/energy/energy-consumption (accessed 7 April 2014).

Elgendy, K. (2015) 'Doha has just three days supply: are water shortages the biggest threat to the Middle East', *City Metric,* 16 July. Available online at www.citymetric.com/

horizons/doha-has-just-three-days-supply-are-water-shortages-biggest-threat-middle-east-1234 (accessed 20 December 2015).

Emirates Group (2011). *Environmental Report 2010–2011, Dubai*. Available online at www.emirates.com/english/images/The%20Emirates%20Group%20Environment%20 Report_tcm233-701728.pdf (accessed 14 July 2014).

Emirates 24/7 (2012) *'UAE is world's second largest desalination producer'*, Emirates 24/7, 24December. Available online at www.emirates247.com/business/uae-is-world-second-largest desalination-producer-2012-12-24-1.488486 (accessed 14 July 2014).

Emirates 24/7 (2015) *'Legoland Dubai gets new water park'*, *Emirates 24/7*, 22 April. Available online at www.emirates247.com/news/emirates/legoland-dubai-gets-new-water-park-2015-04-22-\1.588250 (accessed 15 August 2015).

Essex, S., M. Kent and R. Newnham (2004) 'Tourism development in Mallorca: is water supply a constraint?', *Journal of Sustainable Tourism*, 12(1): 4–28.

Fennel, D. A. and K. Ebert (2010) 'Tourism and the precautionary principle', *Journal of Sustainable Tourism*, 12(6): 461–479.

Feulner, G. R. (2006) 'Goby gone for good', *Tribulus: Journal of the Emirates National History Group*, 16(2): 34.

Filipino Times (2014) *'Dubai beach clean-up yields a nasty load of butts'*, *Filipino Times*, 11 March. Available online at http://filipinotimes.ae/breaking-news/2014/03/11/dubai-beach-clean-up-yields-a-nasty-load-of-butts/ (accessed 15 May 2014).

Gladstone, W., B. Curley and M. R. Shokri (2013) 'Environmental impacts of tourism in the Gulf and the Red Sea', *Marine Pollution Bulletin*, 72(2): 375–388.

Glass, N. and G. Webster (2012) 'Counting the carbon cost of bringing water to the desert', *CNN*, 20 January. Available online at http://edition.cnn.com/2012/01/20/world/meast/ carbon-cost-water-uae/index.html (accessed 4 August 2013).

Golden, L. L. (2007) 'Hotels in Dubai use 225 per cent more energy than European hotels', 19 May. Available online at www.ameinfo.com/120582 (accessed 4 August 2013).

Gössling, S., P. Peeters, C. M. Hall, J-P. Ceron, G. Dubois, L. V. Lehmann and D. Scott (2012) 'Tourism and water use: supply, demand and security. An international review', *Tourism Management*, 33(1): 1–15.

Gottdiener, M. (2011) 'Socio-semiotics and the new mega spaces of tourism: Some comments on Las Vegas and Dubai', *Semiotica*, 2011(183): 121–128.

Gulf Business (2015) 'AW Rostamani group's car rental unit to invest Dhs 400m in Expansion', *Gulf Business*, 9 August. Available online at www.gulfbusiness. com/articles/industry/aw-rostamani-groups-car-rental-unit-to-invest-dhs-400m-in-expansion/ (accessed 3 January 2016).

Gulf News (2007) 'Dubai hotels rank low in energy efficiency-study', *Gulf News*, 20 May. Available online at http://gulfnews.com/business/tourism/dubai-hotels-rank-low-in-energy-efficiency-study1.179153 (accessed 15 September 2014).

Gulf News (2014) 'Dubai unveils Dh700m road projects', *Gulf News*, 17 March, p. 4.

Gulf News (2015) '45% of taxis booked through automated channels in Dubai', *Gulf News*, 23 August. Available online at http://gulfnews.com/news/uae/transport/45-of-taxis-booked-:through-automated-channels-in-dubai-1.1571543 (accessed 22 December 2015).

Hamdan, S. (2013) 'Abu Dhabi company searches for greener method of desalination', *New York Times*, 23 January. Available online at www.nytimes.com/2013/01/24/ world/24/world/middleeast/abu-dhabi-company-searches-for-greenerdesalination. html?ref=desalination&_r=0 (accessed 2 August 2015).

Ignatieva, M. (2011) 'Plant material for urban landscapes in the era of globalization: Roots, challenges and innovative solutions', in M. Richter and U. Weiland (eds) *Applied Urban Ecology*, Oxford: Blackwell Publishing Ltd, pp. 139–151.

Jennings, K. (2015) 'The real story behind Dubai palm islands', *Condé Nast Traveller*, 23 November. Available online at www.cntraveler.com/stories/2015-11-23/the-real-story-behind-dubai-palm-islands (accessed 15 June 2016).

Kader, B. A. (2014) '7 more UAE beaches receive Blue Flag certification', *Gulf News*, 17 June. Available online at http://gulfnews.com/news/uae/environment/7-more-uae-beaches-receive-blue-flag-certification-1.1425051 (accessed 15 June 2016).

Kazim, A. (2000) *The United Arab Emirates AD. 600 to the Present: A Socio-Discursive Transformation in the Arabian Gulf*, Dubai: Gulf Book Centre.

Kazim, A. (2010) 'Strategy for a sustainable development in the UAE through hydrogen energy', *Renewable Energy*, 35: 2257–2269.

Laws, E. (1995) *Tourist Destination Management: Issues, Analysis and Policies*. London: Routledge.

Macnaghten, P. and J. Urry (1998) *Contested Natures*, London: Sage.

Mahdavinejad, M., A. Zia, A. N. Larki, S. Ghanavati and N. Elmi (2014) 'Dilemma of green and pseudo green architecture based on LEED norms in case of developing countries', *International Journal of Sustainable Built Environment*, 3(2): 235–246.

Meethan, K. (2011) 'Dubai: an exotic destination with a cosmopolitan lifestyle', in J. Mosedale (ed.) *Political Economy of Tourism: A Critical Perspective*, London: Routledge, pp. 175–188.

Mellor, M. (1992) *Breaking the Boundaries*, London: Virago.

Morris, S. and S. Kazi (2016) 'Planning an accessible expo 2020 within Dubai's 5 star hotel industry from legal and ethical perspectives', *Journal of Tourism Futures*, 2(1): 88–94.

Nagraj, A. (2016) 'Dubai's population forecast to rise to five million by 2030', *Gulf Business*, 14 February. Available online at http://gulfbusiness.com/dubai-s-population-forecast-to-rise-to-five-million-by-2030/#.V2PeWOt97IV (accessed 15 June 2016).

Nakheel (2013) 'Artificial reefs'. Available online at www.nakheel.com/en/environment/artificial-reefs (accessed 25 September 2014).

Neuhof, F. (2013) 'Dubai plan to double number of visitors to 20m by 2020', *The National*, 5 May. Available online at www.thenational.ae/business/industry-insights/tourism/dubai-plan-to-double-number-of-visitors-to-20m-by-2020 (accessed 3 August 2013).

Pretes, M. (1995) 'Postmodern tourism: the Santa Claus industry', *Annals of Tourism Research*, 22(1): 1–15.

Pritchard, A., N. Morgan and I. Ateljevic (2011) 'Hopeful tourism: new transformative perspective', *Annals of Tourism Research*, 38(3): 941–963.

Rosenthal, E. and A. W. Lehren (2012) 'Relief in every window, but global worry too', *New York Times*, 20 June. Available online at www.nytimes.com/2012/06/21/world/asia/global-demand-for-air-conditioning-forces-tough-environmental-choices.html (accessed 1 October 2013).

Ryan, C. and M. Stewart (2009) 'Eco-tourism and luxury – the case of Al Maha, Dubai', *Journal of Sustainable Tourism*, 7(3): 287–301.

Sale, P. F., D. A. Feary, J. A. Burt, A. G. Bauman, G. H. Cavalcante, K. G. Drouillard, B. Kjerfve, E. Marquis, C. G. Trick, P. Usseglio and H. V. Lavieren (2011) 'The growing need for sustainable ecological management of marine communities of the Persian Gulf', *AMBIO*, 40: 40–17.

Sambridge, A. (2014) 'Dubai's HMH to launch new budget hotel brand', *Arabian Business. com*, 7 May. Available online at www.arabianbusiness.com/dubai-s-hmh-launch-new-budget-hotel-brand-549383.html (accessed 5 September 2015).

Sampler, J. and S. Eigner (2008) *Sand to Silicon: Going Global-Rapid Growth Lessons for Dubai*, Dubai: Motivate Publishing.

Saseendran, S. (2014) 'Umm Suqeim beach to be partially closed for 9 months', *Khaleej Times*, 17 June. Available online at www.khaleejtimes.com/article/20140616/ article/306169887/1002 (accessed 20 August 2014).

Schmid, H. (2009) *Economy of Fascination: Dubai and Las Vegas as Themed Urban Landscapes*, Berlin: Gebr. Borntraeger Verlagsbuchhandlung Science Publishers.

Sethi, P. K. (2013) 'Fishless oceans within 40 years?', *Gulf News*, 18 November, p. A5.

Shah, M. M. (2011) 'Simplified method of calculating evaporation from swimming pools', *HPAC Engineering*, 1 October. Available online at http://hpac.com/humidity-control/ simplified-method-calculating-evaporation-swimming-pools (accessed 13 August 2013).

Shahbandari, S. (2014) 'Turtles found dead on Dubai's Al Sufouh beach', *Gulf News*, 25 April. Available online at http://gulfnews.com/news/gulf/uae/environment/turtles-found-dead-on-dubai-s-al-sufouh-beach-1.1324151 (accessed 24 June 2014).

Shaw, G. and A. M. Williams (2002) *Critical Issues in Tourism: A Geographical Perspective*, 2nd edn, Oxford: Blackwell Publishers.

Shiva, V. (1998) *Biopiracy: The Plunder of Nature and Knowledge*, Dartington: Green Books.

Steiner, C. (2010) 'From heritage to hyper-reality? Tourism destination development in the Middle East between Petra and the Palm', *Journal of Tourism and Cultural Change*, 8(4): 240–253.

Stephenson, M. L. (2014) 'Tourism, development and destination Dubai: cultural dilemmas and future challenges', *Current Issues in Tourism*, 17(8): 723–738.

Stephenson, M. and J. Ali-Knight (2010) 'Dubai's tourism industry and its societal impact: Social implications and sustainable challenges' (Middle East and North Africa Special Issue), *Journal of Tourism and Cultural Change*, 8(4): 278–292.

Stephenson, M. L., K. A. Russell and D. Edgar (2010) 'Islamic hospitality in the UAE: indigenization of products and human capital', *Journal of Islamic Marketing*, 1(1): 9–24.

Steward, F. (1991) 'Citizens of planet earth', in G. Andrews (ed.) *Citizenship*, London: Lawrence and Wishart, pp. 65–75.

Telegraph (2015) 'Dubai overtakes Heathrow to become world's busiest airport', *Telegraph*, 27 January. Available online at www.telegraph.co.uk/finance/newsb1ysector/ transport/11372616/Dubai-overtakes-Heathrow-to-become-worlds-busiest-airport.html (accessed 20 December 2015).

Thompson, D. (2016) 'Dubai added 1,500 hotel rooms in Q1 2016', *Hotelier Middle East. com*, 9 June. Available online at www.hoteliermiddleeast.com/27342-dubai-added-1500-hotel-rooms-in-q1-2016/ (accessed 12 June 2016).

Todorova, V. (2011) 'Golf clubs count cost of keeping grass green', *The National*. Available online at www.thenational.ae/news/uae-news/environment/golf-clubs-count-cost-of-keeping-grass-green (accessed 14 June 2015).

Townsend, S. (2015) '1,160 tonnes of rubbish collected from Dubai Creek', *Khaleej Times*, 4 June. Available online at www.khaleejtimes.com/nation/general/1-160-tonnes-of-rubbish-collected-from-dubai-creek (accessed 20 December 2016).

TTN *(2008)* 'Dubai to attract 15m tourists by 2015*', Travel and Tourism News Middle East, 26(10): 9.*

Unal, A., Y. Hu, M. E. Chang, M. T. Odman and A. G. Russell (2005) 'Airport related emissions and impacts on air quality: application to the Atlanta International Airport', *Atmospheric Environment*, 39: 5787–5798.

Vedler, S. (2014) 'Free public transit in Tallinn is a hit with riders but yields unexpected results', *Citiscope*, 27 January. Available online at http://citiscope.org/story/2014/ free-public-transit-tallinn-hit-riders-yields-unexpectedresults#sthash.6AIIGp44.dpuf (accessed 3 January 2015).

Walsh, P. (2016) 'Sheraton MOE achieves 17.5% drop in water usage', *Hotelier Middle East.com*, 19 March. Available online at www.hoteliermiddleeast.com/26508-sheraton-moe-achieves-175-drop-in-water-usuage/ (accessed 19 June 2016).

Water Technology (2015) 'GCC to expand desalination capacity by 40 per cent in 5 years', *Water Technology*, 28 October. Available online at www.watertechonline.com/gcc-to-expand-desalination-capacity-by-40-in-5-years/ (accessed 19 June 2016).

Yee, A. (2013) 'Rooftop solar plan for Abu Dhabi', *The National*, 13 December, p. b1.

Zacharias, A. (2013) 'UAE residents living near quarries endure long wait for dust to settle', *The National*, 16 July. Available online at www.thenational.ae/news/uae-residents-living-near-quarries-endure-long-wait-for-dust-to-settle (accessed 15 February 2014).

13 Pilgrimage and tourism development in Saudi Arabia

Understanding the challenges and opportunities

Joan C. Henderson

Saudi Arabia is a highly distinctive international tourist destination where development has followed an unusual pathway shaped by environmental, economic, socio-cultural and political circumstances. There are impediments to inbound leisure travel (see Chapter 7), but millions of Muslims visit the holy cities of Makkah and Madinah for religious reasons and especially during the annual pilgrimage of the Hajj. Makkah is where the Prophet Mohammed was born and is said to have first received God's message, and Madinah is where the Prophet fled to safety with some followers in a journey known as the Hirjah, which is also the location of his tomb. Makkah is a venue for visitors undertaking the Hajj and Umrah, a shortened pilgrimage, and for additional forms of religious tourism or Ziarah. Although not on the formal routes, Madinah is often included in such visits.

Movement on such a scale gives rise to formidable practical problems, while also being a source of commercial opportunities, and meeting rising demand is a dilemma which is set to intensify in the years ahead. Efforts to improve infrastructure and expand visitor capacities are already leading to tensions between development and conservation of heritage which will not be easy to reconcile, raising questions of limits to growth and sustainability. This chapter examines the special qualities of tourism in Saudi Arabia and its management, with specific reference to the Hajj.

Issues of religious tourism, the Hajj and tourism development in Saudi Arabia were considered in an earlier article published by the author (Henderson 2011). Here, information is updated, and the focus concerns the ongoing challenges of managing the Hajj, as well as identifying future opportunities for this form of pilgrimage tourism. The event is shown to be exceptional in many ways related to its obligatory character, spatial dimensions, degree of government intervention and control and official policies which are reconfiguring sites to maximize pilgrim space. Demand will never, however, be fully satisfied, and there are fears about irreparable physical damage and an erosion in the quality of the spiritual experience. In contrast, leisure tourism unconnected to religion is relatively low, and there have been some tentative steps to explore these markets.

Pilgrimage tourism, the Hajj and its performance

The relationship between religion and tourism has received attention from researchers of assorted disciplinary backgrounds in a manner recounted in the aforementioned article (Henderson 2011), despite the fact that the literature on the interactions between Islam and tourism remains 'fragmented' (Jafari and Scott 2014: 2). It is not only a subject of academic enquiry, as contemporary religious tourists of various faiths are recognized to be a lucrative market (UNWTO 2011). Religious-inspired motivations emerge as very influential in some tourist decision-making and behaviour, and manifestations of religion can entice tourists even if they do not follow the belief system represented, but there is scope for conflict between the two phenomena. One well-established form of religious tourism is pilgrimage, conventionally defined as a 'journey resulting from religious causes, externally to a holy site, and internally for spiritual purposes and internal understanding' (Barber 1993: 1). Although there are definitional ambiguities and evidence of convergence between the secular and religious, more traditional pilgrimages allied to major religions can and should be differentiated from other travel which may or may not incorporate a mystical component. They involve fixed routes and rituals frequently centred on shrines or other physical structures that may be of interest to (and visited by) those without any religious connection, thus adding to the challenges of managing sacred sites (Shinde 2012).

The Hajj exhibits some of these characteristics and is a means of expressing solidarity among Muslims and their submission to God (Ahmed 1992; Eickeleman and Piscatori 1990). It is distinguished by the quantity of people on the move in a delineated span of time whose actions can be termed involuntary. Pilgrimage is central to Islam (Kessler 1992), and completion of the Hajj is the fifth pillar of the faith, accepted as a religious duty for all adult Muslims unless they are prevented from compliance by specified barriers such as infirmity. Women under the age of 45 must be accompanied by a close male relative, and those older are admitted in organized groups provided they have a kinsman's letter of approval authenticated by a notary (US Department of State 2013). Participation is denied to non-believers who are unable to visit the holy cities, endowing the experience and destinations with an exclusivity which sets them apart from many instances where devout pilgrims share spaces with those who follow other religions or none at all. However, these restrictions do not negate concerns about the effective management of the Hajj and its future, which are discussed here following a brief account of the origin and performance of the pilgrimage.

According to Islamic tradition, the Hajj originated around 2000 BC and recalls the tale of Ibrahim (or Abraham) who was instructed by God to leave his second wife Haajar and son Ishmael in the desert as a test of faith. Haajar and Ishmael miraculously found water, surviving the ordeal, and Ibrahim and Ishmael erected a small shrine in commemoration, which was to become the Kaaba or Cube at the heart of the Grand Mosque in Makkah (Figure 13.1). It enticed people of all religions and was rededicated to Allah by Prophet Mohammed on his return to Makkah, after a period of exile in Madinah, when he removed idols left by

Figure 13.1 The Kaaba, which is located in the centre of the Grand Mosque, Al-Masjid al-Haram, in Makkah. Pilgrims circumambulate the Kaaba counterclockwise seven times.

Source: Zurijeta, July 2012 (www.shutterstock.com/pic.mhtml?id=125633117&src=id).

non-Muslims (Peters 1994). Muslims flocked to the spot subsequently (Burns 2007), and travel from afar was facilitated by improvements in shipping, especially the opening of the Suez Canal in 1869, and later, air transport. Pilgrims reached half a million in 1958, 200,000 of whom were from overseas, rising to 2 million at the end of the century. By the new millennium, many more were coming from North Africa as well as traditional pilgrim sources of South and Southeast Asia and the rest of the Middle East. Registered Hajj participants totalled 3.2 million in 2012, and 1.8 million of these were foreigners from over 188 countries (Royal Embassy of Saudi Arabia 2013). Estimates for 2015 were 2 million foreigners from 160 countries (BBC 2015). Totals are higher in reality because of the presence of many unregistered pilgrims, largely from within the Kingdom, despite official endeavours to eradicate the practice (Ascoura 2013). Official sources quoted in the media calculate that over 200,000 pilgrims were without a permit in 2013 (Hotelier Middle East.com 2013).

The Hajj is always undertaken in the last month of the Islamic lunar calendar year, and details of its operation vary depending upon the school of religious thought (Peters 1994). The Ministry of Hajj writes of 'three ways' of completing the Hajj (Ministry of Hajj 2013a), but many aspects seem to be common (Hammoudi 2006). When approaching Makkah, and sometimes earlier in their journey, pilgrims dress in plain white robes signifying egalitarianism and abide by specific rules of behaviour. From Makkah they walk (or are transported) 8 km to the tent city of Mina and then move on 14.4 km at daybreak to the Plain of Arafat for a day of prayer. The Plain of Arafat is the level area surrounding Mount (Jabal) Arafat (Figure 13.2), from where Prophet Mohammed purportedly addressed fellow Muslims in the 'Last Sermon' during the Hajj. The next stop is Muzdalifah, which is around 9 km away, where the night is spent outdoors before returning to Mina at dawn. The day marks the Eid-al-Adha festival when a devil stoning ceremony is held on the Jamarat Bridge, and animals are sacrificed. Pilgrims proceed to Makkah where they walk around the Kaaba anti-clockwise seven times, pointing to or kissing the Black Stone in the corner reputed to be a 'meteorite used by Abraham as a foundation stone' (Government of Saudi Arabia 2013). The area between the hills of Al-Safah and Al-Marwah, now partially flattened, is said to be where Haajar searched for water and is traversed seven times via air-conditioned tunnels. Water is also drunk from the Grand Mosque's Zamzam Well. The rest of the pilgrimage occurs at Mina, where the stoning ritual may be repeated, and Makkah, involving a final circumambulation of the Kaaba. On completion, pilgrims merit the title of Hajji. Many opt to visit Mohammed's tomb in the Mosque of the Prophet in Madinah and other shrines, although these are not formal stipulations (Henderson 2011).

The Hajj thus demands that pilgrims spend almost 2 weeks covering over 80 km, traditionally on foot, in the company of millions of others. Temperatures in Makkah span 64 to 108 degrees Fahrenheit in the Hajj season, and arrivals at the main entry point of Jeddah airport are likely to confront delays, sometimes of 12 hours, in hot and humid conditions (US Department of State 2013). There are also lengthy queues for basic amenities and services throughout the trip, and risks of theft and fraud. Pilgrims are exposed to debility, disease and injury, and the frail and elderly tend to be most vulnerable (Ahmed *et al.* 2006). Overcrowding

Figure 13.2 Mount (Jabal) Arafat, which is located around 20 km southeast of Makkah.

Source: Zurijeta, July 2012 (www.shutterstock.com/pic.mhtml?id=125650148&src=id).

is unavoidable and can trigger serious mishaps. The worst instance in modern times was the death of around 1,400 in 1990 due to a tunnel stampede, and 345 were killed and 600 injured in 2006 (*Aljazeera* 2009a). In 2015, the collapse of a crane at the Holy Mosque in Makkah left over 100 dead, and more than 750 died as a result of a crush at Mina with many additional casualties (Gov.UK 2016). Accident prevention is a priority for the authorities, where the need for better safety is one reason for the expansion in facilities and capacities described later. Irrespective of hardships facing pilgrims, studies reveal perceptions of satisfaction with pilgrim services and facilities (Eid 2012), realization of religious goals and strong feelings of community (Gunlu and Okumus 2010; Haq and Jackson 2009; Metcalf 1990).

Such sentiments may also be incited among those travelling for religious purposes outside the Hajj, although these movements are much less studied despite the large numbers. Estimates of religious tourists in total varied from between 6.9 million to 8 million in 2013 (*Gulf Business* 2014), many of them engaged in the aforementioned Umrah. Umrah centres on the Grand Mosque and shares some of the Hajj rituals (Ministry of Hajj 2014). It can be completed in a few hours, but a trip will usually include other religious sites and, perhaps, more secular pursuits. Umrah activity is spread over a nine-month period, peaking before the Hajj and during Ramadan, so that pilgrim density is less intense and more easily managed (Currie and Shalaby 2012). Participants in Umrah increased from half a million in 1988 to 2.8 million in 2008, where about 36 per cent came from beyond Saudi Arabia, and are forecast to reach 4.2 million in Makkah by 2030 (Kaysi *et al.* 2010).

Managing the Hajj

The numbers involved in the modern era mean that the informal running of the Hajj in the past (Miller 2006; Woodward 2004) gave way to tighter control by the state which declares that it 'shall provide security and care for the visitors thereof to enable them to perform Hajj, Umrah and visit the Prophet's Mosque in peace and tranquility' (Ministry of Hajj 2013b). Policies are executed by the Ministry of Hajj, which plans and oversees the pilgrimage as well as coordinates the many public bodies and government departments which play a part in events. The royal family assumed guardianship of the holy sites since the founding of the Kingdom, a stance disputed by some who resent this appropriation of Islamic heritage (*Aljazeera* 2011).

While a government responsibility and sacred occasion, the Hajj has always been a business and was of particular importance to Saudis as a revenue earner in the pre-oil economy (Miller 2006). Officials must work with commercial operators in Saudi Arabia and overseas which provide accommodation, transport and other services. Service providers employ about 40,000 and include six Tawafa establishments, 450 affiliated field service groups, 17 transportation companies, 70 missions and more than 2,300 extended travel companies and agencies. In addition, there are 230 domestic establishments with 700 branches (Ministry of

Hajj 2015a). Agents abroad and in the Kingdom are licensed to deal with Hajj travel, and the ministry circulates instructions to Hajj missions, urging those making arrangements to educate pilgrims and prepare them properly for the undertaking (Ministry of Hajj 2013c). The maintenance of acceptable standards by the numerous companies is an aim of the ministry, striving to ensure that 'religious duties are not transformed into a commercial commodity' by ventures keen to maximize revenues (Ministry of Hajj 2013b). Nevertheless, it could be argued that religion has inevitably become the raw material for an industry driven by the profit motive, and pilgrims are essential to the commercial success of private enterprises selling goods and services, as exemplified by the souvenir vendors and accommodation sector. Collins and Murphy (2010: 330) conclude that a suitable balance has been struck, and the various elements of the occasion are blended in a 'successful enterprise that is also respectful and spiritually appropriate', but these are, perhaps, matters for participants to judge.

Certain other management challenges are officially acknowledged, such as meeting the spiritual and physical needs of a diverse multitude of pilgrims – from the poorest with little education, to the very rich and sophisticated who desire service levels to which they are accustomed. Differences are apparent in the choice of accommodation, spanning luxury hotels to very modest properties. In practical terms, the Hajj has posed serious logistical problems, and the Development Commission of Makkah, Madinah and Mashair was formed to coordinate planning with a view to maximize safety (Al-Kodamy 2009). There is pedestrian, public and private traffic congestion, especially within the city of Makkah (Kaysi *et al.* 2010). Safety and order are critical issues which require considerable public spending; for example, more than 100,000 troops were deployed in 2013 to deal with security, and 5,000 surveillance cameras were in operation, including 1,500 cameras at the Grand Mosque to monitor flows (*Middle East Online* 2013). Investment has been made in advanced crowd simulation modelling (Currie and Shalaby 2012), and movements on the Jamarat Bridge are being assessed (Ministry of Hajj 2015b).

A quota mechanism is in force, whereby Hajj visas are allocated according to the size of a nation's Muslim population, reported to be one for every thousand and commonly filled by the lottery. Hajj missions overseas deal with about 80 per cent of pilgrims, the remainder are handled by tourism companies and agencies. The scheme permits visitor volumes to be controlled in a manner which authorities looking after sensitive religious sites elsewhere might envy. Nevertheless, the Saudi government is committed to constantly increasing pilgrim numbers. Efforts at capacity expansion, together with ensuing criticisms, are the subject of the final section. Looking ahead, demand for Hajj and Umrah tourism will increase alongside the Muslim population of around 1.6 billion, which accounts for about one-quarter of the world's total and is growing at a relatively fast pace (Pew Research 2012). Economic advances in South Asian countries make travel to Saudi Arabia more affordable for its residents, and a doubling in all the Kingdom's pilgrims is forecast between 2010 and 2019 (Business Monitor International 2013).

Expanding capacity to meet demand

The Ministry of Hajj (2013d) asserts that since 1932, 'no expense has been spared' in developing the two Holy Mosques in Makkah and Madinah. Augmentation of the pilgrimage infrastructure of accommodation, transport and sanitation has also occurred. The reign of King Fahd from 1982 until 2005 was marked by expansion and refurbishment of facilities, notably a multimillion-dollar programme for Makkah's Grand Mosque so that it could accommodate more than 1 million worshippers compared to 48,000 in the 1930s (Ministry of Hajj 2013e). Modifications at Madinah created space for over half a million devotees, up from 17,000 in the 1930s (Government of Saudi Arabia 2013). The 'largest ever expansion' of Makkah's Grand Mosque was announced in 2008 and is designed for a three-fold rise in pilgrims. Capacity is being increased through structural alterations and new courtyards, while enhancements are being made to lifts, air conditioning and security systems. Another scheme is being developed to enable the Prophet's Mosque at Madinah to hold 1.6 million worshippers when finished. The Prophet's tomb, currently at the centre of the mosque, is due to become the east wing of a building eight times the present size. A series of projects are also slated for Mina, including better roads and parking, ground levelling and the widening of the Al Jamarat Bridge (Ministry of Hajj 2013f). Jeddah's King Abdulaziz Airport is being expanded to handle 80 million passengers a year, and a new high-speed rail link will connect Jeddah with the holy cities (Wainwright 2012). The Makkah Metro opened its first rail line in 2010 from Makkah to Arafat via Mina, a journey of just over six hours, which an estimated half a million Hajj pilgrims made in 2012. The ministry has a 25-year strategic plan (*Al Arabiya News* 2014), and there are predictions that arrivals in Makkah will rise from 20 to 30 million when extant projects are completed (Kaysi *et al.* 2010).

These physical changes were not always welcomed formerly by critics within and outside Saudi Arabia (Henderson 2011), who are still complaining about the loss of heritage and erosion of place identity (Taylor 2013). There are worries about irretrievable damage to the oldest parts of Makkah Grand Mosque, illustrated by the removal of Ottoman and Abbasid columns on the eastern side, which is of greatest significance to Islam. Ignoring protests, notably from Turkey, the Ottoman Ajyard Fortress and the hill on which it stood were destroyed to build the modern Jabal Omar complex on the city's western flank. Current plans necessitate the demolition of 1,000 buildings near the Grand Mosque (Ministry of Hajj 2013g). The pace of change has been less rapid in Madinah, yet only two of the seven ancient mosques commemorating the historic Battle of the Trench survive there. The old district around the Prophet's Mosque is no more (Bianci 2000), and the fate of the famous green dome surmounting the Prophet's tomb is reported to be in doubt, given the proposed reconfiguration (Johnson 2014). Public lavatories and a Hilton hotel reportedly now occupy the sites of the houses of the Prophet's wife and one of his companions, respectively, and a large proportion of older structures have been razed to the ground in Makkah since the 1990s (Taylor 2013). Archaeological sites vital to an understanding of the early history of Islam are also disappearing, and mountains are being flattened to enable new construction (Wainwright 2012).

The transformation of Makkah into a city of skyscrapers, dwarfing what is left of the former settlement and obliterating the traditional urban form (*Aljazeera* 2013), has been deplored (Orbasli 2007). Exemplifying this trend is the Abraj Al Bait Complex featuring the Royal Makkah Clock Tower, one of the tallest buildings in the world at 577 m, and housing shops and a hotel abutting the Grand Mosque. The aforementioned Jabal Omar scheme is planned to have eight hotels with 1,255 rooms, 20-storey residential accommodation, 4,360 commercial and retail units and 500 restaurants in a series of towers (*Arabian Business* 2013). Property values, now among the highest globally, have escalated because of the construction boom (Wainwright 2012), and investment in hotels is predicted to surpass US$40 billion in the next ten years (Euromonitor International 2013). Accommodation is priced in correspondence with proximity to and views of the Grand Mosque, showcased in advertising, and can reach US$7,000 per night (*Aljazeera* 2011). Detractors bemoan unacceptable levels of commercialization and the manner in which the affluent are privileged with uninterrupted sight of the Kaaba on an occasion such as the Hajj, when men are purportedly equal before God. Environmental impacts must also be considered, as well as social consequences, whereby some Makkah residents have been relocated and face a lack of affordable housing (Ascoura 2013).

The government approach is partly explained by the Wahhabist suspicion of tangible reminders of the Prophet, deemed to encourage the worship of idols which they condemn as sinful. Officials also say that sanctity is intangible and undiminished by alterations to the physical environment, which are necessary to cater to the ever-growing number of pilgrims (*Aljazeera* 2009b). The decision to amend plans for Madinah to save three old mosques hints at responsiveness to the conservationist cause, and there is talk of a comprehensive strategic plan for Makkah and its environs, but extant built heritage is seriously endangered (Usborne 2014). There is also a reluctance to speak out too vehemently against the regime's actions at home, given the prevailing political culture. Foreign governments with reservations may be fearful of having their Hajj visa quotas reduced, as well as mindful of the state's influence on the international stage. Archaeologists and historians, too, are anxious to retain access to the sites and information, which might be jeopardized if the authorities are antagonized (Taylor 2012a; 2012b). Politics and religion thus intersect in the theatre of the Hajj, as they do in everyday life in the Kingdom, and political-religious dynamics operating internally and externally will continue to have profound effects on the pilgrimage and its administration.

The opportunities of pilgrimage tourism

The growth trajectory outlined already and possible negative consequences indicate the immense challenges ahead regarding managing religious tourism in Saudi Arabia. Writing about land use and transportation planning, Kaysi, Shalaby, Mahdi and Darwish (2010: 38) describe the likelihood of adverse impacts with respect to 'mobility and accessibility' as well as 'safety, security, equity, sustainability and economy'. They claim that pilgrims are at risk from pedestrian overcrowding, very heavy road traffic, air and noise pollution, fire, terrorism, robbery and riots, while groups such as the elderly, disabled, poor and those who do not speak Arabic or English are in danger of exclusion. However, not all scenarios are bleak, as there have been some attempts to minimize harmful outcomes. Greater use is being made of sophisticated technologies to handle crowds and visa processing, and investment is occurring in the necessary transport infrastructure to create a modern system. Pilgrims are being educated about more responsible behaviour, and licensing machinery should help to check mismanagement by the Hajj and Umrah industries. Promoting Umrah travel could help alleviate disappointment at failing to secure a Hajj visa and offset problems of seasonality. There is also scope for combining religious devotions with other vacation activities, which would be a boost for the tourism sector overall.

Awareness of the importance of the conservation of natural and cultural heritage is increasing and may influence policy to a greater degree in the future. The work of agencies such as the Centre of Research Excellence in Hajj and Umrah in data collection and critical analysis is encouraging and, hopefully, will be expanded on in the future. An event such as the Hajj deserves to be celebrated for its ability to unite the Muslim community, which is sometimes divided by sectarianism and has to negotiate hostile public perceptions in much of the world. Sharing information about the pilgrimage experience and its spiritual meaning with non-Muslims could also assist in cross-cultural understanding and breaking down barriers.

Importantly, Saudi Arabia's potential as a tourism destination, in which the primary motive is not religion, should be recognized. Accordingly, the country has much to offer international visitors searching for locations that are rich in history and natural features (see Chapter 7).

Conclusion and research implications

Saudi Arabia is defined by its economic, socio-cultural and political differences with much of the rest of the world. These inhibit inbound leisure tourist flows, but do not preclude pre-eminence as a religious tourist destination which hosts a pilgrimage of an exceptional character. Participation in the Hajj is mandated by Islam, and millions of pilgrims follow a pre-ordained timetable and join in set rituals at locations from which non-believers are barred. Activity is tightly controlled by an authority that has political and religious power, whose leaders have styled themselves as protectors of the holy cities, interpreted as encompassing the right to institute fundamental changes to historic sites. Radical expansion of worshipping space and supporting infrastructure is being authorized in the professed interests of the global Muslim community. Such development is taking precedence over conservation and, indeed, effacement of certain built heritage appears to be sanctioned by the dominant religious ideology. The subject of the Hajj is thus a fascinating one, which merits continued and more exhaustive study to enhance knowledge of the characteristics and consequences of this unique manifestation of tourism and the destination where it is practiced.

Issues to address include the expectations of pilgrims about spiritual and physical experiences and satisfaction afforded by completion of the Hajj. Of interest are reactions to encroaching and aggressive commercialization, embodied in new buildings oriented towards making money, and the erasure of structures and landscapes. Resultant information would help to test the validity of concerns that place identities are being undermined and links severed with the past, thereby confounding appreciation of history and disinheriting future generations. Awareness of social divisions and widening inequalities between rich and poor pilgrims, reflected in the choice of accommodation, could also be assessed. Patterns of urbanization are another avenue for exploration, considering the applicability of conventional models of tourist city evolution, and embracing issues of sustainability and liveability. Finally, the politics of the Hajj in terms of internal decision-making and external relations is worthy of attention. Some of these areas might be deemed sensitive, and the challenges of the research environment should, perhaps, be acknowledged. Nevertheless, there is a need for further work on tourists, destinations, policy and industries in the Arab world conducted by native scholars and accessible to an international audience.

References

Ahmed, Z. (1992) 'Islamic pilgrimage (Hajj) to Ka'aba in Makah (Saudi Arabia): an important international tourism activity', *Journal of Tourism Studies*, 3: 35–43.

Ahmed, Q. A., Arabi, Y. M. and Memish, Z. (2006) 'Health risks at the Hajj', *The Lancet*, 367: 1008–1015.

Al Arabiya News (2014) 'Saudi Ministry of Hajj unveils 25-year strategic plan', *Al Arabiya News*, 29 October. Available online at http://english.alarabiya.net/en/special-reports/hajj-2014/2014/10/29/Ministry-of-Haj-unveils-25-year-strategic-plan.html (accessed 8 February 2015).

Aljazeera (2009a) 'Hajj: major incidents', *Aljazeera*, 19 November. Available online at www.aljazeera.com/news/middlewast/2007/12/2008525172542227691.html (accessed 27 November 2013).

Aljazeera (2009b) 'Improving Mecca's infrastructure', *Aljazeera*, 25 November. Available online at www.aljazeera.com/focus/hajj/2009/11/200911250505146948.html (accessed 12 August 2014).

Aljazeera (2011) 'The mall of Mecca or a new era of growth', *Aljazeera*, 13 October. Available online at http://stream.aljazeera.com/story/comin-soon-mecca-expands-and-develops-what-cost (accessed 26 November 2013).

Aljazeera (2013) 'Mecca construction transforms Holy City', *Aljazeera*, 12 October. Available online at www.aljazeera.com/news/middleast/2013/10/mecca-construction-transform-holy-city (accessed 26 November 2013)

Al-Kodmany, K. (2009) 'Planning for the Hajj: political power, pragmatism and participatory GIS', *Journal of Urban Technology*, 16(1): 5–45.

Arabian Business (2013) 'Jabal Omar development company', *Arabian Business.com*. Available online at www.arabianbusiness.com/companies/jabal-omar-development-company-66584 (accessed 30 November 2013).

Ascoura, I. E. (2013) 'Impact of pilgrimage (Hajj) on the urban growth of Mecca', *Journal of Educational and Social Research*, 3(2): 255–263.

Barber, R. (1993) *Pilgrimage*, London: The Boydell Press.

BBC (2015) 'Hajj in numbers'. Available online at www.bbc.com/news/world-middle-east-2943590 (accessed 24 March 2016).

Bianci, S. (2000) *Urban Form in the Arab World*, London: Thames and Hudson.

Burns, P. (2007) 'From Hajj to hedonism? Paradoxes of developing tourism in Saudi Arabia', in M. F. Daher (ed.) *Tourism in the Middle East: Continuity, Change and Transformation*, Clevedon: Channel View Publications, pp. 215–236.

Business Monitor International (2013) *Saudi Arabia Tourism Report Q4 2013*, London: Business Monitor International.

Collins, N. and J. Murphy (2010) 'The Hajj: an illustration of 360-degree authenticity', in N. Scott and J. Jafari (eds) *Tourism in the Muslim World*, Bingley: Emerald, pp. 321–330.

Currie, G. and A. Shalaby (2012) 'Synthesis of transport planning approaches for the world's largest events', *Transport Reviews*, 32(1): 113–136.

Eickeleman, D. F. and J. Piscatori (1990) *Muslim Travellers: Pilgrimage, Migration and the Religious Imagination*, London: Routledge.

Eid, R. (2012) 'Towards a high-quality religious tourism marketing: the case of Hajj service in Saudi Arabia', *Tourism Analysis*, 17(4): 509–522.

Euromonitor International (2013) *Travel and Tourism in Saudi Arabia*, London: Euromonitor International.

Government of Saudi Arabia (2013) 'The two Holy Mosques'. Available online at www.info.gov.sa/portals/kingdom/Mosques.html (accessed 26 November 2013).

Gov.UK (2016) 'Foreign travel advice: Saudi Arabia'. Available online at www.gov.uk/foreign-travel-advice/saudi-arabia/safety-and-security (accessed 24 March 2016).

Gulf Business (2014) 'Saudi's Umrah visa extension scheme to launch next month – SCTA', *Gulf Business*, 3 April. Available online at http://gulfbusiness.com/2014/04/saudis-umrah-visa-extension-scheme-launch-next- month (accessed 8 February 2015).

Gunlu, E. and F. Okumus (2010) 'The Hajj experience of Turkish female pilgrims', in N. Scott and J. Jafari (eds) *Tourism in the Muslim World*, Bingley: Emerald, pp. 221–233.

Hammoudi, A. (2006) *A Season in Mecca: Narrative of a Pilgrimage*, New York: Hill and Wang.

Haq, F. and J. Jackson (2009) 'Spiritual journey to Hajj: Australian and Pakistani experience and expectations', *Journal of Management, Spirituality and Religion*, 6(2): 141–156.

Henderson, J. C. (2011) 'Religious tourism and its management: the Hajj in Saudi Arabia', *International Journal of Tourism Research*, 13(6): 541–552.

Hotelier Middle East.com (2013) 'Saudi crackdown on 120,000 illegal Hajj pilgrims', *Middle East Hotelier.com*, 22 October. Available online at www.hoteliermiddleeast.com/18549-saudi-crackdown-on-120000-illegal-hajj-pilgrims/ (accessed 12 August 2014).

Jafari, J. and N. Scott (2014) 'Muslim world and its tourisms', *Annals of Tourism Research*, 44: 1–19.

Johnson, A. (2014) 'Saudis risk new Muslim division with proposal to move Mohamed's tomb', *Independent*, 1 September. Available online at www.independent.co.uk/news/world/middle-east/saudis-risk-new-muslim-division-with-proposal-to-move-mohameds-tomb-9705120.html (accessed 8 February 2015).

Kaysi, I. A., Shalaby Y. Mahdi and. F Darwish (2010) 'Background material toolkit', Makka: Centre of Research Excellence in Hajj and Umrah at UMM Al Qura University.

Kessler, C. S. (1992) 'Pilgrims' progress: the travellers of Islam', *Annals of Tourism Research*, 19: 147–153.

Metcalf, B. D. (1990) 'The pilgrimage remembered: South Asian accounts of the Hajj', in D. F. Eickeleman and J. Piscatori (eds) *Muslim Travellers: Pilgrimage, Migration and the Religious Imagination*, London: Routledge, pp. 85–110.

Middle East Online (2013) 'Pilgrims start leaving Saudi Arabia after incident-free Hajj', Middle East Online, 17 October. Available online at www.middle-east-online.com/english/?id=62008 (accessed 27 November 2013).

Miller, M. B. (2006) 'Pilgrims' progress: the business of the Hajj', *Past and Present*, 191: 189–228.

Ministry of Hajj (2013a) 'The rituals and stages of the Hajj'. Available online at www.hajinformation.com/main/f20.htm (accessed 24 November 2013).

Ministry of Hajj (2013b) 'Responsibilities of the Ministry of Hajj'. Available online at www.hajinformation.com/main/m10.htm (accessed 24 November 2013).

Ministry of Hajj (2013c) 'Instructions regarding agreements between Hajj missions and the Ministry'. Available online at www.hajinformation.com/main/m40.htm (accessed 24 November 2013).

Ministry of Hajj (2013d) 'Kingdom as guardian of the holy places'. Available online at www.hajinformation.com/main/d10.htm (accessed 24 November 2013).

Ministry of Hajj (2013e) 'Modern development of the Holy Mosque'. Available online at www.hajinformation.com/main/j102.htm (accessed 24 November 2013).

Ministry of Hajj (2013f) 'Mina development projects'. Available online at www.haji information.com/main /m90.htm (accessed 24 November 2013).

Ministry of Hajj (2013g) 'Largest ever expansion of the Haram in Makah (2008)'. Available online at www.hajiinformation.com/main/j103.htm (accessed 24 November 2013).

Ministry of Hajj (2014) 'International Umrah procedures'. Available online at http://haj.gov.sa/en-us/Information/AboutMinisry/HajjUmrahProcedures/Pages (accessed 8 February 2015).

Ministry of Hajj (2015a) 'Work arrangements during the Hajj and Umrah seasons'. Available online at http://haj.gov.sa/en-US/Information/AboutMinistry/Pages/WorkIn Ministry.aspx (accessed 8 February 2015).

Ministry of Hajj (2015b) 'Hajj sector work programs'. Available online at http://haj.gov.sa/en-us/Information/AboutMinistry/HajjUmrahProcedures/Pages (accessed 8 February 2015).

Orbasli, A. (2007) 'The "Islamic city" and tourism: managing conservation and tourism in traditional neighbourhoods', in M. F. Daher (ed.) *Tourism in the Middle East: Continuity, Change and Transformation*, Clevedon: Channel View Publications, pp. 161–178.

Peters, F. E. (1994) *The Hajj: The Muslim Pilgrimage to Mecca and the Holy Land*, Princeton, NJ: Princeton University Press.

Pew Research (2012) 'Religion and public life project: the global religious landscape'. Available online at www.pewforum.org/2012/12/18/global-religious-landscape-muslim/ (accessed 22 November 2013).

Royal Embassy of Saudi Arabia (2013) '1,379,531 Pilgrims from 188 countries arrived for Hajj', Available online at www.saudiembassy.net/print/latest_news/news1031302.aspx (accessed 20 November 2013).

Shinde, K. A. (2012) 'Policy, planning and management for religious tourism in Indian pilgrimage sites', *Journal of Policy Research in Tourism, Leisure and Events*, 4(3): 277–301.

Taylor, J. (2012a) 'Why don't more Muslims speak out against the wanton destruction of Mecca's holy sites', *The Independent*, 28 October. Available online at www.independent.co.uk/voices/comment/why-dont-more-muslims-speak-out-against-the-wanton-destruction-of-meccas-holy-sites-8229682.html (accessed 24 March 2016).

Taylor (2012b) 'Medina: Saudis take a bulldozer to Islam's history', *The Independent*, 26 October. Available online at www.independent.co.uk/news/world/middle-east/medina-saudis-take-a-bulldozer-to-islams-history-8228795.html (accessed 24 March 2016).

Taylor, J. (2013) 'The photos Saudi Arabia doesn't want seen', *The Independent*, 15 March. Available online at www.independent.co.uk/news/world/middle-east/the-photos-saudi-arabia-doesnt-want-seen-and-proof-islams-most-holy-relics-are-being-demolished-in-8536968.html (accessed 24 March 2016).

UNWTO (United Nations World Tourism Organization) (2011) *Religious Tourism in Asia and the Pacific*, Madrid: World Tourism Organization.

Usborne, D. (2014) 'Redevelopment of Mecca: bulldozers bear down on site of Mohamed's birth', *The Independent*, 20 February.

US Department of State (2013) *Hajj and Umrah fact sheet*, Bureau of Consular Affairs. Available online at https://travel.state.gov/content/passports/en/go/Hajj.html (accessed 1 December 2013).

Wainwright, O. (2012) 'Mecca's mega architecture cast shadow over Hajj', *Guardian*, 23 October. Available online at www.theguardian.com/artanddesign/2012/oct/23/mecca-architecture-hajj1 (accessed 26 November 2013).

Woodward, S. (2004) 'Faith and tourism: planning tourism in relation to places of worship', *Tourism and Hospitality Planning and Development*, 1(2): 173–186.

14 Transnational heritage in Abu Dhabi

Power, politics and identity

Sarina Wakefield

Nation states are increasingly engaging in global activities. These activities have been predominantly analyzed in terms of their political and economic agendas. However, culture is playing a significant role in the development of cross-border relationships, and this is leading to the development of new forms of transnational heritage. National governments, cultural agencies and professional bodies have recognized the potential of preserving and presenting cultural heritage globally, to develop and reinforce their national identities. A trend that has emerged from this has been the development of museums as a form of 'portable social technology' (Kratz and Karp [2006] 2007: 4). Significantly, these transnational institutions are not geographically bound to the areas in which they are developed (Kirshemblatt-Gimblett [2006] 2007; Harrison 2013). This mobilization of heritage is an important aspect of the transnationalization of heritage, which is markedly different to established heritage processes that emerged predominantly from Western Europe in the nineteenth and twentieth centuries (Harrison 2013). Transnationalization is used throughout this chapter to describe how heritage operates within and across national borders (cf. Hannerz 1996). The author has argued elsewhere that transnational heritage formations in Abu Dhabi are developed using hybrid heritage processes that are based on the promotion of cosmopolitanism, identity and co-production (Wakefield 2013; 2014). The way that transnational heritage is defined and put to use sheds light on the ways in which cultural heritage is implicated within globalization and the development of global contemporary identities.

This chapter is specifically concerned with one aspect of the transnationalization of heritage, the international franchising of museums and how they operate as a global heritage institutions. This chapter draws from the author's PhD research, which explored the processes and cultural effects of cultural heritage franchising in the United Arab Emirates (UAE) through four years of detailed ethnographic multi-sited research. It will explore how the franchise model has developed and how it is connected to globalization, cosmopolitanism and the production of soft power. It will discuss how the process of cultural heritage franchising challenges the local versus the global nexus and what this means in the context of producing heritage in non-Western contexts. It will then go on to explore how this relates to globalization and the co-production of heritage across borders. Next, it will discuss how global heritage formations, such as cultural heritage franchises, are connected to cosmopolitanism and what the implications of this are for the production of transnational identities. Finally, it will analyze how politics and power are connected to the process of cultural heritage franchising.

The cultural heritage franchise

The Solomon R. Guggenheim Foundation (hereafter SRGF) was the first organization to develop cultural heritage franchises. In 1949, it expanded its operations from its first site, the Guggenheim Museum in New York, by opening a global site in Venice, Italy (SRGF n.d.). Then came the Deutsche Guggenheim Berlin, followed in 1991 by the Guggenheim Museum Bilbao (hereafter GMB) (SRGF n.d.). Alvarez Sainz (2012: 101) noted that, 'in the ten years since the GMB opened more than ten million people have visited'. This amount was unprecedented in the history of SRGF's effort to establish museum franchises. Arguably, then, it was the development of GMB and the subsequent increase of tourism in the Basque region that helped to establish SRGF's global brand (Alvarez Sainz 2012). More broadly, the partnership set the framework for cultural heritage franchising, which at the time of writing (May 2016) was being used as the model for both the Guggenheim Abu Dhabi and the Louvre Abu Dhabi.

As part of a broader initiative to develop Abu Dhabi's tourism industry, and more generally to enhance the city's image and reputation, the government developed a strategy to facilitate the growth of the cultural heritage industry. This strategy forms part of the government's economic development plan, 'Plan Abu Dhabi 2030' (Abu Dhabi Urban Planning Council 2007). A key development within the government's plans is the Cultural District, which will form part of the Emirate's Saadiyat Island development. Saadiyat Island will feature seven distinct districts: (1) the Cultural District, (2) Saadiyat Beach, (3) Saadiyat Marina, (4) Saadiyat Reserve, (5) Saadiyat Promenade, (6) Saadiyat Lagoons and (7) Saadiyat Retreat (Tourism Development Investment Corporation). The Cultural District will include the development of four of the island's five planned large-scale cultural institutions: (1) Guggenheim Abu Dhabi museum, (2) Louvre Abu Dhabi museum, (3) Performing Arts Centre and (4) Zayed National Museum. The fifth institution, the Maritime Museum, will be located in the island's Marina District (Al Saadiyat n.d.). The planned museums are being developed in partnership with several international branded museums: the Louvre Museum in the case of the Louvre Abu Dhabi, the SRGF in the case of the Guggenheim Abu Dhabi and the British Museum in the case of the Zayed National Museum. It is important to note that the British Museum partnership is different to the Louvre Abu Dhabi and the Guggenheim Abu Dhabi as it is providing consultancy services towards the development of the Zayed National Museum, rather than franchising its brand name. The way in which the cultural heritage developments are being presented suggests that Abu Dhabi, perhaps in competition with Qatar, with similar cultural heritage development objectives, is to position the Emirate as a place for cultural tourism within the Gulf. What is unique within Abu Dhabi is the strategic use of both autochthonous and global heritage formations.

The franchising literature suggests that the process of franchising creates a 'common identity', whereby the franchisee uses the franchise partnership to draw on the established identity of the franchisor to develop the brand in a different area (Bradach 1998: 16). The value of this is connected to the provision of a familiar product that is instantly credible and recognizable (Ritzer [1999] 2010). McDonald's operates, as George Ritzer's analysis illustrates, 'through four main strategies – efficiency, predictability, calculability and control – providing familiarity and creating a preference towards known quantities' ([1999] 2010: 4). An important aspect of cultural heritage franchising comes from the association of established international branded museums, and the cultural experiences that are anticipated from a visit to such institutions (Wakefield 2014). This is similar to the attitudes and expectations that people have towards World Heritage Sites (Harrison 2013; Ryan and Silvanto 2011). Global heritage such as cultural heritage franchising and World Heritage Site Listing creates a global grouping, which is used to define national identity and position the nation within the global heritage economy.

Transnational power relations

Within the transnational heritage economy it is not just about how, in what form and where heritage moves to that matters (while these are still important elements); more crucially, it is about the inherent power relations that are contained within different heritage mobilities. Sociologist Zygmunt Bauman (1998: 2) suggests that mobility has become an important aspect of modernity, which has an impact on social equality and access. The use of heritage in global terms can be seen, in part, as a form of 'soft power' and, in this sense, transnational heritage is used to signify and present a nation's 'cultural credentials to the world' (Labadi and Long 2010: 6). More recently, Winter (2015: 997) has highlighted the need for 'a framework of heritage diplomacy', which recognizes 'heritage as an arena of governance, of institutions, and as a space of both cooperation and contestation'. The trade of transnational heritage brands is therefore an important indicator of a nation's economic wealth and power. In Abu Dhabi, the development of cultural heritage franchises signifies a measured move to produce and exert its power through cultural ownership. It is, essentially, a symbolic display of Abu Dhabi's modernity, its wealth and its global power.

Wakefield (2014) suggests that bilateral relations are playing a significant role in the production of cross-border partnerships. For example, France and the UAE have established a number of bilateral agreements, which include the opening of a French military base in Abu Dhabi, the Paris-Sorbonne University, and the planned Louvre Abu Dhabi (Cody 2009). The way in which these partnerships are presented as cross-cultural dialogues suggests that global heritage is based upon cosmopolitan ideologies (Wakefield 2014). According to Appiah, cosmopolitanism is founded on 'an obligation to others', which emphasizes the 'value' of other people's 'practices and beliefs' ([2006] 2007: xiii). The idea of 'global citizenship' is applied to heritage through the promotion of 'global shared heritage'. UNESCO has most famously promoted the idea of global heritage through its categorization and World Heritage Listing. This can be observed in the way in which national cultural heritage is presented in Abu Dhabi. Wakefield (2013; 2014) has observed that Abu Dhabi's heritage discourse draws heavily on cosmopolitanism, universalism and transnationalism and is used by both the government and heritage institutions to present the nation as an active global actor. Kirshenblatt-Gimblett argues that 'world heritage is a vehicle for envisaging and constituting a global polity' ([2006] 2007: 161). Heritage works in this way to establish Abu Dhabi's identity and value system within the processes of globalization. Transnational heritage is, therefore, set up as a system of global exchange and connection. In this sense, nations use global heritage processes to define their identities and their membership of humanity.

On a practical level, this cosmopolitan shift has altered the way in which heritage is produced and presented. Meskell (2009: 3–4) argues that 'rooted cosmopolitanism' has the potential to 'acknowledge attachments to place and particular social networks, resources and cultural experiences that inhabit that space'. Within Abu Dhabi, cultural heritage is utilized to position the nation's past within a universal heritage discourse and to strengthen national identity. In this sense, cultural heritage development is a strategic process that works to symbolize Abu Dhabi's place within the global system by positioning the Emirate's cultural identity, both past and present, within transnational terms.

Cosmopolitanism, then, is a political process that is connected to the way in which heritage is produced and 'authorized' by the state (Wakefield 2013). The result is that it excludes alternative ideas and representations of heritage that do not fit, or may challenge, the 'official view' (Harrison 2013; Smith 2006), which ultimately undermines the ethical stance of cosmopolitanism and the hybrid heritage processes that it produces. The cosmopolitan discourse is therefore highly selective and elitist, since global heritage is 'officially sanctioned' by nation states (Harrison 2013; Smith 2006). Absent from the heritage narratives are more problematic histories. For example, heritage narratives do not account for the many migrant workers who live (and were born) in the UAE. This is ironic, given the fact that migrant workers have over many years been involved in the construction of the city itself, and perhaps more so due to their significant involvement in the construction/reconstruction of the heritage infrastructure. Cosmopolitan approaches to heritage must, therefore, be analyzed carefully in order to understand the dynamics that are at play within hybrid heritage contexts.

As noted earlier, the transnational heritage economy in Abu Dhabi is largely focused around exclusive and high-profile partnerships with powerful nations, namely the United Kingdom, the United States and France. Philippe Reginier, editor of the French *newspaper Journal des Arts*, writing in the *Guardian* newspaper, argued that the Louvre Abu Dhabi partnership was 'about France's presence in the region and its economic concerns' (Chrisafis 2006) rather than cultural development per se. The political and financial imperatives of franchise partnerships rarely go unnoticed and, as a result, have come under heavy criticism (Bradley 1997; Lowry 2004). When the Louvre Abu Dhabi project was announced, it received significant criticism from the international media and the cultural sector (Cachin *et al.* 2006; Rykner 2007), which led to an online petition being set up by French art website, *La Tribune de l'Art* (Rykner 2006)

The international press also criticized the plans by questioning why tourists would want to visit the Louvre Abu Dhabi or the Guggenheim Abu Dhabi, when they can go and see the original museums in Paris and New York (Riding 2007). In this sense, cultural heritage franchising is seen as a process of 'reproduction' that 'dilutes' the 'original'. This has led some to call such cultural heritage franchises 'McGuggenheims' (Zulaika 1997), which is seen as a derogatory label. It is connected to the dominant view that globalization works exclusively along Western terms of reference (Nederveen-Pieterse 1995: 47). However, Staiff and Bushell (2003) have suggested that translation is not about producing an authentic copy. Rather, they argue that the process of translation 'is always a cultural, social and political intervention by the translator', therefore, 'who undertakes the translation and how it is undertaken are therefore critical issues' (Staiff and Bushell 2003: 117). Accordingly, archaeologist Denis Byrne (2011) notes that in Thailand the construction and restoration of Thai stupas is not only a process of conservation but also one that re-develops and re-inscribes the past in contemporary society. He suggests that 'the traditional way of restoring stupas, for instance, simply encases the old object inside another much bigger one. The original in this sense is consumed by the restoration' (2011: 146). This suggests that the way in which the past is valued in the present is a matter of judgement, calling into question the assumption that branded museums are copies of the original. The implications of this are that it overlooks the complexity and nuances that are present within the processes of developing cultural heritage franchises.

Heritage and globalization

The idea that global heritage processes, such as cultural heritage franchises, result in homogenized representations connects to debates that have emerged within studies of globalization. These debates question whether globalization results in the disappearance of cultural differences and the production of homogenized cultural forms (Featherstone 1990: 1–14). Fibiger (2011) suggests that Islamic critiques of globalization in the Gulf have focused on the argument that modernization, globalization and Westernization represent a threat to Islamic values and local traditions. He argues that such views 'fail to acknowledge the global role that Islam plays as a world religion and a globalized practice' (2011: 194). This highlights how Islam, like heritage, is bound up in both local and global processes. Until recently, debates within the heritage literature have tended to position the development of localism as a defence against the threat of globalization (see Asfour 2006; Harvey 1989). This then creates a divide where 'unofficial heritage' comes to be seen as a threat to the state and 'officially' sanctioned heritage discourses (Graham, Ashworth and Tunbridge [2000] 2004; Harrison 2010). Within the Gulf, this has manifested itself in what academics have termed 'heritage revivalism' (Fox *et al.* 2006; Khalaf 2002), where the establishment and growth of heritage practices in the Gulf represent a direct response to rapid changes in society as a consequence of economic development, population diversity and migration, and the importation of foreign goods and services. Khalaf (2002) argues that the production of Dubai's Heritage Village was a result of the threat of globalization to Emirati identity.

More recently, arguments that set the West and the East, and the global and the local against each other have been challenged. Anthropologist Anna Tsing (2005) argues that globalization should be seen as a process of 'friction'. She suggests that by seeing globalization in this way allows us to explore the dynamics that work towards global formations and the resultant effects that this has socially, economically and politically. Sociologist Roland Robertson asserts that globalization 'refers to both the compression of the world and the intensification of consciousness of the world as a whole' (1995: 8). This is particularly significant for heritage as it draws attention to the ways in which local and global heritage processes interact and enmesh. Importantly, Winter (2014: 557) emphasizes that heritage studies need to be pluralized to 'better address the heterogeneous nature of heritage, for both the West and the non-West' and that this should occur within a consideration of broader 'geopolitical and geocultural' change. Appadurai (1990: 6) has suggested that:

> The new global cultural economy has to be seen as a complex, overlapping, disjunctive order, which cannot any longer be understood in terms of existing center-periphery models (even those which might account for multiple centers and peripheries).

Robertson (1995) has also argued that local and global forces intersect and that the result is 'glocalization', which produces new and specific expressions of global cultural interaction. According to Beck (2006: 72–73), cosmopolitanism is a 'dialectical process in which the universal and particular, the similar and the dissimilar, the global and the local are to be conceived, not as cultural polarities but as interconnected and reciprocally interpenetrating principles'.

Heritage can thus be seen as a socially constructed process. This process is also hybrid because as it draws on both global and local processes to produce what is essentially a new system of heritage categorization and professionalization. The co-production of heritage in transnational settings contradicts the global versus local binary that has dominated the heritage debates. Bhabha (1996) and Clifford (1997) suggested that hybrid cultural contexts emerge, which can be defined and identified as 'contact zones'. This implies that zones of contact can be easily recognized and demarcated from other aspects of cultural production and interaction. This, however, is rarely the case, as cultural encounters and interpretations are highly variable and subjective. Therefore, in the case of Abu Dhabi, not only is the museum used as an arbitrator of transnational identity, but it is also tied to the ways in which heritage is used in the economic and political processes of the state. This process of producing heritage represents a form of de-colonization, where the old imperial powers of the West are seen as translators of cultural production by the Gulf, but are subject to the power and control of the Gulf through the sale of their brand services and the cultural restrictions imposed upon their practices. Rather than being seen as distinctive and separate categories, local and global heritage is part of a hybrid process that produces a transnational heritage identity. In this sense, transnational heritage operates to produce a heritage identity that speaks of both the nation at home and the nation as envisaged within the global.

Garcia Canclini (1990; 1995a; 1995b) argues that hybridity involves both the past and the present, which are used in the construction of contemporary hybrid identities and global modernity. This concept is particularly relevant in Abu Dhabi, where 'traditional' tribal structure and 'global practices' work together, though not always in harmony, to shape the city's social, economic and political development (Davidson 2009; Fox *et al.* 2006). For example, Fox *et al.* (2006: 9) illustrate how 'globalization meshes with traditionalism rather than being an imported total package of lifestyles and values' in the Gulf states. The implication of this for heritage production is that global processes and categorizations are used in a way that 'fits' with local social structures and norms. The formations of what is produced, and by whom, are still a matter of debate. The role that the Abu Dhabi government plays in driving heritage developments is very much state driven and, arguably, top down, illustrating that Abu Dhabi is active in the process of hybrid heritage production.

Conclusion and research implications

This chapter has shown that cultural heritage franchising is a deeply political and complex process that is intimately connected to the global cultural economy. The discussion of cultural heritage franchising has shown how this process challenges ideas that have largely developed out of Western Europe, about how museums should operate in the contemporary world. It suggests that cultural heritage fran chises should be considered in relation to their distinct cultural settings, and how they challenge the notion of authenticity in non-Western contexts. This challenges the idea that globalization leads to the eradication of difference by arguing that the co-production of cultural heritage produces new forms of cultural formations and identities. These formations emerge not only from the movement of cultural producers and things but also from the ideological promotion of cosmopolitanism. As this chapter has shown, cosmopolitanism is used to promote global heritage and to encourage nations around the world to contribute to the making of that global heritage. This system of global heritage production is exclusive and serves to promote established standards and methods that do not necessarily fit, or ben-efit, all nations. The chapter discussed how power is implicated within cultural partnerships, emphasizing that hybrid heritage is intimately connected to political power and the development and consolidation of bilateral relations. The example of cultural heritage franchising, particularly the planned Louvre Abu Dhabi, illustrates that transnational cultural partnerships are often politically motivated. In this sense, the process of cultural heritage franchising is utilized to reinforce and extend bilateral relations. Accordingly, cultural heritage franchise partnerships, arguably, work as a form of cultural diplomacy. Perhaps more importantly in the case of Abu Dhabi, cultural partnerships are used to position the city as cultural producer capable of purchasing and exerting control over other nations' cultural heritage.

The work has demonstrated how dominant models of heritage, bounded by national and local borders (Harrison 2013), are no longer the only means of exploring heritage processes. Instead, it has been suggested that the co-production and dissemination of transnational forms of cultural heritage require more in-depth research. This is important because as globalization continues to inform much of the way people live their lives in the contemporary world, so too will global heritage processes continue to increase. It has been argued that transnational heritage production is a hybrid process involving the co-production of heritage across national borders by multiple actors. These hybrid processes are far from static and, as such, will vary depending upon the socio-political circumstances from which they emerge.

Therefore, more research needs to be undertaken into comprehending the different ways that hybrid heritage processes develop and are engaged with, in diverse global settings. Moreover, more interdisciplinary studies are required in order to be able to explore and make linkages across diverse subject areas. This enquiry, for example, draws on academic debates from commercial franchising literature, critical heritage studies, sociology and citizenship theory. Ultimately, greater attention needs to be paid to the ways in which global heritage is co-produced and presented in different regional contexts, and the way in which these developments link to the economic, political and cultural motivations that are embedded within transnational cultural networks.

References

Abu Dhabi Urban Planning Council (2007) *Plan Abu Dhabi 2030*. Available online at www.upc.gov.ae/en/MasterPlan/Plan-AbuDhabi2030.aspx (accessed 4 January 2010).

Al Saadiyat (n.d.) *Saadiyat Cultural District*. Available online at www.saadiyat.ae/en/inspiration-details/1/Saadiyat-Cultural-District (accessed 20 April 2013).

Alvarez Sainz, M. (2012) '(Re)Building an image for a city: is a landmark enough? Bilbao and the Guggenheim Museum, 10 Years Together', *Journal of Applied Social Psychology*, 42(1): 100–132.

Appadurai, A. (1990) 'Disjuncture and difference in the global cultural economy', *Theory, Culture and Society*, 7(2): 295–310.

Appiah, K. A. ([2006] 2007) *Cosmopolitanism: Etics in a World of Strangers*, London: Penguin Books.

Asfour, G. (2006) 'An argument for enhancing Arab identity within globalization', in J. W. Fox, N. Mourtarda-Sabbah and M. Al-Mutawa (eds) *Globalization and the Gulf*, London: Routledge, pp. 141–147.

Bauman, Z. (1998) *Globalization: The Human Consequence*, New York: Columbia University Press.

Beck, U. (2006) *The Cosmopolitan Vision*, Cambridge: Polity.

Bhabha, H. (1996) 'Cultures in between', in S. Hall and P. DuGay, *Questions of Cultural Identity*, London: Sage Publications, pp. 53–60.

Bradach, J. L. (1998) *Franchise Organizations*, Boston, MA: Harvard Business School Press.

Bradley, K. (1997) 'The deal of the century', *Art in America*, 85(2): 128.

Byrne, D. (2011) 'Archaeological heritage and cultural intimacy: an interview with Michael Herzfeld', *Journal of Social Archaeology*, 11(2): 144–157.

Cachin, F., J. Clair and R. Recht (2006) 'Museums are not for sale', *Le Monde*, 13 December. Available online at www.bpe.europresse.com (accessed 5 February 2010).

Chrisafis, A. (2006) 'The race for art island: Louvre and Guggenheim battle it out', *Guardian*, 22 November. Available online at www.theguardian.com/world/2006/nov/22/france.arts (accessed 14 January 2010).

Clifford, J. (1997) *Routes: Travel and Translation in the Late Twentieth Century*, Cambridge and London: Harvard University Press.

Cody, E. (2009) 'First French military base opens in the Persian Gulf', *Washington Post*, 27 May. Available online at http://articles.washingtonpost.com/2009-05-27/world/36882134_1_rafale-french-soldiers-first-military-base (accessed 27 May 2009).

Davidson, C. (2009) *Abu Dhabi: Oil and Beyond*, London: C. Hurst & Co.

Featherstone, M. (1990) 'Global culture: an introduction', in M. Featherstone (ed.) *Global Culture: Nationalism, Globalization and Modernity: A Theory Culture and Society Special Issue*, London: Sage, pp. 1–14.

Fibiger, T. (2011) 'Global display – local dismay: Debating "globalized heritage" in Bahrain', *History and Anthropology*, 22(2): 187–202.

Fox, J. W., N. Moutada-Sabbah and M. al-Mutawa (2006) 'The Arab Gulf region: traditionalism globalized or globalization traditionalized?', in. J. W. Fox, N. Moutada-Sabbah and M. al-Mutawa (eds) *Globalization and the Gulf*, London: Routledge, pp. 3–60.

Garcia Canclini, N. (1990) 'Cultural reconversion', in G. Yudice, J. Franco and J. Flores (eds) *On the Edge: The Crisis of Latin American Culture*, translated by H. Staver, Minneapolis, MN: University of Minnesota Press, pp. 29–44.

Garcia Canclini, N. (1995a) Hybrid Cultures: Strategies for Entering and Leaving Modernity, Minneapolis, MN: Minnesota Press.

Garcia Canclini, N. (1995b) 'Cultural globalization in a disintegrating city', *American Ethnologist*, 22(4): 743–755.

Graham, B., G. J. Ashworth and J. E. Tunbridge ([2000] 2004) *A Geography of Heritage: Power, Culture and Economy*, London: Hodder.

Hannerz, U. (1996) *Transnational Connections: Culture, People, Places*, London: Routledge.

Harrison, R. (2010) 'Multicultural and minority heritage', in T. Benton (ed.) *Understanding Heritage and Memory*, Manchester: Manchester University Press, pp. 238–276.

Harrison, R. (2013) *Heritage: Critical Approaches*, Abingdon and New York: Routledge.

Harvey, D. (1989) *The Condition of Post-Modernity: An Enquiry into the Origins of Cultural Change*, Oxford: Blackwell.

Khalaf, S. (2002) 'Globalization and heritage revival in the Gulf: an anthropological look at Dubai Heritage Village', *Journal of Social Affairs*, 19(75): 13–42.

Kirshenblatt-Gimblett, B. ([2006] 2007) 'World heritage and cultural economics', in I. Karp, C. A. Kratz, L. Szwaja and T. Ybarra-Frausto (eds) *Museum Frictions: Public Cultures/Global Transformations*, Durham, NC: Duke University Press, pp. 161–202.

Kratz, C. A. and I. Karp (2006, 2007) 'Introduction: museum frictions: public cultures/ global transformations', in I. Karp, C. A. Kratz, L. Szwaja and T. Ybarra-Frausto (eds) *Museum Frictions: Public Cultures/Global Transformations*, Durham, NC: Duke University Press, pp. 1–31.

Labadi, S and Long, C. (2010) 'Introduction', in S. Labadi and C. Long (eds) *Heritage and Globalisation*, Abingdon and New York: Routledge, pp. 1–16.

Lowry, G. D. (2004) 'A deontological approach', in J. B. Cuno (ed.) *Whose Muse? Art Museums and the Public Trust*, Princeton, NJ: Princeton University Press, pp. 129–150.

Meskell, L. (2009) *Cosmopolitan Archaeologies (Material Worlds)*, Durham and London: Duke University Press.

Nederveen Pieterse, J. P. (1995) 'Globalization as hybridization', in M. Featherstone, S. Lash and R. Robertson (eds) *Global Modernities*, London: Sage, pp. 45–68.

Riding, A. (2007) 'Abu Dhabi is to gain a Louvre of its own', *New York Times*, 13 January. Available online at http://query.nytimes.com/gst/fullpage.html?res=9E02E5DA1330F9 30A25752C0A9619C8B63&sec=&spon=&pagewanted=2 (accessed 15 August 2011).

Ritzer, G. ([1999] 2010) 'An introduction to McDonaldization', in G. Ritzer (ed.) *McDonaldization*, London: Sage, pp. 3–25.

Robertson, R. (1995) 'Glocalization: time-space and homogeneity – heterogeneity', in M. Featherstone, S. Lash and R. Robertson (eds) *Global Modernities*, London: Sage.

Ryan, J. and S. Silvanto (2011) 'A brand for all the nations: the development of the world heritage brand in emerging markets', *Marketing Intelligence and Planning*, 29(3): 305–318.

Rykner, D. (2006) 'Petition', *La Tribune de l'Art*. 14 December. Available online at www. latribunedelart.com/petition (accessed 17 March 2010).

Rykner, D. (2007) 'The fight continues', *La Tribune de l'Art*. 3 March. Available online at www.latribunedelart.com/le-combat-continue (accessed 17 March 2010).

Smith, L. (2006) *Uses of Heritage*, Abingdon and New York: Routledge.

SRGF (Solomon R. Guggenheim Foundation) (n.d.) 'History'. Available online at www. guggenheim.org/guggenheim-foundation/history (accessed 20 April 2013).

Staiff, R. and R. Bushell (2003) 'Heritage interpretation and cross-cultural translation in an age of global travel: some issues', *Journal of Park and Recreation Administration* (Special Places Issue), 21(4): 104–122.

Tsing, A. L. (2005) *Friction: Ethnography of Global Connection*, Princeton and Oxford: Princeton University Press.

Wakefield, S. (2013) 'Hybrid heritage and cosmopolitanism in the Emirate of Abu Dhabi', in P. Erskine-Loftus (ed.) *Reimagining Museums: Practice in the Arabian Peninsula*, Edinburgh and Cambridge: MuseumsEtc., pp. 98–129.

Wakefield, S. (2014) 'Heritage, cosmopolitanism and identity in Abu Dhabi', in K. Exell and T. Rico (eds) *Cultural Heritage in the Arabian Peninsula: Debates, Discourses and Practices*, Farnham and Burlington: Ashgate, pp. 99–115.

Winter, T. (2014) 'Heritage studies and the privileging of theory', *International Journal of Heritage Studies*, 20(5): 556–572.

Winter, T. (2015) 'Heritage diplomacy', *International Journal of Heritage Studies*, 21(10): 997–1015.

Zulaika, J. (1997) 'The seduction of Bilbao', *Architecture*, 86(12): 59–62.

15 A critical evaluation of the potentiality of tourism and destination development in Failaka Island

Cody Morris Paris

Failaka Island is located approximately 20 km off the coast of Kuwait City and 50 km from the Iraqi coast. It is one of the largest Kuwaiti islands in the Arabian Gulf, with a landmass of 43 sq km. Failaka Island has a rich history and rugged natural landscapes. It possesses the most important ancient sites in the country, including remnants of the Bronze Age Dilmun civilization. Alexander the Great's general Nearchus established a settlement on the island in the fourth century BC, which lasted for over 200 years. The name of the island is thought to come from 'fylakio', the Greek word for 'outpost' (Lawler 2013). Archaeologists have excavated several important Greek sites, as well as early Christian and Islamic settlements.

Failaka Resort was opened on 16 March 1982 and built on approximately 5 million sq m of land adjacent to the coastline. The resort included 472 private chalets, of which 213 were for daily rental and the rest for annual rental. The resort was short-lived, however, as it was abandoned in 1990 due to the Iraqi invasion (see Figure 15.1). Today, it resembles the rest of the island structures, with many of the chalets displaying bullet holes and other scars of war. During the Iraqi invasion, 2,000 residents were forced from their homes, and the island was used as a military base. The Kuwaiti and the US military have recently had a large presence on the island, and in 2002 the island made international news when US marines were gunned down by militants with reported ties to Al-Qaeda (Schmitt 2002).

The development of Failaka Island is an integral part of Kuwait's future tourism development plans. The planned development of Failaka Island, as a central focal point in the tourism strategy for Kuwait, concerns the goal to create an 'iconic' destination that will move Kuwait onto a competitive plane with other leading Gulf destinations, such as Dubai, Abu Dhabi and Qatar, for international long-haul, regional and domestic tourists. Accordingly, there has been some progress nationwide, especially in terms of recent economic reforms and a rejuvenated proposed mega-project development strategy: the 'Kuwait Vision 2035'. This plan will attempt to remove bureaucratic barriers to the private sector, and increase government agency effectiveness and access to land, among other high impact reforms (Al-Jazzaf and Al-Mutairi 2009) (see also Chapter 11). The plan's main aim is to address economic pressures felt since the start of the global economic recession in 2008 by decreasing the country's dependence on oil. Nonetheless,

Figure 15.1   Resort on Failaka that was abandoned during the Iraqi invasion.
Source: C. Morris Paris, May 2012.

planning directives for the development of Failaka Island actually date back to the 1960s, though hampered by the political and economic landscape of Kuwait. The magnitude of the more recent development plans, however, also poses a challenge of balancing the large-scale development of the island and the preservation of the natural environment and historical richness of the island. Nonetheless, although the last decade witnessed the re-emergence of large-scale development plans, they have been held up by bureaucratic deadlock, disagreements between the government and the private sector investors and the global economic recession.

The chapter initially highlights the island's heritage and then the implications of the Iraqi invasion on tourism development. The mid-section of the work then examines other emerging concerns relating to the development of Failaka Island as a tourism destination. The latter section of the main body of the chapter attempts to focus on the how Failaka Island can develop as a tourism destination through pursuing a sustainable pathway addressing the preservation of its complex history and culture.

Failaka Island heritage

Failaka Island has a lengthy history of settlement and trade dating back 4,000 years. There is a large-scale ongoing archaeological mission on Failaka that is working to excavate, document and preserve sites. The Kuwaiti Department of Antiquities and the Museum of the National Council for Culture, Arts and Letters commissioned several international archaeological missions. More than 180 different sites were identified and mapped. Recently, a Danish team uncovered the earliest settlement on the island, a Mesopotamian settlement dating back to around 2000 BC that has provided evidence that the island was home to an important trading post of Mesopotamian merchants (Lawler 2013). The Dilmun civilization emerged around 2300 BC in the surrounding islands of Bahrain (UNESCO 2012) and by 1900 BC had extended to Failaka Island, either driving out or succeeding the Mesopotamians on the island (Lawler 2013). Archaeological excavations have uncovered Dilmun Barbar temples that suggest a strong cultural similarity between Failaka and Bahrain during the early second millennium BC (Hojlund 2012). During this time, Failaka was an important hub of the Dilmun civilization. Archaeological evidence also indicates encounters with the Sumerians from Mesopotamia, Harappans from the Indus Valley and Magans from Oman. Archaeologists have excavated a large Dilmun temple and are currently working on a nearby palace (UNESCO 2013). There is even some academic debate over whether Failaka Island is the Garden of Eden from the Babylonian epic and biblical story of Gilgamesh (Tetreault 2013).

In the fourth century BC, Nearchus, Alexander the Great's general, had established the island as an outpost for Alexander's army (Arun 2007). A Greek colony was located on Failaka Island between 325 BC and 150 BC and was part of the Ptolomeic era maritime trade route. Reportedly, Alexander the Great named the island Ikaros due to its similar size and shape of the Aegean island of the same name (Lawler 2013). Recently, French archaeologists discovered a fort surrounding a well, with a well-preserved quintessential Greek temple inside. The fort and temple had been built by Antiochus I, a third-century BC ruler of the Seleucid Empire, and has elements of both traditional Ionic design combined with Persian Archaemenid style, a rare fusion of Greek and Eastern cultural influences. Surrounding the fort and temple, a larger port town grew until the end of the first century BC (Lawler 2013). This temple is one of the best preserved and excavated sites on the island.

Failaka also was home to a small Christian community, possibly Nestorian, until the ninth century. Two churches were excavated in the centre of the island at the Al-Qusur (Bernard and Salles 1991), and other excavations uncovered early Islamic settlements dating from the eighth and ninth century (Pieta *et al.* 2009). However, there is still a lot of work required to uncover the more recent history on the island. Several teams of archaeologists are working at sites dating from the seventeenth to the nineteenth century that show evidence of a Portuguese fort and/or a possible base used by Arab pirates to attack the lucrative trading and shipping lanes emanating from Basra (Lawler 2013). At present, Failaka is host to archaeological teams from several countries including Poland, France, Denmark and Italy, some of whom have been enticed to Kuwait as their work in such places as Iraq and Syria has been disrupted due to political volatility and conflict (Lawler 2013).

Failakawans and the Iraqi invasion

During the modern times, Failaka supported a population of several thousand residents. Prior to the Iraqi invasion, the main village of Az Zawr was considered one of the oldest continuously inhabited locations in Kuwait. The local population was largely comprised of fishermen and their families, who had a strong identity tied to the island itself. Many Kuwaitis who can trace their roots to the island share its name, al-Failakwi. The inhabitants on Failaka Island developed small towns, schools and seaports for fishing. One particularly notable structure, included on the United Nations Educational, Scientific and Cultural Organization (UNESCO) World Heritage application, is the Sheikh Ahmed Al Jaber Rest House. This building was built in 1927 with a unique design not seen elsewhere in the Gulf (UNESCO 2013). During Iraq's invasion of Kuwait in 1990, the island was attacked by Iraqi forces, and around 2,000 residents had to resettle on the mainland. Failaka became a military outpost for about 1,400 Iraqi soldiers. During the short occupation of Failaka, the Iraqis removed and/or destroyed some of the most important archaeological artifacts from the Greek Temple (see Figure 15.2). They also mined the area, preventing scientific access for many years after the occupation (Tetreault 2013). Beaches were also turned into minefields.

The scars from the conflict are clearly visibly today, over 25 years since the invasion. The village, Az Zawr, itself is full of bullet-ridden and bombed out structures (Figure 15.3). These 'memorabilia of warfare sites' (Smith 1998) are central components of the 'tourist gaze', particularly as they are significantly located in close proximity to the ferry port where visitors arrive. These remnants are clear reminders of the political role of the island in the Gulf's contemporary history, and the complex heritage landscape of Failaka Island. These sites are often visited by day-trip visitors, many of whom can be observed taking photos of (and posing next to) these visible reminders of the war. These sites could be categorized as potential 'dark conflict sites' (Stone 2006) that have yet to go through the dark tourism commodification process. The motives for visiting these types of sites vary according to the intensity of their relationship to the conflict (Stone and Sharpley 2008). The lack of any interpretive infrastructure to aid in visitors' 'consumption' of these sites could pose a potential safety hazard for some visitors, as well as diminish the seriousness of the conflict that occurred on the island. Future

Figure 15.2   Greek temple on Failaka Island.
Source: C. Morris Paris, May 2012.

Figure 15.3   Reminders of the Iraqi invasion and occupation of Failaka within the context of the post-invasion era.

Source: C. Morris Paris, May 2012.

development plans, as well as research concerning tourism on Failaka Island, will need to consider how best to provide visitors with a socially acceptable educational and memorial experience of the island and its recent history. This would help to ensure that visitors are afforded the opportunity to reflect upon and contemplate the meaning of these sites.

After the Allied forces reclaimed the island in 1991, many of its original inhabitants remained in Kuwait City and surrounding areas. While some former residents visit Failaka Island often, officially there are no permanent residents. This may have to do with existing infrastructural damage on the island. Many of the older Failakawans still revisit the island, some nearly every weekend, which could be considered a form of domestic 'nostalgia' or 'memory' tourism (Bartoletti 2010). After the Kuwaiti liberation in 1991, the government gave each of the islanders 150,000 dinar for their old homes. According to one Failakawan, 19 families kept one home, and about 300 Failakawans usually return to spend the weekends. Some of the homes have been rebuilt and appear to be occupied, but this a very small number (Calderwood 2010). In fact, there is significant potentiality in terms of domestic tourism, which is, arguably, an economically sustainable form of tourism.

The recent development plans include, in addition to large-scale tourism and entertainment developments, plans for a permanent population of about 5,000 residents including both Kuwaitis and foreigners, mostly to work and 'give life' to the island. Some of the former residents view the new development plans warily, as one stated: 'We don't agree with any development on the island because anything new is going to bring more people. They're going to destroy the calm, what a problem it is going to be' (Calderwood 2010). Any plans to 'give life' to the island should attempt to understand and take into account the 'embodied memories' and nostalgic emotions (Marschall 2012) of Failakawans. Therefore, future development plans will need to consider issues related to both material manifestations of memory and nostalgia – including land ownership, repossessed buildings, farms and rebuilt buildings – and the socio-psychological and symbolic significance (see Park 2010) of the island's heritage.

Developing Failaka Island into a tourist destination: emerging concerns

The plans to develop Failaka Island have been around since the early master plans for the island in 1960. The most recent plans emerged in the last decade, but have been slow to come to fruition for a variety of reasons related to bureaucratic deadlock and conflicts between private sector investors and the government. Additionally, there are land ownership issues that need to be settled, as some former residents still own homes on the island, and there are currently two small military bases on the island.

A major tourism redevelopment project on Failaka Island was unveiled in 2003 by Dizatt and the Kuwait Islands and Mega Projects Development Team. The project was estimated to cost up to US$5 billion, and due to the size of the proposed project, a build-operate-transfer (BOT) tender was created. For this project, three separate BOT contracts were to be tendered (Ali 2004). The project plans included the construction of tourism facilities, hotels, chalets and entertainment venues. Initially, 15 investor groups submitted expressions of interest in the project. The government was seeking out one primary investor to oversee the project (*Arab News* 2003). Another project on the southern part of the island included the construction of a five-star hotel, a spa and 500 chalets. This particular development, estimated to cost US$138 million, was spearheaded by the government-owned Touristic Enterprises Company and a private real estate company. The third major project was the development of Heritage Village, a residential and tourism complex (Ali 2004).

In 2005, the press started to report on roadblocks facing the developments. One of the major issues was a disagreement between private developers and the government authority overseeing the projects. On one hand, the developers wanted the government to build the infrastructure on the island and extend the 20-year BOT to a 30-year BOT. They argued that 20 years was not enough time to make the investments profitable. On the other hand, the government wanted the investors to build most of the infrastructure, with the government only contributing the power generation (Taqi 2005). Another issue was the size of the main project, with the private investors indicating that the project was far too large to be overseen by just one investor. In the midst of the turmoil that stopped any progress for the projects, Dizatt was suddenly dissolved by the Council of Ministers in June of 2005. The Mega Projects Agency (MPA) was then charged with overseeing the project on Failaka Island, as well as several other major development projects including Bubiyan Island. The first order of business was to salvage the project on

Failaka Island through extending the bid deadline for the nine interested investor groups, creating a separate BOT concession for power and water to the island and considering extending the BOT period up to 50 years; though this would mean a change of law, which is unlikely in the current political climate (Jabr 2013). The MPA was steadfast regarding the requirement for the investor group to keep the overall project as a single project, rather than to break it up. The rest of the infrastructure requirements were kept intact, including constructing ministry buildings and a military barracks, and making the island more accessible by expanding the marine transport facilities (*MEED* 2005).

While the new agency allowed a little flexibility, the project has not seen a lot of progress. The only project that has seen any work has been the continued development of the Failaka Heritage Village, which is an educational visitor attraction that celebrates its history and natural beauty. The heritage project, launched with the support of the late Emir Sheik Jaber and the 'Father Emir' Sheikh Saad, was focused on renovating and restoring the palace of the late Emir Sheikh Abdullah Al Salim Al Sabah, the ruler of Kuwait between 1950 and 1965 (Heritage Village Failaka 2013). In 2001, the development of the heritage village was initiated by Masharee Al Khair, the charitable foundation of the Kuwait Projects Company, one of the largest holding companies in the Middle East and North Africa (MENA) region. There were consistent improvements and expansions to the village, including restored traditional houses from the 1950s, a horse stable, a fleet of catamarans, restaurants, a small hotel and a recreational beach offering water sports and mini golf (Heritage Village Failaka 2013). The village has become a popular weekend getaway for overnight and day visitors from the mainland. Due to the natural and manufactured attractions on Failaka Island, it has become one of the most visited 'tourist attractions' in the country, although most visitors are Kuwaitis and resident expatriates. The rest of the island has seen little progress in midst of the political schism and deadlock in the National Assembly, the global economic crisis and the ongoing conflict in Iraq.

The combination of the historic sites and the items recovered by the archaeological missions can provide substantial content for the establishment of a museum on the island. Several of the archaeologists working at the site viewed the future development plans for Failaka Island as a trade-off of potential benefits and negative impacts. On one hand, there was consensus that tourism development could bring recognition, exposure and preservation of the sites, especially if the development proceeds in a responsible manner. On the other hand, however, they saw large-scale modern development plans as being potentially destructive of already uncovered sites and an obstacle to future research and excavations. Alarmingly, as many sites were not fully explored this would lead to a significant historical loss. Within the recent 'mega-development' plans put forth by the government, there was a lack of plans for the development of museums or other cultural/heritage sites based on the island's rich history, or even for steps to be taken for the preservation of the important historical sites uncovered on the island.

In addition to posing a threat to the heritage sites of the island, proposed large-scale developments on Failaka Island and other coastal areas in Kuwait pose an environmental threat. Research has been undertaken to develop a comprehensive assessment of the island's coast, resulting in a coastal zone management map and guidelines for future costal development of Failaka Island (Al-Sarawi *et al.* 1996). However, in Kuwait there are no adequate coastal management policies or dedicated institutions responsible for coastal management (Baby 2013), and thus no planning for sustainable coastal development. While there have been some improvement in the regulations and law in regards to the environment over the last decade, some experts have stated that the advances are still inadequate and that the current framework and judiciary system lack a desired capacity in environmental law (Baby 2013). Failaka Island was the longest consistently inhabited place in Kuwait, with a history extending 4,000 years, partly due to its abundant fresh water and arable land. During the last century, as the Kuwaiti population has become concentrated and sprawled along the coast, Failaka Island has seen its access to fresh water disappear, as the island shares the same water table as Kuwait City. Any future development of the island would need to incorporate desalinization and/or piped water from the mainland. Future developments on the island and other coastal areas in Kuwait will also need to take into consideration threats posed by the rising sea level due to climate change. According to a study by Neelamani (2014), Failaka Island could face high levels of costal inundation with just a small rise in sea levels.

The large-scale US$5 billon Failaka Island project failed to proceed beyond the planning phase due to legislative changes in 2008, the global financial crisis (Egbert 2009) and the lack of reforms to address remaining issues with the public-private partnership (PPP) and BOT process in Kuwait. In 2010, 42 companies participated in contract bidding for the project (Kuwait Mega Projects 2010). However, due to the challenges within the current BOT system, no contracts were awarded (Jabr 2013). The challenges faced by the proposed development could turn out to be opportunities for a more environmentally, socially and culturally responsible development plan to emerge.

Transformation and sustainable ways forward

Within the vacuum created by the stalled US$5 billion dollar development plan for Failaka Island, several people have started to lobby for the protection for all of Failaka Island. Calls for the island's history to be preserved and for archaeologists to continue their research and excavations have intensified. One of the most vocal proponents of protecting the island is the director of the Department of Antiquities and Museums, whose efforts have drawn the research teams from more than half a dozen countries to the island, and the government has set aside more than US$10 million dollars to fund their work. Another huge step towards preservation and conservation was evident when the National Council for Culture, Arts and Letters submitted an application to UNESCO on 27 February 2013 for the recognition and listing of the areas of Sa'ad and Sae'ed as a World Heritage

Site (UNESCO 2013). These areas are where most of the archaeological sites are actually located. While several more steps are required in the review process before the sites can be listed, this is an important way forward in ensuring that future developments on the island incorporate the preservation and conservation of these sites. According to the statement of integrity on the World Heritage Site application:

> Since the liberation of Kuwait in 1991, the island remains significantly under-developed, giving way to current policies of cultural tourism to further shape future scenarios for the Island, and support strategic development projects aligned with keeping the island as an archeological record.
>
> (UNESCO 2013)

In February 2014, as part of the country's five-year plan for the travel and tourism sector, the Partnership Technical Bureau (PTB) announced that the development of Failaka Island was a top priority in achieving the goal of attracting 1 million international tourists (Navdar 2014). Taking its direction from the Kuwait National Development plan, the PTB is moving forward with the planned PPP development of the island. While the project will still be overseen by various government bodies, including the Ministry of Public Works, the 'handing over' of the project to the PTB represents a renewed focus on the private sector being involved in the plans. After an assessment period of 27 months in late 2013, when the PTB was assessing and surveying the island's land ownership, farms, repossessed buildings and other properties and archaeological sites, the PTB published an extension of the request for proposals for advisory services to develop a new master plan for the island. The renewed Kuwait Failaka Island Project (KFIP) appears to be progressing more responsibly than previous plans for the island. According to the PTB website (PTB 2014):

> The government of Kuwait is planning the implementation of the Kuwait Failaka Island Project (KFIP) as a PPP. The project will transform Failaka Island into a premier, state of the art leisure and tourist destination. Preservation and promotion of the Island's outstanding heritage and archeology are drivers of the project. Cultural facilities will be integrated with regular tourist and leisure facilities such as hotels and leisure parks. This will comprise of the developments of hotels suited for week-long stays as well as a town center for commerce, food & beverage, retail and other activities.

At a meeting of the Supreme Council for Planning and Development in December 2015, plans to establish economic free zones on five of Kuwait's main Gulf islands, including Failaka, were announced. According to the proposal, the free zones would provide an economic and cultural gateway to the northern Gulf, and would reflect the emir's plans of transforming and diversifying the economy of Kuwait. Establishment of the free zones would also, as suggested in the proposal, limit the dependence on government funding and open up the project to local, regional and international private sector investment (KUNA 2015). The plan to diversify the country's economy and reduce the reliance on oil production has also become more urgent, especially given the global decline in oil prices. Accordingly, there has been a 68 per cent decline in Kuwait's foreign trade surplus in the fourth quarter of 2015 compared to the fourth quarter of 2014, as well as a 2016–17 draft budget produced that forecasts a US$40.2 billion deficit (*Arabian Business* Staff Writer 2016).

Given the current economic climate, there is a chance that planning and projects maybe entered into a bit hastily. The value of Failaka Island as a tourism destination stems from its potential as a heritage site and potential as a small island destination. For the long-term *sustainability* of tourism development on Failaka Island, a deliberate plan will need to ensure that the construction and operation of hotels and other tourist infrastructure prioritize an environmentally friendly agenda. Moreover, the preservation of the social continuity of the island's heritage must also be given due attention. This includes not only the preservation of the archaeological heritage sites but also the representation of the tangible and intangible aspects of the island's more recent past.

Conclusion and research implications

This chapter argues that tourism development on Failaka Island faces multiple economic, environmental and social challenges, but also provides the most practical and reasonable potential for developing a large-scale tourist destination to drive international, regional Gulf Cooperation Council and domestic tourism demand. The development of Failaka Island into a large-scale tourism destination is a central component of the recent government initiatives to expand the tourism sector within Kuwait. The focus on developing the island is not new, with plans extending back to the 1960s. However, the island has since faced a whole series of challenges, from the Iraqi invasion of Kuwait to failed and stalled plans in the last decade, including a multi-billion US dollar development plan.

While many obstacles concerning the island's development have been highlighted in this chapter, together with bureaucratic logjams and the economic world crisis, for any planned development to come to fruition there needs to be a clear economic framework in place to support investment (infrastructural or otherwise) and subsequent change. There is some hope that the Kuwait Vision 2035 will allow the state to move past the economic obstacles that have stalled its development thus far.

The failure of the planned US$5 billion development to move the island's development agenda beyond the planning process could actually prove to be an advantage in the long term. Recently, there has been a much stronger level of support for preservation, conservation and research into the island's heritage sites. It is hoped that that the historical and cultural sites of the island will be a key focal point for the destination and for sustainable development. However, even if the development process does not reach full fruition, the island's important historical sites and fragile desert island ecosystem will be seriously threatened.

Future studies should focus on assessing the prospects and success factors of incorporating heritage and environmental preservation and conservation into the island's tourism development agenda. With a particular focus on domestic tourism, resident surveys could provide useful information concerning the current domestic tourism activities, behaviour, attitudes and expenditures that would assist the planning and marketing of the island domestically. Additionally, surveys and interviews of current Failaka Island visitors could provide insights into travel motivations and behaviours of visitors. Another area that needs further consideration is the BOT system, PPPs and the wider political-economic landscape in Kuwait, particularly in the context of the development tourism and other non-petroleum economic sectors.

This chapter illustrates potentialities of the development of the tourism projects on Failaka Island and ways in which these can contribute, no doubt, to the wider diversification plans for the Kuwaiti economy. The future for tourism development in Kuwait can be viewed optimistically, where the strategic development of the tourism industry represents an opportunity to emerge as a progressive economic power where PPPs can create a foundation for a sustainable economic future. While it may be inevitable for Kuwait to diversify its oil-dominated economy, there is not yet a sense of urgency for this to happen (see Chapter 6). Thus, there is still time for Failaka Island to adopt a progressive development pathway, and if this is done right, then Failaka could be transformed into a leading heritage/historical destination in the Gulf.

Acknowledgements

A special note of thanks to my close friend, Mr Abdulrahim Alawadi, for his invaluable expert guidance, support and contribution to this project and to Mr Simon Rubin for his early collaboration and contribution to this project.

References

Ali, J. (2004) 'Kuwait begins to explore the country's tourism potential', *Gulf News*, 30 October. Available online at http://gulfnews.com/business/opinion/kuwait-begins-to-explore-the-country-s-tourism-potential-1.337123 (accessed 10 March 2012).

Al-Jazzaf, M. and E. Al-Mutairi (2009) *Kuwait Team's Report: Developing Knowledge Economy Strategies to Improve Competitiveness*, Alexandria: World Bank Institute.

Al-Sarawi, M. A., Y. R. Marmoush, J. M. Lo and K. A. Al-Salem (1996) 'Coastal management of Failaka Island, Kuwait,' *Journal of Environmental Management*, 47(4): 299–310.

Arab News (2003) 'Kuwait unveils investment plan to develop Failaka Island,' *Arab News*, 13 May. Available online at http://archive.arabnews.com/?page=6&section=0&article=26155&d=16&m=5&y=2003 (accessed 10 March 2012).

Arabian Business Staff Writer (2016) 'Kuwait's foreign trade surplus shrinks 68% in Q4,' *Arabian Business*, 18 March. Available online at www.arabianbusiness.com/kuwait-s-foreign-trade-surplus-shrinks-68-in-q4-624012.html (accessed 1 May 2016).

Arun, N. (2007) 'Alexander's Gulf outpost uncovered', *BBC News*, 7 August. Available online at http://news.bbc.co.uk/2/hi/europe/6930285.stm (accessed 10 March 2012).

Baby, S. (2013) 'Findings and discussion on coastal evolution of Kuwait, review of laws and perspective of developed strategies', *Journal of Image and Graphics*, 1(1): 17–33.

Bartoletti, R. (2010) '"Memory tourism" and the commodification of nostalgia', in P. Burns, C. Palmer and J. A. Lester (eds) *Tourism and Visual Culture*, vol. 1, Wallingford: CABI Publishing, pp. 23–42.

Bernard, V. and J. Salles (1991) 'Discovery of a Christian church at Al-Qusur, Failaka (Kuwait)', *Proceedings of the Seminar for Arabian Studies*, Oxford, July 24–26, 1990.

Calderwood, J. (2010) 'Depopulated Kuwaiti Island with rich past looks to brighter future', *The National*, 19 May. Available online at www.thenational.ae/news/world/middle-east/depopulated-kuwaiti-island-with-rich-past-looks-to-brighter-future (accessed 10 March 2012).

Egbert, C. (2009) 'Top 10 Kuwait projects', *Construction Week Online*, 9 May. Available online at www.constructionweekonline.com/article-5153-top-10-kuwait-projects/ (accessed 10 March 2012).

Heritage Village Failaka (2013) 'About us', Failaka: the Heritage Village. Available online at http://heritagevillagefailaka.com/aboutus.asp (accessed 17 May 2014).

Hojlund, F. (2012) 'The Dilmun temple on Failaka, Kuwait', *Arabian Archaeology and Epigraphy*, 23(2): 165–173.

Jabr, A. (2013) 'Politics eclipses Kuwait development hopes-BOT law amendments on hold', *Kuwait Times*, 25 December. Available online at http://news.kuwaittimes.net/politics-eclipses-kuwait-development-hopes-bot-law-amendments-hold/ (accessed 17 May 2014).

KUNA (2015) 'Kuwait to launch free economic zone on islands – PM chairs meet', *Arab Times*, 18 December. Available online at www.arabtimesonline.com/news/kuwait-to-launch-free-economic-zone-on-islands-pm-chairs-meet/ (accessed 1 May 2016).

Kuwait Mega Projects (2010) Kuwait Mega Projects 2010–2014: Kuwait Five Year Plan. Available online at http://kuwait-embassy.or.jp/pdf/kuwait-five-year-plan.pdf (accessed 10 March 2012).

Lawler, A. (2013) 'Archaeology island', *Archaeology Magazine*, March/April. Available online at www.archaeology.org/issues/78-1303 (accessed 1 August 2014).

Marschall, S. (2012) 'Tourism and memory', *Annals of Tourism Research*, 39(4): 2216–2219.

MEED (2005) 'Agents of fortune: The newly formed public body will be pulling out all the stops this summer in an effort to get the giant Failaka and Bubiyan projects underway', *Middle East Economic Digest*, 49(26): 44–48.

Navdar, P. (2014) 'Kuwait allocates $13 billion for infrastructure projects in five-year plan', *Arabian Industry*, 19 February. Available online at www.arabianindustry.com/hospitality/news/2014/feb/19/kuwait-allocates-13-billion-for-infrastructure-projects-in-five-year-plan-4606134/ (accessed 1 August 2014).

Neelamani, S. (2014) 'The expected sea-level rise scenarios and its impacts on Kuwaiti coast and estuarine wetlands', *International Journal of Ecology and Development*, 29(3): 32–43.

Park, H. Y. (2010) 'Heritage tourism: emotional journeys into nationhood', *Annals of Tourism Research*, 37(1): 116–135.

Pieta, K., A. Shehab, J. Tripak, M. Bielich and M. Bartik (2009) 'Archeological and geophysical survey in deserted early Islamic village Al-Qusur (Failaka, Kuwait)', *ArcheoSciences*, 33: 155–157.

PTB (2014) 'Kuwait Failaka island development', Partnerships Technical Bureau. Available online at www.ptb.gov.kw/en/Kuwait-Failaka-Island-Development (accessed 1 August 2014).

Schmitt, E. (2002) 'Threats and responses: skirmish; U.S. marine is killed in Kuwait as gunmen strike training site', *New York Times*, 9 October. Available online at www.nytimes.com/2002/10/09/world/threats-responses-skirmish-us-marine-killed-kuwait-gunmen-strike-training-site.html (accessed 13 January 2015).

Smith, V. (1998) 'War and tourism: an American ethnography', *Annals of Tourism Research*, 25(1): 202–227.

Stone, P. (2006) 'A dark tourism spectrum: towards a typology of death and macabre related tourist sites, attractions, and exhibitions,' *Tourism Review*, 54(2): 145–160.

Stone, P. and R. Sharpley (2008) 'Consuming dark tourism: a thanatological perspective', *Annals of Tourism Research*, 35(2): 574–595.

Taqi, A. (2005) 'Major Kuwaiti tourism project hits roadblock,' *Gulf News*, 12 March. Available online at http://gulfnews.com/business/tourism/major-kuwaiti-tourism-project-hits-roadblock-1.280482 (accessed 10 March 2012).

Tetreault, M. (2013) 'Failaka Island: unearthing the past in Kuwait', *MEI Insights*. Middle East Institute, National University of Singapore. Available online at http://nus_mei.theadventus.com/publications/mei-insights/failaka-island-unearthing-the-past-in-kuwait (accessed 1 August 2014).

UNESCO (United Nations Educational, Scientific and Cultural Organization) (2012) 'Qal'at al-Bahain – ancient harbor and capital of Dilmun', UNESCO World Heritage Centre. Available online at http://whc.unesco.org/en/list/1192 (accessed 20 May 2014).

UNESCO (United Nations Educational, Scientific and Cultural Organization) (2013) 'Sa'ad and Sae'ed Area in Failaka Island', UNESCO World Heritage Centre. Available online at http://whc.unesco.org/en/tentativelists/5800/ (accessed 20 May 2014).

Afterword

Beyond petromodernity: excavating pathways for *Khaleeji* tourism studies

Waleed Hazbun

Even though you might be holding in your hands a volume focused exclusively on aspects of the tourism sector in the context of Gulf Cooperation Council (GCC) states, the study of tourism in this region remains highly underdeveloped. Strides have been made in recent years, of which this volume is surely a major contribution. However, consider the extraordinarily rapid growth of the travel and tourism infrastructure in the region, as well as the massive volume of flows of tourists and tourism capital. Accordingly, the study of tourism in the Gulf region ought to be its own growth industry. Its results can offer valuable insights to the broader field of tourism studies and become an important component of the emerging interdisciplinary field of Gulf studies.

We might pause first to note that scholars of tourism in the region face considerable obstacles and barriers. As noted in the contributing chapters, especially Timothy in Chapter 2, travel to most of the states of the GCC can be difficult for a range of non-GCC citizens due to visa restrictions. Researchers, like tourists, face transportation challenges due to the lack of public transportation in many areas, as indicated in Chapter 4 by Batzner and Stephenson. Political and cultural norms often obstruct researchers who explore and ask questions about tourism development. Many of the spaces of tourism in the GCC are interior not public. They exist behind walled compounds, on luxury resorts and inside exclusive malls and recreation areas. Moreover, the monocratic nature of these regimes and the geopolitical environment of the region, particularly in the context of the post-Arab uprisings in the Middle East, means that these states do not fully encourage the open flow of information. Other limitations that exist for those conducting fieldwork concern the weather and environmental factors. The climate can be forbidding at times, and the commonly spoken languages beyond English, such as Arabic and South Asian languages, are difficult to grasp for non-natives. While these various factors help explain the slow development of the field, they also suggest how much potential remains for Gulf tourism studies. The purpose of this afterword is to highlight those needs and suggest avenues to advance towards the potential within the field.

While Saudi Arabia, Oman and other GCC states possess fabulous archaeological sites, heritage resources and natural landscapes with tourist potential, the main driver of tourism development across the GCC has been the influx and circulation of petrodollars. In this sense, patterns of tourism development can be viewed as a product of 'petromodernity'. The ample flow of oil receipts allowed regional governments to promote development and modernization efforts that rapidly sought to craft local versions of 'modern' institutions found elsewhere. These local versions, which are significantly staffed by foreign workers, tend to follow international (rather than local) forms of architecture.

Within the literature on the 'rentier state', scholars have attempted to outline how access to oil receipts shapes 'state building' and political change. Yet as Gray in Chapter 1 explains, petrodollar-fuelled 'state building' is a dynamic process with different pathways and variations. As much as tourism development is a product of these flows, it is often also touted as a strategy for regional states to seek a post-rent future. The Emirate of Dubai, long drained of substantial oil incomes, has famously forged a development model based on transport services, telecommunications, retail, commercial real estate, tourism and hospitality. We might then ask if a decline in oil incomes across the region will provoke similar moves towards diversification, or else drain the region of the petrodollars needed to sustain these forms of economic expansion. In any case, a critical question for further investigation concerns the sustainability of the existing GCC political economies and the role that tourism plays in them. Tourism, often viewed as a vehicle for economic diversification, is also a driving force behind patterns of urban change and development that might strain the sustainability of the *Khaleeji* or 'Gulf' model of development (see Hanieh 2011). In his essay, 'Right to the City', the Marxist geographer David Harvey (2008: 30) was concerned with the 'absurd mega-urbanization projects' being developed to take advantage of 'the surplus arising from oil wealth', especially in a manner that he believed was not socially equitable nor environmentally sustainable.

While leisure tourism can be accused of being wasteful, building from Stephenson and Vyas in Chapter 12, the GCC region needs to fully account for the long-term environmental consequences of the different aspects of tourism development – from water consumption to carbon dioxide emissions of air travel – across the diverse cases. Sustainability and resource use are two of the many areas where studies of the GCC can be brought into comparative perspective. Such research, for example, might engage the work of Hal Rothman, an environmental historian of the American West (also a historian of tourism), who challenged a popular assumption by arguing that 'the Las Vegas Strip is the most economically efficient use of water in Nevada' because it sustains the most income per unit of water and the highest level of job creation (Rothman 2005). Furthermore, despite the challenges facing a move towards ecotourism development, as outlined in Chapter 9 by Al-Riyami, Scott, Ragab and Jafari, the development of commercial leisure activities in fragile desert environments represents a deep concern for a sustainable future.

The relationship between the future of tourism development and geopolitical developments also remains unclear (see Chapter 5 by Bagaeen and Chapter 3 by Timothy). Will the continued wars in the wider region disrupt existing patterns of tourism flows? Alternatively, however, will the economies of the GCC states benefit from the general perception that these places largely remain stable places in the region?

Tourism scholars of any locality, but especially of the GCC region, can use their research on tourism to provide an insight on other issues, such as those highlighting how tourism is part and parcel of the broader process of globalization that is reshaping GCC economies and societies. While many urban areas of the GCC region have become highly connected to the global circulation of capital, commodities and media across the GCC, these flows pass through what anthropologist Ahmed Kanna (2007) calls a 'jagged' landscape of hierarchies, exclusion and, often, 'immobility'.

As we trace the travel itineraries and experiences of tourists, scholars also need to explore the range of migrant and expatriate workers who staff the sector – from cleaning crews to executive managers. This population includes such a diversity of communities and social classes than any researcher is likely only to be able to map a small portion of it. To these we have to add the point of view of the citizens of host societies, often outnumbered by foreign workers. What are their views of tourism trends? What sorts of leisure tourism do they engage in? The context of the GCC does not easily fit into the host-guest models that have defined much research on tourism in the developing world. The profiles of middle- to high-income expatriates often match those of tourists, while some GCC citizens might spend more tourism dollars abroad than most visitors to the GCC. Rather than thinking of the context of the GCC as 'exceptional', scholars of tourism in the GCC have the opportunity and challenge of approaching common questions found elsewhere using newly discovered or underexploited data. These questions often involve the sorts of boundary ambiguities that define research on host-guest relations, distinctions between religious pilgrimage and tourist travel and the division between what economic transactions count and what do not as part of the tourism sector.

Within the context of tourism development in the Gulf, we can witness the prevalence of not only the commodification of cultures, experiences, environments and local places, but also the 'branding' of cities and states that are being marketed as emerging entities within the global political economy and mediascapes (see Chapter 8 by Scharfenort and Chapter 14 by Wakefield). Across the GCC, but most notably in the United Arab Emirates (UAE), these processes take a large-scale material form, including the creation of artificial islands, massive real estate and infrastructure projects and iconic architectural forms. Nevertheless, the tourism ecosystems that have resulted are often fragmented with poor connections between the elements that sustain tourism economies (see Atalla and Nasr 2013). Limited tourism-focused planning, marketing and transportation infrastructures often hinder the easy flow of visitors between places and tourism-related activities. To address these issues, interdisciplinary scholars need to explore planning policies, infrastructure development, political economy and cultural trends. To complement these top-down and macro-oriented approaches, Gulf tourism studies should develop tools and research that explore the landscape from the ground-up.

The field of Gulf tourism studies would clearly benefit from efforts to conduct rich ethnographic fieldwork, thus shedding light on many rarely viewed and poorly understood aspects of Gulf societies. To address many of the broader questions of political economy, as noted already, tourism scholars will need to build from national case studies found in this volume and begin to map the transnational and transregional processes and networks that shape most of the flows of tourists, capital, commodities and images that pass through and across the GCC states. The rise of hotel management firms, airlines and cultural institutions in the region, for example, has given policymakers and entrepreneurs in the region tools to forge tourism sectors that are not as fully dependent on metropolitan multinational firms, as is the case with most developing economies first seeking to promote tourism development.

With its studies of heritage, museums, transport, destinations and tourism planning, this volume advances the production of knowledge within the field of tourism studies. In the past, however, we have seen much of the accessible information, journalism and even, at times, scholarship about the region resemble public relations 'boosterism' and corporate marketing, or else in the case of some foreign media outlets, Gulf-bashing. Informed scholars need to meet the challenge of filling in the middle ground with critical but accurate information. As implied in Chapter 3 by Feighery, one useful way forward concerns the capacity to deconstruct tourism representations through crucially acknowledging the way in which formal tourism and mainstream representations fall short of projecting competing social realities and cultural diversities, and varied socio-cultural identities.

The book addresses every state with at least one contribution and includes studies of what might seem unlikely topics to interest academic journals, but nevertheless offer critical insights into the dynamics of tourism development (in the region and elsewhere). While studies of opposition to aspects of tourism development, such as those led by environmental and indigenous-rights activists, are readily found in the literature, there has been little study of the issue of 'ambivalence'. Several contributors address the issue most starkly framed by Kelly (Chapter 6), but also by Burns and Bibbings (Chapter 11). As Kelly shows, the issue in the Gulf turns out to be a complex and revealing one with clear resonances. Accordingly, issues range from a lack of pressing need for hard currency and inadequate institutional capacity to societal concerns about the cultural impact of expanded visitor flows. At a deeper level, this ambivalence represents the absence of efforts to convert the experience of a place into a commodity that then becomes circulated and valued within the international marketplace. In the age of neoliberalism, this almost Polanyian sensibility, for better and worse, rarely makes its way into the discussion of tourism development where scholars tend to focus on interested advocates and committed opponents.

The volume also addresses two disparate but related features of tourism in a region that is predominately Muslim. First, it recognizes the deep historical and cultural notion of travel as serving as a means to develop meaningful religious and spiritual knowledge (Chapter 13 by Henderson, for instance). Second, the text also highlights efforts to commodify those experiences and norms, such as in the formation of Halal tourism, conforming to Islamic laws, that have become a means to brand certain activities, create 'added value' and market them to different audiences (see Chapter 10 by Ashill, Williams and Chathoth; and Chapter 7 by Ekiz, Oter and Stephenson). Accordingly, there are clear opportunities to strengthen Islamic tourism and heritage. Nonetheless, there are also archeological demands and heritage truths that could strengthen claims to ensure that the tourism industry acknowledges the Arabian Peninsula's co-presence with European and Christian heritages. The destination case study concerning Failaka Island (Chapter 15 by Paris), for instance, indicates the past ethnic diversities and transformative cultural histories that are associated with the island.

Last, as I noted already, the most productive and useful future research pathways for tourism studies in the GCC will likely be those that avoid tropes of exceptionalism and dig deeper to explore what are, more often than not, ambiguities and seeming contradictions. For example, many GCC states and institutions have self-images, or at least marketed brands, that seem at odds with other aspects of their realities. They boast opulent resorts but also religious traditions of modesty. Such seeming 'contradiction' is often found in discussions of the question of cosmopolitanism in the Gulf. Consider how a commentator in *Foreign Policy* magazine notes that the 'Hello Tomorrow' ad campaign by Emirates airline:

> evokes the world of the creative class: globalized, multicultural travelers, attending fashion shows and raves, trolling through neon-lit shopping centers in Tokyo, stealing romantic moments on rooftops in Brooklyn, or jumping on a crowded bus in India. It has become a global brand icon. (Molavi 2015)

This seeming cosmopolitanism is a product of what I have referred to as petromodernity. It suggests a local version of a Western or modern form created rapidly or seemingly 'all at once' due to access to abundant petrodollars. At the same time, it is a cosmopolitanism that is often only accessible in confined enclaves, in interior spaces and at high income and social status levels (see Hazbun 2008: 222–225). To this 'enclave' or elite cosmopolitanism we can contrast the appreciation offered by Laleh Khalili of what she calls 'sha'bi (or popular; or from-below) cosmopolitanism'. In a blog post reflecting on her travels on a cargo ship through the Gulf, Khalili (2015) writes that this kind of 'cosmopolitanism occurs because of longstanding ties across the sea (including the trade in humans and in indentured labour). But it also occurs because of mercantile relations that long predate stories of modern capitalist "globalisation"'. Khalili goes on to offer the sorts of critical observations that can provide the foundations for a post-petromodernity approach to understanding the social and economic dynamics of the Gulf:

> This cosmopolitanism is an everyday cosmopolitanism or conviviality of a port city. This is of course classed, and always already taut with tensions of history, memory, power. But there is also a port city's openness. Its proximity, accessibility, to those who escape or arrive. It is the survival of languages, of pidgin forms of communication, or hybrid or mixed foods, hybrid or mixed

styles of life. It is walking through Souq Mubarakiyya in Kuwait and hearing a distinctly Kuwaiti-accented Farsi in the mouth of people whose ancestors migrated to Kuwait several generations back. It is to see meyveh (dried fish mixed with herbs and spices) being sold not as an Iranian condiment, but as the thing eaten by Kuwaitis, spelling it in distinct ways, preparing it differently than Iranians do.

Likewise, beyond the walled tourist resorts, carefully crafted museum exhibits and state-managed mega events, the Gulf is also home to diverse forms of everyday 'sha'bi' travel and tourism from people of different classes and backgrounds. *Khaleeji* tourism studies could make important contributions to the broader field by excavating these itineraries and experiences, broadening our definition and understanding of tourism across the globe.

References

Atalla, G. and A. Nasr (2013) *Reinventing Tourism in the GCC, Building the Tourism Ecosystem*, Abu Dhabi/Beirut: Booz & Company/strategy&. Available online at www.strategyand.pwc.com/media/file/Reinventing-tourism-in-the-GCC.pdf (accessed 22 May 2015).

Hanieh, A. (2011) *Capitalism and Class in the Gulf Arab States*, London: Palgrave.

Harvey, D. (2008) 'The right to the city', *New Left Review*, 53 (September/October), 23–40.

Hazbun, W. (2008) *Beaches, Ruins, Resorts: The Politics of Tourism in the Arab World*, Minneapolis, MN: University of Minnesota Press.

Kanna, A. (2007) 'Dubai in a jagged world', *Middle East Report*, 243 (Summer). Available online at www.merip.org/mer/mer243/dubai-jagged-world (accessed 22 May 2015).

Khalili, L. (2015) 'Sha'bi cosmopolitanisms', *The Gamming Blog*, posted 14 January. Available online at http://thegamming.org/2015/01/14/shabi-cosmopolitanisms/ (accessed 22 May 2015).

Molavi, A. (2015) 'The Arab battle for U.S. skies', *ForeignPolicy.org*, 4 May. Available online at http://foreignpolicy.com/2015/05/04/dubai-qatar-etihad-emirates-fair-skies-open-skies-american-delta-united/ (accessed 22 May 2015).

Rothman, H. (2005) 'Water ways', *Las Vegas Sun*, 13 October. Available online at http://lasvegassun.com/news/2005/oct/13/columnist-hal-rothman-water-ways/ (accessed 22 May 2015).

Index

For Product Safety Concerns and Information please contact our EU
representative GPSR@taylorandfrancis.com
Taylor & Francis Verlag GmbH, Kaufingerstraße 24, 80331 München, Germany

www.ingramcontent.com/pod-product-compliance
Ingram Content Group UK Ltd.
Pitfield, Milton Keynes, MK11 3LW, UK
UKHW021011180425
457613UK00020B/901